GRE®

GRADUATE RECORD EXAMINATIONS

DATE DUE	
Reg 10/03/05	

KAPLAN

PUBLISHING

New York

© 2011 Kaplan, Inc.

Published by Kaplan Publishing
395 Hudson St., 4th Floor
New York, NY 10014

Printed in the United States of America

10 9 8 7 6 5 4 3 2 1

ISBN-13: 978-1-60714-848-7

Kaplan Publishing books are available at special quantity discounts to use for sales promotions, employee premiums, or educational purposes. For more information or to order books, please call the Simon & Schuster special sales department at 866-506-1949.

Contents

How To Use This Book

More people get into graduate school with a Kaplan course than via any other major test prep company. The techniques and approaches from Kaplan's classroom and tutoring programs are distilled in this book in a clear, easy-to-grasp format. Here's the plan to get you started!

1. IDENTIFY YOUR STRENGTHS AND OPPORTUNITIES

Take the practice test at the end of this book, and then evaluate your test results.

To evaluate your results, first look at the summary of your performance at the end of the test to get a sense of

- the number of questions you got right, wrong, skipped, or didn't answer—overall and by section;
- how long it took you to answer each question; and
- how much you changed your mind.

Next, read the answer explanations for each question. Make a list of your personal strengths and opportunities by identifying whether or not

- you know and understand the concepts being tested;
- you find certain GRE question types especially challenging; and
- you are answering questions quickly enough.

2. GET TO KNOW THE GRE AND CREATE YOUR STUDY PLAN

First, read Chapter 1 of your book, "Introduction to the GRE" to get familiar with important details about the test, including structure, scoring, and registration information. Next, choose a test date and register! This will secure your spot in the test center.

At that point, you can work back from your test date to figure out how much time you have to prepare.

Divide that preparation time in half. Start with the key concepts and GRE question types you need to focus on. Go through the lessons in this book, take the practice sets, and read the answer explanations.

Once you've improved on those, devote time to reinforcing your strengths through lesson reviews and practice sets. Also, plan time to practice with the essay prompts, even if writing is your best subject. Understanding the essay requirements and practicing periodically will help you deliver the right paragraphs on test day, when it really counts.

As soon as you are comfortable with the question types and Kaplan Methods, take another full-length practice test by accessing your Online Companion.

3. PRACTICE, PRACTICE, PRACTICE

If you're looking for more practice, pick up a copy of *Kaplan GRE Math Workbook* or *Kaplan GRE Verbal Workbook*. You'll get a review of core concepts, as well as additional testlike practice questions to help build speed and accuracy.

You can also go to **kaptest.com/gre** and take the free practice test provided there.

Good luck!

PART ONE

Getting Started

CHAPTER 1

Introduction to the GRE

This book will explain more than just a few basic strategies. It will prepare you for practically everything that you are likely to encounter on the GRE. This may sound too good to be true, but we mean it. We are able to do this because we don't explain questions in isolation or focus on particular problems. Instead, we explain the underlying principles behind *all* of the questions on the GRE. We give you the big picture.

UNDERSTANDING THE GRE

Let's take a look at how the GRE is constructed. The GRE, or Graduate Record Examination, is a computer-based exam required by many graduate schools for admission to a wide variety of programs at the graduate level. You need to know firsthand the way this test is put together if you want to take it apart. In this section, you will learn about the purpose for the test and ways you can learn to be successful on the GRE. For the latest, up-to-the-minute news about the GRE, visit Kaplan's website at kaplanGRE.com/newGRE.

THE PURPOSES OF THE GRE

The GRE is designed to assess readiness for a wide variety of graduate programs. The ways in which graduate schools use GRE scores vary. Scores are often required as part of the application packet for entrance into a program, but they also can be used to grant fellowships or financial aid. Each section of the GRE is designed to assess general skills necessary for graduate school. Some of these skills include the ability to read complex informational text and understand high-level vocabulary words in the Verbal Reasoning section, the ability to respond to an issue in written form in the Analytical Writing section, and the ability to apply general mathematical concepts to a variety of problem types in the Quantitative Reasoning section. Graduate school admissions officers often view the GRE score as an important indicator of readiness for graduate-level studies. In addition, graduate school admissions officers are comparing hundreds or even thousands of applications, and having a quantitative factor, such as a GRE score, makes the job of comparing so many applicants much easier. Just by having this book and making a commitment to yourself to be as well prepared as possible for this exam, you've already taken the crucial first step toward making your graduate school application as competitive as possible.

THE SECRET CODE

Doing well on the GRE requires breaking down the "secret code" upon which each and every test is constructed. Like all of the tests created by the Educational Testing Service (ETS), the GRE is based on psychometrics, the science concerned with creating "standardized" tests. For a test to be standardized, it must successfully do three things. First, the test must be reliable. In other words, a test taker who takes the GRE should get approximately the same score if he or she takes a second GRE (assuming, of course, that he or she doesn't study with Kaplan materials during the intervening period). Second—and this is closely related to our first point—it must test the same concepts on each test. Third, it must create a "bell curve" when a pool of test takers' scores are plotted; in other words, some people will do very well on the test, and some will do very poorly, but the great majority will score somewhere in the middle.

What all this boils down to is that to be a standardized test, the GRE has to be predictable. And this is what makes the GRE and other standardized tests so coachable. Because ETS has to test the same concepts in each and every test, certain vocabulary words appear over and over again, as do variations of the same exact math questions. Moreover, the GRE has to create some questions that most test takers will get wrong—otherwise, it wouldn't be able to create its bell curve. This means that hard questions will usually contain "traps"—wrong answer choices that will be more appealing than the correct answer to a large percentage of test takers. Fortunately, these traps are predictable (this is what we mean by the secret code), and we can teach you how to recognize and avoid them. The goal of this comprehensive program is to help you break the code.

ACQUIRE THE SKILLS

It is a valid argument that the GRE isn't a fair or decent predictor of the skills a person needs for graduate-level study. In fact, this is one of the main criticisms this revision to the test is intended to address. And you may be concerned that your scores on the GRE will not be a fair or accurate representation of the strong work you will do in your advanced degree program. Take heart: none of the GRE experts who work at Kaplan were *born* acing the GRE. No one is. That's because these tests do not measure innate skills; they measure *acquired* skills. People who are good at standardized tests are simply people who've already acquired these skills, maybe in math class, or by reading a lot, or by studying logic in college, or perhaps the easiest way—in one of Kaplan's GRE courses. But they have, perhaps without realizing it, acquired the skills that spell success on tests like the GRE. And if *you* haven't, you have nothing whatsoever to feel bad about. It's time to acquire them now.

SAME PROBLEMS—BUT DIFFERENT

As we noted, the test makers use some of the same problems on every GRE. We know it sounds incredible, but it's true—only the words and numbers change. They test the same principles over and over. Here's an example.

Quantity A	Quantity B

$$2x^2 = 32$$

x	4

This is a type of math problem known as a Quantitative Comparison. (Look familiar? It might, if you've taken the SAT. This question type used to appear on the SAT, although ETS decided to drop this question type from the SAT starting in 2005.) Your job is to examine the relationship and pick **(A)** if the term in Column A is bigger, **(B)** if the term in Column B is bigger, **(C)** if they're equal, or **(D)** if not enough information is given to solve the problem.

Most people answer **(C)**, that the quantities are equal. They divide both sides of the centered equation by 2 and then take the square root of both sides to get $x = 4$. Wrong. x doesn't have to be 4. It could be 4 *or* −4. Both work, so the answer is **(D)** because the answer cannot be determined from the information given. If you just solve for 4, you'll get this problem—and every one like it—wrong. ETS figures that if you get burned here, you'll get burned again next time. Only next time, it won't be $2x^2 = 32$; it will be $y^2 = 36$ or $s^4 = 81$.

The concepts tested on any particular GRE—right triangles, simple logic, word relationships, and so forth—are the underlying concepts at the heart of *every* GRE. ETS makes changes only after testing them exhaustively. This process is called *norming*, which means taking a normal test and a changed test and administering them to a random group of students. As long as the group is large enough for the purposes of statistical validity and the students get consistent scores from one test to the next, then the revised test is just as valid and consistent as any other GRE.

That may sound technical, but norming is actually quite an easy process. We do it at Kaplan all the time—for the tests that we write for our students. The test at the back of this book, for instance, is a normed exam. While the interactive, computer-based test experience of the GRE is impossible to reproduce on paper, the paper-based test in our book is a normed exam that will produce an equivalent score.

HOW THE GRE IS ORGANIZED

The Graduate Record Examination (GRE) is administered on computer and is approximately 3 hours and 45 minutes long. The exam consists of six sections, with different amounts of time allotted for you to complete each section.

Basics of the GRE	
Exam Length	3 hours, 45 minutes
Scoring Scale	130–170 (1 point increments) for Verbal and Quantitative; 0–6 for Analytical Writing
Format	Multi-stage test (MST), a computer based format that allows students to navigate forward and backward within each section of the test
Number of Test Sections	6 sections, including an experimental or research section
Analytical Writing	One section with two 30-minute tasks: analyze an issue, and analyze an argument
Verbal Reasoning	Two 30-minute sections with approximately 20 questions each
Quantitative Reasoning	Two 35-minute sections with approximately 20 questions each; on-screen calculator available

Your test will also contain an experimental section—a second Verbal Reasoning or Quantitative Reasoning section that ETS puts on the test so that they can norm the new questions they create for use on future GREs. That means that if you could identify the experimental section, you could doodle for half an hour, guess in a random pattern, or daydream and still get exactly the same score on the GRE. However, the experimental section is disguised to look like a real section—there is no way to identify it. All you will really know on the day of the test is that one of the subject areas will have three sections instead of two. Naturally, many people try to figure out which section is experimental. But because ETS really wants you to try hard on it, it does its best to keep you guessing. If you guess wrong, you could blow the whole test, so we urge you to treat all sections as scored unless you are told otherwise.

Lastly, in lieu of an experimental section, your test could contain a research section. This section is unscored, and will be indicated as such. If you have a research section on the test, it will be the last section. Pay careful attention to the directions at the beginning of the section.

SCORING

The Analytical Writing section is scored on a scale of 0–6 in half-point increments. (See Chapter 15, "Introduction to Analytical Writing," for details on this scoring rubric.) The Verbal Reasoning and Quantitative Reasoning sections each yield a scaled score within a range of 130 to 170 in one-point increments. You cannot score higher than 170 for either the Verbal Reasoning or the Quantitative Reasoning sections, no matter how hard you try. Similarly, it's impossible to score lower than 130 for Verbal Reasoning or Quantitative Reasoning.

But you don't receive *only* scaled scores; you will also receive a percentile rank, which will rate your performance relative to that of a large sample population of other GRE takers. Percentile scores tell graduate schools just what your scaled scores are worth. For instance, even if everyone got very high scaled scores, universities would still be able to differentiate candidates by their percentile scores.

The relative frequency of high scaled scores means that universities pay great attention to percentile rank. It's important that you do some real research into the programs you're thinking about. Admissions officers from some top graduate school programs consider the GRE the most important factor for graduate school admissions. Many schools have cut-off scores below which they don't even consider applicants. But be careful! If a school tells you they look for applicants scoring an average of 150 per section, that doesn't mean those scores are good enough for immediate acceptance. Some students will be accepted with scores slightly below that average, and some students may be denied admission even with scores that are slightly higher. Consider the score of 150 per section as a target score, but also be sure the rest of your application is strong. You owe it to yourself to find out what kinds of scores *impress* the schools you're interested in and work hard until you get those scores. You can definitely get there if you want to and if you work hard enough. We see it every day.

Another thing to keep in mind is that historically, student scores drop after a test revision. When the GRE last made updates in 2002, median scores dropped seven points and continued to decline for the next five years. Over time, test takers will get better at the new format, but expect that your old scores and new scores may not compare. That's another reason why your percentile rank is so important!

A final note about percentile rank: the sample population that you are compared against to determine your percentile is not the group of people who take the test on the same day as you do. ETS doesn't want to penalize an unlucky candidate who takes the GRE on a date when everyone else happens to be a rocket scientist. So they compare your performance with that of a random three-year population of recent GRE test takers. Don't worry about how other people do – strive for your best score. We often tell our students, "Your only competition in this classroom is yourself."

CANCELLATION AND MULTIPLE SCORES POLICY

Unlike many things in life, the GRE allows you a second chance. If at the end of the test, you feel that you've definitely not done as well as you could have, you have the option to cancel your score. The trick is that you must decide whether you want to keep your scores before the computer shows them to you. If you cancel, your scores will be disregarded. (You also won't get to see them.) Canceling a score means that it won't count; however, it will appear on your score report as a canceled test.

Two legitimate reasons to cancel your score are illness and personal circumstances that may have caused you to perform unusually poorly on that particular day.

But keep in mind that test takers historically underestimate their performance, especially immediately following the test. They tend to forget about all of the things that went right and focus on everything that went wrong. So unless your performance has been terribly marred by unforeseen circumstances, don't cancel your test. If you do cancel, your future score reports will indicate that you've canceled a previous score. Because the canceled test was never scored, your score will never appear on any subsequent score report. However, a canceled score can be a red flag to the admissions team, so only cancel if you absolutely must do so.

If you take more than one test without canceling, then all the scores will show up on each score report, so the graduate schools will see them all. Requested score reports are sent to schools within 10–15 days after the exam. All GRE testing administrations will be listed (and usable) in your ETS record for five years. Most grad schools will consider the highest score you have for each section for your application, although there are a few exceptions. Check with individual schools for their policies on multiple scores.

TEST REGISTRATION

You should first obtain a copy of the *GRE Registration Bulletin*. This booklet contains information on scheduling, pricing, repeat testing, cancellation policies, and more. You can receive the booklet by calling the Educational Testing Service at (609) 771-7670 or by downloading it from **gre.org**.

The computer-based GRE General Test is offered year-round. To register for and schedule your GRE, use one of the following options. (If you live outside the United States, Canada, American Samoa, Guam, the U.S. Virgin Islands, or Puerto Rico, visit **gre.org** for instructions on how to register.)

Register Online

You can register online (if you are paying with a credit card) at **gre.org**. Once the registration process is complete, you can print out your voucher immediately (and can reprint it if it is lost).

Register by Phone

Call 1-800-GRE-CALL or 1-800-529-3590 (TTY). A confirmation number, reporting time, and test center location will be given to you when you call. Registering earlier is strongly recommended because spaces often fill quickly. Payments can be made with a Visa, MasterCard, or American Express card.

Register by Mail

Complete the Authorization Voucher Request Form found in the GRE Registration Bulletin. Mail the fee and signed voucher request form in the envelope provided to the address printed on the voucher.

ETS advises that you allow up to four weeks for processing before you receive your voucher in the mail. When you receive your voucher, call to schedule an appointment. Vouchers are valid for one year from the date of issue. When you register, make sure you list a first- and second-choice test center. If you register online, you can confirm test center availability in real time.

GRE CHECKLIST

Before the Test

- Choose a test date.
- Register online at **gre.org**, by phone at 1-800-GRE-CALL, or by mail.
- Receive your admission voucher in the mail or online.
- Check out your test center.
    - Know the kind of workstation you'll be using and whether the room is likely to be hot or cold.
    - Know the directions to the building and room where you'll be tested.

- Create a test-prep calendar to ensure that you're ready by the day of the test.
  - If you skipped it, go back and read "How to Use This Book."
  - On a calendar, block out the weeks you have to prepare for the test.
  - Based on your strengths and weaknesses, establish a detailed plan of study and select appropriate lessons and practice. (Don't forget to include some days off!)
- Stick to the plan; as with any practice, little is gained if it isn't methodical. Skills can't be "crammed" in the last minutes.
- Re-evaluate your strengths and weaknesses from time to time and revise your plan accordingly.

The Day of the Test

- Make sure you have your GRE admission voucher and acceptable ID.
- Leave yourself plenty of time to arrive at the test site stress-free.
- Arrive at the test site at least 30 minutes early for the check-in procedures.
- Don't stress; you're going to do great!

GRE SUBJECT TESTS

Subject Tests are designed to test the fundamental knowledge that is most important for successful graduate study in a particular subject area. To do well on a GRE Subject Test, you must have an extensive background in the particular subject area—the sort of background you would be expected to have if you majored in the subject. Subject Tests enable admissions officers to compare students from different colleges with different standards and curricula. Not every graduate school or program requires Subject Tests, so check admissions requirements at those schools in which you're interested.

ORGANIZATION, SCORING, AND TEST DATES

All Subject Tests are administered in paper-and-pencil format and consist exclusively of multiple-choice questions that are designed to assess knowledge of the areas of the subject that are included in the typical undergraduate curriculum.

On Subject Tests, you'll earn one point for each multiple-choice question that you answer correctly, but lose one-quarter of a point for each incorrectly answered question. Unanswered questions aren't counted in the scoring. Your raw score is then converted into a scaled score, which can range from 200 to 990. The range varies from test to test.

Some Subject Tests also contain subtests, which provide more specific information about your strengths and weaknesses. The same questions that contribute to your subtest scores also contribute to your overall score. Subtest scores, which range from 20 to 99, are reported along with the overall score. For further information on scoring, you should consult the relevant Subject Test Descriptive Booklet, available from ETS. Subject Tests are offered three times a year: in October, November, and April. Note that not all of the Subject Tests are offered on every test date; consult **gre.org** for upcoming test dates and registration deadlines.

Subjects

Currently, eight Subject Tests are offered. A list of them follows, along with a brief description of each.

Biochemistry, Cell, and Molecular Biology

This test consists of 175 questions and is divided among three subscore areas: biochemistry, cell biology, and molecular biology and genetics.

Biology

This test consists of about 200 questions divided among three subscore areas: cellular and molecular biology, organismal biology, and ecology and evolution.

Chemistry

This test consists of about 130 questions. There are no subscores, and the questions cover the following topics: analytical chemistry, inorganic chemistry, organic chemistry, and physical chemistry.

Computer Science

This test consists of approximately 70 questions. There are no subscores, and the questions cover the following topics: software systems and methodology; computer organization and architecture; theory and mathematical background; and other, more advanced topics, such as numerical analysis; graphics; and artificial intelligence.

Literature in English

This test consists of 230 questions on literature in the English language. There are two basic types of questions: factual questions that test the student's knowledge of writers typically covered in the undergraduate curriculum and interpretive questions that test the student's ability to read various types of literature critically.

Mathematics

This test consists of 66 questions on the content of various undergraduate courses in mathematics. Most of the test assesses the student's knowledge of calculus, abstract algebra, linear algebra, and real analysis. About one quarter of the test, however, requires knowledge in other areas of math.

Physics

This test consists of 100 questions covering mostly material from the first three years of undergraduate physics. Topics include classical mechanics, electromagnetism, atomic physics, optics and wave phenomena, quantum mechanics, thermodynamics and statistical mechanics, special relativity, and laboratory methods. About 9 percent of the test covers advanced topics, such as nuclear and particle physics, condensed matter physics, and astrophysics.

Psychology

This test consists of 210 questions drawn from courses most commonly included in the undergraduate curriculum. Questions fall into three categories. The experimental or natural science-oriented category includes questions in learning, cognitive psychology, sensation and perception, ethology and comparative psychology, and physiological psychology. The social or social science-oriented category includes questions in abnormal psychology, developmental psychology, social psychology, and personality. Together, these make up about 85 percent of the test, and each of the two categories provides its own subscore. The other 15 percent or so of the questions fall under the "general" category, which includes the history of psychology, tests and measurements, research design and statistics, and applied psychology.

For more information, you should consult ETS's Subject Test section at **gre.org**. You can also visit the Kaplan website **(kaptest.com)** for a more detailed description of each Subject Test and some free sample questions.

CHAPTER 2

MST Test Mechanics

The MST, or multi-stage test, introduced in fall of 2011, differs in some critical ways from the older tests, and we at Kaplan have some useful insights into why the GRE has been revised. Firstly, the GRE may have been structured to look more like the GMAT, the test for entry into business school, because the skills tested are so similar. The revised GRE contains more high level reasoning skills, similar question types, including critical reasoning and argumentation questions, and data inference questions drawn from tables and graphs. Secondly, the GRE scoring scale did not match well with percentile scores. The new scoring scale is designed to align the scaled scores with percentile scores.

The content and scoring scale aren't the only things ETS tweaked for the revised GRE. The old GRE featured a CAT (Computer-Adaptive Test) that varied the difficulty of the question based upon how you answered the preceding one (the computer adapted to your answers). Its big disadvantage was that you couldn't go back to change your answer. Not so with the revised GRE. You'll be able to move about freely within the section of the test you're currently working on, and you can mark questions you are unsure of and return to them when you have time. This will more closely approximate the experience of a traditional exam. The whole idea is to make the process much friendlier and more natural, and also less unpleasant (to the extent that that's possible for a standardized test!).

MST MECHANICS

The biggest changes to the structure of the test are mechanical in nature. Let's start with them. A MST, or multi-stage test, is a computer-based test that you take at a special test center at a time you schedule. You're probably already at least a little bit familiar with the old test design, the CAT. Below is a chart that highlights some of the key differences between the old and new GRE test design:

CAT (old)	MST (new)
The test adapts one question at a time	The test adapts one section at a time
You cannot change your answer, or go back to a previous question	You can return to previous questions within a section
You are not allowed a calculator	An on-screen calculator is provided for the Quantitative Reasoning sections
No Mark or Review buttons	Mark & Review buttons are available
Scored on a scale from 200–800	Scored on a scale from 130–170
About 3 hours	About 3 hours, 45 minutes

A CAT "adapts" to your performance, making the old GRE quite different from the traditional paper-and-pencil tests you've probably taken all your academic life. On a test with a CAT design, instead of having a predetermined mixture of basic, medium, and hard questions, the computer selects questions for you based on how well you are doing. The first question may be of medium difficulty. If you get it right, the second question may be a little harder; if you get it wrong, the second will be more basic. If you keep getting questions right, the test will get harder and harder. If you make some mistakes, the test adjusts and starts giving you easier problems, but if you answer them correctly, it will go back to the hard ones.

The idea was for the test to give you enough questions to ensure that scores were not based on luck. If you got one hard question right, you might just have been lucky, but if you got ten hard questions right, then luck had little to do with it. So the test was self-adjusting and self-correcting. Because of this format, the CAT was very different structurally from a paper-and-pencil test. After the first problem, every new problem was determined by, among other factors, how you answered the prior problem. That meant you couldn't return to a question once you'd answered it. Once you answered a question, it became part of your score, for better or worse.

The revised GRE allows you to move around within the section you're working on. You can use the Mark and Review buttons to tag questions. This way, if you are struggling with an answer or you just can't concentrate on a challenging passage, you can mark a question for review, and come back to it later when you know you've answered at least a few other questions correctly and you have regained the confidence to tackle the passage. Questions that you have "marked" will appear with check marks next to them. At any point during the section, you will have the option to look at the review screen for that section and see how many questions you have left. It also helps you to budget your time. If you see that you're almost halfway through your allotted time, but have answered only a few questions, you'll know to pick up the pace!

SECTION MANAGEMENT TECHNIQUES

At first, you will get a lot of mileage from the standard strategy of approaching questions based on their level of difficulty. It won't be spelled out for you explicitly, but as you progress through the questions, you should have a good idea of how you're doing. If you've practiced a lot on the questions in this book and used other test preparation materials to study, it will be even easier to gain a pretty clear sense of the difficulty level of your questions and to eliminate answer choices accordingly.

Try as best you can to approach the exam as you would a paper-based one. After all, that is the idea of the MST. It should feel more comfortable and familiar, given that you can move about freely within a section. Use this to your advantage. If a question looks too daunting, you can skip it and come back to it. You can also use the Mark button to indicate to yourself that you should come back and review your answer, if you have time at the end of that section. You can do this whether or not you've answered the question. This way, you can better organize your time by keeping track of which questions you are done with, and which ones need a second look.

Finally, the timer in the corner can work to your advantage, but if you find yourself looking at it so frequently that it becomes a distraction, you should turn it off for 10 or 15 minutes and try to refocus your attention on the test. You may be concerned about losing track of time, but if you are so distracted by it that you can't get through the questions, it will be just as damaging to your score as will running out of time. As with a traditional, paper-and-pencil test, you don't want to get hung up on clock management.

NAVIGATING THE GRE MST: COMPUTER BASICS

Let's preview the primary computer functions that you will use to move around on the MST. ETS calls them "testing tools." They're basically tabs that you can click with your mouse to navigate through the section. The following screen is typical for a multi-stage test.

Directions: Choose the word or set of words for each blank that best fits the meaning of the sentence as a whole.

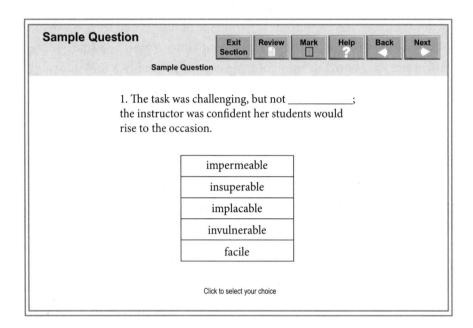

Here's what the various buttons do:

The Time Button (not pictured)

Clicking on this button turns the time display at the top of the screen on or off. When you have five minutes left in a section, the clock flashes, and the display changes from hours and minutes to hours, minutes, and seconds.

The Quit Test Button (not pictured)

Hitting this button ends the test prematurely. *Do not* use this button unless you want all of your scores canceled and your test invalidated.

The Exit Section Button

This allows you to exit the section before the time is up. Try not to end the section early—use any extra time to review any particular problems you flagged or felt concerned about.

Review Button

This button will allow you to view your progress on all the questions you have looked at so far within the section you're working on. The items you have marked for review will have a check mark next to them. The chart on the screen will also have a column indicating whether or not you have answered a question.

Mark Button

This button allows you to 'mark' a question for review later. The question will have a check mark next to it in the review section.

The Help Button

This button leads to directions and assistance from the tutorial. *But beware*: the test clock won't pause just because you click on Help.

The Back Button

This button allows you to return to previous questions within the section. Note that this allows you to go back to questions *only* in the section you're currently working on.

The Next Button

Hit this when you want to move on to the next question. You cannot proceed until you have hit this button.

Calculator (not pictured; Quantitative Reasoning section only)

This button opens the on-screen calculator for you on Quantitative Reasoning sections. It's a pretty basic calculator, and the questions are more conceptual in nature, but it still should help you to avoid basic computational errors. Note that you can click on the "Transfer Display" button in the calculator to transfer your answer into a numeric entry box.

MST: THE UPSIDE

There are many good things about the MST, such as the following:

- You are given more time to answer each question than test takers were given on the old pencil-and-paper exam.
- There will be only a few other test takers in the room with you—it won't be like taking it in one of those massive lecture halls with distractions everywhere.
- You get a one minute break between each section. The break is optional, but you should always use it to relax and stretch.
- You can sign up for the GRE just two days before the test (though we recommend signing up much earlier!), and registration is very easy.
- The MST is convenient to schedule. It's offered at more than 175 centers three to five days a week (depending on the center) all year long.
- You don't have to take it on the same day as a Subject Test, so you can avoid fatigue.
- Perhaps the MST's best feature is that it gives you your unofficial Verbal Reasoning and Quantitative Reasoning scores immediately.

MST: THE DOWNSIDE

There are also some less attractive features about the MST:

- The MST is a long test requiring lots of endurance.
- As with any computer-based test, you can't cross off an answer choice to use the process of elimination. Use your scratch paper to avoid reconsidering choices you've already eliminated.
- You have to scroll through Reading Comprehension passages and read them on-screen.
- You may need to scroll down to see graphs or Reading Comprehension passages, which may feel somewhat overwhelming.
- You'll be given scratch paper to make notes or perform calculations, but if you need more, you'll have to turn in the scratch paper that you've already used before obtaining new paper.
- Many people find that computer screens tire them and cause eyestrain—especially after three hours.
- Having a calculator provided for you on the Quantitative Reasoning sections may seem like a gift, but it comes with a price. The questions on the Quantitative Reasoning section will now be more conceptual and less calculation-based. Basically, you won't have to worry about doing long division, but the problems will be less straightforward.
- Whenever a test changes—and we at Kaplan have seen this in recent years for the SAT and LSAT—scores tend to drop for the first several years until students adapt.
- Being able to go back and change your answers may be a plus, but it can lead to pacing issues for some test takers, who will leave questions blank and then forget to come back to them or run out of time.
- You cannot take the GRE as frequently: you can only test every 60 days. So if you're on a tight deadline and you don't get the scores you need the first time, you need to wait two months until you can test again.

KAPLAN'S MST STRATEGIES

Using certain MST-specific strategies can have a direct, positive impact on your score:

- Use the computer tutorial to your advantage. Spend some time to make yourself comfortable with the computer before you begin the actual test. Once the test is underway, if you click on Help to review the directions or a summary of the tutorial, it will count against your allotted time for that section of the test.

- Make good use of the new Mark and Review buttons; you can use these to effectively manage your time. You're no longer obliged to answer the question that's presented to you. You can mark it for review and come back to it later. This isn't the only way to use the buttons, though. If you're only 50% sure about an answer, you can mark it as a note to yourself to come back to it later. This way, you can indicate which questions might need a second look.

- The MST does not have an easily predictable order for the difficulty of its questions. Always be on the lookout for traps! It's just like the SAT you took in high school; if an answer looks too good to be true, it very well could be.

- Guess intelligently and strategically—eliminate any obviously wrong answer choices and guess among those remaining.

- Sometimes it's necessary to give up on a tough, time-consuming question. It's difficult to do, but let it go and move on to the next question. That's how you score points on the GRE. Don't agonize over one question that's chewing up precious minutes.

PAPER-AND-PENCIL STRATEGIES

If you are located outside of the United States, Canada, American Samoa, Guam, the U.S. Virgin Islands, or Puerto Rico, you will take the paper-and-pencil version of the GRE test (check **gre.org** for test dates). It is comprised of six sections: two Analytical Writing sections, two Verbal Reasoning sections, and two Quantitative Reasoning sections. There is no experimental or research section on the paper-based GRE.

Note that registration for the paper-and-pencil test fills up much more quickly than for the MST. You will need to plan ahead to register in advance of the test.

You have approximately 3 hours and 30 minutes to complete the entire test. The test-taking strategies for the paper-based test are different from those for the MST. One strategy we recommend is to keep track of your answers—particularly ones you've eliminated—by crossing out wrong answer choices. This will also help you grid your answers more accurately. You can also say the question number and answer choice (silently, of course) to yourself as you grid, to help make sure you're gridding carefully. Here are some targeted strategies for each section of the paper-based GRE.

ANALYTICAL WRITING

For the Analytical Writing section, if you are not using a transcriber, you will have to handwrite your essay, so we suggest you write clearly and legibly. For more tips and strategies for conquering the Analytical Writing section, refer to Chapter 15.

VERBAL REASONING SECTION

Before you start a Verbal Reasoning section, glance over it completely, but quickly, to familiarize yourself with it. With Reading Comprehension, you can preview question stems to help guide your reading, but don't try to memorize them or answer the questions without reading the passages. We recommend that you answer the questions you're most comfortable with first. Make sure you set aside about 15 minutes in each Verbal Reasoning section for Reading Comprehension.

Always try to be aware of how difficult the question you're working on is. If you find yourself running into trouble with a particular group of questions, move on and come back to them if you have time. Don't get hung up on hard questions. Mark those questions to return to them later; you want to give yourself every opportunity to answer as many questions as you are capable of answering correctly.

The Verbal Reasoning sections for the paper-and-pencil test have 25 questions, five more than each section on the MST. The new question types, Text Completion and Sentence Equivalence, and the new question format, One-or-More, will be on the paper-and-pencil test. The question format that requires you to highlight a sentence, Select-in-Passage, will not be available.

QUANTITATIVE REASONING SECTION

As with the Verbal Reasoning questions, it will behoove you to be aware of the difficulty level of each question. This will help you determine how much time you should be spending on the question and whether it's a question that should have an obvious answer. Calculators will now be permitted on the GRE revised General Test. They will be provided at the testing center, but still don't forget to utilize your scratch paper. Feel free to skip around within this section as well and do all the problems you can do; then come back to the harder ones.

The Quantitative Reasoning sections of the paper-and-pencil test have 25 questions, five more than each section on the MST. The new question formats, All that Apply and Numeric Entry, will be on the paper-and-pencil test. You will also mark all of your answers directly in the test book, which means no more answer grid!

Now you have an understanding of the GRE MST and paper-and-pencil formats. Let's now turn to the test sections and get you ready for each one.

Verbal Reasoning

CHAPTER 3

Introduction to Verbal Reasoning

OVERVIEW

The Verbal Reasoning section of the GRE is designed to place most of its emphasis on complex reasoning skills and your ability to analyze the relationships between words and sentences as they are used in context. Vocabulary will be tested contextually, and the reading passages are both dense and written with a sophisticated level of diction. The goal of the test's content and emphasis upon analytical skills is to make the test an accurate indicator of your ability to understand what you're reading and apply reasoning skills to the various question types. These skills will translate directly to a graduate level of study.

In this section of the book, we'll take you through all the types of Verbal Reasoning questions you'll see on the GRE and give you the strategies you need to answer them quickly and correctly. Also, many of the vocabulary words you'll encounter on the test are included in the "GRE Resources, Verbal Reference section" in the Appendix at the back of this book. Think of the glossary and word lists there as building blocks for the questions you will see on the test.

VERBAL REASONING QUESTION TYPES

The GRE contains two Verbal Reasoning sections with approximately 20 questions each. Each section will last 30 minutes and be composed of a selection of the following question types:

- Text Completion
- Reading Comprehension
- Sentence Equivalence

The Verbal Reasoning portion of the GRE draws heavily upon your vocabulary and your facility with understanding and analyzing written material. Specifically, it evaluates your ability to:

- analyze sentences and paragraphs.
- derive a word's meaning based upon its context.
- detect relationships among words.
- understand the logic of sentences and paragraphs.
- draw inferences.
- recognize major, minor, and irrelevant points.
- summarize ideas.
- understand passage structure.
- recognize an author's tone, purpose, and perspective.

Within each section of Verbal Reasoning questions on the GRE, you will see an assortment of question types.

PACING STRATEGY

As a multi-stage test, the GRE allows you to move freely within each section, which can be a big advantage on test day. If you get stuck on a particular question, you can tag it and come back to it later when you have time. You only score points for correct answers, so you don't want to get bogged down on one problem and lose time you could have used to answer several other questions correctly.

You will have 30 minutes to work on each Verbal Reasoning section. The 20 questions in each section will be an assortment of Text Completion, Sentence Equivalence, and Reading Comprehension items. However, these types of questions are not distributed equally. The chart below shows how many questions you can expect of each type, as well as the average amount of time you should spend per question type.

	Text Completion	Sentence Equivalence	Reading Comprehension
Number of Questions	approx. 6	approx. 4	approx. 10
Time per Question	1 to 1.5 minutes, depending on the number of blanks	1 minute	1-3 minutes, depending on the length, to read the passage and 1 minute to answer each question

Try to keep these time estimates in mind as you prepare for the test. If you use them as you work on the practice items, you will be comfortable keeping to the same amounts of time on test day. Additionally, you will be prepared to use the Mark and Review buttons to your advantage while taking the actual test.

NAVIGATING THE VERBAL FOUNDATIONS AND CONTENT REVIEW SECTION

The chapter immediately following this one is on Verbal Foundations and Content and will review the classic verbal concepts and topics that you may encounter on the GRE. This section of the book also includes individual chapters on Text Completion, Sentence Equivalence, and Reading Comprehension questions. Each chapter includes an introduction and definition of the relevant question types, and a review and examples of the strategies to follow to answer those questions quickly and correctly. In addition, you'll find a practice set of questions with answers and explanations for each of the question types you'll encounter on the GRE.

Finally, at the end of this section, you'll find the Verbal Reasoning Practice Sets, two sets of 60 Verbal Reasoning questions along with answers and explanations. Use the Verbal Reasoning Practice Sets to test your skills and pinpoint areas for more focused study. When you are finished with this section of the book, you should be thoroughly prepared for any question you might encounter on the Verbal Reasoning section of the GRE.

CHAPTER 4

Verbal Foundations and Content Review

INTRODUCTION TO VERBAL FOUNDATIONS AND CONTENT REVIEW

The GRE tests your mastery of sophisticated language and a wide range of comprehension skills. These concepts include:

- Vocabulary Concepts
  - Basics of Vocabulary Building
  - Word Groups
  - Use your Thesaurus
  - Greek and Latin Roots
  - Words in Context
  - Parts of Speech
  - The Test Maker's Favorite Words

- Reading Comprehension Strategies
  - Read the First Third of the Passage
  - Determine the Topic, Scope, and Author's Purpose
  - Read Strategically

This chapter will cover all these vocabulary concepts, as well as specific Reading Comprehension strategies to conquer any questions you might have pertaining to each concept.

THE KAPLAN APPROACH TO VOCABULARY CONCEPTS

The vocabulary words found on the GRE are usually members of a very particular class of prefixed and suffixed words which typically are derived from Latin or Greek. You probably remember from middle school English that prefixes and suffixes are attached to the stem of a word to change its meaning. For instance, _contraindicate_, a verb meaning "to give an indication against," is a great GRE word. So is _contradict_, another verb meaning "to assert the contrary." Recognizing the prefix "contra," meaning "against," in one of these words can help you to figure out other words with the same prefix (contravene, contraband, contraceptive, et cetera). A solid knowledge of prefixes and suffixes will help you derive the meaning of thousands of words you're not familiar with, especially when they're used in context.

The GRE words used in context in this vocabulary section will appear in **boldface**. One of the points of emphasis of the GRE is understanding words in context. This means that the questions will have a more conceptual bent to them, and you'll be able to deduce answers from contextual clues. So if you see a word in this book—or anywhere in your reading—that's unfamiliar, take a moment to make a note of it. A good practice for acquiring vocabulary is to keep a vocabulary journal of unfamiliar terms and then practice using them so as to integrate them into your own working vocabulary.

BASICS OF VOCABULARY BUILDING

Most people build their vocabulary by hearing or reading words in context. Reading is ultimately the best way to increase your vocabulary, but it also takes a great deal of time. You should get into the habit of reading publications that are aimed at well-educated readers, such as _Scientific American_, the _Economist_, and the _New York Times_. Because your GRE passages will appear on the computer screen, reading these publications online can be especially helpful while you prepare for the GRE. When you come across words you don't know and can't figure out from the context, look them up in the dictionary, or use a dictionary add-on for your browser, or a web-based dictionary, and make a note of them in your vocabulary journal. It sounds tedious, but it's definitely worth the time and effort come test day. You can even keep your journal on your computer or smartphone and refer to it during spare moments throughout the day.

While any word can appear on the GRE, some words are more common than others. Many of the words you'll encounter most often during your prep can be found in an appendix of this book. This handy reference tool contains thousands of the words that you're most likely to find on the GRE. Studying words is a more effective way to build the kind of vocabulary you need than reading the dictionary from aardvark to zygote.

There are a couple of techniques you can use to quickly build a more robust vocabulary. In your vocabulary journal, you should be noting words in your reading that aren't familiar to you. As a mental exercise, generate a list of synonyms and antonyms. By compiling such lists, you'll be able to build your vocabulary into a structure in which it'll be organized in your head. It will also be easier to assimilate new words into your active vocabulary if you can easily relate them to other words (e.g. its synonyms and antonyms). For example, if you know what *progressive* means, you'll understand *regressive* immediately if you think of it as the antonym of progressive. Making these kind of cognitive connections will go a long way to stockpiling your vocabulary vault.

One final study exercise for vocabulary building is to practice using each unfamiliar word in a sentence. This will help you to internalize the word and its meaning because you'll be using it *in context.*

We'll be going over some of these concepts in more detail later in this chapter, but for now you should be aware of the following tools for vocabulary building while you're studying for the GRE:

- Record and define unfamiliar words.
- Generate synonyms and antonyms.
- Put unfamiliar words in context by using them in sentences.

Word Groups

The GRE does not test whether you know *exactly* what a particular word means. If you have only an idea of what a word means, you have as good a chance of correctly answering a question as you would if you knew the precise dictionary definition of the word. The GRE isn't interested in finding out whether you're a walking dictionary. While it is helpful to have a broad and diverse (but classically-rooted) vocabulary, such as you would be likely to encounter in a graduate-level degree program, your critical reasoning skills are more important. Learning words in groups based upon similar meaning is an excellent way to expand your useful vocabulary. If you have an idea of what a word means, you can use contextual clues to help nail down the nuance of the correct answer choice.

The words in the list below all mean nearly the same thing. Some of them are different parts of speech, but that's OK. They all have something to do with the concept of criticism, which often appears on the GRE. The goal is to be able to identify words that have similar meaning.

CRITICIZE/CRITICISM

aspersion	impugn
belittle	inveigh
berate	lambaste
calumny	objurgate
castigate	obloquy
decry	opprobrium
defamation	pillory
denounce	rebuke
deride/derisive	remonstrate
diatribe	reprehend
disparage	reprove
excoriate	revile
gainsay	tirade
harangue	vituperate

On the test, for instance, you might see a Sentence Equivalence question like this one:

Select the **two** answer choices that, when inserted into the sentence, fit the meaning of the sentence as a whole **and** yield complete sentences that are similar in meaning.

The angry pedestrian _____ the careless driver for his recklessness.

A remonstrated

B reviled

C atoned

D vouchsafed

E lauded

F reproved

The correct answers to this Sentence Equivalence question are *remonstrated* **(A)** and *reproved* **(F)**—if you know that *remonstrate* means something like "criticize," that should be enough to know that *reprove* (which means "chastise") will yield a sentence that means nearly the same thing. *Reviled* is a tempting but deceptive choice. *Reproved* and *remonstrated* both have a connotation suggestive of criticism. *Reviled*, meaning "despised," would produce a sentence that makes sense (especially under the circumstances), but does not yield an equivalent sentence. The charge of the word *reviled* is far stronger than the other two, and produces a sentence that is much more strident in tone.

You can certainly add to the word lists provided in the appendices to this edition, or you can start to generate your own. In addition to synonyms and antonyms, you can also put together lists grouped by etymology, similar meaning, positive and negative connotations.

USE YOUR THESAURUS

The *criticize* group is not the only group of synonyms whose members appear frequently on the GRE. There are plenty of others. And lists of synonyms are much easier to learn than many words in isolation. Learn them with a thesaurus. Make synonym index cards based on the common groups of GRE words and **peruse** those lists periodically.

If you think this suggestion might be **fallacious**, consider the following: the words in the following list all have something to do with the concept of falsehood. Their precise meanings vary: *erroneous* means "incorrect," whereas *mendacious* means "lying." But the majority of test questions won't require you to know the exact meanings of these words. You will most likely get the question right if you simply know that these words have something to do with the concept of falsehood. If you do have to differentiate between different shades of meaning, that's where contextual clues will help you out.

FALSEHOOD

apocryphal	fallacious
canard	feigned
chicanery	guile
dissemble	mendacious/mendacity
duplicity	perfidy
equivocate	prevaricate
erroneous	specious
ersatz	spurious

Consider this Text Completion question:

Though he was prone to ———, the corrupt executive was still capable of moments of honesty.

- Ⓐ displeasure
- Ⓑ mendacity
- Ⓒ failure
- Ⓓ levity
- Ⓔ histrionics

You might not know the exact denotation of **mendacity**, but, because you studied word groups, you'll know that it has the connotation of "*false*," which will be enough to get the question right. Additionally, you'll be able to **intuit** the fact the answer is going to have to have the opposite meaning of "honesty," if you recognize that the word "though" is signaling that the answer will be contrasted with "honesty." Additionally, even if you have no clue what "mendacity" means, you can still eliminate all the other answers as incorrect.

GREEK AND LATIN ROOTS

Because GRE words are so heavily drawn from Latin and Greek origins, learning roots can be extremely useful, both in **deciphering** words with **obscure** meanings and in guessing intelligently. Studying Latin and Greek roots can allow you to figure out the definitions of words you've never even seen before!

You'll learn more words in less time if you learn them in groups. Once you know that the root PLAC means "to please," you have a hook for remembering the meanings of several words: *plac*ate, im*plac*able, *plac*id, *plac*ebo, and com*plac*ent.

Sometimes you can use roots to figure out the meaning of an unfamiliar word. Suppose, for example, you come across the word **circumnavigate** and don't know what it means. If you know that the root CIRCUM means "around" and that the root NAV means "ship, sail," then you can guess that *circumnavigate* means "to sail around," as in "*circumnavigate* the globe." Once you've learned the root, you will be able to recognize the meanings of other words with that root, such as "circumvent" or "circuitous."

Consider the word **panoptic**. It comes from the Greek PAN, meaning "all," and OPTIC, meaning "to see/observe." If you put it all together, you'll arrive at a definition like "everything visible in one view." If you know that, you have an advantage in deconstructing other words that incorporate similar constituent parts. You'll have an easier time **parsing** language with words like **panacea**, **optician**, and **pandemonium**.

Roots offer a common denominator for words thousands of years old—but language changes a lot over time, and words take on new meanings or lose old meanings. Roots don't always give accurate clues about meaning. For example, **affinity** seems to contain the root FIN, meaning "end," but *affinity* means "a kinship" or "attractive force."

There are other problems with using roots to pinpoint a definition. Looking at the **etymology** of a word is a great trick if you know Greek, Latin, or French. For example, DEM in Greek means "people." **Democracy** essentially means "government of the people." This approach can be helpful, but it's not without complications. Most notably, there are exceptions.

> Example: The word **venal**. The root VEN/VENT means "to come" or "to move toward." But **venal** means "corrupt or capable of being bought." **Adventure,**

convene, event, avenue, advent, and *circumvent* clearly spring from the root meaning. *Venal* is a bit of a stretch.

Example: The word *pediatrician* has PED for a root. PED has to do with the foot. But a *pediatrician* is a children's doctor. A *podiatrist* is a foot doctor. It turns out that PED in regards to feet is a Latin root but PED in regards to children is a Greek root.

The good news is that these **aberrations** are precisely that: exceptions that prove the rule. More often than not, you should be able to use etymology to your advantage.

WORDS IN CONTEXT

Learning words in context is one of the best ways for the brain to retain word meanings. In GRE Resources at the back of this book, we've not only listed the top 200 GRE words with their definitions, but we've also used all of these words *in context* to help you to remember them. After all, the test is trying to measure how well prepared applicants are for graduate-level academic study. Most graduate students spend the balance of their time deciphering dense, high-level writing. Given that, your best bet is to read material written for an educated audience and written at the graduate level.

Reading is ultimately the best way to increase your vocabulary, although it also takes the most time. Of course, some types of reading material contain more GRE vocabulary words than others. You should get into the habit of reading publications written in a sophisticated register with dense prose, such as the *Wall Street Journal* and the *New York Times*. And because you'll have to read from the computer screen on test day, Kaplan recommends that you start reading these publications online, if possible. You might as well start getting accustomed to reading in the testing mode.

This is also a good place to incorporate a technique mentioned earlier: composing practice sentences using the words you're studying. This will ingrain the words in your mind by situating them within a meaningful context.

PARTS OF SPEECH

The GRE never directly tests your ability to classify words by part of speech, but you will get a higher score on test day if you can distinguish nouns, adverbs, adjectives, and verbs. If you know how an answer choice must fit into a sentence, you'll be better equipped to narrow down the possible answer choices. Use your understanding of grammar and syntax to help you arrive at the correct answer.

Words With Multiple Meanings

Remember that words can have more than one meaning, and they can also function as more than one part of speech. Here's a single word used as a noun, adjective, and verb:

As the test tube rested overnight, some *precipitate* formed. (noun)
It would be better to proceed with caution than to take *precipitate* action. (adjective)
Passage of the resolution could well *precipitate* rebellion. (verb)

The reason you should care about being able to identify the part of speech of a word is that it can help you on the test. If you're able to identify parts of speech, as well as the spelling changes words undergo when they function as a different part of speech, you'll have one more weapon in your arsenal for attacking Sentence Equivalence and Text Completion questions. In those question types, if you know that the correct answer choice must function as a verb, then you can cross off choices that can only function as nouns, for example.

Nouns

A noun names a person, place, or thing, and answers the questions "who?" "where?" or "what?" A noun can function as the subject ("The *eulogy* was eloquent") or object of a verb ("He wrote an eloquent *euology*").

If you know the meaning of a word, you can tell if it's a noun by thinking about the way it would be used in a sentence.

- If the word can function as the subject of a sentence, it's a noun.
- If it can be replaced by a nominative pronoun (he, she, it, or they), it's a noun.
- If you can put the word "a," "an," or "the" in front of it, it's a noun.
- If you don't know the meaning of a word, but it has one of the following suffixes, then it's probably a noun.

-ACY	-HOOD	-OGY
-AGE	-ICE	-OR
-ANCE	-ICS	-RY
-ANCY	-ISM	-SHIP
-DOM	-IST	-SION
-ENCE	-ITY	-TION
-ENCY	-MENT	-TUDE
-ERY	-NESS	-URE

Adjectives

An adjective describes a noun, answering the questions "what kind?" "which one?" or "how many?" In a sentence, you will generally find adjectives right in front of the nouns they describe ("The book is full of *sophomoric* humor") or after a form of the verb *to be* or some other verb that links subject and adjective. ("The book's humor is *sophomoric*").

If you know the meaning of a word, you can tell if it's an adjective by thinking about the way the word would be used in a sentence. If the word can be used to describe a noun, it's an adjective. Some adjectives have comparative and superlative forms (for *rife, rifer* and *rifest;* and for *sanguine, more sanguine* and *most sanguine*). You should also be able to identify adverbs, which function in the same way as adjectives, except that they describe verbs, adjectives, whole sentences, or other adverbs. Most adjectives can be turned into adverbs by adding *-ly* (*harshly*.)

If you don't know the meaning of a word, but it has one of the following suffixes, then it's probably an adjective.

-ABLE	-OUS	-ISH
-AL	-FUL	-IVE
-ANE	-IBLE	-LESS
-ANT	-IC	-OSE
-AR	-ILE	
-ENT	-INE	

Verbs

A verb is a word that represents an action, state, or relationship between two or more things. Every sentence must have at least one verb. The main verb usually comes right after the subject ("They *squander* their fortunes"), but sometimes it is separated from the subject ("The contestant with the second highest vote total *wins* the consolation prize"), and sometimes it even precedes the subject ("Quickly *flow* the years.")

If you don't know the meaning of a word, but it has one of the following suffixes, then it's probably a verb.

-EN	-IFY
-ESCE	-IZE

THE TEST MAKER'S FAVORITE GRE WORDS

The research team at Kaplan keeps tabs on GRE vocabulary words and determines which words appear more frequently than others. The following words all turn up time and again on the GRE, so it makes sense to memorize these words if you don't already know them. Of course, some words appear on the GRE more frequently than others.

The top 12 words on the GRE are:

ANOMALY	ASSUAGE	ENIGMA
EQUIVOCAL	ERUDITE	FERVID
LUCID	OPAQUE	PLACATE
PRECIPITATE	PRODIGAL	ZEAL

The next 20 most popular words are:

ABSTAIN	ADULTERATE	APATHY
AUDACIOUS	CAPRICIOUS	CORROBORATE
DESICCATE	ENGENDER	EPHEMERAL
GULLIBLE	HOMOGENOUS	LACONIC
LAUDABLE	LOQUACIOUS	MITIGATE
PEDANT	PRAGMATIC	PROPRIETY
VACILLATE	VOLATILE	

The Top GRE Words in Context section at the end of this book reviews these and 150 other top GRE words. Make sure you spend the time to get to know these words. At least some of them are bound to appear on the GRE you take.

VOCABULARY CONCEPTS PRACTICE SET

Directions: For each sentence below, choose one word for each set of blanks. Select the word or words that best fit(s) the meaning of the sentence as a whole.

1. Historical biographies are not merely restricted to objective assessments and empirical (i) _____. There is an inherently subjective aspect to the genre that often (ii) _____ the biographer's claim to objective neutrality.

	Blank (i)		Blank (ii)
A	reminiscences	D	disparages
B	data	E	belies
C	speculations	F	bolsters

2. The aging engineer found it strange that the (i) _____ etching process she studied as a student of technology was still considered (ii) _____ today.

	Blank (i)		Blank (ii)
A	porous	D	antiquated
B	innovative	E	translucent
C	implausible	F	novel

3. Auctions have a (i) _____ reputation. The most high-profile sales are the rarest ones when (ii) _____ prices are achieved for unique items; however, there are (iii) _____ occasions when items are sold well below their estimates and buyers get great bargains.

	Blank (i)		Blank (ii)		Blank (iii)
A	prestigious	D	incongruous	G	somber
B	infamous	E	unprecedented	H	myriad
C	contradictory	F	pretentious	I	quixotic

Directions: For each of the following questions, choose **two** of the answer choices below that, when used to complete the sentence, produce two completed sentences that are similar in meaning.

4. Celebrities often make themselves the subject of _____ as a result of their behavior in public.

- A gossip
- B derision
- C provocation
- D calumny
- E commendation
- F prestige

5. Though the scientist was cognizant of the fact that such vicissitudes were
_____ to the field of quantum mechanics, she was not discouraged.

- [A] salient
- [B] salubrious
- [C] inherent
- [D] helpful
- [E] opprobrious
- [F] endemic

6. High-quality treatment for neuropathic pain is not consistently implemented
in the medical community because the results of scientific investigations
for treatment are not currently reliable; they include strong _____ in the
populations studied, especially in children, which renders them incomparable.

- [A] zeal
- [B] propriety
- [C] nuance
- [D] differentials
- [E] variance
- [F] justification

VOCABULARY CONCEPTS PRACTICE SET ANSWERS AND EXPLANATIONS

1. B, E

A key phrase in the first sentence is "objective assessments," and the missing word parallels this phrase—this missing word is connected to "objective assessments" with the conjunction "and."

Reminiscences **(A)** and *speculations* **(C)** are wrong. Neither correlates with "objective assessments" as well as *data* **(B)** does—both are dispassionate enumerations of facts, whereas *reminisces* and *speculations* are subjective in nature.

Paraphrase the second complex sentence to predict the correct answer: "There is a subjective aspect that _____ their claim to objectivity." A good prediction is "denies." Choice **(E)**, *belies*, means "to contradict," so it's the correct answer. Choices **(D)** and **(F)**, *disparages* and *bolsters*, have different connotations that are either too negative or too positive, respectively, for the context of this sentence, so they're incorrect.

2. B, F

This seemingly straightforward sentence is actually a bit deceptive. The first blank is fairly easy: an engineer would not have studied a **(A)** *porous* (full of holes) or **(C)** *implausible* (difficult to believe) etching process, so the answer can only be **(B)**, *innovative*. While the word *strange* might at first indicate a direct contrast between the two blanks, such as **(D)**, *antiquated*, would have it, an engineer would actually *not* find it strange if the etching process she studied as a student was currently considered *antiquated*. She would, however, find **(F)**, *novel*, quite strange. If the technique was revolutionary quite some time ago, the engineer would be surprised that it was still currently novel.

3. C, E, H

The first sentence doesn't have enough information in it for you to fill in the first blank so you have to go to the second sentence for clues. Fortunately, it includes a detour road sign ("however") that contrasts "rare" auctions where unique items sell for a certain price with auctions whose items sell for less than anticipated. The word in the first blank that best characterizes these dissimilar auctions is choice **(C)**, *contradictory*. Choices **(A)** and **(B)**, *prestigious* and *infamous*, would inaccurately complete the meaning of the sentence.

For the second blank, you can paraphrase in order to predict the blank: "There are rare auctions where 'high' prices are paid for unique items, but at other auctions, items sell for below their estimate." If you scan the answer choices, none of the words means exactly that, but **(E)**, *unprecedented*, "like nothing that has come before," best completes the meaning of the sentence. A high price for a unique item isn't necessarily **(D)**, *incongruous* ("incompatible"), or **(F)**, *pretentious* ("pompous"), because at least one person—the buyer—thought the item was worth what he paid.

Finally, the third blank describes occasions when items sell for less than their estimated value. You know from the detour road sign that this sentence includes a contradiction.

Sales where prices are high are described as "rare," so sales where items sell below estimate must be frequent. The answer choice that best matches "frequent" is **(H)**, *myriad*, "a great number." Choices **(G)**, *somber* ("gloomy"), and **(I)**, *quixotic* ("foolishly idealistic"), make no sense in context.

4. B, D

Celebrities who behave poorly will make themselves vulnerable to *derision* and *calumny*, which both have a negative connotation of criticism. These two words work well in context, giving the resulting sentences a similar meaning. They're the right answers.

Note that the words **(E)** *commendation* and **(A)** *gossip* also work well in this sentence: If they behaved well, they could be commended. But there's no other term that produces a sentence with a meaning similar to that created by using "commendation," so it cannot be the correct answer. You need two words that have similar meanings and fit in the sentence. The same applies for "gossip." The two answer choices must produce sentences that have an equivalent meaning, and **(D)** *calumny* ("slander") and **(B)** *derision* ("ridicule") are the only two that will do so.

5. C, F

The sentence itself is relatively straightforward; there is something that is discouraging about studying the field of Quantum Mechanics, i.e. the undefined "vicissitudes" to which it is subject. **(A)** *salient* does not work because there is no other answer choice that means the same thing, and **(B)** *salubrious* and **(D)** *helpful* do not work, because they have a positive connotation, which does not make sense when used with "discouraging." **(C)** *inherent* and **(F)** *endemic* both mean "naturally a part of," and therefore both produce sentences that have the same meaning. Note that **(E)** *opprobrious* yields a sentence that makes sense, but there is no other term that will make a sentence of similar meaning to that one.

6. D, E

This passage is explaining why certain treatment protocols for neuropathy cannot be implemented. The end of the sentence suggests they are not used consistently because the results are very different in the populations studied, making them impossible to compare. Hence, you're looking for two words that have the meaning of "differing" or divergent. Both will produce sentences that have the meaning of "the results are based on populations with too many differing characteristics to be reliable." Choices **(D)** and **(E)**, *differentials* and *variance*, do that nicely. Note that you didn't need to know the *exact* definition of either *variance* or *differentials*. But you knew what the correct answers would have to mean, roughly. Knowing the roots of "differential" and "variance" (differ and vary) makes the problem much easier.

THE KAPLAN APPROACH TO READING COMPREHENSION

You're going to spend a great deal of your time breaking down dense, complicated prose passages while taking the GRE. These skills, and the ability to wrestle with some very difficult reading, are exactly what you'll need for your work in graduate school. Even engineering and science majors will need to read obtuse technical documents or lab reports, so the best way to excel on the test is to review the skills you'll need to analyze such texts.

BREAKING DOWN THE TEXT

As noted, the texts you'll encounter on the GRE Verbal Reasoning sections are similar to the complex reading you'll encounter in graduate school. For this reason, you will need to use the following steps when approaching a Reading Comprehension passage.

These principles hold true for every type of question you'll come across in GRE Reading Comprehension. Keep them in mind as you work through the passages and question sets.

1. Read the first third of the passage.

The first third of a Reading Comprehension passage usually introduces its topic and scope, the author's main idea or primary purpose, and the overall tone. It almost always hints at the structure that the passage will follow. Before diving into the rest of the passage, try to get a handle on the structure of the passage by reading the first third of it carefully. Look for key words such as *however*, *thus*, or *likewise*. These will help to indicate the direction, shape, and thrust of the passage. Pay close attention to how these key words affect the passage's tone and structure:

> **Structure and Tone.** A key strategy for Reading Comprehension is to understand not only the passage's purpose, but also its structure and tone. Many question sets will contain a question that concerns how the author organizes or expresses his or her ideas. Here are some classic GRE passage structures:
>
> - arguing a position (often a social sciences passage)
> - discussing something specific within a field of study (for example, a passage about Shakespearean sonnets in literature)
> - explaining some significant new findings or research (often a science passage)

"Tone" refers to an author's attitude towards his or her topic, or how he or she expresses his or her point of view. In passages that cite significant new findings or research, the tone is likely to be academic and detached. In passages that argue a position, the tone may be more forceful and opinionated. In some passages, the author may be describing the opinions of someone else. In this case, the tone might be narrative or descriptive. The tone would be argumentative if the author mentions the opinions of others in order to then debunk them. The correct answer choice for a "tone" question will use language similar to that found in the passage; a correct answer choice will not use language more extreme than that used in the passage.

2. Determine the topic, scope, and author's purpose.

Every passage boils down to one or more main ideas. Your job is to cut through the prose and find it. Often, the main idea is presented in the first third of the passage, but occasionally the author builds up to it gradually. Everything else in the passage supports the main idea. Almost every type of Reading Comprehension question will be easier to answer once you establish the main idea, because correct answer choices will be consistent with it, and incorrect choices will not. You can break down the main idea of a passage by determining the topic, scope, and purpose of a passage:

Topic vs. Scope. A topic is broad; its scope is focused. Scope is particularly important because answer choices that go beyond it will always be wrong. The broad topic of "James Joyce's *Ulysses*," for example, would be a lot to cover in 200 words. So if you encounter a passage about *Ulysses*, ask yourself, "What aspect of this topic does the author focus on?" Because of length limitations, it must be a narrow aspect. Whatever it is—the author's use of stream-of-consciousness, the novel's Homeric influences, its aftermath, the principal characters—is the passage's scope. Answer choices that deal with anything outside this narrowly defined aspect of the topic will be wrong.

Author's Purpose. As an author writes a passage, he or she chooses to develop it by including certain aspects of the topic at hand and excluding others. Those choices reflect the author's purpose and main idea. From the broadly stated topic (for example, solving world hunger), identify the narrower scope (a high-yield farming technique for doing so). That scope leads you to the author's purpose (to describe a new farming technique and its promise) and main idea (that the technology currently exists to solve the problem of world hunger). If you can uncover the author's purpose, you will be better able to answer the harder questions associated with a particular passage. Knowing the author's purpose will allow you to more easily answer questions about the author's main idea. It will also help you to make inferences about his or her reason for including a particular passage or paragraph.

As you read each passage, remember to do the following:

- Identify the topic.
- Narrow it down to its precise scope.
- Make a prediction about why the author is writing and where he or she is going with the passage.

3. Read strategically.

This principle highlights the difference between passive and active reading. Most reading is done passively. For example, you might read a magazine article or novel from beginning to end, without assimilating the details, themes, or connections. That kind of reading is inappropriate for the GRE.

Instead, you'll need to read *actively*. This means you'll have to get good at paraphrasing, looking for key words, and anticipating the direction the author is taking. These strategies help you think carefully about what you read *as you read it*. When you read actively, you don't just absorb the passage, you attack it! You can be an active reader by:

- Thinking about what you're reading
- Paraphrasing complex ideas
- Asking yourself questions about the passage as you read
- Jotting down notes about the author's arguments and counterarguments

Now that you have a grip on the argument(s) being made in support of the author's position, try to identify the counterarguments. The Verbal Reasoning portion of the GRE obliges you to wrestle a bit with the text. That's part of reading actively, which is exactly what you'll be doing in graduate school. It's not enough just to acknowledge and accept what's presented in the text as received wisdom. Note that how you engage with and analyze a passage will inevitably vary from passage to passage.

Try your hand at a short passage to get the hang of breaking it down. You can use the steps of the process above to help you deconstruct Reading Comprehension passages such as this one:

> The admissions policy at Carver City University stipulates that in considering applications for freshman admission from potential students who meet the entrance requirements, preference will be given to high school graduates who are permanent residents of Carver City. This policy is followed consistently by all admissions officers; however, although over 600 students have graduated from Carver City's high schools in the past year, some slots in the freshman class of 200 are filled by students who are not permanent residents of Carver City.

1. Read the first third of the passage.

The topic here is readily obvious: it's college admissions. The first sentence sets up the basic facts of the situation. The key word to take note of is *however*; that should be your first clue. It indicates that the author is setting up a conclusion that contradicts what you might expect from the evidence. In a passage this short, the structure is fairly simple as well. The first sentence presents the information you need about the admission process, and the second presents an outcome that is counterintuitive to that evidence.

2. Determine the topic, scope, and author's purpose.

As noted above, the topic is fairly obvious: college admissions at Carver City University. The specific scope is its admissions policy relating to high school graduates from Carver City itself. The author seems to be concerned mostly with the dearth of freshmen at Carver City University who are also permanent residents of Carver City. The author cites the friendly admissions policy for local applicants as part of his or her argument.

3. Read strategically.

Now, let's nail down what the author is actually saying. Trying to figure out the author's position tests our understanding of the passage's complicated logic. It's a bit tricky with this particular passage because the position is not explicitly stated. There's not a succinct "thesis statement," so you'll have to unpack things a bit. The author is trying to assert something about the high school graduates who are permanent residents of Carver City. The author makes sure you know that in the last year 600 students have graduated from Carver City's high schools. If any qualified Carver City resident who wants a slot in the class may have one, but not every slot in the class is filled by a Carver City resident, something must be amiss, as the freshman class consists of only 200 students. Since Carver City high school grads have preference, and there are more than enough of them (600 to fill 200 spots), they must either be unqualified in some way or they must not be applying to Carver City University. Remember the admission policy states that successful applicants must meet entrance requirements. Therefore, some of the slots in the freshman class must have been filled by applicants who both met entrance requirements and were not permanent residents of Carver City. You could paraphrase the position as, "there were some slots in the freshman class for which no qualified permanent resident applied."

Now consider what the author is implying. Though the author does not explicitly state it, he or she is intimating something about the previous year's graduating class. It could be that not enough qualified applicants chose to apply or that those who did apply did not meet entrance requirements. This is the kind of "active reading" of the text you'll need to do on the Reading Comprehension questions on the GRE.

READING COMPREHENSION STRATEGIES PRACTICE SET

Questions 1 through 3 are based on the passage below.

> Among the earliest published literature by African Americans were slave narratives—autobiographical accounts of the lives of slaves who lived primarily

in the American South in the early to mid-1800s. The themes addressed in these accounts, which consist of letters, notes, or a diary, frequently included escapes, slave auctions, interactions with plantation owners and abolitionists, and the forced separation of family members, often parents and children. Some of the best known slave narratives were written by Josiah Henson and Frederick Douglass. In the last three decades, a renewed awareness of the lives of enslaved African Americans has prompted a wave of novels and biographies, sometimes called "neo-slave narratives," in which modern writers such as Toni Morrison and Olivia Butler offer a historical or fictional representation of the lives of slaves.

1. According to the passage, each of the following could be described as a slave narrative EXCEPT:

    (A) an autobiography by a free-born African American man who lived in New Orleans in the 1830s

    (B) personal papers of African American field hands who were enslaved in Alabama

    (C) an account of two sisters being auctioned to different plantation owners in rural Georgia

    (D) a letter smuggled to an escaped slave from her brother, a slave in South Carolina

    (E) the diary of a Mississippi slave who was captured while attempting to escape

2. Consider each of the following choices separately and select all that apply. What distinction(s) does the author make between slave narratives and neo-slave narratives?

    [A] No neo-slave narratives were published in the early to mid-1800s.

    [B] Neo-slave narratives are written primarily by women, while most slave narratives were written by men.

    [C] Some neo-slave narratives are fictional, but all slave narratives are firsthand accounts.

3. The author's description of the characteristics of a slave narrative suggests which of the following conclusions?

    (A) The work of abolitionists in the northern states helped bring about the publication of slave narratives.

    (B) All of the narratives published in the early to mid-1800s were written by slaves living in southern states.

    (C) Most slave narratives were not published until over a century after they were written.

    (D) In the mid-1900s, fewer people knew about slave narratives than did people in the late 1900s.

    (E) The work of neo-slave narratives such as those by Butler and Morrison has helped to bring attention to older narratives by other writers.

Questions 4 through 6 are based on the passage below.

The problematic relationship between Heidegger's political views and his seminal status as a philosopher is a continuing point of contention in the historical assessment of his achievements. His contributions to Continental Philosophy in works such as *Sein und Zeit* have been read, in some circles, through the critical lens of his affiliation with National Socialism in Nazi Germany during the Second World War. His writing during that time covered a broad range of subjects, including philosophy, politics, and aesthetics. His work on ontology directly influenced his contemporary philosophical thinkers, such as Jean-Paul Sartre. Though he is widely regarded within philosophical circles as one of the preeminent luminaries, along with Husserl, in the modern development of ontology, there are scholars and thinkers in certain intellectual circles that militate against the value of his thought in its entirety. To regard Heidegger's work highly would be, in their eyes, to absolve him for his support of the politics of Nazism, even though he is being evaluated solely on the basis of his contributions to the study of philosophy, and not in any political context.

4. Select the sentence in the passage in which the author indicates the current attitude of critical reaction to Heidegger from the academic community in general.

5. Consider each of the following choices separately and select all that apply. The author asserts which of the following about Heidegger's work:

   A   Some academics view him positively for both his political and philosophical work.

   B   His legacy has been affected by his actions during World War II.

   C   Some academics in some circles view him positively for his contributions to philosophy, while other cannot countenance them at all because of his connection to the Nazis.

6. Which conclusion is implied by the author in his description of the status of Heidegger's legacy?

   A   Heidegger's work should not be given serious recognition due to his political views.

   B   The Second World War fostered a climate of intellectual innovation in Europe.

   C   It is possible to critically evaluate Heidegger's contributions to philosophy while not absolving him for his political views.

   D   Scholars should consider the entire body of work of a thinker, in every field to which he or she contributed, when assessing that thinker's legacy in any one field.

   E   It is impossible to divorce the study of politics from the study of philosophy.

READING COMPREHENSION STRATEGIES PRACTICE SET ANSWERS AND EXPLANATIONS

1. A

The first two sentences outline defining characteristics of slave narratives and provide examples of the kind of content they might include. Of the answer choices, the only one that falls outside the scope of the question is **(A)**; slave narratives were written by enslaved people, not by free people. Choices **(B)**, **(C)**, **(D)**, and **(E)** all fit the passage's criteria in terms of subject matter, authorship, and geography; choice **(A)** is the only one that deviates.

2. C

The passage's last sentence tells us that neo-slave narratives have been published in the last three decades, but nothing in the passage says the neo-slave narratives were born recently, only that there has been a wave recently. We can't assume there weren't any earlier. So, choice **(A)** is incorrect. Although the authors of slave narratives mentioned are both men, and the authors of neo-slave narratives mentioned are both women, there's no basis for us to conclude that this distinction holds true on a broader scale, **(B)**. Only choice **(C)** addresses a distinction the author draws between slave and neo-slave narratives. The passage supports the statement that all slave narratives were autobiographical, whereas neo-slave narratives may be biographical or fictional.

3. D

This question asks us to evaluate which conclusions follow logically from what the author says. The mention of "renewed interest" implies a previous lapse or reduction in interest, so **(D)** is a reasonable conclusion. The passage doesn't mention abolitionists or the process that led to the narratives' publication, so **(A)** is out of scope. The language of **(B)** is too extreme; you're told that the narratives were primarily, not completely, authored by slaves from the South. Choice **(C)** directly contradicts the first sentence of the passage. Choice **(E)** reverses the order of events presented in the passage; renewed interest in the narratives led to Butler and Morrison's writing, not the other way around.

4. Though he is widely regarded within philosophical circles as one of the preeminent luminaries, along with Husserl, in the modern development of ontology, there are scholars and thinkers in certain intellectual circles that militate against the value of his thought in its entirety.

The sentence you're looking for one that sums up how the intellectual community, as a whole, views Heidegger. This means it should encompass all parties, both those that are receptive to him and those that view him negatively. The second sentence, "His contributions to Continental Philosophy in works such as *Sein und Zeit* have been read, in some circles, through the critical lens of his affiliation with National Socialism in Nazi Germany during the Second World War" is tempting, but this is telling you the way in which his work has been interpreted, not the reactions or attitudes of the academic community. The last sentence provides justification for *why* certain scholars view him as they do, but does not account for the other schools of thought. The next-to-last sentence, "Though he is widely regarded within philosophical circles as one of the preeminent luminaries, along with Husserl, in the modern development of ontology, there are scholars and thinkers in certain intellectual circles that militate against the value of his thought in its entirety," sums up the complete range of reaction to Heidegger across the academic community.

5. B, C

Choice **(A)** is incorrect. The author nowhere explicitly states nor implies that anyone has a positive reaction to Heidegger's political views. He only intimates that scholars working in the study of philosophy have been influenced by his work in that field. Choice **(B)** is correct, because the author states that Heidegger's work, even in philosophy, has been viewed through this "critical lens." Answer choice **(C)** is also correct. The author cites philosophers, such as Sartre, as those who have reacted positively to his philosophy, and asserts that those who view him negatively do so because that cannot abide "absolving him" for his support of the Nazis.

6. C

This question asks you to engage the text at a deep level, and to infer what the author is suggesting. The conclusions available are all implied, so it will be important to pay close attention to the author's tone. The passage's main idea is the evaluation of a thinker's body of work by academic scholars in different fields. The author points out both Heidegger's tremendous accomplishments in the field of philosophy, and also his less-than-admirable involvement with the Nazi party. Choice **(B)** is dealt with nowhere in the passage. Choice **(E)** goes beyond the scope of the passage. Choice **(A)** is incorrect, because the author emphasizes Heidegger's influence on philosophers like Sartre, and makes certain to point out that it is in "their eyes" that Heidegger is so viewed, not the author's own. Choice **(D)** is incorrect because it is the opposite of what the author implies. Choice **(C)** is the correct answer because, in the last sentence of the passage, the author stresses that it is only Heidegger's contributions to philosophy that are being considered, not his political views. He seems to be suggesting that the two can be judged apart from one another.

In the chapters that follow this one, you will learn how to approach the three basic types of Verbal Reasoning problems on the GRE. Although the format of these problems—Text Completions, Sentence Equivalence, or Reading Comprehension—varies from problem to problem, one thing is true: they are all built on the foundations you studied in this chapter.

CHAPTER 5

Text Completion

INTRODUCTION TO TEXT COMPLETION

In the Text Completion question type, you will be asked to select one entry for each blank from the corresponding column of choices. Each question may include as many as three blanks.

You will find about six Text Completions in each Verbal Reasoning section. In each of these questions, one or more words from the sentence will be missing. This question type tests your ability to read critically—to recognize the point of the sentence and find the best word(s) to fit this meaning.

The directions for Text Completions will look like this:

> Each sentence below has one or more blanks, each blank indicating that something has been omitted. Beneath the sentence are five words for one-blank questions, and sets of three words for each blank for two- and three-blank questions. Choose the word or set of words for each blank that best fits the meaning of the sentence as a whole.

A Text Completion question with one blank will look like this:

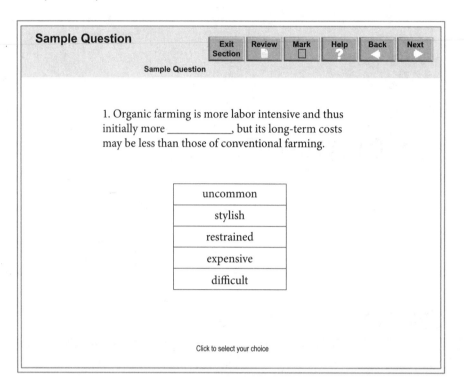

A Text Completion question with two blanks will look like this:

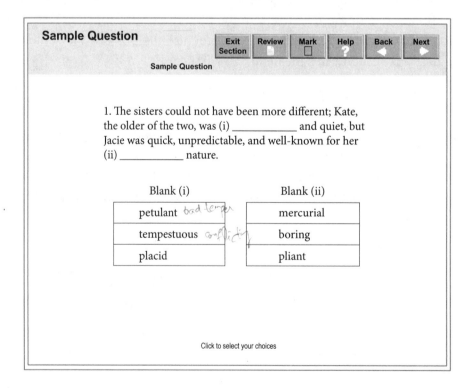

A Text Completion question with three blanks will look like this:

Sample Question

| Exit Section | Review | Mark | Help | Back | Next |

Sample Question

1. As a result of the (i) _____ pace of life, urban living (ii) _____ many young professionals the opportunity to (iii) _____ their lives with a sense of constant excitement.

Blank (i)	Blank (ii)	Blank (iii)
intrinsic	instigates	eschew
ephemeral	affords	inter
frenetic	arrogates	imbue

Click to select your choices

THE KAPLAN METHOD FOR TEXT COMPLETION (ONE-BLANK)

STEP 1   Read the sentence, looking for clues.

STEP 2   Predict an answer.

STEP 3   Select the choice that most closely matches your prediction.

STEP 4   Check your answer.

HOW THE KAPLAN METHOD FOR TEXT COMPLETION (ONE-BLANK) WORKS

Now let's discuss how the Kaplan Method for Text Completion (One-Blank) works:

❯❯ STEP 1
Read the sentence, looking for clues.

There are always clues in the sentence that will point you to the right answer. The missing words in Text Completion questions will usually have a relationship similar to or opposite from key words in the sentence.

On the GRE, a semicolon by itself always connects two closely related independent clauses. If a semicolon is followed by a road sign, then that clue word determines the direction. There are road signs in the GRE that tell you to go straight ahead and those that tell you to take a detour.

"Straight-ahead" road signs are used to make one part of the sentence support or elaborate another part. They continue the sentence in the same direction. The positive or negative connotation of what follows is not changed by these clues.

"Detour" road signs change the direction of the sentence. They make one part of the sentence contradict or qualify another part. The positive or negative connotation of an answer is changed by these clues.

Knowing the following lists of road signs will help you to determine which way the sentence is going and to predict what words will best complete the blank(s).

Straight-ahead road signs:	Detour road signs:
And	But
Since	Despite
Also	Yet
Thus	However
Because	Unless
; (semicolon)	Rather
Likewise	Although
Moreover	While
Similarly	On the other hand
In addition	Unfortunately
Consequently	Nonetheless
	Conversely

Key words and key phrases are the descriptors that lead to the meaning of the missing words.

STEP 2
Predict an answer.

Once you've found the road sign and the key word(s) relevant to the blank, predict an answer for the blank. Your prediction does not have to be a sophisticated or complex word or phrase, but simply a paraphrase that logically fits into the sentence. By predicting, you avoid the temptation of trying every answer choice on its own, which can take up valuable time on test day.

STEP 3
Select the choice that most closely matches your prediction.

Quickly go through the choices and see which one most closely matches, and eliminate whichever choices do not fit your prediction. If none of the choices match your prediction, you should reread the question and revisit Steps 1 and 2.

STEP 4
Check your answer.

This step is simply double-checking that you did your work correctly, and that your answer choice is correct in context. If your answer makes sense when you read your choice back into the sentence, you can confirm and move on. If your choice does not make sense when you read it back into the sentence, you should reread the question and revisit Steps 1 through 3.

How to Apply the Kaplan Method for Text Completion (One-Blank)

Now let's apply the Kaplan Method to a Text Completion (One-Blank) question:

1. The yearly financial statement of a large corporation may seem _____ at first, but the persistent reader soon finds its pages of facts and figures easy to decipher.

   (A) bewildering

   (B) surprising

   (C) inviting

   (D) misguided

   (E) uncoordinated

⟩ STEP 1
Read the sentence, looking for clues.

The sentence contains the detour road sign *but*, which indicates that the correct answer will mean the opposite of another key word or key phrase in the sentence. The key phrase to note in this example is "easy to decipher."

⟩ STEP 2
Predict an answer.

Knowing that the blank must contrast with the phrase "easy to decipher," you can predict that the blank will be similar to "difficult to understand."

⟩ STEP 3
Select the choice that most closely matches your prediction.

Quickly go through the choices and see which one most closely matches "difficult to understand," which in this case is choice **(A)**, *bewildering*.

⟩ STEP 4
Check your answer.

Plugging the word *bewildering* into the sentence fits the context: "The yearly financial statement of a large corporation may seem *bewildering* at first, but the persistent reader soon finds its pages of facts and figures easy to decipher."

Now let's apply the Kaplan Method to a second Text Completion (One-Blank) question:

1. Although the initial cost of installing solar panels to produce electricity can be _____, the financial benefits are realized for years to come in the form of reduced electric bills.

   (A) encouraging

   (B) minimal

   (C) exciting

   (D) misleading

   (E) exorbitant

❯❯ STEP 1

Read the sentence, looking for clues.

The sentence contains the detour road sign *although*, which indicates that the correct answer will mean the opposite of a key word or key phrase in the sentence. The key phrase to note in this example is "reduced electric bills."

❯❯ STEP 2

Predict an answer.

Knowing that the blank must contrast with the phrase "reduced electric bills," you can predict that the blank will be similar to "increased or high payments or costs."

❯❯ STEP 3

Select the choice that most closely matches your prediction.

Quickly go through the five choices and see which one most closely matches "increased or high payments or costs," which in this case is choice **(E)**, *exorbitant*.

❯❯ STEP 4

Check your answer.

Plugging the word *exorbitant* into the sentence fits the context: "Although the initial cost of installing solar panels to produce electricity can be *exorbitant*, the financial benefits are realized for years to come in the form of reduced electric bills."

THE KAPLAN METHOD FOR TEXT COMPLETION (TWO-BLANK AND THREE-BLANK)

STEP 1   Read the sentence, looking for clues.

STEP 2   Predict an answer for the easier/easiest blank.

STEP 3   Select the answer choice that most closely matches your prediction.

STEP 4   Predict and select for the remaining blanks.

STEP 5   Check your answers.

HOW THE KAPLAN METHOD FOR TEXT COMPLETION (TWO-BLANK AND THREE-BLANK) WORKS

Now let's discuss how the Kaplan Method for Text Completion (Two-Blank and Three-Blank) works:

▶ STEP 1
Read the sentence, looking for clues.

There are clues in the sentence that will point you to the right answer. The missing words in Text Completions will usually have a relationship similar or opposite to other words in the sentence. Now that you have multiple blanks to contend with, it is even more important to watch your road signs. Different signs will point different ways, and you will also need to keep track of your key words and key phrases. Remember, you need to get the answer choices for *all* the blanks right for the question to be scored as correct.

On the GRE, a semicolon by itself always connects two closely related independent clauses. If a semicolon is followed by a road sign, then that road sign determines the direction. There are road signs in the GRE that tell you to go straight ahead and others that tell you to take a detour.

"Straight-ahead" road signs are used to make one part of the sentence support or elaborate another part. They continue the sentence in the same direction. The positive or negative connotation of what follows is not changed by these clues.

"Detour" road signs change the direction of the sentence. They make one part of the sentence contradict or qualify another part. The positive or negative connotation of an answer is changed by these clues.

Refer to the list of road signs in the previous section to help you to determine which way the sentence is going and to predict what words will best complete the blank.

STEP 2
Predict an answer for the easier/easiest blank.

Identify the easier/easiest blank to work with. Once you've found the road sign and the key word(s) relevant to the easier/easiest blank, predict an answer for that blank. Your prediction does not have to be a sophisticated or complex word or phrase, but simply a paraphrase that logically fits into the sentence. By predicting, you avoid the temptation of trying every answer choice on its own, which can take up valuable time on test day.

STEP 3
Select the answer choice that most closely matches your prediction.

Quickly go through the choices and see which one most closely matches your prediction. Simultaneously, eliminate whichever answer choices do not fit your prediction. If none of the choices match your prediction, you should reread the question and revisit Steps 1 and 2. If one does match, you should proceed to Step 4.

STEP 4
Predict and select for the remaining blanks.

Once you have completed the easier/easiest blank, you provide a context in which to interpret the remaining blanks.

For two-blank Text Completions, use the context to help you choose the answer for the remaining blank. If the answers for the second blank are not working out, you know you need to go back to Step 2.

For three-blank Text Completions, select the easier of the two remaining blanks and predict which choice will most logically complete the sentence. You now have two blanks to provide context for the last, most difficult blank. This way, your approach to two and three-blank questions is just a logical extension of your approach to one-blank questions.

STEP 5
Check your answers.

This step is simply double-checking that you did your work correctly, and that your answer choices are correct in context. If your answers make sense when you read your choices back into the sentence, you can confirm and move on. If your choices do not make sense when you read them back into the sentence, you should reread the question and revisit Steps 1 through 4.

HOW TO APPLY THE KAPLAN METHOD FOR TEXT COMPLETION (TWO-BLANK AND THREE-BLANK)

Now let's apply the Kaplan Method to a Text Completion (Two-Blank) question:

1. Everyone believed the team was favored with athletic talent and a seasoned, successful coaching staff; consequently, it was difficult to (i)_____ why the team was (ii) _____ so badly against one of the worst teams in the division.

Blank (i)		Blank (ii)	
A	fathom	D	elevating
B	reveal	E	dominating
C	explore	F	floundering

➤ STEP 1

Read the sentence, looking for clues.

In this sentence, the straight-ahead road sign *consequently* indicates that the correct answer will support, or elaborate on another word or phrase in the text. The key word to note in this example is "badly."

➤ STEP 2

Predict an answer for the easier/easiest blank.

Knowing that the second blank must support or elaborate on the phrase "so badly," you can predict that the blank will be similar to "not doing very well."

➤ STEP 3

Select the answer choice that most closely matches your prediction.

Quickly go through the three choices and see which one most closely matches "not doing very well," which, in this case, is choice **(F)**, *floundering*.

➤ STEP 4

Predict and select for the remaining blanks.

Once you have completed the easier blank, you have a context in which to interpret the remaining missing word.

For the remaining blank, select the choice that will most logically complete the sentence. The first clause in the sentence indicated that the team should be good, but it is doing poorly, and this is "difficult" for everyone, because it does not make sense. In other words, it is hard to understand. The answer choice most like "understand" is **(A)**, *fathom*.

❯❯ STEP 5
Check your answers.

Plugging the selected words into the sentence fits the context: "Everyone believed the team was favored with athletic talent and a seasoned, successful coaching staff; consequently, it was difficult to *fathom* why the team was *floundering* so badly against one of the worst teams in the division."

Now let's apply the Kaplan Method to a Text Completion (Three-Blank) question:

It seemed there would be no resolving the matter, since both sides felt they had reached an (i) _____; neither side would (ii) _____, and the resulting (iii) _____ would keep their relationship strained and fragile for years to come.

Blank (i)		Blank (ii)		Blank (iii)	
A	apogee	D	capitulate	G	acrimony
B	epiphany	E	regress	H	cacophony
C	impasse	F	impugn	I	sinecure

❯❯ STEP 1
Read the sentence, looking for clues.

In this sentence, there are clues in the phrases "no resolving the matter" and "strained and fragile," which, along with the straight-ahead road signs "since" and "and," suggest that the correct answers are going to describe or support a conflict between disagreeing parties. In this example, you may already sense the words that complete at least one of the blanks just from the construction of the sentence.

❯❯ STEP 2
Predict an answer for the easier/easiest blank.

Determine that the answer for the first blank must support or elaborate on the phrase "no resolving the matter."

❯❯ STEP 3
Select the answer choice that most closely matches your prediction.

Quickly go through the choices and see which one most closely matches "no resolving the matter." You can predict the answer will be **(C)**, *impasse*.

STEP 4
Predict and select for the remaining blanks.

For the remaining blanks, select the choice that will most logically complete the sentence. The sentence tells us the sides are at an *impasse*, or blocked path. Predict the answers for the second and third blanks by thinking how groups at an impasse would feel and act. Determine that they are not willing to **(D)** *capitulate*, or give in on their demands, and that the result would be **(G)** *acrimony*, or bitter feelings, between the two sides.

STEP 5
Check your answers.

Plugging the words *impasse*, *capitulate*, and *acrimony* into the sentence fits the context: "It seemed there would be no resolving the matter, since both sides felt they had reached an *impasse*; neither side would *capitulate*, and the resulting *acrimony* would keep their relationship strained and fragile for years to come."

KAPLAN'S ADDITIONAL TIPS FOR TEXT COMPLETION QUESTIONS

Look for What's Directly Implied and not an Ambiguous Interpretation
The questions you'll encounter are written in sophisticated but still logical and straight-forward prose. Therefore, the correct answer is the one most directly implied by the meanings of the words in the sentence. These sentences are constructed to allow you to identify the answer using the inferential strategies you just practiced.

Don't Be Too Creative
Read the sentence literally, not imaginatively. Pay attention to the meaning of the words, instead of any associations or feelings that might come up for you.

Paraphrase Long or Complex Sentences
You may encounter a sentence that, because of its length or structure, is hard to get a handle on. When faced with a complex sentence, slow down and put it in your own words. You could break it into pieces as well and tackle one phrase at a time.

Use Word Roots
In the Resource section of this book, you can learn the Latin and Greek roots of many common GRE words. If you can't figure out the meaning of a word, take a look at its root to try to get close to its meaning. Etymology can often provide clues to meaning, especially when you couple a root definition with the word in context.

TEXT COMPLETION PRACTICE SET

Try the following Text Completion questions using the Kaplan Method for Text Completion. If you're up to the challenge, time yourself; on test day, you'll want to spend only 1 to 1.5 minutes on each question depending on the number of blanks.

1. The young man always had to have the last word; he would rather be disliked than _____.

   A gainsaid

   B selfish

   C remembered

   D praised

   E different

2. The giant squid's massive body, adapted for deep-sea life, breaks apart in the reduced pressures of higher ocean elevations, making the search for an intact specimen one of the most _____ quests in all of marine biology.

   A meaningful

   B elusive

   C popular

   D expensive

   E profitable

3. Although situated in the same neighborhood, the little brick house seemed (i) _____ compared to the ornate, almost (ii) _____ new house beside it.

	Blank (i)		Blank (ii)
A	impressive	D	translucent
B	dilapidated	E	diminutive
C	desirable	F	ostentatious

4. The (i) _____ gave such an ingenious speech that the crowd seemed moved to (ii) _____.

	Blank (i)		Blank (ii)
A	orator	D	despair
B	miscreant	E	duress
C	interloper	F	ebullience

5. His explosive, rude remarks convinced many that he was (i) _____ and of (ii) _____ character, suddenly making his future as a politician seem (iii) _____.

	Blank (i)		Blank (ii)		Blank (iii)
A	indifferent	D	courageous	G	guaranteed
B	charming	E	virtuous	H	precarious
C	volatile	F	ignoble	I	facetious

TEXT COMPLETION PRACTICE SET
ANSWERS AND EXPLANATIONS

1. A

The semicolon between these clauses is a straight-ahead road sign; these two ideas are closely related or elaborate upon each other. Since the blank is in the second clause, look to the first for direction. There you discover that this person always has to be right, or have the last word in an argument. The second clause will be consistent with this notion; it explains just how much he needs the last word. He would rather be disliked than have what happen? A good prediction would be: "He'd rather be disliked than contradicted."

Choice **(A)** *gainsaid* matches the prediction, but look at the others just to be sure. Scanning the other choices quickly, you see that all of the remaining options do not support the first part of the sentence. None of these other choices reinforces the idea that he always has to be right, so even if you aren't familiar with the word *gainsaid* you can still get the right answer.

2. B

The key word here is "intact," which means that although specimens have been collected, they have rarely (if ever) been in one piece when recovered. You can fairly assume that recovering an intact specimen is difficult. When you look for a synonym for "difficult" in the answer choices, you recognize *elusive* **(B)** as your answer.

3. B, F

In this case, the second blank is easier to predict than the first, so start with that one. The word "almost" before the second blank tells you the correct choice will be a word that means the nearly same as "ornate." Something *ostentatious* is considered showy, excessive, or ornate, so the correct choice is **(F)**.

There are several road signs, key words, and phrases in this sentence that give clues. "Although" and "compared" tell you there is something the same, and also something different about the two houses. The detour road sign "although" tells us the choice in the first blank will have a meaning opposite of "ornate", and will be a synonym for "run-down." The state of being "run-down" is not considered *impressive* **(A)**, or *desirable* **(C)**, so the correct choice is **(B)**, *dilapidated*.

4. A, F

The key phrase for the first blank is "ingenious speech." You can tell the correct answer for the first blank is someone who can speak well. *Miscreants* **(B)** and *interlopers* **(C)** are not usually thought of as excellent speakers, but *orators* are. The correct choice is **(A)**.

For the second blank, the key words are "ingenious" and "moved," which tell you the speaker's words had a positive effect on the crowd. Since *despair* **(D)** and *duress* **(E)** are not positive, the answer is **(F)** *ebullience*.

5. C, F, H

For the first blank, the key phrase is "explosive, rude remarks." Choice **(A)** *indifferent* suggests neutrality, but being explosive and rude is far from being neutral. The second choice, *charming* **(B)**, does not make sense because someone who is "explosive" and "rude" is not usually seen as being charming. Choice **(C)** *volatile* means "unstable," the same as explosive.

Since we know the subject of the sentence is explosive, rude, and volatile, we can predict his character will be seen in negative ways. Because *courage* and *virtue* have positive connotations, choice **(F)** *ignoble* is the correct choice.

With the information that he is explosive, rude, volatile, and ignoble, predict what kind of "future as a politician" he will have. This is the key phrase for identifying the third blank. His character suggests he may not be popular, so we can conclude his future is not **(G)** *guaranteed*. Choice **(I)** *facetious*, means "*witty*," which does not fit with the negative description of the speaker. Choice **(H)** *precarious*, means "uncertain", which fits the context of the sentence and is the correct choice.

CHAPTER 6

Sentence Equivalence

INTRODUCTION TO SENTENCE EQUIVALENCE

Each Verbal Reasoning section features approximately four Sentence Equivalence questions. In each sentence, one word will be missing, and you must identify two correct words to complete the sentence. The correct answer choices, when used in the sentence, will result in the same meaning for *both* sentences. This question type tests your ability to figure out how a sentence should be completed by using the meaning of the entire sentence.

The directions for Sentence Equivalence will look like this:

> Select the **two** answer choices that, when inserted into the sentence, fit the meaning of the sentence as a whole **and** yield complete sentences that are similar in meaning.

A Sentence Equivalence question will look like this:

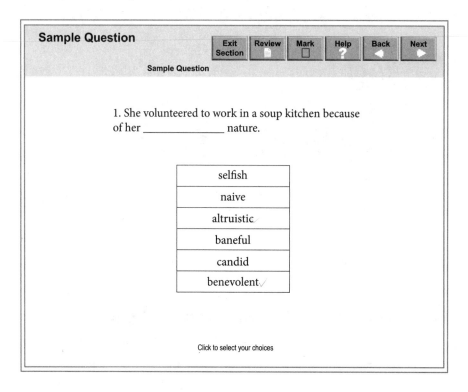

THE KAPLAN METHOD FOR SENTENCE EQUIVALENCE

STEP 1 **Read the sentence, looking for clues.**

STEP 2 **Predict an answer.**

STEP 3 **Select the two choices that most closely match your prediction.**

STEP 4 **Check your answers to see if the sentence retains the same meaning.**

HOW THE KAPLAN METHOD FOR SENTENCE EQUIVALENCE WORKS

Now let's discuss how the Kaplan Method for Sentence Equivalence works:

◆ STEP 1

Read the sentence, looking for clues.

As you read the sentence, pay attention to the part of speech that the answer choice will be, and compare it with the answer choices. Also look for specific words in the sentence that will help you to understand its meaning. These are called "key words" or "road signs"—descriptive phrases or contextual clues that suggest the meaning of the missing word.

Words that connect one part of a sentence to another ("straight-ahead" road signs) include:

And	*Also*
Similarly	*Thus*
In addition	*Because*
Consequently	*Likewise*
Since	*Moreover*

Words that show one part of the sentence contradicts another part of the sentence ("detour" road signs) include:

But	*Although*
Despite	*While*
Yet	*On the other hand*
However	*Unfortunately*
Unless	*Nonetheless*
Rather	*Conversely*

Being aware of these road signs will help you to figure out the meaning of the sentence.

◆ STEP 2
Predict an answer.

Once you have read the sentence and identified clues to words that will complete the sentence, predict an answer. Your prediction should be a word that you choose on your own BEFORE you look at the answer choices. The prediction word should also be a simple word that logically completes the sentence.

◆ STEP 3
Select the two choices that most closely match your prediction.

Quickly review the six answer choices and choose the two words that, when plugged into the sentence, most closely match the intended meaning of the sentence with your prediction. Eliminate the answer choices that do not fit your prediction. Sometimes you will need to adjust your prediction in order to find two answer choices that match each other.

◆ STEP 4
Check your answers to see if the sentence retains the same meaning.

Read the sentence with each answer choice to check that you have selected the correct answers. Make sure that both answer choices make sense in the context of the sentence. Pay close attention to the charge of a word's meaning. For example, "dislike" and "despise" both mean the same thing, but "despise" has a much *stronger* degree of charge to that meaning. Each sentence should have the same meaning. If one or both of your answers does not make sense when you reread the sentence, revisit the question and repeat Steps 1, 2, and 3.

How to Apply the Kaplan Method for Sentence Equivalence

Now let's apply the Kaplan Method to a Sentence Equivalence question:

1. She volunteered to work in a soup kitchen because of her _____ nature.

   A selfish

   B naive

   C altruistic

   D baneful

   E candid

   F benevolent

◆ STEP 1

Read the sentence, looking for clues.

One clue to the correct answer in this sentence is to figure out the part of speech of the missing word. The missing word in this sentence is an adjective. Another clue in this sentence is the key word "volunteer." A volunteer is someone who offers his or her time or skills without pay. The blank will be an adjective with a positive connotation that describes the type of person who volunteers.

◆ STEP 2

Predict an answer.

Knowing that the blank must describe someone who offers his or her time or skills without pay, you can predict that the blank will be similar to "helpful."

◆ STEP 3

Select the two choices that most closely match your prediction.

Quickly review the six answer choices to see which two words most closely match "helpful," which in this case are choice **(C)** *altruistic* and choice **(F)** *benevolent*.

◆ STEP 4

Check your answers to see if the sentence retains the same meaning.

Plug each answer choice into the sentence to see if it matches the context. Make sure that each sentence has the same meaning:

"She volunteered to work in a soup kitchen because of her altruistic nature."

"She volunteered to work in a soup kitchen because of her benevolent nature."

Now let's apply the Kaplan Method to a second Sentence Equivalence question:

1. While the first speaker at the conference was confusing and unclear, the second speaker was _____.

   - A articulate
   - B experienced
   - C melancholy
   - D ambiguous
   - E eloquent
   - F vociferous

❱❱ STEP 1
Read the sentence, looking for clues.

In this sentence, the clue word "while" is a detour road sign. "While" indicates that the second part of the sentence will mean the opposite of the first part of the sentence. The first speaker was described as "confusing" and "unclear," which are the key words in this question. The correct answer means the opposite.

❱❱ STEP 2
Predict an answer.

Knowing that the blank will mean the opposite of "confusing" and "unclear," you can predict that blank will be similar to "clear."

❱❱ STEP 3
Select the two choices that most closely match your prediction.

Quickly go through the six answer choices and see which two words most closely match "clear" in the context of speaking, which in this case are choice **(A)** *articulate* and choice **(E)** *eloquent*.

❱❱ STEP 4
Check your answers to see if the sentence retains the same meaning.

Plug each answer choice into the sentence to see if it matches the context. Make sure that each sentence has the same meaning:

"While the first speaker at the conference was confusing and unclear, the second speaker was <u>articulate</u>."

"While the first speaker at the conference was confusing and unclear, the second speaker was <u>eloquent</u>."

KAPLAN'S ADDITIONAL TIPS FOR SENTENCE EQUIVALENCE

Consider All Answer Choices

Make sure to read and check all answer choices in the sentence before making your final choice. An answer may fit well in the sentence and closely match your prediction, but if there is no other answer choice that also completes the sentence with the same meaning, it isn't correct.

Paraphrase the Question

If you rephrase a difficult or longer sentence into your own words, it will be easier to make a prediction for the answer. Paraphrasing will also make sure that you understand the meaning of the sentence.

Look Beyond Synonyms

Simply finding a synonym pair in the answer choices will not always lead you to the correct answer. Answer choices may include a pair of words that are synonyms, but do not fit in the context of the sentence. Both of those two choices will be incorrect. The meaning of each sentence must be the same and correct. Be sure to try both words in the sentence, checking that each sentence has the same meaning, before making your final choice.

Use Prefixes, Suffixes, and Roots

Think about the meaning of the prefixes, suffixes, and roots in words that you know if you are struggling to figure out the definition of a word.

SENTENCE EQUIVALENCE PRACTICE SET

Try the following Sentence Equivalence questions using the Kaplan Method for Sentence Equivalence. If you're up to the challenge, time yourself; on test day, you'll want to spend only about one minute on each question.

1. She was unable to move her arm after the stroke; in addition, it _____ her ability to speak.

   A appeased
   B satisfied
   C impeded
   D helped
   E hindered
   F assisted

2. Although the lab assistant openly apologized for allowing the samples to spoil, her _____ did not appease the research head, and she was let go.

   A insincerity
   B frankness
   C falsehoods
   D candor
   E inexperience
   F hesitation

3. Afterwards, the late man's wife could not stop crying; similarly, his daughter was very _____.

   A overjoyed
   B morose
   C abashed
   D lucid
   E nonplussed
   F sullen

4. Her last-minute vacation was _____ compared to her usual trips, which are planned down to the last detail.

   A expensive

   B spontaneous

   C predictable

   D satisfying

   E impulsive

   F atrocious

5. After staying up all night she felt extremely _____; however, she still ran three miles with her friends.

   A apprehensive

   B lethargic

   C controversial

   D sluggish

   E vigorous

   F energetic

76

SENTENCE EQUIVALENCE PRACTICE SET ANSWERS AND EXPLANATIONS

1. C, E

The straight-ahead road sign "in addition" in this sentence is a clue that both parts of the sentence are related. Since the missing word is in the second part of the sentence, the first part gives a clue to what your prediction should be. The person had a stroke and was unable to move her arm.

Use this to make a prediction such as: "She was unable to move her arm after the stroke; in addition, it <u>prevented</u> her ability to speak."

Quickly review the answer choices looking for two words that closely match your prediction. **(C)** *Impeded* and **(E)** *hindered* both have the meaning "to interfere," and produce sentences with equivalent meaning. The other four choices do not have meaning anywhere close to "prevented." Choices **(A)** *appeased*, **(B)** *satisfied*, **(D)** *helped*, and **(F)** *assisted*, all have too positive a connotation to be correct. *Appeased* has the same meaning as *satisfy*, and *helped* and *assisted* both mean "to aid."

2. B, D

The clue in this sentence is the detour road sign "although," which indicates contrast. Knowing that the second half of the sentence will be the opposite of the first half, you can predict that the blank will be similar to "honesty." Choices **(A)**, **(C)**, **(E)**, and **(F)** are not synonyms for "honesty," leaving choices **(B)** and **(D)**. **(B)** *frankness* and **(D)** *candor* both carry the meaning of "forthright." They're your answers.

3. B, F

The word "similarly" in this sentence is a straight-ahead road sign that you can use to figure out the blank. It indicates that the sentence will continue to move in the same direction, and the word that goes in the blank will have a similar meaning. In the sentence, the wife was crying, and her daughter felt the same way.

Use this to make a prediction such as: "Afterwards, the late man's wife could not stop crying; similarly, his daughter was very <u>depressed</u>."

Choice **(A)**, *overjoyed*, is the opposite of depressed, so it does not make sense. Someone who feels *abashed*, choice **(C)**, is embarrassed. A *lucid* person, choice **(D)**, is very clear-headed, and *nonplussed* **(E)** means perplexed.

4. B, E

The phrase "compared to her usual trips" is a clue that the first half of the sentence will have an opposite meaning.

You can use this phrase to make a prediction such as: "Her last minute vacation was <u>unplanned</u> compared to her usual trips, which are planned down to the last detail."

Something that is unplanned is done without much preparation or careful thought. Both choice **(B)** and choice **(E)** match this prediction. Choice **(B)** *spontaneous* means something that happens without planning, and choice **(E)** *impulsive* means doing something without careful thought. Choice **(A)** *expensive*, doesn't fit with "unplanned"; nor does **(C)** *predictable* (the opposite); **(D)** *satisfying*; or **(F)** *atrocious*.

5. B, D

When someone stays up all night, he or she is usually very tired. The detour road sign in this sentence is "however," in the second clause. It indicates that the person in the sentence went running, which takes a lot of energy, even though he or she was up all night.

You can use this clue to make a prediction such as: "After staying up all night she felt extremely <u>tired</u>; however, she still ran three miles with her friends."

Choices **(E)** *vigorous* and **(F)** *energetic* are the opposite of tired. Choice **(A)** *apprehensive* can be used to describe someone who is anxious, but not tired. Choice **(C)** *controversial* can be used to describe something that is open to debate.

CHAPTER 7

Reading Comprehension

INTRODUCTION TO READING COMPREHENSION

Reading Comprehension is the only question type that appears on all major standardized tests, and with good reason. No matter what academic discipline you pursue, you'll have to make sense of dense, complex written material. This means that being able to understand and assess what you read is a critical skill for every graduate student.

To make the test as relevant as possible, and to better evaluate your ability to understand graduate-level material, ETS adapts its content from "real-world," graduate-level documents. The GRE traditionally takes its topics from four disciplines: social sciences, biological sciences, physical sciences, and the arts and humanities.

The GRE includes roughly ten reading passages spread between the two Verbal Reasoning sections of the test. Many of these passages are one paragraph in length, although a few are longer. Each passage is followed by one to six questions that relate to that passage. These questions will test your ability to ascertain the author's purpose and meaning, to consider what inferences can properly be drawn from the passage, to research details in the text, and to understand the meaning of words and the function of sentences in context.

A sentence that tells how many questions are based on each passage will appear in boldface before the passage, like this:

Questions 1-3 are based on the passage below.

A Reading Comprehension passage will look like this:

> Many baseball enthusiasts are aware of the story of how Abner Doubleday invented the game of baseball with some friends in 1839 and introduced it to a nation during the Civil War. However, most baseball historians now agree that this story is a convenient fiction, propagated by Albert Spalding, a player, manager, owner, and one of the first manufacturers of sporting equipment. Spalding's desire to distinguish baseball, which so keenly mirrored American interests and pursuits, from similar games played in England, such as cricket and rounders, led Spalding to seek out a purely colonial origin to the sport. Spalding's entire basis for the foundation of baseball history lay in a hand-written letter in 1907 that he said came from a man who claimed to have gone to school with Doubleday and attributed the invention to him. Despite the speculative and dubious claims of the letter, Spalding and other members of his commission were quick to adopt the narrative as gospel and began to market their sport to the masses as a truly American pursuit.

Reading Comprehension questions will take one of three forms. The first will ask you to select the best answer from a set of five possible answers. A Reading Comprehension question of this type will look like this:

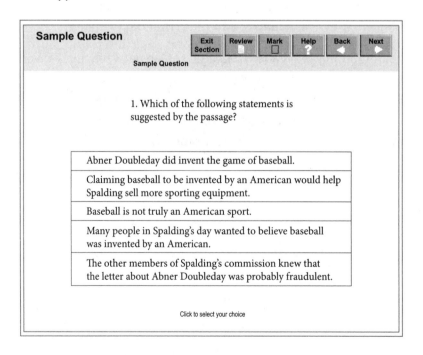

The second type of question gives you three different answers, one or more of which are true. You will be asked to mark down all correct answers. All correct answers must be selected, and no partial credit will be given for only getting some of the right answers. The directions for this type of question will look like this:

> Consider each of the following choices separately and select all that apply.

A Reading Comprehension question of this type will look like this:

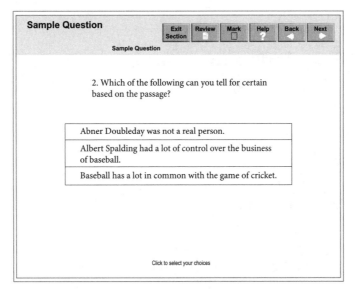

A third type of question asks you to select a sentence within the passage that best demonstrates the function or information requested by the question. A Reading Comprehension question of this type will look like this:

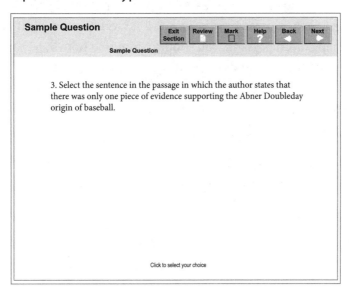

THE KAPLAN METHOD FOR READING COMPREHENSION

STEP 1   Read the passage strategically.

STEP 2   Analyze the question stem.

STEP 3   Research the relevant text in the passage.

STEP 4   Make a prediction.

STEP 5   Evaluate the answer choices.

How the Kaplan Method for Reading Comprehension Works

Now let's discuss how the Kaplan Method for Reading Comprehension works:

STEP 1
Read the passage strategically.

Reading strategically means identifying the topic, scope, and purpose of a passage, as well as noting the passage's structure and main points. The topic is the general subject matter, and the scope is the specific aspect of the topic that the author focuses on. The topic of the passage above is Abner Doubleday and baseball, but the scope is limited to the myth about his role in creating the sport.

In order to nail down topic, scope, and purpose, you should target the bones of the piece in the form of the passage's main ideas, primary arguments, secondary arguments, supporting statements or evidence, and conclusions. At this point you should start making your passage map or at least take notes on scratch paper about the points discussed above. For each paragraph, write a 1–2 sentence summary that highlights the main points. For any given passage, you should be able to both summarize the text and identify the main points in your own words before proceeding. It is also important to use the key words and phrases connected to the sentences to identify the important ideas and statements.

With each passage, you need to look for the purpose of the text: why was it written? While there will be numerous facts provided in any given piece, not all passages are purely informative. There will be some degree of persuasive elements to each passage, if only to convince you that the subject is important. The key is to identify early on whether the piece is primarily informative or argumentative. This can be done by recognizing the tone the author uses. Tone, loosely defined, is the attitude the author has towards his or her subject. Tone is indispensible in nailing down an author's purpose, especially if his or her purpose is not entirely explicit. If the author makes use of comparisons (*better, more effective*) or assertions (*should, must, need to*), then the author is likely trying to persuade you. If the author writes in a more straightforward style with no persuasive or judgmental terminology, the piece is likely informative. Pieces written in that tone are more likely to have the purpose of explanation or description in mind. Purpose is itself important, as it is closely tied to the author's *opinion* on the subject matter. This is of crucial importance for Inference questions.

In general, a social sciences piece is likely to argue a position, as the complex nature of human behavior and interaction is open to wide interpretation. Likewise, a discussion of a piece of art or literature will likely contain arguments as the author asserts an interpretation of these art forms. Scientific articles, on the other hand, will be mainly informative, seeking primarily to explain a scientific concept or discovery. Still, there may be arguments or conclusions drawn about the importance of these discoveries or principles in daily application. Therefore, you should pay close attention to tone, as it greatly informs the argument.

STEP 2
Analyze the question stem.

Many test takers attempt to "shortcut" the process of a Reading Comprehension passage by reading the question stems before reading the passage itself in hopes of giving themselves a "clue" about what to look for as they read. This is almost always a mistake. All Reading Comprehension requires an active awareness and understanding of what is being read, as described in Step 1. The nature of the question stem should not dissuade you from making your own interpretations prior to reading the passage. Therefore, you should be cautious and try not to allow the nature of the stem to influence your interpretation of a passage.

Also, one question stem following the passage may concern itself with a passage's tone, whereas another question may focus on a vocabulary term in context. Trying to read with these questions in mind will affect your sense of priority in interpreting the main ideas of the passage. It is more important for you to be able to use the question stem to know where to look in researching the passage for details than for you to try to use the stem as a roadmap in advance. Your passage map and/or notes will organize the reading well enough to allow you to find the correct answer(s) quickly.

The purpose of analyzing a question stem is to look for guidance as to the specificity and uniqueness of the answer being sought. Some questions are general questions that you may already have the answer to, such as "what is the purpose of this passage?" or "which of these mirrors the author's conclusion?" By having followed Step 1, you may already have the information needed to answer this question.

In many cases, however, there is a relationship between the answers that is indicated in the question stem and that should serve as a warning as to how to proceed. If a question asks for the "best" answer or one that "most closely describes" something in the passage, there may be more than one answer that arguably applies, but only one answer that most closely fits the question stem.

The question stem might also require you to go a step further and make a contrasting judgment against an idea in the passage. A question that asks for the "least likely" or answer that "differs" from the author's perspective would require you to understand the author's conclusions or viewpoints well enough to select the choice that is most opposed to that idea.

STEP 3
Research the relevant text in the passage.

Once you have analyzed and fully understood the question stem, you should already have an idea of where in the passage the answer will be found, due to your active reading in Step 1. You should not consider any more text from the passage than is necessary to answer the specific question. If the question is about vocabulary in context, you should not need to look much further than the sentence in which it appears, and possibly the preceding sentence, to arrive at the answer.

STEP 4
Make a prediction.

Many of the questions will, by design, test your comprehension of what you have read and not just your ability to go into the passage and mine for the correct details. As such, you will often have the ability to formulate a prediction as to the answers of many questions that deal with the main idea, conclusions, arguments, author's meaning, tone, and implications of the information provided. Before moving on to the provided answer choices, try to either form a response in your own mind or perhaps target a section in the passage that you think will be most likely to contain the answer.

There will be occasions in which you will have to infer an answer based on clues provided in the text that come in the form of details or author's tone. In these cases, if the question prompts you to consider a particular facet of the passage, you should first create your own hypothesis regarding that facet before moving on to the answers. The relevant sections of the passage for Step 3 are those that provide evidence or details to support (or refute) your conclusion. One note of caution: making a specific prediction is sometimes not possible for Inference questions. Instead, refer back to the passage or your passage map as necessary as you evaluate the answer choices.

❯ STEP 5
Evaluate the answers.

Even if there is an answer that clearly matches the prediction you have made, or an answer that jumps out at you as resoundingly correct, it is important to read and consider each answer choice. Eliminating incorrect answers not only helps narrow down options for questions that are hard to answer, it also validates the selection you are considering.

In absolute uncertainty, you should begin by identifying answers that are demonstrably wrong in answer to the question. Eliminating the answers can be done using the same steps above as for finding the right answer: by weighing them against the criteria set forth by your own reading and interpretation, the wording of the question stem, the relevant portions of text, and your predicted response, which can now be weighed against the remaining choices before repeating the steps above.

HOW TO APPLY THE KAPLAN METHOD FOR READING COMPREHENSION

Now let's apply the Kaplan Method to a Reading Comprehension passage and questions:

Many baseball enthusiasts are aware of the story of how Abner Doubleday invented the game of baseball with some friends in 1839 and introduced it to a nation during the Civil War. However, most baseball historians now agree that this story is a convenient fiction, propagated by Albert Spalding, a player, manager, owner, and one of the first manufacturers of sporting equipment. Spalding's desire to distinguish baseball, which so keenly mirrored American interests and pursuits, from similar games played in England, such as cricket and rounders, led Spalding to seek out a purely colonial origin to the sport. Spalding's entire basis for the foundation of baseball history lay in a hand-written letter in 1907 that he said came from a man who claimed to have gone to school with Doubleday and attributed the invention to him. Despite the speculative and dubious claims of the letter, Spalding and other members of his commission were quick to adopt the narrative as gospel and began to market their sport to the masses as a truly American pursuit.

1. Which of the following statements is suggested by the passage?

    Ⓐ Abner Doubleday did invent the game of baseball.

    Ⓑ Claiming baseball to be invented by an American would help Spalding sell more sporting equipment.

    Ⓒ Baseball is not truly an American sport.

    Ⓓ Many people in Spalding's day wanted to believe baseball was invented by an American.

    Ⓔ The other members of Spalding's commission knew that the letter about Abner Doubleday was probably fraudulent.

❱ STEP 1

Read the passage strategically.

If you were only to skim the beginning and end sentences of the passage, you would surmise that the topic is baseball, but could get tricked early on into thinking that the passage is about Abner Doubleday in scope. The key word "However" in the second sentence is indicative that it is the following sentence that is of greater importance. Indeed, the sentence does introduce the true point of focus: Albert Spalding and his impact on baseball. You might also note that while there are some judgmental terms (*speculative, dubious*) in the passage, the text's tone is that of an informative passage.

❱ STEP 2

Analyze the question stem.

The key phrase is "suggested by," which tells us that the answer is not explicitly stated in the text, but can be discerned by an accurate reading of the text. Each possible answer will have to be considered on its own merits. Remember that the answer has to be determined based on the information in the text alone, which must be assumed to be true for the purpose of answering the question, regardless of any outside knowledge.

❱ STEP 3

Research the relevant section in the text.

In this case, the relevant portions of the text will not become clear until after the answers are read, because the question stem did not give us a point of focus in its own regard. Here we see how the Kaplan method sometimes requires cycling through the steps in order to arrive at the right answer.

STEP 4
Make a prediction.

Although the question stem does not initially seem to provide enough information about its intent to allow you to make a prediction without seeing the answers, if you have been actively reading, it is likely that you have made some conclusions of your own regarding the text, such as to the veracity of the Abner Doubleday story and Albert Spalding's motivations—the unsaid implications of the text. These can serve you well in analyzing the answers.

STEP 5
Evaluate the answers.

Each given answer reflects a portion of the passage. With each, you should return to Step 3 and target the appropriate sections of the passage that help support or refute an answer. Choice **(A)** can immediately be eliminated because it is in direct opposition to the main idea of the piece, stated within the first two sentences. Similarly, choice **(C)** can be eliminated as being in disagreement with the passage. Even if the sport of baseball had its origins in other sports and other countries, the author states that baseball "mirrored American interests and pursuits" and implies that it is firmly embraced by American culture. Remember that you must decide based only on the passage, and even if another author might make the claim of answer **(C)**, the author of the passage doesn't. Choices **(B)** and **(E)** can both be eliminated because there is no evidence to support these claims within the text. The speed and willingness of Spalding and his commission to adopt the Doubleday story does provide evidence, however, for the correct answer, **(D)**.

How to Apply the Kaplan Method for Reading Comprehension

Now let's apply the Kaplan Method to a second Reading Comprehension question (based on the previous passage):

> Consider each of the following choices separately
> and select all that apply.

2. Which of the following can you tell for certain based on the passage?

      A   Abner Doubleday was not a real person.

      B   Albert Spalding had a lot of control over the business of baseball.

      C   Baseball has a lot in common with the game of cricket.

◈ STEP 1
Read the passage strategically.

One of the first steps in strategic reading is to determine the tone of the passage. In this case, it is informative. You are allowed the use of scratch paper, and creating a passage map is encouraged. With an informative piece, you should be identifying the main ideas and facts of the issue. Doing this will help to answer a multiple selection question such as this one.

◈ STEP 2
Analyze the question stem.

Even though the question says "which of the following," the directions for the question remind us that there may be more than one answer. The question stem also mentions "based on the passage," but for the purposes of the test, this is <u>always true</u>, even when not stated. The key phrase for this question is "can you tell for certain." This tells us that we should eliminate any answer choices that are not absolutely confirmed by the text.

◈ STEP 3
Research the relevant section in the text.

Again, each answer will have to be considered on its own merits, but your outline will tell you where to search for the answer. As you determined from analyzing the question stem, the passage must contain the evidence you need to select each choice, or it is not a valid answer.

◈ STEP 4
Make a prediction.

In a way, you have done this with your passage map. In order to answer this question, you must be able to distill the facts from the passage. Your predictions can start with the most important information revealed in the passage and work down in importance. With these facts in mind, you will probably have a gut reaction to the veracity of each possible answer, but certainly know where to look in the text to find out.

◈ STEP 5
Evaluate the answers.

Since each answer must be considered independently of the others, let's go in order. Choice (A) can quickly be dismissed because the passage concerns itself with Double-day only as far as his involvement in inventing baseball. The text never disputes his existence. Choice (A) is not a correct answer. Choice (B) concerns itself with Spalding, the primary figure in the piece. The passage states that he was a player, a manager, an owner, and a sporting goods manufacturer. It says that he appointed a commission. And, above all, the passage states that Spalding was responsible for a pervasive myth. All of these defend choice **(B)** as a valid answer. Choice **(C)** can quickly be confirmed because the author states outright that baseball is similar to cricket. The correct answers are **(B)** and **(C)**.

HOW TO APPLY THE KAPLAN METHOD FOR READING COMPREHENSION

Now let's apply the Kaplan Method to the third example question (based on the previous passage):

3. Select the sentence in the passage in which the author states that there was only one piece of evidence supporting the Abner Doubleday origin of baseball.

❯❯ STEP 1
Read the passage strategically.

Again, making a passage map, at least a mental one, is critical. Each sentence of the passage plays at least some purpose in the text, and your outline and identification of main ideas and supporting details will give you a roadmap to find the sentence you need for this type of question.

❯❯ STEP 2
Analyze the question stem.

There are several key terms here that will guide your search. The term "states" tells us that the information is clearly given, and not implied or suggested, making it easier to find. Because the question, like the passage, must be accepted as true in order to take the test, the phrase "only one piece" means that you only need find one sentence with such evidence.

❯❯ STEP 3
Research the relevant text in the passage.

With the idea in mind that there is only one piece of evidence to find, and a passage map created through your critical reading, you should have no trouble finding the section near the end of the passage that begins "Spalding's entire basis for the foundation of baseball history lay...."

◆ STEP 4
Make a prediction.

For this question, the ability to make a prediction is easier than for the other two questions for this passage, because if you have been paying attention, you would almost certainly recall the letter mentioned in the text, and know where to look for it.

◆ STEP 5
Evaluate the answer choices.

For a question of this sort, there are no answer choices *per se*, but each sentence of the passage is a potential option, so if there is any uncertainty in answering the question, each sentence may have to be considered as a choice. However, if you have been following the previous steps, having to evaluate each sentence should be unlikely, and you should be able to quickly find and click on "Spalding's entire basis for the foundation of baseball history lay in a hand-written letter in 1907 that he said came from a man who claimed to have gone to school with Doubleday and attributed the invention to him."

KAPLAN'S ADDITIONAL TIPS FOR READING COMPREHENSION QUESTIONS

Express the main idea in your own words.
Summarizing the main idea of the passage for yourself will not only help form the foundation of your comprehension of the passage, it will also be the starting point of all your text evaluation for the questions. While not every passage has a specific main idea, each passage does have a topic and scope, both of which you should discern by the end of the first paragraph. If you are halfway through a passage and still have not identified these elements, you may be reading too fast and not outlining or identifying key words and phrases in the text.

Focus on retaining ideas, not facts.
Unlike in your coursework, you do not have to memorize or retain any of the dates, details, or minutiae of each passage. If you are asked a question about a specific term or detail within the text, such as a date or place, you have the text there to refer back to, and in that sense it is like an open-book test. It is your job to concern yourself with the ideas, arguments, and conclusions the author presents so as to assess the questions accurately and examine them within the context of the passage.

Concentrate on using only what the passage gives you.

In some sense, a passage about a topic completely foreign to you can serve as a benefit to a smart test taker. Whatever the information is about, it is still presented using familiar systems of information presentation or persuasive writing. This is your guide to Reading Comprehension passages.

A danger occurs within topics where you have pre-existing knowledge. This knowledge can confuse or muddle your ability to answer a question by clouding or expanding the scope of the piece beyond what is written. To best handle the questions, you must be concerned only with what can be gleaned from the text itself and not be influenced by outside knowledge that can put you at odds with the established answer as defined by the passage and the question stem.

Also, while you should approach a text in a way that causes you to question and examine the authority or credibility of something in print, such as a magazine article or an op-ed piece in a newspaper, you must surrender that critical reading style during the test and accept the information given in informative passages as true in order to answer the questions. Even with persuasive passages, regardless of your opinion in relation to the author's, you must use only the evidence and arguments given as the groundwork for answering the questions.

Do not approach Bolded Sentence questions differently.

In Bolded Sentence questions, two sentences in the passage are highlighted, and you are asked to determine the function of both. Some of the functions a sentence might serve are:

- development of an argument
- conclusion of an argument
- evidence supporting a conclusion
- evidence supporting part of a conclusion
- evidence supporting an objection to the conclusion
- a secondary argument or support for a secondary argument

However, while it is a natural instinct on the part of some to focus primarily or only on the boldfaced sentences, the entire passage should be handled with the same strategy as any other question. As you read the passage, read strategically to determine the position taken by the author. Identify the argument and its conclusion, and note how are they supported or refuted. While the bolded lines are in essence the relevant text, the surrounding material still provides key context.

Remember to make a prediction before evaluating the answer choices, and then move on to evaluating and eliminating obviously incorrect answers. Each answer has two parts, one for each highlighted sentence; both must be correct in order for the answer to be correct. If you are unable to predict an answer, or if your prediction is not among the answer choices, you should be able to eliminate most of the wrong answer choices by looking carefully at the two parts. You may find a mischaracterization of the role of a sentence, a reversal of the sentences' roles, a reference to a sentence not highlighted, or a description of something that does not appear in the passage. Once you have eliminated the obviously incorrect answers, you should more easily be able to identify the answer that best describes the roles of the sentences.

Do not get misled by variations on standard question stems.

While most questions concern themselves with what is true about the passage, some questions will ask you to find the item that is not supported by the passage. A question that states that all of the answers EXCEPT one apply will have several "right" answers in that they are supported by the text, but if you forget to look for the erroneous answer, you may pick a "right" answer that is, in fact, incorrect for the purposes of the question.

Also, while the passage must be assumed to be true, and the question must be assumed to be true, all answer choices are initially to be regarded with suspicion. Any new information that is given only in the context of an answer choice cannot be given the benefit of being true. Answer choices that attempt to insert additional information are almost certainly wrong.

For multiple choice questions involving boldfaced sentences, the standard question is to ascertain the relationship between the two sentences, but some questions simply ask for the purpose of each sentence within the passage. You must, through your own active reading, be able to discern the purpose of boldfaced sentences independently of the question in order to best answer the question.

READING COMPREHENSION PRACTICE SET

Try the following Reading Comprehension questions using the Kaplan Method for Reading Comprehension. If you're up to the challenge, time yourself; on test day, you'll want to spend only 1–3 minutes reading each passage and 1 minute on each question.

Questions 1 and 2 are based on the passage below.

The idea of medical nanotechnology often conjures up the potentially troubling image of tiny machines and devices that both exist and operate far outside the scope of unmagnified human vision. Yet much of what constitutes nanotechnology is purely biological in form and function. For example, strands of DNA and the proteins that make up its structure are mere nanometers thick. Many of the basic functions of life occur on the nanoscale level. Efforts to understand or affect these functions are among the primary fields of nanotechnology. Gene study and gene therapy, two byproducts of medical nanotechnology, have already proven useful for identifying and treating a number of different diseases, sometimes even before symptoms of those diseases present themselves. **Even so, genetic nanotechnology and treatments can give as much cause for concern as the idea of microscopic machines at work in the body.** The possibility of altering an organism's genetic structure has been a subject of much debate as to what extent such an alteration would be both safe and ethical.

1. In the passage above, what roles do the boldfaced sentences serve?

    (A) The first sentence is the main idea, and the second sentence restates the main idea.

    (B) The first sentence makes the central argument of the passage, and the second sentence supports the argument.

    (C) The first sentence provides the primary argument, and the second sentence is the secondary argument.

    (D) The first sentence is a secondary argument and the second sentence is evidence against that argument.

    (E) The first sentence introduces the topic and the second sentence is the conclusion.

2. According to the passage, all of the following statements are true EXCEPT:

   (A) Medical nanotechnology is a field of nanotechnology that is 100% biological in practice.

   (B) Nanotechnology has already led to medical practices that are currently in use.

   (C) There are valid concerns regarding the use of nanotechnology.

   (D) Most of what happens on the nanoscale is naturally occurring.

   (E) Gene therapy would not be possible without medical nanotechnology.

Questions 3 through 5 are based on the passage below.

Although it is an imperfect model for describing a complex market, the theory of supply and demand is a reasonably accurate method of explaining, describing, and predicting how the quantity and price of goods fluctuate within a market. Economists define supply as the amount of a particular good that producers are willing to sell at a certain price. For example, a manufacturer might be willing to sell 7,000 sprockets if each one sells for $0.45, but would be willing to sell substantially more sprockets, perhaps 12,000, for a higher price of $0.82. Conversely, demand represents the quantity of a given item that consumers will purchase at a set price; in the most efficient market, all buyers pay the lowest price available and all sellers charge the highest price they are able. The intersection of these occurrences is graphically represented in supply and demand curves that show the prices at which a product becomes too expensive or too readily available.

3. Which one of the following best expresses the main idea of the passage?

   (A) explaining why buyers in a given market tend to seek the lowest price on available goods

   (B) offering a dissenting perspective on an obsolete economic model

   (C) persuading readers that the model of supply and demand is the best method for understanding market forces

   (D) providing an explanation of the two primary elements of an economic model and how they intersect

   (E) analyzing the fluctuation of supply and demand within a market

Part Two: Verbal Reasoning
Reading Comprehension | **95**

> Consider each of the following choices separately and
> select all that apply.

4. If the producer of sprockets nearly doubles his prices as described in the passage, it follows that

    A buyers in the market will be likely to purchase more of the sprockets being sold

    B the price of sprockets will continue to increase

    C buyers in the market will be likely to purchase fewer of the sprockets being sold

5. Select the sentence in the passage that illustrates an abstract concept presented by the author.

READING COMPREHENSION PRACTICE SET ANSWERS AND EXPLANATIONS

1. E

(E) is the best answer not only through process of elimination, but because the piece is not truly a persuasive piece. The arguments presented are mainly those of others, not the author, and so as an informative piece, any answers indicating the existence of arguments are suspect. Only in the second bolded sentence does the author draw a conclusion or give a slight acknowledgement of people's concerns over medical nanotechnology. **(A)**, **(B)**, and **(C)** can be passed over quickly because the first sentence is not the main idea, and its contents are contradicted by the following sentence, which is directed more at the central focus. **(D)** can be dismissed in that the second bolded sentence to some degree supports people's concerns about nanotechnology and does not refute it like the choice suggests.

2. A

A careless test taker can be tripped up here because this is a question that is reversed from the standard form. In it, there are four true statements and one false. It is the false one that must be found, so each of the true ones should be evaluated and confirmed in the text. Choice **(A)** is the early favorite for the right answer because the second sentence mentions that much of nanotechnology is biological, but not all, and nothing else in the text gives any indication that this does not apply to medical nanotechnology as well. All other choices can be confirmed within the text through explicit or easily implied information.

3. D

The passage as a whole discusses the basic elements of the model of supply and demand, defining the two terms and describing how they work. That's choice **(D)**. Choice **(A)** is too narrow, focusing on only one of the two forces described. Choice **(B)** is out of scope because there's no mention of the model being obsolete, and the author simply describes the model—he or she doesn't dissent from its contentions. The passage makes no effort to persuade readers, so you can rule out **(C)**. Although the theory of supply and demand does allow for the analysis of market forces, **(E)**, the passage itself provides only description, not analysis.

4. C

You are told that producers want to charge as much as possible and buyers want to pay as little as possible, so it makes sense that as prices rise, demand falls, choice **(C)**.

Choice **(A)** is the opposite of what the passage implies; demand decreases as prices rise. There's no evidence that this change in price will lead to further price increases, so you can rule out **(B)**.

5.   For example, a manufacturer might be willing to sell 7,000 sprockets if each one sells for $0.45, but would be willing to sell substantially more sprockets, perhaps 12,000, for a higher price of $0.82.

The abstract concepts addressed in the passage are those of supply and demand, and the only example that illustrates supply and demand occurs in Sentence 3. Sentence 1 introduces the supply and demand model. Sentence 2 defines the term "supply." Sentence 4 explains demand, and Sentence 5 describes a graphical representation of the two forces.

CHAPTER 8

Verbal Reasoning Practice Set

In this section, you will take a practice test made of 120 questions. This section has been divided into two parts to allow you to check your answers at the halfway mark. You will use a diagnostic tool at that point to help you learn from your mistakes and continue on with more awareness of the traps you may encounter in the second set.

REVIEW OF THE KAPLAN METHOD FOR VERBAL REASONING QUESTION TYPES

Review the steps and strategies you have studied for answering each type of question quickly, efficiently, and correctly before starting your Practice Sets.

THE KAPLAN METHOD FOR TEXT COMPLETION (ONE-BLANK)

STEP 1 Read the sentence, looking for clues.

STEP 2 Predict the blank.

STEP 3 Select the choice that most closely matches your prediction.

STEP 4 Check your answer.

THE KAPLAN METHOD FOR TEXT COMPLETION (TWO-BLANK AND THREE-BLANK)

STEP 1 Read the sentence, looking for clues.

STEP 2 Predict an answer for the easier/easiest blank.

STEP 3 Select the answer choice that most closely matches your prediction.

STEP 4 Predict and select for the remaining blanks.

STEP 5 Check your answers.

THE KAPLAN METHOD FOR SENTENCE EQUIVALENCE

STEP 1 Read the sentence, looking for clues.

STEP 2 Predict an answer.

STEP 3 Select the two choices that most closely match your prediction.

STEP 4 Check your answers to see if the sentence retains the same meaning.

THE KAPLAN METHOD FOR READING COMPREHENSION

STEP 1 Read the passage strategically.

STEP 2 Analyze the question stem.

STEP 3 Research the relevant text in the passage.

STEP 4 Make a prediction.

STEP 5 Evaluate the answer choices.

THE KAPLAN METHOD FOR ANALYTICAL WRITING

STEP 1 Take the issue/argument apart.

STEP 2 Select the points you will make.

STEP 3 Organize, using Kaplan's essay templates.

STEP 4 Type your essay.

STEP 5 Proofread your work.

VERBAL REASONING PRACTICE SET I

Directions: Each sentence below has one or more blanks, each blank indicating that something has been omitted. Beneath the sentence are five words for one-blank questions and sets of three words for each blank for two- and three-blank questions. Choose the word or set of words for each blank that best fits the meaning of the sentence as a whole.

1. In spite of its popularity, *The Merchant of Venice* remains a (i) _____ play, with many critics (ii) _____ the extent of Shakespeare's anti-Semitism.

Blank (i)		Blank (ii)	
A	controversial	D	assuaging
B	celebrated	E	augmenting
C	histrionic	F	debating

2. The cotton gin played a (i) _____ role in advancing the textile industry, (ii) _____ its negative effects can be seen in the rapid development of slavery as the economic base of the American South.

Blank (i)		Blank (ii)	
A	controversial	D	although
B	crucial	E	so
C	trivial	F	therefore

3. Although Thomas Paine was (i) _____ his political pamphlets, he was in fact (ii) _____ writer on many different subjects.

Blank (i)		Blank (ii)	
A	inimical concerning	D	an abstruse
B	condemned regarding	E	a prolific
C	famous for	F	a terrible

4. St Elmo's fire is a weather phenomenon which, (i) _____ it was documented from ancient times, was not (ii) _____ until recently.

Blank (i)		Blank (ii)	
A	because	D	accepted
B	since	E	reported
C	although	F	understood

5. Though the poet's work was praised highly by critics, sales of his anthologies were (i) _____; it is possible the poor sales were due to his language being too (ii) _____ to be readily understood.

Blank (i)	Blank (ii)
A scanty	D lucid
B robust	E prosaic
C singular	F abstruse

6. (i) _____ its many difficult and mature themes, *Hamlet* nevertheless remains a (ii) _____ choice for introducing teenagers to Shakespeare.

Blank (i)	Blank (ii)
A Due to	D neglected
B Despite	E popular
C Because of	F spurned

7. Because she was so _____, Mary rarely spoke in groups of people.

(A) reticent

(B) congenial

(C) brusque

(D) gregarious

(E) scurrilous

8. The patterns of the stock market seem _____ to many beginners, but can be decoded with dedication and patience.

(A) unwelcoming

(B) arcane

(C) harmonious

(D) shocking

(E) lucid

9. The band's new album was universally panned by critics, with many _____ their change to a simpler sound.

    (A) lauding

    (B) ignorant of

    (C) tolerating

    (D) deriding

    (E) apathetic to

10. Because he was convinced of his own _____, Adam never accepted criticism.

    (A) genius

    (B) acclamation

    (C) shrewdness

    (D) infallibility

    (E) popularity

11. She was appalled at the mayor's policy, feeling he _____ the promises made during his campaign.

    (A) challenged

    (B) exaggerated

    (C) misunderstood

    (D) hindered

    (E) abjured

12. Much to his _____, he was forced to acknowledge the flaw in his reasoning; he responded gracefully, however, and soon returned with a new defense of his argument.

    (A) irritation

    (B) befuddlement

    (C) chagrin

    (D) bemusement

    (E) resentment

13. Jen was disappointed when she was passed over for a promotion, but when she learned that the sister of her manager had been promoted instead she became irate, claiming _____.

    Ⓐ altruism

    Ⓑ peerage

    Ⓒ malfeasance

    Ⓓ ingratitude

    Ⓔ nepotism

14. Given the gravity of the situation, Terrence's _____ quips were inappropriate; he did not seem to realize it was not the time or place for sarcasm.

    Ⓐ supercilious

    Ⓑ coarse

    Ⓒ sardonic

    Ⓓ fatuous

    Ⓔ ribald

15. Historians often use the merciless Russian winter as _____ for various failed military invasions of Russia; they cite the armies of Charles XII of Sweden, Napoleon Bonaparte, and Adolf Hitler as examples of forces who suffered heavy causalities due to the harsh conditions.

    Ⓐ a defense

    Ⓑ an excuse

    Ⓒ a justification

    Ⓓ an explanation

    Ⓔ a rationalization

16. Although he _____ the image of anti-authoritarianism, Johnny Cash was a frequent visitor to the White House and friends with several Presidents during his life.

    Ⓐ advocated

    Ⓑ cultivated

    Ⓒ patronized

    Ⓓ supported

    Ⓔ snubbed

17. (i) _____ mushrooms are popular in many cuisines, it is
    (ii) _____ to eat those found in the wild, as many frequently found
    mushrooms resemble edible mushrooms but are, in fact, (iii) _____.

Blank (i)		Blank (ii)		Blank (iii)	
A	Considering	D	imprudent	G	poisonous
B	While	E	cheaper	H	bland
C	Because	F	ingenuous	I	toothsome

18. Considered one of his most (i) _____ works, its incomplete status at
    the time of his death has given Mozart's Requiem Mass in D Minor a certain
    (ii) _____ in Western culture, and many (iii) _____ stories
    have arisen surrounding it; unfortunately, the truth is lost to us.

Blank (i)		Blank (ii)		Blank (iii)	
A	ignominious	D	obscurity	G	fraudulent
B	inconspicuous	E	indifference	H	apocryphal
C	famous	F	mystique	I	verified

19. The octopus is remarkable for its (i) _____, demonstrating
    exceptional problem-solving skills and memory; beyond its mental
    (ii) _____, the octopus possesses exceptional physical
    (iii) _____, allowing it to precisely manipulate objects.

Blank (i)		Blank (ii)		Blank (iii)	
A	physiology	D	acumen	G	brilliance
B	intelligence	E	acridity	H	genius
C	creative	F	trenchancy	I	dexterity

Directions: For the following questions, select the **two** answer choices that, when inserted into the sentence, fit the meaning of the sentence as a whole **and** yield complete sentences that are similar in meaning.

20. Known to all as having a silver tongue, audiences are easily distracted from the meaning of his words by his _____ speech.

    A mellifluous

    B flowing

    C stumbling

    D laconic

    E euphonic

    F strident

21. When the underdogs so soundly beat the team favored to win, it _____ the entire sports world.

    A horrified

    B electrified

    C shook

    D bored

    E alienated

    F stunned

22. Despite the efforts made by the municipal government to increase public transportation usage, many people of the city continued to drive their own vehicles, complaining that the bus schedules were too _____ to be relied upon.

    A irregular

    B exacting

    C circuitous

    D rigid

    E isolated

    F erratic

23. Word painting is a musical technique in which the progression of the notes _____ the meaning of the lyrics; a famous example of this can be found in Handel's *Messiah* in which the notes rise with the mention of "mountains" and fall with the mention of "low."

    A sustains

    B mimics

    C contrasts

    D reflects

    E opposes

    F reinforces

24. After naturally occurring smallpox was eradicated, the World Health Organization chose to _____ the remaining samples of the virus in hopes that they may be later used in developing means to combat other viruses.

    A eliminate

    B duplicate

    C preserve

    D retain

    E extirpate

    F cultivate

25. The *Magna Carta* was one of the most _____ political declarations of the Middle Ages because it declared the monarch's powers to be limited by the law; although its practical effects were not immediate, it is commonly seen as the genesis of constitutional law in England.

    A remarkable

    B immense

    C pivotal

    D recondite

    E ancient

    F momentous

26. Though _____ filled the streets, people seemed unconcerned with the appearance of their city.

    A detritus

    B refuge

    C gaudiness

    D bedlam

    E refuse

    F barrenness

27. G. K. Chesterton's wit is exemplified in his often _____ responses to his friend and rival George Bernard Shaw.

    A punctilious

    B vociferous

    C waggish

    D vicious

    E scathing

    F lighthearted

28. Electrotherapy has been used for over 150 years in various physical rehabilitation programs, even though many of its precise effects remain _____.

    A uncertain

    B disputed

    C disproved

    D unstudied

    E elusive

    F precarious

29. Despite a long career at famous establishments, the noted croupier chose instead to join the new casino, where he felt he was properly appreciated for his professional _____ and efficiency at the table.

    A articulation

    B demeanor

    C reputation

    D history

    E mien

    F dexterity

30. Although the river itself had vanished, the banks and bed were _____ years of erosion from running water.

    A repudiation of

    B witness to

    C coarsened by

    D an attestation to

    E vindicated from

    F recovered from

31. While he was still _____, the doctors advised Phillip to remain home, lest he was contagious, even though his symptoms had receded.

    A impaired

    B ailing

    C convalescing

    D nauseous

    E enfeebled

    F recuperating

32. The advent of the Internet has created an unprecedented increase in communication _____ , as it allows for the near-instant transmission of information.

   A potential

   B controversies

   C theories

   D litigation

   E prospects

   F revolutions

33. Although she did not approve of her father's smoking, she was forced to admit that the smell of his pipe tobacco was _____ her youth.

   A poignant for

   B redolent of

   C debilitating during

   D pungent of

   E odorous of

   F evocative of

34. Her fractured wrist made the aspiring flutist _____ about her future career; however, her doctor assured her it would heal without long-term damage.

   A alarmed

   B truculent

   C panegyrical

   D timorous

   E ebullient

   F phlegmatic

35. Although English is the de facto language of the United States of America, it is _____ for it to be made the official language, especially given the diversity of the population, in particular the rapid rise in the Spanish-speaking demographic.

   A liable

   B unlikely

   C improbable

   D impossible

   E plausible

   F preposterous

36. As excited as he was to have been chosen for the reality television show, he was _____ about involving his family, particularly his children, who he felt would not understand the situation fully.

   A thrilled

   B timorous

   C vacillating

   D horrified

   E resigned

   F wavering

37. Because the architect had found evidence of decay in a supporting wall, his official report _____ the structural integrity of the building as a likely cause for the accident.

   A proposed

   B imputed

   C rejected

   D advanced

   E insinuated

   F condemned

38. Max's repertoire of cooking techniques was remarkably broad, allowing him to draw upon many culinary traditions to create _____ dishes.

   A artful

   B catholic

   C dilettantish

   D eclectic

   E savory

   F ambrosial

39. The Space Shuttle is an _____ of human creativity and engineering, unparalleled in its complexity and ingenuity.

   A expression

   B apogee

   C encroachment

   D assertion

   E excess

   F apex

40. He _____ visiting Blarney Castle, fearing the summer tourist crowds, and chose a quieter destination for himself.

   A contemplated

   B eschewed

   C deprecated

   D considered

   E forwent

   F discouraged

Directions: Each passage in this group is followed by questions based on its content. After reading a passage, choose the best answer to each question. Answer all questions following a passage on the basis of what is stated or implied in that passage.

Questions 41 and 42 are based on the passage below.

Criticisms of the automaticity model of reading acquisition include a lack of focus on comprehension as the ultimate goal of reading. Too much focus on fluency to the neglect of comprehension is a correlative criticism. Miscue analysis, tracking students errors or "miscues," has demonstrated that even early readers use prediction as well as translation into dialect as they read, thereby using tools outside of those described in the automaticity model. A third criticism is that dyslexic readers, because of the inherent decoding problems they face, necessarily have trouble following the model and sustaining the reading rates recommended for fluency.

41. The passages suggests that all the following are flaws in the automaticity model of reading acquisition EXCEPT

(A) failure to consider all the methods commonly used by developing readers.

(B) measuring reading ability by reading.

(C) prioritizing efficiency in reading over understanding.

(D) insufficient research.

(E) basic assumptions about the reader's cerebral processes.

42. Based on the passage, which of the following would the author likely recommend as a sign of fluency?

(A) the ability to translate the material into another language

(B) the ability to decode and pronounce the sounds in words

(C) the ability to explain the plot or main idea in a text

(D) the ability to predict the main idea in unread reading material

(E) the ability to read material written in a wide variety of dialects

Questions 43 through 46 are based on the passage below.

It has been commonly accepted for some time now that certain scenes in Shakespeare's *Macbeth* are interpolations from the writing of another author; Act III, scene 5, and parts of Act IV, scene 1 have been determined to be the writing of one of his contemporaries, Thomas Middleton. This can be regarded as both illuminating and problematic, depending upon how the play is being studied. It allows us to infer a great deal about the conventions and practices of writing for the stage at the time. For example, it may have been more collaborative than previously thought or perhaps Elizabethan notions of plagiarism are different from ours. While this is historically significant, it does, however, complicate our interpretation of the characters in the play itself. It is more difficult to assess authorial intention with regard to a character's motives if the text has been redacted by multiple authors.

43. Select the statement or statements that are correct according to the passage.

  A The author feels that Shakespeare is guilty of plagiarism.

  B The interpolations found in plays such as *Macbeth* makes it more difficult to assess the author's motives in writing the play.

  C Our current understanding of plagiarism may have arisen after Shakespeare's time.

44. Consider the following choices and select all that apply. Which of the following could aid in the further study of the interpolations discussed in the above passage?

  A an investigation of thematic and technical irregularities in other plays by Shakespeare

  B an examination of the themes and techniques of other contemporary writers

  C searching through legal history from Shakespeare's time for references to plagiarism or intellectual property rights

45. Consider the following choices and select all that apply. Which can NOT be inferred from the passage?

  A This example of interpolation would be illegal today.

  B Authors and playwrights might have recruited assistance for their compositions.

  C Middleton's writing was used without his consent.

46. Which of the following best describes the relationship between the highlighted phrases?

    (A) concept and example

    (B) cause and effect

    (C) thesis and defense

    (D) thesis and synthesis

    (E) synthesis and antithesis

Questions 47 and 48 are based on the passage below.

In the decades leading up to the 1970s, the primarily French-speaking Canadian province of Québec saw its proportion of native French speakers diminish from year to year. The attrition of French was attributed to preeminence of English in the workplace, particularly in affluent, "white-collar" jobs. The French-speaking majority was economically marginalized within their own province, as it was left with the choice of either working in lower-paying jobs or teaching its children English as a first language. This would further erase its cultural autonomy and singularity within a country that primarily spoke English. Facing the risk of linguistic extinction, the province passed *Loi 101* (Law 101): The Charter of the French Language. It established French as the only official language of the province, established the primacy of French in the workplace, and led to more economic equitability. Since its passage in 1977, the percentage of people who speak French as a first language has begun to rise.

47. Which of the following is suggested as a reason for the decline of French in Québec?

    (A) economic devaluation

    (B) influx of English-speaking immigrants

    (C) efforts to further integrate themselves with Canadian culture

    (D) emigration of French-Canadians

    (E) French was outlawed in the other provinces.

48. *Loi 101* was significant in that it

    (A) was a final, unsuccessful attempt at enforcing the usage of French in Québec.

    (B) curtailed the economic supremacy of English.

    (C) restricted the teaching of English in schools.

    (D) highlighted the uniqueness of the cultural identity of Québec from the rest of Canada.

    (E) provided for bilingual education.

Questions 49 through 51 are based on the paragraph below.

The advent of online education in the first decade of the 21st century was the result of and response to a number of factors that were both internal and external to the field of higher education. Traditional tertiary institutions, especially those that were privately endowed, raised tuition rates far in excess of the rate of inflation. This, in concert with a larger demand for post-secondary education for working adults, helped facilitate the introduction of online learning. However, it should be acknowledged that the relative simplicity of using the Internet as a platform, as well as its cost-effectiveness, was seized upon by entrepreneurs in the private sector. Online education is now largely in the hands of for-profit companies. The question now becomes whether the democratization of higher education is worth the price of removing it from non-profit, research-based universities.

49. The passage is concerned primarily with

    (A) the advent of online education.

    (B) adult-oriented educational systems.

    (C) the usefulness of the Internet in post-secondary education.

    (D) trends in online education.

    (E) the advantages and disadvantages of online education.

50. The author's use of the term "seized upon" evokes an image of _____ on the part of the entrepreneurs.

    (A) accidental realization

    (B) opportunistic tactics

    (C) violent appropriation

    (D) collusive behavior

    (E) predatory business practice

51. The underlined section refers to

    (A) the cost of online education.

    (B) the influence of popularity on online courses.

    (C) the opening of online education to the free market.

    (D) the role of voting in class selection.

    (E) whether or not a democratic society should have online education.

Questions 52 through 54 are based on the passage below.

Thermodynamics is concerned with changes in the properties of matter when we alter the external conditions. An example of this is a gas being compressed by the motion of a piston. The final outcome depends on how the change is made—if the piston is moved in slowly, we say that the compression is "reversible." This means that if we pull the piston back out, we retrace the same sequence of properties but in the reverse order; hence, the temperature of the gas will be the same when the piston has been pulled out as it was before the piston was pushed in. However, if the piston is moved in and out quickly then the initial state (and temperature) will not be recovered—the gas will always be hotter than it was at the beginning. This is a manifestation, although not a statement, of the second law of thermodynamics. It also makes a difference whether there is a transfer of heat between the cylinder of gas and the external surroundings. If the cylinder is insulated, then the gas will heat on compression and cool on expansion (refrigeration uses this principle). On the other hand, if the cylinder can exchange heat with the surroundings, it will remain at the same temperature if the compression is slow enough.

52. The scope of this passage is

  Ⓐ the motion of a piston demonstrating the effects of thermodynamics.

  Ⓑ the conservation of heat during the motion of a piston.

  Ⓒ how the second law of thermodynamics applies to pistons.

  Ⓓ how thermodynamics function.

  Ⓔ reversible compression.

53. Based on this passage, if we were to record the temperature of the gas within the piston of a car engine when we were driving the car at 20 mph, and measure it again after accelerating the car to 40 mph, what would we expect to find?

  Ⓐ The gas would be hotter in the first reading.

  Ⓑ The gas would be hotter in the second reading.

  Ⓒ The gas would be the same temperature in both readings.

  Ⓓ There is no way to accurately predict the change in temperature.

  Ⓔ The gas would be cooler in the second reading.

54. Given the context, what is the meaning of the underlined phrase?

  Ⓐ The second law of thermodynamics is only applicable to objects moving at high speeds.

  Ⓑ The motion of the piston is a confirmation of the second law of thermodynamics.

  Ⓒ The second law of thermodynamics cannot, on its own, explain the change in heat in the cylinder.

  Ⓓ The change in heat inside the cylinder illustrates the second law of thermodynamics but does not prove it.

  Ⓔ The motion of the piston disproves the second law of thermodynamics.

Questions 55 through 57 are based on the passage below.

Towards the end of the 19th century many scientists thought that all the great scientific discoveries had already been made and that there was not much left to do beyond some "tidying up." Max Planck, born in 1858, turned this notion upside down with his study of black-body radiation. Even in a vacuum a hot body will tend come to thermal equilibrium with a colder body by radiative heat transfer. This is the principle by which we derive energy from the sun. However, the theory for black-body radiation in Planck's day predicted an unphysical result at high frequencies. After many years of work devoted to this problem, Planck succeeded in quantitatively explaining the experimental data; his key insight was that energy comes in small discrete packets, called quanta. His theory was the birth of what is called quantum mechanics, the revolutionary theory of matter that is fundamental to the modern understanding of physics, chemistry and molecular biology.

55. Select the sentence that best describes the importance of Max Planck's work.

56. Which of the following would best paraphrase the opening sentence?

   Ⓐ By the late 1800s, much of the scientific community felt it had completed the majority of its work and minor revisions were its only remaining task.

   Ⓑ By 1900, few scientists were still making significant discoveries, and most projects were revising current theories.

   Ⓒ At the end of the 19th century, there was a concern among scientists that they had run out of discoveries to make and could only perfect already proven theories.

   Ⓓ By 1900, the scientific community declared that it had come to understand the natural laws of the universe.

   Ⓔ At the end of the 19th century, scientists ceased trying to formulate new theories.

57. Which of the following best describes the relationship between the highlighted phrases?

   Ⓐ topic and scope

   Ⓑ theory and debunking

   Ⓒ problem and solution

   Ⓓ hypothesis and analysis

   Ⓔ thesis and synthesis

Questions 58–60 will be based on the passage below.

At the atomic scale, all matter exhibits properties commonly associated with both waves and particles. The classic experiment that demonstrates wave-like properties is the double-slit experiment, first performed by Thomas Young at the beginning of the 19th century. If a beam of light passes through two narrow slits and is projected onto a screen behind the slits, a pattern of light and dark fringes can be observed. The explanation for this is based on an analogy with ripples in water. If a stone is dropped into a pond, we see a circular pattern of ripples emanating from the place where the stone hits the water. If we drop two stones some distance apart, the ripples start to interfere with each other, sometimes amplifying, when two crests or troughs meet, sometimes canceling when a crest meets a trough. A similar explanation holds for interference effects with visible light—the two slits act as independent sources, in the same way as the stones in water. This experiment provided convincing evidence in support of Christian Huygens' wave theory of light, which eventually supplanted the older particle theory of Isaac Newton. However, in the 20th century Einstein showed that Newton was not entirely wrong. His analysis of the photoelectric effect showed that light could behave as a particle as well as a wave. Surprisingly, electrons, which we tend to think of as particles, also demonstrate interference effects, showing that they too are waves as well as particles.

58. Which of the following best summarizes the findings of Young's experiment?

   (A) Two light sources can cancel each other out creating the observed dark fringes.

   (B) The waves from independent light sources interact with one another in predictable patterns.

   (C) Light exhibits properties of both particles and waves.

   (D) Newton's theory was permanently debunked.

   (E) Newton's theory was correct all along.

59. Based on the passage, what would we expect the light fringes in Young's experiment to represent?

　　Ⓐ the amplification created by the combination of both sets of waves of light

　　Ⓑ the combination of the light particles from both slits onto the screen

　　Ⓒ the projection onto the screen where the light is not blocked out by the object with the slits

　　Ⓓ the amplification created by light particles

　　Ⓔ the projection onto the screen where the light is blocked by the object with the slits

60. What is the relevance of the underlined phrase to the passage as a whole?

　　Ⓐ It demonstrates a comparison between electrons and light.

　　Ⓑ It is proof that Newton, to some degree, was correct in his theory of light as particles.

　　Ⓒ It is a rephrasing of the first sentence that matter at the atomic level functions as both waves and particles.

　　Ⓓ It refutes Newton's theory.

　　Ⓔ It disconfirms particle-wave duality.

ANSWERS AND EXPLANATIONS

1. A, F	17. B, D, G	33. B, F	49. D
2. B, D	18. C, F, H	34. A, D	50. B
3. C, E	19. B, D, I	35. B, C	51. C
4. C, F	20. A, E	36. C, F	52. A
5. A, F	21. C, F	37. A, D	53. B
6. B, E	22. A, F	38. B, D	54. D
7. A	23. B, D	39. B, F	55. "His theory was the birth of . . ."
8. B	24. C, D	40. B, E	
9. D	25. C, F	41. D	56. A
10. D	26. A, E	42. C	57. C
11. E	27. C, F	43. C	58. B
12. C	28. A, E	44. A, B, C	59. A
13. E	29. B, E	45. A, C	60. C
14. C	30. B, D	46. B	
15. D	31. C, F	47. A	
16. B	32. A, E	48. B	

Diagnostic Tool

Tally up your score and write your results below.

Total

Total Correct: _____ out of 60 correct

By Question Type

Text Completions (questions 1–19)_____ out of 19 correct

Sentence Equivalence (questions 20–40) _____ out of 21 correct

Reading Comprehension (questions 41–60) _____ out of 20 correct

DIAGNOSE YOUR RESULTS

Look back at the questions you got wrong and think about your experience answering them.

> ### STEP 1
> #### Find the Road Blocks

If you struggled to answer some questions, to improve your score you need to pinpoint exactly what "road blocks" tripped you up. To do that, ask yourself the following two questions.

Am I weak in the skills being tested?

The easiest way to determine this is to think of it in terms of what skills are required for each question type. If you're having trouble with Sentence Equivalence or Text Completion, you probably need to review your vocabulary word lists. Maybe you need to brush up on using word etymology to your advantage. If Reading Comprehension items are bothersome, you need to work on your critical reading skills. If you know you need to brush up on your verbal skills, try the *Kaplan GRE Exam Verbal Workbook*, which contains a focused review of all the verbal reasoning concepts tested on the GRE, as well as practice exercises to build speed and accuracy.

Was it the question type that threw me off?

Then you need to become more comfortable with them! Sentence Equivalence questions have a unique format, and Reading Comprehension questions can be daunting with their dense, complex passages. If this was a problem for you, go back to the beginning of this chapter and review the Kaplan principles and methods for the question types you struggled with. Make sure you understand the principles and how to apply the methods. These strategies help to improve your speed and efficiency on test day. Remember, it's not a reading or vocabulary test; it's a critical-reasoning test (even though your reading habits and command of vocabulary are indispensible tools that will help you earn a high score).

Also, get as much practice as you can so that you grow more at ease with the question type formats. For even more practice, try the *Kaplan GRE Exam Verbal Workbook*, which includes practice sets for each question type.

STEP 2
Find the Blind Spots

Did you answer some questions quickly and confidently but get them wrong anyway?

When you come across wrong answers like these, you need to figure out what you thought you were doing right, what it turns out you were doing wrong, and why that happened. The best way to do that is to **read the answer explanations!**

The explanations give you a detailed breakdown of why the correct answer is correct and why all the other answer choices are wrong. This helps to reinforce the Kaplan principles and methods for each question type and helps you figure out what blindsided you so it doesn't happen again. Also, just as with your "roadblocks," try to get in as much practice as you can.

❱❱ STEP 3
Reinforce Your Strengths

Now read through all the answer explanations for the ones you got right. You should check every answer because if you guessed and guessed correctly without having any idea how to solve, reading the explanations makes sure that whatever needs fixing gets fixed. Work through them one more time. Again, this helps to reinforce the Kaplan principles and methods for each question type, which in turn helps you work more efficiently so you can get the score you want. Keep your skills sharp with more practice.

As soon as you are comfortable with all the GRE question types and Kaplan methods, complete a full-length practice test under timed conditions. In this way, practice tests serve as milestones; they help you to chart your progress! So don't save them all for the final weeks. For even more practice, you can also try the Kaplan GRE Quiz Bank. You get more than 1,000 questions that you can access 24/7 from any Internet browser, each with comprehensive explanations. You can even customize your quizzes based on question type, content, and difficulty level. Take quizzes in Timed Mode to test your stamina or in Tutor Mode to see explanations as you work. Best of all, you also get detailed reports to track your progress.

Visit **kaptest.com/gre** for more details on our Quiz Bank and for more information on our other online and classroom-based options. If the Verbal Reasoning section is where you need the most help, you should check out the new Kaplan course, GRE Verbal Advantage—Anywhere. It's available online anywhere you are, *and* you can get live instruction from an expert Kaplan GRE teacher.

VERBAL REASONING PRACTICE SET I
ANSWER AND EXPLANATIONS

1. A, F

Begin by making note of the phrase "in spite of," which suggests that there will be two opposing ideas in the sentence. The sentence describes the play as popular so you can rule out choices **(B)** *celebrated* and **(C)** *histrionic* for the first blank because you are looking for a word contrasting with its popularity. Based on the remaining option, **(A)** *controversial*, you are looking for a solution to the second blank that implies uncertainty. Choices **(D)** *assuaging* and **(E)** *augmenting* are not possible, given that neither carries a connotation of uncertainty. It is therefore answer choice **(F)** *debating* for the second blank.

2. B, D

Looking at the sentence and choices, you know that the second word will be some kind of conjunction to connect the two parts of the sentence. You can see from the second part that there were negative effects, while in the first part of the sentence you see mention of technological advances, suggesting that a contrasting conjunction is likely. From the perspective of the first blank, you can safely rule out choice **(C)** *trivial* because we know that it had some notable effects from the second part of the sentence. Choice **(A)** *controversial* is tempting, but can be ruled out for the reason that you are looking for a positive sense for the first clause to contrast with the second clause. Choice **(B)** *crucial* is the only positive option for the first blank.

For the second blank, answer choice **(D)** *although* is an appropriate contrasting conjunction. Choices **(E)** and **(F)** are poor choices because they are contingent on the second clause being a necessary result of the first, and none of the answer choices allow for that possibility (nor does the sentence make sense in that way).

3. C, E

Although, a detour road sign, heads off the sentence, indicating that the ideas of the first and second clause will be opposites. While external knowledge might tell you that he was, in fact, a famous writer, it is important to remember that the answer is derived from clues in the sentence alone. Choice **(B)** *condemned regarding* makes no sense unless the sentence is a personal opinion (which you won't find on the exam), and you have no reason to believe choice **(A)** *inimical concerning* works for the first blank based on the material given alone. That leaves you with answer choice **(C)** *famous for*.

Choices **(D)** *abstruse* and **(E)** *terrible* could work in a different sentence, but there is no choice for the first blank that will allow the resulting sentence to make sense. The answer will always be clear and definite—choices **(C)** *famous for* and **(E)** *prolific* create a sentence that makes sense without requiring any other knowledge or qualifications.

4. C, F

Based on the choices, you know that there will be some connection between the clauses of the first and second blanks. The contrast of "ancient times" and "recently" tells you to expect to find a word for the first blank that suggests contrast (something like "despite the fact that"), which eliminates choices **(A)** *because* and **(B)** *since*, leaving you with answer choice **(C)** *although*.

You know it has been documented for a long time, so discount choices **(E)** *reported* and **(D)** *accepted* for the second blank. That leaves **(F)** *understood*, which makes sense given the conjunction "although."

5. A, F

The semicolon allows you to focus solely on the first half of the sentence. This is because a semicolon functions as a road sign for the direction the sentence is going to take. Within the first half of the sentence you are given the detour road sign "though" to contrast the high praise with the sales—thus choice **(C)** *singular* cannot be correct because you can assume that sales failed to match the high praise. For similar reasons eliminate choice **(B)** *robust*, leaving answer choice **(A)** *scanty*, which fits perfectly with "poor sales" later in the sentence.

The second half of the sentence offers a possible explanation for why the sales were poor, suggesting that it was too hard to understand his language, which immediately removes choice **(D)** *lucid*. Choice **(E)** *prosaic* might trip you up; however, answer choice **(F)** *abstruse* is clearly the better choice for the second blank—it is an adjective indicating that the prose is difficult to understand.

6. B, E

The first blank means something like "although" because of the "nevertheless," which allows you to reject choices **(A)** *Due to* and **(C)** *Because of*, as they have no sense of contradiction. Answer choice **(B)** *Despite* matches the prediction for the first blank, as "despite" and "although" are synonyms. **(B)** is the best option.

The final clause tells you Hamlet is widely read in high school, so you can assume that the second blank means something similar to "popular"—choices **(F)** *spurned* and **(D)** *neglected* can be eliminated for the second blank. Choice **(E)** matches the prediction exactly.

7. A

Mary is quiet when in groups, so you should look to find a related word. You can thus quickly rule out choices **(B)** *congenial* and **(D)** *gregarious*. Answer choice **(A)** *reticent* properly matches the sense of the second clause, whereas choices **(C)** *brusque* and **(E)** *scurrilous* would require information beyond her being quiet in groups to be good choices.

8. B

The key phrase here is "but can be decoded"—you are looking for an answer that suggests something incomprehensible, which rules out choices **(C)** *harmonious*, **(D)** *shocking*, and **(E)** *lucid*. Choice **(A)** *unwelcoming* is a possibility, but it refers more to a sense of unpleasantness rather than perplexity. Answer choice **(B)** *arcane* is a perfect fit for the sense of something that cannot be easily understood.

9. D

The critics do not approve of the band's change, so look for something that suggests criticism or rejection. This eliminates choices **(A)** *lauding* and **(C)** *tolerating*; furthermore, you know that the reception was strongly negative based on the phrase "universally panned," so you can eliminate choices **(B)** *ignorant of* and **(E)** *apathetic to* because both of these require general lack of interest. This leaves answer choice **(D)** *deriding*, which provides the sense of a strong, negative reaction.

10. D

Criticism implies that there is something wrong, so you can assume that Adam does not want to admit to being wrong. Choices **(B)** *acclamation* and **(E)** *popularity* can be immediately discounted because they have nothing to do with being right or wrong. Choices **(A)** *genius* and **(C)** *shrewdness* may seem related to being right but they are also too closely related to be able to make a clear distinction between them (they are both related to mental quickness). Furthermore, answer choice **(D)** *infallibility* directly opposes the notion of being wrong.

11. E

The key word is "appalled," from which you can take two things: that she is displeased with the mayor's policy and that it is a very strong displeasure. Choices **(A)** *challenged*, **(B)** *exaggerated*, and **(C)** *misunderstood* could all be argued based on the second clause. However, **(D)** *hindered* and **(E)** *abjured* are both better fits, so you can eliminate the first three. Choices **(D)** *hindered* and **(E)** *abjured* both have similar ideas, but answer choice **(E)** *abjured* is significantly stronger—to reject entirely rather than to just impede—and this better agrees with the strength of "appalled."

12. C

You are immediately granted two key facts: he recognized that he was wrong and that he was graceful about it. Thus you are searching for a word that suggests he was embarrassed about being wrong but not angry. That he was graceful about it allows you to reject choices **(A)** *irritation* and **(E)** *resentment*. Choices **(B)** *befuddlement* and **(D)** *bemusement* cannot be the correct answer because he recognizes why he was wrong, leaving answer choice **(C)** *chagrin*, which matches the expectation to be embarrassed but not angry.

13. E

This is a test of vocabulary nuances, with shades of meaning playing the biggest role. All the options are characterizations of the sister's promotion. Based on this, you can simply select answer choice **(E)** *nepotism* because it is the only one that emphasizes the familial relationship.

14. C

Based on the sentence, you know that Terrence has an affinity for sarcasm in inappropriate situations. While all of the options provide possibly inappropriate comments, you are looking for a word that is connected to sarcasm. The only possible option here is answer choice **(C)** *sardonic*—choices **(A)** *supercilious*, **(B)** *coarse*, **(D)** *fatuous*, and **(E)** *ribald* are all unrelated.

15. D

This sentence is taken from the perspective of history, and uses nationally diverse examples, so look for a word that has a dispassionate sense to it—"explanation" would be a good prediction, and sure enough answer choice **(D)** *an explanation* is among the options. You can eliminate the other choices based on the personal involvement of the historians that would be implied in each.

16. B

You are given a contrast in this sentence about the way Johnny Cash presented himself—"the image of anti-authoritarianism" versus being closely connected with various politicians. Judging by the sentence, you would expect a term akin to "encouraged" (you can therefore remove **(E)** *snubbed* from the list); furthermore you know it is his own image, not the image of others. It is based on this latter fact that we can make a choice. Choices **(A)** *advocated*, **(C)** *patronized*, **(D)** *supported* all imply outward action—to encourage the image in someone else. Answer choice **(B)** *cultivated* is the best choice because it most clearly refers to developing his own image.

17. B, D, G

Three blank sentences take a little longer to work out. Looking at the first blank, you can see that it is a conjunction, but you cannot be sure of which until you solve the rest of the sentence. The best place to begin in this sentence is actually at the end—you are given a very useful hint with the contradicting conjunction "but," telling you that blank three will be an antonym to "edible". Looking through the choices, you can easily see that the correct answer is answer choice **(G)** *poisonous*—while you might not want to eat something **(H)** *bland*, this is not a direct antonym to edible and makes little sense in the sentence. Choice **(I)** *toothsome* means palatable or desirable and is the opposite of what the blank needs.

From here work backwards to the second blank. Since you now know that you are talking about eating possibly poisonous mushrooms, you can predict that blank two will say that it is "unwise" to do so. Choice **(E)** *cheaper* is irrelevant to the context (and no mention of money is made elsewhere), and choice **(F)** *ingenuous*, meaning innocent or sincere, is unrelated to the meaning of the sentence. Answer choice **(D)** *imprudent* is a synonym of "unwise" and is therefore the answer you need.

Return to the first blank in the sentence. You know that mushrooms are popular in many cuisines and that you are looking for an answer that connects the two ideas—predict a meaning of roughly "*although* mushrooms are popular in many cuisines, it is imprudent . . ."; what you are looking for is a conjunction marking this contradicting idea. Answer choice **(B)** *While* is clearly the correct choice. For sentences with three blanks, especially, it is important to reread the sentence with all the blanks filled in: "*While* mushrooms are popular in many cuisines, it is *imprudent* to eat those found in the wild, as many frequently found mushrooms resemble edible mushrooms but are, in fact, *poisonous*." The sentence makes perfect sense both grammatically and thematically.

18.   C, F, H

When there are so many missing parts, it is often best to begin with whatever complete clause you can find, in this case the final one. This will allow you to fill in the third blank. You are told that we do not know the truth, which allows you to eliminate both choices **(G)** *fraudulent* and **(I)** *verified*, because both indicate that there exists concrete knowledge on the matter. Answer choice **(H)** *apocryphal* is the only possible answer and allows you to make further progress into completing the sentence. If you know that many apocryphal stories arose surrounding the work, you can make headway into both of the other blanks.

For the first blank, assume that if many stories are made about something, it is widely talked about—this eliminates choice **(B)** *inconspicuous* without a doubt, and between choices **(A)** *ignominious* and **(C)** *famous*, the choice is fairly straightforward. When you know something is much talked about but little else, you can suppose that a synonym of "well-known" is going to be much more likely than a synonym of "shameful."

Finally, for the second blank, you can reject choices **(D)** *obscurity* and **(E)** *indifference* because you know the composition is well known, so answer choice **(F)** *mystique* is the only logical choice (which is supported by the mention of *apocryphal* stories). Let's check our answers: "Considered one of his most *famous* works, its incomplete status at the time of his death has given Mozart's Requiem Mass in D Minor a certain *mystique* in Western culture, and many *apocryphal* stories have arisen surrounding it; unfortunately, the truth is lost to us." Everything fits in perfectly when you read back the sentence with the correct answer choices.

19.   B, D, I

The first clause in this allows you to answer the first blank—you know you are talking about mental abilities so you can rule out choice **(A)** *physiology* immediately. **(C)** *creative* might seem tempting, but be careful: it's the wrong part of speech. "Creativity" might be a fitting answer, but that is not what is offered. Answer choice **(B)** *intelligence* is an easy blank to begin with.

For the next blank, you know you are still referring to its intelligence and you are looking for a noun modified by "mental" to give us a sense of sharpness of mind. All three options refer to sharpness, but **(E)** *acridity* and **(F)** *trenchancy* both refer to a sharpness of taste or smell (think acidic), and "mental *acumen*," choice **(D)**, is a relatively commonly heard phrase.

By contrast, you now switch to its physical abilities, which (as the clause indicates) are also exceptional. **(G)** *brilliance* doesn't make sense in a physical context, and **(H)** *genius* is likewise inappropriate—**(I)** *dexterity* is the clear option. "The octopus is remarkable for its *intelligence*, demonstrating exceptional problem-solving skills and memory; beyond its mental *acumen*, the octopus possesses exceptional physical *dexterity*, allowing it to precisely manipulate objects." This is exactly what you need.

20.   A, E

The key here is that the sentence tells us that his "silver tongue" makes it hard to concentrate on the meaning of his words. To have a silver tongue is to be noted for the pleasantness of one's speech, so you are looking for a pair of answers that mean "pleasing." **(C)** *stumbling*, **(D)** *laconic*, and **(F)** *strident* all are unrelated to the pleasantness of his tone, and while **(B)** *flowing* may certainly be an attribute of a skilled orator, it will not create a similar sentence to one created by any other of the possible answers. **(A)** *mellifluous* and **(E)** *euphonic* both mean to be sweet or pleasing, and are both often used in reference to speech.

21.   C, F

For the favorite to lose is a surprise, so you already know you are looking for choices that are synonyms of "surprised." Choice **(A)** *horrified* has a negative connotation not implied in the sentence, and likewise the emotions conveyed in choices **(B)** *electrified*, **(D)** *bored*, and **(E)** *alienated* all would require further information than you are given to be considered as possible answers. Answer choice **(C)** *shook* is often used in a metaphorical sense when a surprising event occurs, as is answer choice **(F)** *stunned*, and the two are synonyms of one another and of "surprised."

22.   A, F

This is a good example of a sentence in which you are given more information than you need. In fact, the only clue you need lies in the final phrase "to be relied upon." Your answers will be antonyms of "reliable," which eliminates choices **(B)** *exacting*, **(C)** *circuitous*—a tempting choice because of the relationship between bus routes and the root word "circuit," but the meaning is not related to the sentence—and **(D)** *rigid*. Out of the three remaining options, you can see that all three would be accurate, however **(E)** *isolated* implies that the buses are few and far between, whereas **(A)** *irregular* and **(F)** *erratic* both suggest that they are unreliable and, again as is often (but not necessarily) the case with these questions, they are synonyms of each other.

23.   B, D

While you might have no background in musical techniques, the example you are given tells us that the progression of notes in the music seem to somehow imitate the words of the lyrics. So, you need a word that gives the meaning "the progression of the notes mirrors the meaning of the lyrics." Choices **(C)** *contrasts* and **(E)** *opposes* are antonyms to our desired answer, and while the remaining four options may all, arguably, be indicative of the notes meshing well with the lyrics, choices **(A)** *sustains* and **(F)** *reinforces* are both without synonyms in the remaining options and do not properly refer to the desired meaning of "mirrors." Answer choices **(B)** *mimics* and **(D)** *reflects* do, however, and you can thus know that they are your desired choices.

24. C, D

While you might be tempted to stray towards the answers meaning "destroy" due to the previous mention of eradication and due to the danger of the subject material (smallpox), you must carefully read through the sentence, which informs us that there is hope that the samples may have further uses, so you know they must be preserved. You can thus reject **(A)** *eliminate* and **(E)** *extirpate*. You are left with two pairs of synonyms, choices **(B)** *duplicate* and **(F)** *cultivate* as well as **(C)** *preserve* and **(D)** *retain*, so you must choose one of the sets. You are able to do this by focusing on what is in the sentence alone—there is no mention of expanding the collection of samples, so answer choices **(C)** and **(D)** are correct.

25. C, F

With strong words like "most," "declarations," and "genesis," you can immediately know that the answer will be likewise a word of emphatic meaning. Furthermore, the sentence tells us of the importance of the *Magna Carta*, so you anticipate synonyms of "significant" or "revolutionary." Choices **(D)** *recondite* and **(E)** *ancient* are both meaningless in the sentence, and you can ignore them. Choice **(B)** *immense* can likewise be dismissed because there is nothing to describe the size of the *Magna Carta*, nor are there any synonyms among the other options. While choice **(A)** *remarkable* is tempting to consider, both answer choices **(C)** *pivotal* and **(F)** *momentous* possess a connotation of a significant turning point, which **(A)** lacks—these choices are further backed by the description in the final clause as a "genesis."

26. A, E

The key sign here is that the appearance of the city seems to be lacking, so you are looking for words that imply a deficiency in charm or physical beauty. Choice **(D)** *bedlam* could only make sense without the second clause, and choice **(F)** *barrenness* is too poetic and without relation to the rest of the sentence to make a good choice; furthermore, both are lacking synonyms in the other options. Choice **(C)** *gaudiness* does imply a lack of taste, but it is without a synonym as well. **(A)** *detritus* means waste or debris, which is an excellent option for the blank, and with further investigation you can see it has a synonym in **(E)** *refuse*. **(B)** *refuge* is a trap for the careless, resembling *refuse* and right below a synonym of *refuse*—be careful when you read the answers!

27. C, F

The first thing you notice is that you are looking for solutions that demonstrate Chesterton's particular style of wit. While you might not know anything of his style of wit, you are given a further clue to the answer in the description of Shaw as his "friend and rival." With this description in mind, you can easily dismiss choices **(B)** *vociferous*, **(D)** *vicious*, and **(E)** *scathing* as behavior unlikely to be shown towards a friend—remember, if the solution would demand further qualification such as "Chesterton was known to be as harsh to his friends as to his critics," then it is highly unlikely to be the correct answer. **(A)** *punctilious* is not a synonym of the remaining two answer choices, **(C)** *waggish* and **(F)** *lighthearted*.

28. A, E

The key word to focus on here is "precise"—you are looking for a word to contrast with this, so you can predict a synonym of "vague" or "unknown." You can thus eliminate choices **(C)** *disproved* and **(D)** *unstudied* as they convey too excessively an absolute sense for the sentence. The remaining words provide us with three reasonable options: **(A)** *uncertain*, **(B)** *disputed*, and **(E)** *elusive*—**(F)** *precarious* can also be dismissed because nothing about the dangers or consequences of electrotherapy is discussed in the sentence. With these remaining options, you can confidently select **(A)** and **(E)** because **(B)** *disputed* conveys a meaning of controversy that is also without support in the sentence. Answer choices **(A)** and **(E)** are both synonyms of your prediction of "unknown," and are therefore the correct answers.

29. B, E

While it might help to know the role of the croupier in a casino, it is not necessary to decipher the meaning of the sentence. You are told that he feels he should be highly esteemed for his behavior. You can anticipate finding, then, a pair of solutions that evoke a sense of professionalism or proper etiquette. **(A)** *articulation* is without synonym among the answers, as is **(F)** *dexterity*. **(C)** *reputation* and **(D)** *history* are similar to one another, but too vague to be confidently chosen for this blank, and they have little to do specifically with behavior. The remaining two words, answer choices **(B)** *demeanor* and **(E)** *mien* both relate to one's composure and match the prediction of "behavior."

30. B, D

The first indication you have of the structure of the sentence is the concession "Although," so you can expect the second clause to create some contradiction to the first. The first clause tells us that the river has now vanished, and based on what you are told in the second clause you can judge that the effect of the river is still apparent. You can expect, then, that the solutions will indicate that the physical legacy of the river is still visible, so you need to look for synonyms of "visible" (as opposed to "vanished"). **(A)** *repudiation of* and **(E)** *vindicated from* suggest a level of intent that is unlikely in non-sentient objects, so you can eliminate them as possibilities. **(B)** *witness to* provides us with one possible solution, implying that the effect of the river is still manifest, and you have a possible second solution in **(D)** *an attestation to*. **(C)** *coarsened by* does describe a physical effect, but it makes no sense in context and is without synonym among the other choices. **(F)** *recovered from* also contradicts the idea of a lasting effect, which confirms answer choices **(B)** and **(D)** as the only possible options.

31. C, F

You must be careful here—you know that Phillip is still confined to his house, so it is tempting to assume that this would imply that he is still ill, which is supported by the clause "lest he was contagious." However, you are also told that his symptoms had receded, and so you should not be looking for solutions that indicate he is still sick, but rather that he is healing. This eliminates choices **(B)** *ailing* and **(D)** *nauseous*. **(A)** *impaired* and **(E)** *enfeebled* are synonyms and signs of being sick, but you are again explicitly told that the symptoms had abated. **(C)** *convalescing* and **(F)** *recuperating* describe the stage of recovery in which one is healing but possibly still contagious; these choices match your prediction that he is in the process of recovering.

32. A, E
Without any limiting words, you must make your prediction based on the sentence as one unified idea; hence, the correct answers would be what allows for near-instant transmission of information. You are told nothing more in the sentence about other effects or consequences of the internet, so you can expect the answers to focus solely on the options the internet makes available. **(A)** *potentials* is an excellent option, and also possesses a synonym in **(E)** *prospects*. You can eliminate the other possibilities because **(B)** *controversies*, **(D)** *litigation*, and **(F)** *revolutions* all imply a conflict that is nowhere described in the sentence, and **(C)** *theories* is likewise unrelated to the scope of the sentence.

33. B, F
The detour road sign "Although" informs us that the answer will indicate that she finds something positive in the smell of her father's pipe tobacco to contrast with her disapproval. Choices **(D)** *pungent of* and **(E)** *odorous of* both have a negative connotation that would not, then, make sense because you are looking for words with a positive connotation—the smell, you expect, will remind her of her youth. Likewise, **(A)** *poignant for* bears the sense of painful longing, which would also conflict with our anticipated positive connotation. Choice **(B)** *redolent of* is a possible answer, and you have a synonym in answer choice **(F)** *evocative of*, both of them suggesting that the smell reminds her of her childhood. Choice **(C)** *debilitating during* cannot be the correct answer because it lacks a synonym and has no relevance to the sentence.

34. A, D
A broken wrist would certainly hinder a flutist's ability to play, so you can expect our answers to be signs of her worry for her career. **(A)** *alarmed* is a possible answer, but you can easily determine choices **(B)** *truculent*, **(C)** *panegyrical*, and **(E)** *ebullient* are all incorrect because they carry meaning different from that of alarmed or worried. Answer choice **(D)** *timorous* also conveys the strength of her concern and is a synonym to choice **(A)**. Choice **(F)** *phlegmatic* cannot be correct because it implies she is apathetic.

35. B, C
Given the structure of the sentence, you can know that the solution will provide a clause describing the possibility of English being made the official language in contrast to the status of English as the de facto language. You are therefore looking for answers than imply doubt. Choices **(A)** *liable* and **(E)** *plausible* can then be rejected because they are

the opposite of what you need. Choices **(D)** *impossible* and **(F)** *preposterous* are too strong of words because you need solutions that convey a sense of uncertainty. Answer choices **(B)** *unlikely* and **(C)** *improbable*, then, are the correct synonyms to match your prediction of doubt or poor probability.

36.   C, F

From the concession of the first clause, you know that his feelings of involving his family are in direct opposition to his excitement, so you can expect to find answers describing doubt or even concern. You can then dismiss choice **(A)** *thrilled* because you are looking for a pair of answers that suggest he is not pleased or unsure of involving his family—probably a synonym of "worried." Choices **(D)** *horrified* and **(E)** *resigned* can be likewise eliminated because they do not match our expected meaning and are without synonym among the answers. From the remaining three options you can see that the correct answers must be answer choices **(C)** *vacillating* and **(F)** *wavering* because these two are synonyms—meaning to move unsteadily from one side to the other—whereas **(B)** *timorous* has a slightly different meaning, and no answer choice for it to pair with.

37.   A, D

They key here is "official report"—you are looking for answers that use neutral language to describe the relation of "decay" to "accident" (indicated by "Because"). You are looking for a word to describe the possible role that the building's structural integrity had in the accident, which based on the sentence you can expect to be a synonym of "offered" or "suggested." **(A)** *proposed* is one good choice because it means to suggest and has an official, neutral tone to it. Choices **(B)** *imputed*, **(E)** *insinuated*, and **(F)** *condemned* are all too definitive (or loaded with personal emotion) to be what you are looking for, and between the remaining choices you can see that answer choices **(A)** and **(D)** *advanced* are the correct answers—**(C)** *rejected* is the opposite of what you need.

38.   B, D

Based on the structure of the sentence, you know that Max can create many dishes as a direct result of his broad repertoire of techniques. Thus, you can predict that the answer will be a synonym of "diverse" or "varied." Choices **(A)** *artful*, **(E)** *savory*, and **(F)** *ambrosial* are all positive descriptions of someone's cooking, but none of them are related to the scope of the sentence. **(B)** *catholic* seems unusual, but the key thing to note here is that catholic with a lower-case c means diverse or widespread (only with an upper case C does Catholic refer to the branch of Christianity), and it matches our prediction. You can reject **(C)** *dilettantish* because it implies a level of superficiality that would contradict the meaning of the sentence. Answer choices **(B)** and **(D)** *eclectic* are therefore the correct answers.

39.   B, F

The structure of the sentence indicates that you are looking for answers that reflect how the Space Shuttle is unparalleled in its complexity and ingenuity. Because of the strength of "unparalleled" you are looking for other words that emphasize the Space Shuttle as being the "pinnacle" of human creativity and engineering. Choices **(A)** *expression* and **(D)** *assertion* are too weak for the meaning of the sentence, and **(C)** *encroachment* and **(E)** *excess* make no sense in the context. Answer choices **(B)** *apogee* and **(F)** *apex* both mean the pinnacle, or the very top of, and are the answers you are looking for.

40. B, E
Based on the final clause you are told two key things to deciphering this sentence: he went elsewhere (chose) and is on his own (for himself). You need answers that would render the clause "He decided against visiting" or "He avoided visiting." Choices **(A)** *contemplated* and **(D)** *considered* could be correct answers if you had some kind of contrasting conjunction ("but" or "although") between the clauses, but because you instead have "and," you know these cannot be the correct answers. Choice **(B)** *eschewed* means to avoid or shun and matches our prediction, likewise for **(E)** *forwent*; they are also synonyms of each other. Choices **(C)** *deprecated* and **(F)** *discouraged* could both be possible answers, but you have already seen that he was choosing for himself not for someone else, so it would make little sense for him to discourage the visit to himself.

41. D
Reading through the passage, you can determine answer choice **(D)** to be the correct answer, because there is no mention of amount of research done or needed concerning the automaticity model. Choices **(A)**, **(B)**, and **(C)** are explicitly stated in the passage: **(A)** may be found in the description of early readers, and **(B)** and **(C)** may be found in the criticism of focusing on fluency over understanding. Choice **(E)** can be derived from the third criticism about dyslexia, which is that the automaticity model does not account for irregularities in cerebral processing.

42. C
(A), the ability to translate, might be tempting because of the phrase "translation into dialect," however there is no mention of other languages, so you can eliminate **(A)**. **(B)** is likewise seemingly relevant because the passage makes multiple mention of fluency and reading speed; however, the author is critical of such standards and you are told nothing of average reading rates. Based on this, you can also reject **(D)** and **(E)**, leaving us with **(C)** as the only option. Answer choice **(C)** suggests that the author values the ability to explain the material in the reading, which is a commonly accepted sign of comprehension, and your correct answer.

43. C
For this style of question, you are given three statements and asked to select which ones are true. Break it down statement by statement. You can see that statement **(A)** is untrue because the term "plagiarism" is used in the passage in the phrase "perhaps Elizabethan notions of plagiarism are different from ours"—which tells us that you cannot be certain

of what might have constituted plagiarism at the time. Statement **(B)** is a bit of a trap: you see the phrase in the passage "It is more difficult to assess authorial intention with regard to a character's motives," and if you are reading carelessly, statement **(B)** might seem to say the same thing. However, statement **(B)** declares that it is difficult to assess the motives of the author in writing the play—which is outside of the scope of the text. You can wonder, based on such interpolations, how much you can know of the author's intended motives for the characters, but there is nothing to indicate the motive for writing the play as a whole. Statement **(C)** is correct because you are told that the notion of plagiarism that you use might have been different than the notion of plagiarism in Shakespeare's time. There is nothing to indicate that the very concept of plagiarism did not exist until after Shakespeare, but that *our current understanding of it did.*

44. A, B, C

This question asks us about where you might direct further study into questions about such interpolations as referenced in the passage. This asks us to consider possibilities *based* on what is in the text but not necessarily *within* it. **(A)** the search for other possible interpolations in Shakespeare, is a good possibility—if there is one case of it, it is not unreasonable to at least look for more. **(B)** to familiarize ourselves with the style of other writers who might have helped write or had their work used in the writing of Shakespeare's plays would also prepare us to determine from whence the irregularities you are searching for in **(A)** might come. Finally, **(C)** is an interesting alternative to a strictly literary study and would help to solve the question posed in the text of what constituted plagiarism in the Elizabethan era. All three are good choices for further study.

45. A, C

This is an exclusion question, so you must select which of the answers you cannot infer from the passage. **(A)**, that this example of interpolation would be illegal today, is impossible to tell and this is specified by the author's *questioning* of the difference in notions of plagiarism between now and then; furthermore, it is not specified whether or not Middleton was consciously assisting the composition. **(B)** is suggested within the passage in the supposition that writing such as *Macbeth* might have, in fact, been collaborative—this allows you to eliminate choice **(B)**. **(C)** you know to be also a correct response for the same reason you specified for **(A)**—you do not know precisely his role in the composition. Answer choices **(A)** and **(C)** are both right.

46. B

In this question, you are asked to consider the relation between two phrases. Looking at the passage, you can see that the first highlighted phrase is used as an example of the *interpolations* that the first clause in its sentence mentions. The second highlighted phrase gives an example of the *problems* that arise based on the discovery of such interpolations. In short, the relationship is cause and effect, which you can see offered in answer choice **(B)**. You know **(A)** to be incorrect, because while the second phrase is an example of sorts, the first phrase is not a concept put forth by the author, nor would the second phrase be considered a relevant example. **(C)** is also incorrect because the first phrase is a statement of fact, not an argument or proposal.

47. A

This question asks you to summarize the first few lines of the paragraph—that French had declined in Québec and that there are ascertainable reasons for it. **(A)**, *economic devaluation*, is specified in the description of the "preeminence of English in the workplace." **(B)**, however, you know to be untrue because nothing of immigrant populations is mentioned. This also allows you to reject choices **(D)** and **(E)**, which are also not mentioned. However, it is always important to read through the options, so examine **(C)**: you are told in the passage that a primary concern of the Québécois is *maintaining* their cultural autonomy within Canada, so you know **(C)** to also be untrue. Answer choice **(A)** is the only correct option.

48. B

This question asks you to summarize the significance of the law mentioned in the latter part of the passage. Based on the final sentence of the passage (which mentions the rise in French as the primary language), you can see that **(A)** is untrue—it was not an unsuccessful attempt. You can see **(B)** to be true because the passage specifies that the law "established the primacy of French in the workplace." No mention is made of language in schools, so you can quickly dismiss options **(C)** and **(E)**. Finally, while the cultural identity of Québec is mentioned in the passage, the only results of *Loi 101* specified are the economic equitability of the languages and the rise in the usage of French, so you can also reject **(D)** as a possible answer. Answer choice **(B)** is the only option that is based on what is in the passage.

49. D

You must be careful here. Just because **(A)** is a direct quotation of the opening of the passage does not make it the right answer and, indeed, the passage moves away from the origins of the online education and into other facets of its expansion. **(B)** is likewise not discussed in the passage, even though the author makes note that the demand for adult-oriented education was one of the contributing factors in the rise of online learning. **(C)** and **(E)** are similar ideas, which make them unlikely options to begin with. Furthermore, neither properly describes the entire scope of the passage. Only answer choice **(D)**, "trends in online education," can be said to encompass the entirety of the passage.

50. B

Here you are called to define the words used based on their context. What you are looking for is an answer that accurately reflects what is described in the passage: that is, that the entrepreneurs saw an untapped potential for profit in the unanswered demand for online learning and "seized upon" it. **(A)** is a poor choice because it implies that their success in capitalizing on the demand was unintentional. **(B)** is a much better solution because it evokes the image of the entrepreneurs taking the opportunity available. **(C)** is highly unlikely because no mention of violence is made in the passage (and, indeed, in reference to online education this would be an unlikely choice to begin with). Similarly, choices **(D)** and **(E)** are too strong and must be rejected. Answer choice **(B)** is the only possible answer.

51. C

This type of question asks you to define the phrase based on the context. The key word here is "democratization," and you must find to what it refers in the passage. While the cost-effectiveness of online education is mentioned earlier in the passage, it is unlikely that **(A)** *the cost of online education* is the correct answer because the sense of the final sentence is that "it remains to be seen whether *opening control of higher education to the public* is worth the price of removing it from non-profit, research-based universities." Based on this, you can also discount **(B)** *the influence of popularity* and **(D)** *the role of voting* because while they may be linked to the term "democracy," the context tells us this would be an incorrect usage. Answer choice **(C)** *the opening of online education to the free market* matches our prediction and properly clarifies the usage of the underlined phrase in the passage. You can also discount **(E)** because it goes well beyond the scope of the passage.

52. A

Remember, the first thing to do with any passage is to identify the topic and the scope. The topic is the broad subject of the passage—in this case "thermodynamics." This is why you can immediately rule out **(D)** because it speaks of the topic rather than the scope. The scope of the passage focuses on the application of thermodynamics to the motion of a piston—which is what answer choice **(A)** states and is the correct answer. Choices **(B)** and **(C)** both refer to specific subjects mentioned in the passage but do not refer to the passage as a whole.

53. B

The passage informs you that the faster a piston is moving in and out of a cylinder, the hotter the gas will become. Based on this, you can infer that the when the car is moving faster, the gas will become hotter because the pistons will be moving more quickly. Thus, the correct answer choice is **(B)**. Even if you are unsure of the concepts described in a passage, sometimes you can make a reasonable guess at an answer based on common sense. In this case, you can assume that the parts of a car's engine will be hotter when the car is going faster, without having to apply what you have learned in the passage about thermodynamics.

54. D

The key contrast to make note of here is the difference between "manifestation" and "statement"—that is, the difference between an appearance of something and a declaration of it. What the underlined phrase, then, says is that the motion of the piston is an appearance—an example, if you will—of the second law of thermodynamics but it is not an explanation or proof of it. Choice **(A)** you can immediately reject because a universal law cannot be applied to only certain circumstances. While **(B)** might suggest an excellent example to demonstrate the second law of thermodynamics, it is not proof of it—**(B)** is, in fact, the opposite of our desired answer; furthermore, it would be a poorly worded answer in that it suggests the second law of thermodynamics as relating to the physical object of the piston rather than the gas within the cylinder. **(C)** is also inaccurate because the underlined phrase tells us that the change in heat in the cylinder is an example of the second law of thermodynamics. Answer choice **(D)**, however, states that the change in heat is an example rather than a proof of the second law of thermodynamics, and is our correct answer.

55. "HIS THEORY WAS THE BIRTH OF WHAT IS CALLED . . . "
This sentence provides a summary of the importance of his work.

56. A
While reading the paragraph, you ought to be paraphrasing the words in your head to make sure you understand them. The key aspect of this sentence is that, at the time, there were a number of scientists who believed that the major discoveries had been made and the remaining scientific work was to tweak and perfect current theories. With that in mind, you can look through the options to see which best fits this idea. Answer choice **(A)**, you can see immediately, is an excellent paraphrase of the sentence. **(B)** is problematic because there is a fundamental difference between scientists believing all the great discoveries to have been made and scientists making few new significant discoveries. You can also reject choices **(C)**, **(D)**, and **(E)** because their description of "scientists" and the "scientific community" as a whole is too broad. The original sentence only states "many scientists," suggesting that there were dissenters, such as Planck.

57. C
What you must keep in mind here is that you are asked for the relation between the two phrases, not their relation to the sentence as a whole. A good way to attack this sort of problem is to paraphrase each of the phrases and identify what it is saying on its own. The first phrase states an issue: that the current theory was not applicable at high frequencies because it produced an "unphysical result." The second phrase tells us of Planck's breakthrough discovery of quanta. Thus, you can predict that the answer will be the one that tells us the relationship is between the limitations of the current theory and Planck's solution. **(A)** is a trick answer because it uses words you frequently see elsewhere and are admonished to remember when considering any reading comprehension passage. However, topic and scope are totally irrelevant to this question and choice **(A)** can be dismissed. **(B)** is tempting because of the words "theory" and "debunking," however based on the wording of the first phrase, it is clear that the issue with the current theory was recognized by the scientific community, and thus Planck's solution was not a challenge to a widely accepted belief and "debunking" is not appropriate. In answer choice **(C)** you are given "problem" and "solution," which matches your prediction and is the correct answer. **(D)** is out of scope; a hypothesis is not brought up here, nor is that hypothesis being explained

further. **(E)** is incorrect since the first highlighted sentence is not a thesis, or summary, of the paragraph, but rather an issue that needs to be addressed.

58. B

The key to this question lies in the analogy provided in the passage, with the effects of ripples in the water, where two troughs or crests amplify each other, but one trough and one crest negate each other. Likewise, with the light waves, the two separate light sources produce waves that interact with one another and, like the crests and troughs of the water, have predictable results—the light and dark fringes. Answer **(A)** describes a part of his findings, but you must reject it because it does not adequately describe the whole of his findings. Choice **(C)** cannot be the correct answer either, because the passage notes that it was not until Einstein that particle theory was returned to the theory of light. And likewise for choice **(D)**, you are told that Einstein proved that Newton's theory was not entirely inaccurate, and so it was not permanently debunked. Similarly, you cannot claim he was entirely correct, so **(E)** is out as well. This leaves answer choice **(B)**.

59. A

The answer, again, comes from the ripple analogy—where the two meeting crests are amplified. Thus you can immediately see that **(A)** is likely to be the correct answer. You can dismiss **(B)** because Young's experiment is concerned solely with light as a wave, not as a particle, and answer **(C)** fails to take into account the purpose of his experiment—separating a single light source split into two and recombined on the screen. As for choice **(D)**, amplification of light particles is mentioned as a possibility, but this is out of scope with the question. Choice **(E)** refers to Huygen's wave theory of light, but not Young's experiment. You have a clear and decisive solution in **(A)**.

60. C

The underlined sentence reminds you of the topic of the paragraph—that all matter at the atomic level displays properties of waves and particles (the scope being the example of light, particularly the discovery of it demonstrating wave-like properties). While it is true, then, that there is a similarity between electrons and light in that they both demonstrate properties of waves and particles, **(A)** fails to take the full passage into perspective. **(B)** is also incorrect, because while the author was previously describing Einstein's proof that Newton's theory was, in part, accurate, the sentence is not about light at all, but about electrons. **(C)**, however, accurately describes the place of the underlined phrase in the passage: it is a reminder that all matter demonstrates properties of both waves and particles at the atomic level. **(D)** and **(E)** can also, be eliminated as neither fits the sentence.

VERBAL REASONING PRACTICE SET 2

Directions: Each sentence below has one or more blanks, each blank indicating that something has been omitted. Beneath the sentence are five words for one-blank questions, and sets of three words for each blank of two- and three-blank questions. Choose the word or set of words for each blank that best fits the meaning of the sentence as a whole.

1. With the rise of automated support, reference workers in many fields feel that their services are being inadvertently _____; reference service, they argue, is not something that can be so easily predicted, but a case-by-case effort that requires a skill set built upon training and experience.

    (A) belittled

    (B) tarnished

    (C) ridiculed

    (D) vituperated

    (E) impaired

2. The spice saffron is made from the stigma of the *Crocus sativus* plant; the (i) _____ number of blossoms required to produce saffron and the (ii) _____ of the flower makes it the most expensive spice in the world.

Blank (i)		Blank (ii)	
A	vast	D	color
B	meager	E	hardiness
C	unique	F	delicacy

3. The field of cryptozoology is the search for animals unknown to science and for which we have no scientific attestation; (i) _____ physical evidence, it relies upon (ii) _____ sightings for proof of creatures such as the Loch Ness Monster.

Blank (i)		Blank (ii)	
A	ignoring	D	anecdotal
B	lacking	E	imagined
C	needing	F	nominal

4. The humor of Oscar Wilde remains a classic example of _____ wit; his terse remarks and deadpan delivery belied an acerbic sarcasm and brilliant insight into the world around him.

   Ⓐ ostentatious

   Ⓑ pointed

   Ⓒ brusque

   Ⓓ orotund

   Ⓔ laconic

5. The neglect of the old theater was (i) _____ in the extreme (ii) _____ of the building, which was no longer safe to enter.

Blank (i)		Blank (ii)	
A	hinted at	D	dilapidation
B	suggested	E	depilation
C	manifest	F	radiance

6. The Battle of Thermopylae has been one of the most (i) _____ battles in history, and has become so surrounded in anecdotes and exaggerations that it is often difficult to tell what is history and what is recreated; nevertheless, its cultural impact on the western world cannot be (ii) _____.

Blank (i)		Blank (ii)	
A	sensationalized	D	doubted
B	intriguing	E	supported
C	sanguine	F	arrogated

7. (i) _____ property insurance, there was little he (ii) _____ do when the earthquake struck but accept his losses and move on.

Blank (i)		Blank (ii)	
A	Due to	D	cared to
B	Lacking	E	could
C	Protected by	F	wanted to

8. Stonehenge is arguably the most widely recognized megalithic site in the world, and, despite many popular images, was completed more than a millennium before the Celtic druids arrived in Britain; the (i) _____ can likely be traced to William Stukeley, a pioneer of British archaeology who (ii) _____ the druids for many megalithic sites.

	Blank (i)		Blank (ii)
A	revelation	D	ignored
B	proof	E	blamed
C	misconception	F	credited

9. They predict _____ temperatures for this summer and caution against overexposure to the heat without adequate protection and hydration.

    (A) muggy

    (B) brisk

    (C) torrid

    (D) crisp

    (E) unusual

10. The Book of Kells is one of the most magnificent and famous extant illuminated manuscripts of the Middle Ages; combining masterful artwork and superb calligraphy, it is truly _____ artifact of the past.

    (A) a mythical

    (B) an august

    (C) a famous

    (D) an underappreciated

    (E) a quaint

11. Although many developments have been made in the burgeoning field of artificial intelligence, the ultimate goal of matching human intelligence remains elusive, and its actual _____ remains unknown.

    (A) morality

    (B) popularity

    (C) feasibility

    (D) ethics

    (E) price

12. Their friendship has been tested many times; however, today I can see that
they are _____ each other.

    (A) inseparable from

    (B) estranged from

    (C) distancing from

    (D) acrimonious to

    (E) ambivalent to

13. The modern apartment building can be traced back to the *insulae* of ancient
Rome, where the stories above business establishments were _____
the lower classes who could not afford to own their own residences.

    (A) squatted by

    (B) sold to

    (C) given to

    (D) leased to

    (E) inhabited by

14. Tired of being _____ by her family, she left home at an early age in
order to become more independent.

    (A) neglected

    (B) cosseted

    (C) chastised

    (D) overlooked

    (E) mollified

15. Although unfinished at the time of his death, Chretien de Troyes' *Perceval*
was an immediate success in medieval literature, _____ a fascination
in the knightly quest for the Holy Grail, which it introduced to the European
imagination.

    (A) continuing

    (B) renewing

    (C) advancing

    (D) igniting

    (E) demonstrating

16. Her _____ personality made her an effective organizer, but sometimes left her uncomfortable in informal social situations because she expected others to choose their words as carefully as she did.

    (A) punctual

    (B) reticent

    (C) meticulous

    (D) efficient

    (E) sophisticated

17. As we seek alternative energy sources, one of the most _____ is the use of photovoltaic material on the exterior of buildings, thereby providing an affordable energy source for residential, business, and other structures.

    (A) costly

    (B) advanced

    (C) environmental

    (D) economical

    (E) conscientious

18. The countless (i) _____ days left everyone (ii) _____ for the sudden downpour; the deluge brought traffic to a halt, (iii) _____ the roads.

Blank (i)	Blank (ii)	Blank (iii)
A arid	D waiting	G inundating
B calm	E unprepared	H soaking
C humid	F fearing	I spraying

19. They (i) _____ the scientist's (ii) _____, suspecting his (iii) _____ had affected the study, and he was later found to have tampered with the data to better fit his desired results.

Blank (i)	Blank (ii)	Blank (iii)
A decried	D objectivity	G biases
B discounted	E dedication	H guile
C challenged	F rhetoric	I conduct

20. Although (i) _____ small amounts of seawater is not dangerous to humans, the high salinity of the water makes it (ii) _____ to consume in large quantities; it is from this that comes the (iii) _____ lamented by the narrator of *The Rime of the Ancient Mariner*: "Water, water, everywhere,/Nor any drop to drink."

Blank (i)	Blank (ii)	Blank (iii)
A guzzling	**D** harsh	**G** setting
B quaffing	**E** difficult	**H** quandary
C imbibing	**F** inadvisable	**I** tragedy

Directions: For the following questions, select the **two** answer choices that, when inserted into the sentence, fit the meaning of the sentence as a whole **and** yield complete sentences that are similar in meaning.

21. As modern scholarship continues to dim the possibility that Homer was a single historic figure, the question of authorship of his works has been raised; although we might never know who wrote them, scholars still need some way to refer to the author or authors of the *Iliad* and *Odyssey*, so the term "Homeric Tradition" has been _____ as a possible new terminology.

- [A] selected
- [B] established
- [C] appropriated
- [D] bestowed
- [E] suggested
- [F] proposed

22. _____ commercial arsenic usage has diminished, its ongoing presence in water and soil continues to be a major public health concern, given the extremely high toxicity of the substance.

- [A] After
- [B] Whereas
- [C] Inasmuch as
- [D] Subsequent
- [E] While
- [F] Because

```
ROUTE ITEM FOR HOLD
              GRE : graduate record
              examinations.
              LB2367.4 .G7253 2011
Enumeration

              1
              39424055395682
Route To:     KOERNER circulation
              CURRENT
```

23. Early sewing machines were poorly received by textile workers who feared the technology would _____ the demand for their skills; however, despite their protests, the sewing machine became popular both in the factory and in the home.

    A overwhelm

    B diminish

    C obviate

    D mitigate

    E eliminate

    F belittle

24. The protest march, which began as a peaceful demonstration, quickly turned into a riot, and in the response by police, several people on either side were killed and dozens more wounded; it would later be _____ remembered by both sides as a tragic accident, and no blame would be assigned.

    A indignantly

    B mournfully

    C spitefully

    D bitterly

    E soberly

    F melancholically

25. Regardless of his limited success, the philosopher was _____ in his search for understanding and continued to think and write.

    A content

    B disaffected

    C dogged

    D triumphant

    E perseverant

    F derided

26. The ascent of Mount Everest was first conquered nearly sixty years ago, but it nevertheless remains a symbol of _____ struggle in the popular psyche, demanding incredible determination and physical endurance.

    A arduous

    B Daedalean

    C colossal

    D adamant

    E Herculean

    F Gordian

27. Carl enjoyed the music and culture surrounding the opera house, but, possessing a _____ attention span, he secretly wished the performances could be slightly truncated.

    A limited

    B interminable

    C picayune

    D finite

    E paltry

    F infinitesimal

28. Facing the pressure of an impending deadline, Sarah was afflicted with a case of _____ writer's block; she could not think of a single word to write.

    A middling

    B thorough

    C consummate

    D unmitigated

    E customary

    F egregious

29. "Leaf viewing" is a popular outing in New England, where one can behold the magnificent fall colors in the changing of the leaves; this remarkable sight can be attributed to the _____ of green chlorophyll in leaves, allowing the carotenoids to show through.

    A expulsion

    B consumption

    C abatement

    D irradiation

    E ebbing

    F nourishment

30. Building trust is a crucial, yet difficult aspect of friendship; it can take years to be _____ but only moments to be broken.

    A accomplished

    B edified

    C fostered

    D acquiesced

    E capitulated

    F undertaken

31. James _____ that his efforts in the project had earned him a prolonged vacation, but when his boss rejected the idea, James returned to work without complaint.

    A demanded

    B contended

    C ventured

    D insisted

    E averred

    F opined

32. The doctor's handwriting was entirely _____, much to the frustration of the other staff of the hospital, but some wondered whether it was not intentionally so, in order to prevent forgery of prescriptions.

    A rudimentary

    B indecipherable

    C lucid

    D hieroglyphic

    E unprofessional

    F rustic

33. While all the coworkers participated in the attempted merger of the company with a rival, after their proposal collapsed, he was the one _____ as a scapegoat in the resulting chaos and was forced to leave the company.

    A blamed

    B ostracized

    C voted

    D allotted

    E excommunicated

    F chosen

34. Although the stems of the rhubarb plant have various culinary and medicinal uses, the leaves are in fact poisonous, making it a plant best grown only by those familiar with both its _____ and dangers.

    A benefits

    B treatments

    C purposes

    D contingencies

    E utilities

    F exigencies

35. Because William had left no will, after the funeral, _____ arose among his children over ownership of the family heirlooms; it was tragic to see such bitterness among the family in a time of mourning.

    A a conflagration
    B repudiation
    C dissension
    D contention
    E a Rubicon
    F a squall

36. Seeing that the student had clearly rushed through the assignment at the last minute, the professor returned the paper with a failing grade, and cautioned the student to dedicate more time to his studies and to avoid handing in such _____ work in the future.

    A jaunty
    B sloppy
    C pithy
    D burnished
    E slipshod
    F blithe

37. The difficulty in describing its unique flavor, as well as its slogan "Love it or hate it," makes Marmite a perfect example of _____ taste.

    A a refined
    B an idiosyncratic
    C an acquired
    D a novel
    E an endowed
    F a mediocre

38. Given his long history of penny-pinching behavior, we could not help but feel that his refusal to donate to the charity only reinforced his _____ image.

   A parsimonious

   B avaricious

   C covetous

   D penurious

   E selfish

   F rapacious

39. Although we are constantly beset by stories of exploitation and abuse during widespread catastrophes, it is important also to _____ the good Samaritans who may be found in these same times of crisis.

   A commend

   B recall

   C expound

   D remember

   E pronounce

   F proscribe

Questions 40 through 43 are based on the passage below.

The origins of the English language can be traced back to the Saxon and other Germanic settlers in Britain beginning in the 5th century A.D. Its unusual nature can be attributed to the diverse linguistic origins of the groups that contributed to its development and their role in English society. Although it belongs to the Germanic language family, and its grammatical and syntactical rules reflect this, English vocabulary can be seen to be from multiple origins. In fact, a large part of the vocabulary can be seen to not be derived from the Germanic languages at all, but is rather of Latin origin. This can be explained by the influence on Old English of Old French and Latin during the Norman Invasion in the 11th century. By the time of the Norman Invasion, Old English was already a language, with both its grammar and vocabulary based in the Germanic language family. However, the establishment of a ruling class who spoke a Romance language caused significant changes in the indigenous tongue. It is also interesting to note that there is a distinct trend between the length of a word and its origin—most of the shorter words in the English language are derived from the Germanic languages, whereas the longer words are from a Latin background. One theory to explain this is that the more elaborate and complex words were primarily used by the elite after the Norman Invasion—who would have favored a Latin-based (or Romance) vocabulary—whereas words with the same meaning in the Old English were used primarily by the lower classes, and thus fell into disuse. Modern English words, then, concerning more complex and theoretical, rather than utilitarian, ideas (astronomy, poetry, and epistemology) can generally be found to be of Romance origin, whereas more mundane words, such as pronouns and auxiliary verbs, can be traced to back to Germanic origin.

40. Which of the following best describes the relationship between the highlighted phrases?

   Ⓐ The argument and its counterargument

   Ⓑ Two examples of the scope of the passage

   Ⓒ The topic and scope of the passage

   Ⓓ The scope of the passage and an example

   Ⓔ The topic of the passage, and an example

41. Read the following answer choices and select all that apply. Based on the passage, of what origin would we expect the word "they" to be?

   A Germanic

   B Romance

   C Norse

42. Based on the passage, what is a likely reason as to why English has not been reclassified as a Romance language?

   Ⓐ It was originally developed as a Germanic language in its first incarnation, Old English.

   Ⓑ The core of the language, its grammar and syntax, are still Germanic.

   Ⓒ A larger portion of the English vocabulary is Germanic rather than Romance.

   Ⓓ The Normans felt an affinity for the local tongue, which was Germanic.

   Ⓔ Neither linguistic heritage has a claim to preeminence.

43. Read the following choices and select all that apply. Which of the following can we infer from the passage?

   A Searching for meaning based on the Latin root of the word is less likely to be useful in shorter words.

   B The language spoken by the Saxon and Germanic settlers entirely supplanted the indigenous tongue of 5th century Britain.

   C The discussion of complex ideas during the Norman era in England was primarily the domain of the ruling class.

Questions 44 through 48 are based on the passage below.

The term *Telos* is that for which something is done or that toward which animate beings strive. Thus, an eye is for seeing, a walk for health, a house for shelter, and a book for reading. Little 't' teleology so conceived, though, mustn't be confused with big 't' Teleology, according to which the whole of nature is either progressing, by virtue of some world-historical or cosmic force, toward some overarching purpose or is already the embodiment of some divine plan.

That teleology needn't entail Teleology was evolutionary theory's great insight. From the moment that organic life first appeared on Earth some 4.5 billion years ago, natural selection has been an inexorable, unceasing, and entirely mindless process of winnowing and sifting through a set of design plans. The geological record is littered with plant and animal species falling extinct under the pressures of climatic and geographical changes. Only those designs that natural selection has blindly hit upon and that have worked, designs that are well-adapted to the specific environment and that therefore confer upon certain organisms or certain species some ostensible advantage, will be inheritable by their progeny. This implies that there is no Higher End, no Higher Purpose that governs the actions of intelligent and unintelligent life, only local purposes fitting into the materialist picture of "selfish genes" seeking to pass on genetic information to their descendants *ad infinitum*. There is therefore no Teleology from on high, only teleology all the way down. And there is no more need for what Daniel Dennett has called the "mind-first" hypothesis either.

Nothing under the sun is exempt from the process of natural selection—not eyes or wings and certainly not minds. Thanks to research in evolutionary theory over the past 150 years, it is no longer mysterious how an ignorant, mindless machine, by means of chance, trial and error, and gradual modifications taking place over long swaths of time, could have produced sophisticated, cognizant machines able to reflect upon the process itself. What recommends the evolutionary story of the emergence of intelligent life is not just its plausibility; it is the fact, confirmed time and again by studies in geology, genetics, cell biology, zoology, and botany, that it is true.

44. According to the passage, the principal difference between teleology and Teleology could be understood in terms of the difference between

    Ⓐ quality and quantity.

    Ⓑ example and concept.

    Ⓒ property and object.

    Ⓓ cause and effect.

    Ⓔ part and whole.

45. The primary purpose of the passage is to show how

    Ⓐ new species come into being through a process called natural selection.

    Ⓑ evolution represents a change in our comprehension of all forms of life.

    Ⓒ natural selection shows us how evolution through a set of randomly generated, rather than intentional, procedures is possible.

    Ⓓ intelligent and sentient creatures are the inevitable results of natural selection.

    Ⓔ absolute ignorance works to create living beings much in the same way that absolute wisdom does.

46. Read the following choices and select all that apply. For which of the following topics does the passage provide supporting evidence?

    Ⓐ the plurality of species

    Ⓑ the complex nature of some organisms

    Ⓒ the evolution of sentience

47. Based on information in the passage, it can be inferred from the author's statement that evolution has no need for the "mind-first" hypothesis that

   Ⓐ the first appearance of living things did not involve an intelligent being.

   Ⓑ unintelligent beings necessarily follow from an intelligent being.

   Ⓒ in human beings, mental life came before physical existence.

   Ⓓ living beings had to have come from multicellular organisms.

   Ⓔ experiments in ordering organic life finally yielded intelligent design.

48. Read the following choices and select all that apply. Based on the passage, it can be inferred that the theory of Intelligent Design would be an example of

   A teleology.

   B Teleology.

   C the fact that Teleology must follow from teleology.

Questions 49 through 52 are based on the passage below.

John Finnis developed his theory of natural law based on the structure that Thomas Aquinas provided, filling in areas where he felt that Aquinas's theory was lacking; he also amended other aspects of the theory to respond to a world much more culturally diverse than the one in which Aquinas lived. Unlike Aquinas, who gives only a vague account of the first precepts of the natural law, Finnis locates a specific number of basic human goods. Finnis avoids the charge that his theory falls into the "naturalistic fallacy" by asserting that these goods are not moral in themselves, but become moral through human participation in them. In addition, these goods are not hierarchical, which allows a much greater range of freedom in choosing actions. Finally, Finnis's theory does not require the presence of God. Though curiosity about the nature of the universe is one of his basic human goods, the actual existence of God is not required by his theory. Finnis's theory creates as many problems as it solves. While formulating an interesting answer to the "is/ought" problem and giving a much more robust definition of human volition than Aquinas, his solutions create their own problems as well. His account of the goods is stripped of any method for evaluation. The boundaries of each good are difficult to discern. Further, by asserting that each good is self-evident and equal to all the others, Finnis makes any action taken in furtherance of any of them equivalent morally. Finally, by removing the precepts of natural law from our natural habits and inclinations, placing them instead in self-evident goods, <u>Finnis seems not to be describing our nature at all.</u>

49. Based on the passage, what is the most likely meaning of "good" according to Finnis?

    Ⓐ a physical object, such as foodstuffs or textiles

    Ⓑ morally correct action as determined by God

    Ⓒ actions which help us achieve a desirable, material end

    Ⓓ something self-evident which we ought to strive to embrace

    Ⓔ what is naturally occurring

50. According to the passage, which is likely to undermine Finnis's definition of "goods"?

    Ⓐ the study of the existence of God

    Ⓑ goods that demand opposing actions

    Ⓒ the embracing of our natural desires

    Ⓓ defining additional goods

    Ⓔ the lack of a method for their evaluation

51. Read the following answer choices carefully and select all that apply. According to the passage, which of the following is not an improvement of Finnis's theory of natural law over Aquinas's?

    Ⓐ avoiding the "naturalistic fallacy"

    Ⓑ removing the necessity of God in his definition of "good"

    Ⓒ curtailing freedom in human actions

52. Based on the passage, which of the following is a paraphrase of the reason for the criticism in the underlined passage?

    Ⓐ Since his list of goods are not determined by an absolute force, they must be from some source beyond our nature.

    Ⓑ There is no way to adequately evaluate what makes breaking away from our impulses worthwhile.

    Ⓒ If natural law is created by human participation, it cannot be beyond our nature.

    Ⓓ The boundaries of each "good" are nebulous.

    Ⓔ Finnis erringly decontextualizes the precepts of natural law by removing them from their human context.

Questions 53 through 56 are based on the passage below.

The place of *Claf Abercuawg* in relation to the larger body of Middle Welsh poetry attributed to Llywarch Hen (that is, as narrator rather than author) is a matter of debate, and one that is not likely to be soon settled—bluntly put, there is no way of knowing with certainty. It seems that the association is based largely on the similarity of the structure of *Claf Abercuawg* to the structure of other laments found in the Llywarch Hen cycle, in addition to its presence immediately preceding the Llywarch Hen material in extant manuscripts. However, modern scholarship has called the connection of this poem to the Llywarch Hen cycle into question, and indeed, there is nothing in the poem itself that necessitates a connection. Nevertheless, nature poetry like *Claf Abercuawg* does not form a complete work of poetry itself, but is rather used as a prologue to another type of poem, and so separating this poem from the Llywarch Hen cycle would require another tradition for its origin. This problem is further exacerbated by the fact that there seems to be the implication of an otherwise unknown history behind the current condition of the narrator, as suggested by his reference to his previous life in the court of a king. Nor can the striking similarity of imagery to poems in the Llywarch Hen cycle, such as *Gwên ap Llywarch a'i dad* be ignored. Finally, the appellation *Claf Abercuawg* is a modern creation, and in the manuscripts there is simply a break in the line and an ornate initial letter to signal the beginning of a new piece. Thus, to speak of it as a clear entity is misleading—it is simply one poem the precedes a number of interrelated poems.

This is not to claim that *Claf Abercuawg* must have originated from the same tradition as the Llywarch Hen material, but rather that, if they did come from different traditions, the evidence found in the themes, the imagery, and the placement of these poems in the manuscripts makes it increasingly difficult to believe that the scribes would place *Claf Abercuawg* immediately preceding the Llywarch Hen cycle without the intent to connect the two. And so while it is impossible to say whether the "original" *Claf Abercuawg* was intended to be a part of the Llywarch Hen cycle, by the time of the assembly of the extant manuscripts it was clearly considered to be so.

53. According to the passage, which of the following is NOT a difficulty in ascertaining the connection between *Claf Abercuawg* and the Llywarch Hen cycle of poetry?

  Ⓐ The similarity in literary technique between the works.

  Ⓑ The unlikelihood of *Claf Abercuawg* being a standalone work.

  Ⓒ Both works have anonymous narrators.

  Ⓓ The placement of the poems in the manuscripts.

  Ⓔ The implied background of the narrator of *Claf Abercuawg*.

54. Based on the passage, what seems to be the author's response to the question of the connection between the works?

  Ⓐ The connection is clear based on the extant manuscripts.

  Ⓑ The connection is more likely than not.

  Ⓒ It is fruitless to examine because it can never be known.

  Ⓓ The connection is implied in the extant manuscripts.

  Ⓔ The connection is possible but unlikely.

55. The primary purpose of this passage is to

  Ⓐ describe the poem *Claf Abercuawg*.

  Ⓑ outline the origins of the poem *Claf Abercuawg*.

  Ⓒ contrast other Middle Welsh poetry with *Claf Abercuawg*.

  Ⓓ explain the connection between *Claf Abercuawg* and the Llywarch Hen poetry.

  Ⓔ describe all the Llywarch Hen poetry.

56. Which of the following is an accurate paraphrasing of the underlined phrase?

  Ⓐ The poem *Claf Abercuawg* was recently rewritten.

  Ⓑ The poem originally had a different title than *Claf Abercuawg*.

  Ⓒ The poem was only given the title *Claf Abercuawg* recently.

  Ⓓ The poem should not be called *Claf Abercuawg*.

  Ⓔ The poem as it now stands has been heavily redacted.

Questions 57 through 60 are based on the passage below.

There is an anthropological theory that states that societies may be divided into one of two broad categories by their cultural motivators—shame or guilt. In a shame-based society, the ethical motivations are primarily external—one's behavior is governed based on the potential effects on the social group (such as dishonoring one's family). By contrast, guilt-based societies rely more heavily on internal motivations—one's behavior is governed based on a set of internal guidelines. There is no society where one or the other is entirely absent, but the distinction lies in that, based on the accepted values of the society, one will come to be dominant over the other. It would seem that early Medieval Europe was primarily a shame-based society; indeed, the forms of shame-based motivators in courtly society were extremely highly developed, with express social laws governing various behaviors. This sort of shame may be seen to be divided into many forms, such as positive and negative shame—that is, prospective and retrospective (knowledge of the honor one will accrue or the shame one will avoid through their future actions, and humiliation or other punishment after the action has been done, respectively)—ethical and non-ethical (dealing with higher, such as theological and abstract, concepts, and quotidian matters, respectively), and so on. These social structures may be also found in the contemporary tales of the chivalric world. An example of such may be seen in the frequent plot device of the knight committing adultery with the wife of his lord. Adultery with the wife of one's lord is a matter of treason and an explicit moral wrong, and yet the condemnation in these stories seems to focus on the perpetrator's violation of social norms (treason) rather than moral standards (adultery).

57. Based on the passage, what can we infer about a society that focuses primarily upon a code of moral right and wrong?

   Ⓐ It would be shame-based.
   Ⓑ It would be guilt-based.
   Ⓒ It would tolerate adultery.
   Ⓓ It would not have laws governing behavior.
   Ⓔ It would have extremely draconian laws dealing with wrongdoing.

58. Select the sentence that describes the scope of the passage.

59. Review each of the following choices and select all that apply. Which of the following can NOT be inferred from the passage?

    A Early Medieval Europe was unconcerned with moral codes.

    B There are some cultures which fall under neither category.

    C Guilt-based societies have few laws.

60. Based on the passage, a society that prizes the harmony of the social group would most likely be

    Ⓐ shame-based.

    Ⓑ guilt-based.

    Ⓒ extremely permissive.

    Ⓓ governed by a chivalric order.

    Ⓔ bereft of citizens with an internal code of moral right and wrong.

ANSWERS AND EXPLANATIONS

1. A	17. D	33. B, E	49. D
2. A, F	18. A, E, G	34. A, E	50. B
3. B, D	19. C, D, G	35. C, D	51. C
4. E	20. C, F, H	36. B, E	52. E
5. C, D	21. E, F	37. B, D	53. C
6. A, D	22. B, E	38. A, D	54. D
7. B, E	23. C, E	39. B, D	55. A
8. C, F	24. B, F	40. D	56. C
9. C	25. C, E	41. A	57. B
10. B	26. C, E	42. B	58. "It would seem that early Medieval…"
11. C	27. A, D	43. A	
12. A	28. B, D	44. C	59. A, B, C
13. D	29. C, E	45. C	60. A
14. B	30. A, B	46. A, B, C	
15. D	31. C, F	47. C	
16. C	32. B, D	48. B	

Diagnostic Tool

Tally up your score and write your results below.

Total

Total Correct: _____ out of 60 correct

By Question Type

Text Completions (questions 1–20) _____ out of 20 correct

Sentence Equivalence (questions 21–39) _____ out of 19 correct

Reading Comprehension (questions 40–60) _____ out of 21 correct

DIAGNOSE YOUR RESULTS

Look back at the questions you got wrong and think about your experience answering them. Refer back to the Steps given at the end of Practice Set 1 to pinpoint the trouble and make use of the suggestions given there.

VERBAL REASONING PRACTICE SET 2
ANSWER KEY

1. A

The increase in automated support suggests a decline in demand for reference workers, and the second half of the sentence tells you that you are looking for an answer that indicates that their services are being undervalued. **(B)** *tarnished*, **(C)** *ridiculed*, and **(D)** *vituperated* all suggest, beyond a negative image, a directly hostile one, which is not indicated by the sentence. **(E)** *impaired* might be acceptable from the first part of the sentence alone, but the value of their services implied by the second half can only support **(A)** *belittled*.

2. A, F

The first half of the sentence is just background, so it is from the second half that you must take your clues. It tells us that producing saffron is very costly, so you can anticipate that the number of blossoms required is a large rather than small number. Based on this, you can reject **(C)** *unique* and **(B)** *meager* for the first blank, leaving **(A)** *vast*.

The second blank implies a quality of the flower that makes it difficult to cultivate—faced with the comparison of **(A)** *vast*, the choice for the final blank is **(F)** *delicacy*. **(D)** *color* and **(E)** *hardiness* are irrelevant in that consideration.

3. B, D

The hint you are given immediately is that cryptozoology lacks "scientific attestation," that is that is has no scientific reason to be supported, so for the first blank you are looking for a word that means "without." **(A)** *ignoring* would mean an intentional rejection of scientific evidence, rather than an absence thereof. **(C)** *needing* would work, but there is no choice for blank (ii) that has to do with physical evidence. Furthermore, "relies upon" points us to a limitation of their evidence. Therefore **(B)** *lacking* makes the most sense for blank (i).

With regard, again, to scientific attestation, you can infer that the second blank implies that the sightings are not backed by scientific data, so you are looking for a solution that means "unscientific" or "unreliable." Out of the two remaining options, **(E)** *imagined* makes little sense, because it implies the sightings are not just inadequate, but fictitious. **(D)** *anecdotal* provides us with the sense of unverifiable sightings and completes the first blank with "lacking" for the sense of being without. **(F)** *nominal* does not fit at all, as it means negligible, or in name only.

4. E

Based on the semicolon, you know that the second half of the sentence directly supports the statement made in the first, so you are looking for a word that implies the usage of few words and a dry delivery of his wit. **(A)** *ostentatious* and **(D)** *orotund* can be rejected on the grounds of the terseness of his remarks, and the remark that the biting nature of his wit is not readily apparent can allow us to discount **(B)** *pointed* and **(C)** *brusque*. Checking our final remaining option, **(E)** *laconic*, you find that it fits the meaning of the sentence.

5. C, D

The key word here is "extreme," which indicates that you are looking for words with very strong meaning in the first blank. Furthermore, you know that the building is no longer safe to enter, so the second blank must refer to some sense of structural decay. Thus, you can expect the full the sentence to be something like "the neglect of the old theater was apparent in the extreme deterioration of the building." For the first blank, **(A)** *hinted at*, and **(B)** *suggested* can both be eliminated because their first words are too weak in meaning for "extreme." **(C)** *manifest* makes the most sense.

Out of the options for the second blank, you can see that **(D)** and **(E)** are very similar words, but only **(D)** *dilapidation* refers to buildings—**(E)** *depilation* refers to hair removal. They are similar-looking words with entirely different meanings; always be careful to look at the words properly! **(F)** *radiance* is the opposite of what you need.

6. A, D

The first indication of meaning you are given is the construction of "most . . . . battles in history," which tells us that the battle was unusual in some way, which the following clause reveals: it has many stories surrounding it, and not all of them are reliable. Choice **(C)** *sanguine* does not have the meaning of reworked or retold. You can reject **(B)** *intriguing* for the same reason. **(A)** *sensationalized* works.

The contrast implied in "nevertheless" tells us that the second blank refers to something in spite of the fictionalization of the battle. So you are looking for a complete sentence that means "The Battle of Thermopylae has been one of the most (reworked or retold) battles in history, and has become so surrounded in anecdotes and exaggerations that it is often difficult to tell what is history and what is recreated; nevertheless, its cultural impact on the western world cannot be called into question." **(D)** *doubted* is the only answers supported by only what is in the text. **(E)** *supported* is the opposite of what you are looking for, and **(F)** *arrogated* has the meaning of "hijacked."

7. B, E

The connection of property insurance to earthquake indicates that if he had it, he would not have to be overly concerned about damage from the earthquake. However "accept his losses" points to the likelihood that he did not have it. This eliminates **(C)** *Protected by* and **(A)** *Due to* for the first blank. **(B)** *Lacking* makes the most sense, because the second clause has no sense of replacing property insurance.

You can predict a sentence meaning: "Because he did not have property insurance, there was little he was able to do when the earthquake struck but accept his losses and move on." **(E)** *could* matches our expected meaning and can be selected as the only possible answer for the second blank.

8.   C, F

The first sign to make note of is that the connection between the druids and Stonehenge is a mistaken one (using the word "despite" as a clue). Thus you can infer the second half of the sentence will have a meaning of approximately "the incorrect idea can likely be traced to William Stukeley, a pioneer of British archaeology who believed that the druids constructed and maintained many megalithic sites." **(B)** *proof* can be immediately dismissed, because the implication is that the popular images are not true. **(A)** *revelation* makes no sense for similar reasons. By process of elimination, **(C)** *misconception* works best.

In the second blank, because the implication is that he attributed the megalithic sites to the druids, **(D)** *ignored* and **(E)** *blamed* yield the sense that he was attacking the druids for their construction of megaliths. You are left, then, with **(F)** *credited*, which provides you with "the *misconception* can likely be traced to William Stukeley, a pioneer of British archaeology who *credited* the druids for many megalithic sites," which supports the initial prediction.

9.   C

The major sign you are given here is that the upcoming summer is expected to be extremely hot, so you are looking for an answer that demonstrates this. **(A)** *muggy* is a matter of humidity, not heat, **(B)** *brisk* and **(D)** *crisp* both refer to cool air (and are close synonyms, at that, so you could not choose one of the two), and while **(E)** *unusual* could refer to the exceptional aspect of the weather, it does not have any sense of temperature. **(C)** *torrid* means very hot and is the correct answer.

10.   B

From the sentence, you know that the Book of Kells is very well known and very beautiful, so you are looking for a word that means "sumptuous." **(C)** *famous* you can immediately eliminate because the word was already used in the sentence and will not be reused; be careful for traps like this, which test to make sure you've clearly read the sentence before you choose an answer. **(D)** *underappreciated* and **(E)** *quaint* both contradict the importance and impressiveness of the book, so you are left with **(A)** *mythical* and **(B)** *august*. You are told that the Book of Kells is still in existence today, so **(A)** *mythical* cannot be the correct answer. **(B)** *august* is a synonym of magnificent and is the only option that matches the expected meaning of "sumptuous."

11.   C

The important indication here is that the development of artificial intelligence is not yet complete, and is in fact "elusive," which tells us you are looking for a word that would render the final clause "and its actual capability remains unknown." **(A)** *morality*, **(B)** *popularity*, **(D)** *ethics*, and **(E)** *price* are issues not touched upon in the sentence. **(C)** *feasibility* matches the expectation of "capability" and is the correct answer.

12. A

The first sign to make note of is the detour road sign "however," so you know that the second half of the sentence will be in contrast to the first half. Given the first clause, you can expect the answer to provide us with a clause meaning "however, today I can see that they are still friends." **(B)** *estranged from*, **(C)** *distancing from*, **(D)** *acrimonious to*, and **(E)** *ambivalent to* all oppose this idea, and you can plug **(A)** *inseparable from* into the sentence, confirming it to be the right choice.

13. D

Given the comparison to modern apartments, you can infer that the *"insulae"* were places of residence belonging to someone other than the inhabitants, who rented the space from the owner. Thus, you are expecting to find an answer meaning "rented by." **(A)** *squatted by*, **(C)** *given to*, and **(E)** *inhabited by* fail to specify the financial relation of owner to inhabitant, and you can reject **(B)** *sold to* based on the note at the end of the sentence that the inhabitants did not have the money to own their residences. **(D)** *leased to* matches the sense of the prediction and fits the sentence perfectly.

14. B

The primary road sign you are given here is the word "independent," which indicates what she felt was lacking while living with her family. You are looking for an answer choice that says that her family was too involved in her life, probably a synonym of "restricted by." **(A)** *neglected* and **(D)** *overlooked* mean the opposite of the prediction, and **(C)** *chastised* and **(E)** *mollified* both imply a conflicting relationship with her family which is not even hinted at in the sentence. **(B)** *cosseted* matches the prediction "restricted by" in that she was doted upon by her family to a level that likely felt oppressive to someone who wished "to become more independent." Even if you are not familiar with the term "cosset," the other four options are common words or come from easily derivable roots (such as molli- the Latin root of mollify, meaning "soft").

15. D

From reading the sentence, you can learn that *Perceval* was the first mention of the quest for the Holy Grail, which allows you to anticipate an answer meaning "beginning." In addition, the fact that it was an immediate success suggests that the fascination was a strong one. Based on this, you are looking for a word that would render a phrase "beginning with energy." **(A)** *continuing*, **(B)** *renewing*, **(C)** *advancing*, and **(E)** *demonstrating* all imply a preexisting fascination and can be thus dismissed, leaving **(D)** *igniting*, which matches both the sense of a beginning and the intensity of the fascination.

16. C

The key to this sentence is the stipulation that she was extremely exacting in her choice of words, so you are looking for a word that means "precise" or "carefully chosen." While **(E)** *sophisticated* might seem like a good choice, some of sophisticated speech can also be very verbose or grandiose in their word choice, so you must eliminate this option.

(A) *punctual* and **(D)** *efficient* imply precision, but have little to do with choosing carefully, and **(B)** *reticent* could agree with her behavior in informal social situations but is unrelated to the meaning of the sentence. **(C)** *meticulous* is the correct answer because it means "to demonstrate exacting attention to detail."

17.   D
Based on the description of photovoltaic material, you can know that the key to answering this question is the phrase "affordable energy source"; you would expect the solution to be a synonym. **(C)** *environmental* and **(E)** *conscientious* can both accurately describe the use of photovoltaic material, but are not relevant—remember, the answer will always be specified by the sentence. **(A)** *costly* is an antonym of our anticipated answer, and **(B)** *advanced* is something also unspecified by the sentence, as there is nothing to indicate the place of photovoltaic material in technological development. **(D)** *economical* remains the only possible option and is a synonym of "affordable."

18.   A, E, G
While you expect the final clause, which is preceded by a semicolon, to be related thematically to the rest of the sentence, grammatically it stands on its own. You can therefore figure out the third blank first without needing the other two. The key here is the word "deluge"—you know this is beyond a simple light rain. Hence, for the third blank, you can reject both **(H)** *soaking* and **(I)** *spraying* because both are much weaker words than **(G)** *inundating*.

For the second blank the key clue is "sudden." If it was sudden, then you can assume people were not expecting it—you can thus predict a word synonymous with "not expecting." **(D)** *waiting* and **(F)** *fearing* would both imply they were expecting the downpour on some level; thus **(E)** *unprepared* is clearly the correct choice.

Finally, for the first blank, this word will be the reason that people were not expecting a sudden storm. **(C)** *humid* obviously doesn't work here, but between **(A)** *arid* and **(B)** *calm*, you need to pause for a moment. **(B)** *calm* might work—it certainly contrasts with the eventfulness of the weather that followed—but **(A)** *arid* is a much better answer because it implies that the weather was specifically very dry—the antithesis to the wetness of the storm. Plugging it all in, "The countless *arid* days left everyone *unprepared* for the sudden downpour; the deluge brought traffic to a halt, *inundating* the roads." You can see that everything agrees.

19.   C, D, G
The big hint for the first blank is the word "suspecting," which suggests a sense of doubt. **(A)** *decried* and **(B)** *discounted* are too strong and definitive, whereas **(C)** *challenged* simply means "questioned."

The second blank is a noun modified by "scientist's," and you can immediately predict that **(D)** *objectivity* will be the correct answer because objectivity is of key concern to a scientist. You can be sure of this answer based on the third blank—sometimes, when you cannot be sure about one blank, it is best to pass it over until you have filled in one or more of the others.

The third blank refers to what quality of the scientist is in doubt, and you are informed by the last clause of the sentence that he altered the data of the study. You are thus predicting a word that reflects some personal motivation to force the data to give the results he wanted. **(G)** *biases* is the correct answer to reflect this, and you can be further sure of this because **(H)** *guile* and **(I)** *conduct* are both not specific enough to the discussion of the scientist's personal motivations. Based on this you can return to the second blank and confirm that **(D)** *objectivity* is the correct answer—if his biases led him to alter the study's data, he can be said to be lacking objectivity; **(E)** *dedication* and **(F)** *rhetoric* are both unrelated to this issue. You can read all three choices back into the sentence to check one more time: "They *challenged* the scientist's *objectivity*, suspecting his *biases* had affected the study, and he was later found to have tampered with the data to better fit his desired results." The correct answers all fill in the sentence as desired.

20.   C, F, H
While the first blank seems to have three very similar choices, there is a subtle difference that differentiates them—*guzzling* and *quaffing* both imply drinking large quantities at great speed, which is precisely the opposite of what is discussed in this clause; you can select **(C)** *imbibing* for the first blank.

There is a contradicting sense between the first two clauses, and based on this you can predict that the second blank will reflect the fact that consuming large quantities of seawater is dangerous. You see **(D)** *harsh*, which is close but not quite appropriate to expressing a sense of danger. Likewise for **(E)** *difficult*—drinking large amounts of seawater may be difficult indeed, but this choice fails to address its effects on the human body. **(F)** *inadvisable* doesn't tell us precisely that it is dangerous, but you can infer from its being dangerous that it would also be something not to be done—hence, you can see that **(F)** is the correct answer.

Finally, you are reminded of a famous passage concerning being surrounded by seawater but unable to drink any of it. **(G)** *setting* is too neutral to be "lamented," whereas **(H)** *quandary* properly expresses the difficulty of the situation of being surrounded by non-potable water. **(I)** *tragedy* might be tempting because of "lamented," but fails to capture the proper meaning of the sentence. Finally, you need to reread the whole completed sentence to see how it fits: "Although *ingesting* small amounts of seawater is not dangerous to humans, the high salinity of the water makes it *inadvisable* to consume in large quantities; it is from this that comes the *quandary* lamented by the narrator of *The Rime of the Ancient Mariner*: 'Water, water, everywhere,/Nor any drop to drink'."

21.   E, F
From the sentence you are told that scholars are in need of a new "way to refer to the author or authors"; furthermore, judging by the tone and topic of the sentence, you can

safely assume that the answers you need will have a neutral tone. While it may seem possible for the solutions to render the phrase "the term 'Homeric Tradition' has been rejected," the straight-ahead road sign "so" renders this unlikely. You can predict that the answers will mean "the term has been proffered." The key to this question is the word "possible" at the end of the question stem. **(A)** *selected* and **(B)** *established* cannot be correct because that would mean the term has been decided upon. **(C)** *appropriated* and **(D)** *bestowed* likewise fail to match our prediction, leaving **(E)** *suggested* and **(F)** *proposed* as the choices that suggest that the term has been offered as an option, but no decision has been made. That fits nicely with "possible."

22. B, E

Looking at the sentence and the possible answers, you can see that you are looking for a conjunction. From the meaning of the sentence you can see that the conjunction will render the meaning "commercial arsenic usage has diminished, *but* its ongoing presence is a major health concern." Because the conjunction is placed at the start of the first clause, you need a sense of contradiction that gives the meaning "although." **(A)** *After,* **(C)** *Inasmuch as,* **(D)** *Subsequent,* and **(F)** *Because* are all conjunctions that lack the contradiction you need, leaving only **(B)** *Whereas* and **(E)** *While,* which are synonyms of one another and match the prediction.

23. C, E

The key to this sentence is to make note that the textile workers feared for a negative effect on demand for their skills as a result of the sewing machine. The answer, then, must be indicative of their displeasure with the technology; furthermore, words like "poorly" and "protests" suggest that they felt very strongly about their fear of a decline in their trade, so you must also find words that reflect the strength of their views. **(A)** *overwhelm* is the opposite of what you need and can be rejected easily. **(B)** *diminish,* **(D)** *mitigate,* and **(F)** *belittle* are all possible choices, but none of these words are strong enough to convey the meaning you are looking for. **(C)** *obviate* and **(E)** *eliminate* suggest an absolute removal of demand for their skills, and match both the meaning and the strength of the prediction.

24. B, F

You are told in the final clause that it would be remembered as a "tragic accident" and that no blame was assigned. You are looking for adverbs that reflect this and can expect to find synonyms of "sadly," but you must be careful not to choose answers that suggest vitriol or blame. Based on this, you can see that **(A)** *indignantly,* **(C)** *spitefully,* and **(D)** *bitterly* can all be eliminated. **(B)** *mournfully* is an excellent choice because you often hear about mourning of a tragic accident. **(E)** *soberly,* meaning in this context "clearly," does not have any synonyms among the remaining answers. **(F)** *melancholically* is a direct synonym of **(B)** and matches your predicted answer.

25. C, E

The first word, "Regardless," indicates that the completed sentence will give the meaning "he was unsuccessful but he carried on in his search"; also, based on the phrase "limited success" you can know that he had not accomplished his goal, so you can expect to find answers that give the meaning "he was unrelenting." This allows you to reject **(D)** *triumphant*, and furthermore you can see that **(A)** *content* and **(B)** *disaffected* are without synonyms and do not match the predicted answer. **(F)** *derided* might be a possible answer if you were told more about how the public viewed him, but without further detail and without synonyms, **(F)** must also be eliminated. **(C)** *dogged* and **(E)** *perseverant* both mean to persist unrelentingly and give the desired meaning.

26. C, E

You are told by the final clause that climbing Mount Everest is a challenge both mentally and physically, and you need answers that convey this sense of gargantuan or strenuous effort. **(A)** *arduous* does render the meaning "very difficult struggle," but you have other, stronger options to choose from, so you do not necessarily want to decide upon it yet. You can also see that you have three adjectives all based on names. While this might seem intimidating, it is not too difficult to puzzle out. **(E)** *Herculean* is a term in relatively common parlance, and furthermore matches the prediction of a struggle that is extremely physically demanding. **(B)** *Daedalean* and **(F)** *Gordian* refer to legends, like **(E)** *Herculean*, but they are not related to physical struggle. The story of Daedalus and his son Icarus is well-known, and in it Daedalus is a man of exceptional cleverness, which is not relevant to this sentence. The Gordian Knot is a likewise common story, and refers to a problem whose solution is not readily apparent (and usually lies outside accepted problem-solving convention). Thus, while you can accept **(E)** as a possibility, the other name-based adjectives must be rejected. You are left, then, looking for a likely synonym for **(E)** among the remaining choices: **(C)** *colossal* and **(D)** *adamant*. **(C)** is clearly the correct choice, with the proper strength you need for the adjective, and while **(D)** might imply a quality very necessary to scaling Mount Everest, it is unrelated to the sentence and without synonym.

27. A, D

You are told that the opera performances are too long for Carl, which means you are looking for a word that would describe his attention span as having some limit. The final clause includes the qualifier "slightly" so you must be careful in not choosing a word that is too strong. This allows you to remove **(C)** *picayune*, **(E)** *paltry*, and **(F)** *infinitesimal* because they all suggest he has a minute attention span, which is more than the sentence suggests. **(B)** *interminable* would mean his attention span is very long and can likewise be rejected. **(A)** *limited* and **(D)** *finite* both specify that there is some end to his attention span but do not overly criticize it (as **(C)**, **(E)**, and **(F)** do) or imply too strong a meaning.

28. B, D

The key here is the final clause, which indicates that she could not write anything at all. You are, then, looking for adjectives to describe her writer's block as absolute. **(A)** *middling* is too weak for this sentence, but **(B)** *thorough* fits the meaning perfectly. **(C)** *consummate* does have a strong meaning, but its positive connotations (a consummate writer is a highly accomplished one) do not fit the sentence. **(D)** *unmitigated* is a synonym of **(B)** and it would seem that these two are the answers, but it is always important to read through and consider all the options. **(E)** *customary*, while it could make sense as a tongue-in-cheek commentary on deadlines, is not appropriate to the sentence and is without synonym, and **(F)** *egregious* would imply a strongly negative connotation that would not fit the sentence— the writer's block is an extreme hindrance to her, but it has no particular moral value.

29. C, E

The final words of the sentence give you your biggest clue here—"allowing" and "show through," which suggests that the presence of chlorophyll restricts the visibility of the carotenoids. You can, then, predict that the answers will render the meaning "the reduced presence of green chlorophyll in leaves allows the carotenoids to be visible." **(A)** *expulsion* is very unlikely because you are given nothing to suggest an active removal of the chlorophyll. **(B)** *consumption* might be possible, but since there is nothing in the sentence to suggest that the chlorophyll is consumed, you can safely pass it by. **(C)** *abatement* would render the meaning of "the lessening or reduction of chlorophyll" which is what you're looking for, so now you need to check to see if there are any answer choices that create a sentence similar to the one created by **(C)** in the remaining options. **(D)** *irradiation* refers to an exposure to radiation, so you can assume that isn't what you're looking for. **(E)** *ebbing* is a synonym to **(C)** and the other correct answer choice; both suggest a reduction of chlorophyll. **(F)** *nourishment* makes no sense in the sentence; the chlorophyll is not likely to disappear by being nourished, and the term could only be applied in a poetic or metaphorical sense which is not appropriate here.

30. A, B

The sentence gives you two contrasting pairs of words: "years" and "moments," and whatever fills the blank and "broken." Furthermore, from the first clause you can see that you are looking for a word that explains the building of trust in a friendship, and from "years" you can know that it is a slow process. However, by reading the sentence you can see that the blank only refers to the action of building trust. **(A)** *accomplished* might be a good answer—to achieve a status of trust in friendship—so look through the other options to see if there are possible synonyms. **(B)** *edified* is a very promising option—both **(A)** and **(B)** mean to establish or achieve a goal. **(C)** *fostered* and **(F)** *undertaken* both suggest an ongoing effort, which would not agree with the contrast in the final clause of trust being broken. **(D)** *acquiesced* and **(E)** *capitulated* both imply surrender, and while surrendering to trust might be an arguable notion, the sentence offers nothing to promote such loaded terms. **(A)** and **(B)** are clearly the best options.

31. C, F

All of the options tell you that James asked his boss for a long vacation, but they are all of varying strength in their demand. You are told at the end of the sentence that he quietly returns to work without a fight, so you can predict that you are looking for answers that tell us he asked politely but did not insist or press the issue. Based on this, you can rule out **(A)** *demanded*, **(B)** *contended*, **(D)** *insisted*, and **(E)** *averred* all at once as being too strong. **(C)** *ventured* and **(F)** *opined* both suggest that he offered the idea but was not adamant in his defense of it.

32. B, D

From the word "entirely" you can predict an answer that goes beyond meaning that his handwriting is difficult to read, but is outright illegible. **(A)** *rudimentary* and **(F)** *rustic* both would suggest a crude form of writing—and, given the nature of the doctor's profession, it is unlikely that the sentence is suggesting the doctor is uneducated. **(B)** *indecipherable* is an excellent choice, giving both the correct meaning and strength of the word, and you can see that you have a synonym in **(D)** *hieroglyphic*. Checking the other options, you see that **(C)** *lucid* is an antonym of the prediction, and **(E)** *unprofessional* is a personal accusation that is not relevant to the meaning of the sentence.

33. B, E

The story you are told here is that once the group's efforts had failed, the blame was laid on him (you know this by the term "scapegoat"). Furthermore, you can see that, as the scapegoat, he was driven out of the company. You are looking, then, for an answer that is synonymous with "cast out" or "driven out." **(A)** *blamed* might reflect what happened to him, but it does nothing to indicate his departure from the company. **(B)** *ostracized* is a perfect match to our prediction, and looking down the list you can see a synonym in **(E)** *excommunicated*—while frequently used in a religious sense, "excommunicate" simply means to be removed from the community. **(C)** *voted*, **(D)** *allotted*, and **(F)** *chosen* make no sense because of the mention of the chaos.

34. A, E

The key word here is the word "both"—given the background of the sentence, you know that rhubarb has both positive uses and negative effects, and you are looking for an answer that completes this contrast—you are predicting a noun meaning "good things" to contrast the "dangers." **(A)** *benefits* is clearly a good option, and while **(B)** *treatments* and **(C)** *purposes* might be possible fits, they are not the contrasts of "dangers" for which you are looking. **(E)** *utilities*, however, is a synonym of **(A)** and provides the predicted meaning in the sentence. **(D)** *contingencies* is a throw-away, only tempting because of the similarity to option **(F)** *exigencies*; however, both are unrelated to each other and to the sentence, as they mean "possibilities" and "needs or requirements," respectively.

35. C, D

The key indicators to the solutions here are the fact that there is "bitterness" among the family members and, based on reading the sentence, you can predict the answer will indicate some kind of doubt or question concerning the heirlooms. **(A)** *conflagration* sounds like a good answer, but it actually means "fire." It can also mean "war," but that meaning is too strongly charged to work with "bitterness." **(B)** *repudiation* has a strong, negative meaning, but does not fit the predicted meaning ("repudiate" is "to deny" or "to reject"). **(C)** *dissension*, however, does provide both the predicted meaning of question or doubt, but also conveys a strong feeling (dissent often leads to an argument or fight). Furthermore, you see a synonym in **(D)** *contention* that also agrees with the prediction. **(E)** *Rubicon* can be dismissed because there is no other answer choice that will produce a sentence with similar meaning, and **(F)** *squall* cannot possibly be correct, meaning a storm or tempest (it might be used metaphorically to describe relations between the children, but it is without synonym here).

36. B, E
You can immediately see that the student's work was insufficient and, furthermore, the first clause suggests that the work was noticeably rushed. You can therefore predict an answer that means "shoddy" or is otherwise indicative of work not carefully done. **(A)** *jaunty* and **(F)** *blithe* might be seen as synonyms—especially in reference to speech or writing, however the meanings are closer to "joyous" or "lighthearted," which are not appropriate to the meaning of the sentence. **(B)** *sloppy* is an excellent option, and you can see a synonym in **(E)** *slipshod*, both of which suggest the work was hurried and improperly completed. While **(C)** *pithy* might suggest a brief paper, it does nothing to indicate inadequate work, and **(D)** *burnished* means quite the opposite—that the student had dedicated time to polishing and refining his work.

37. B, D
There's a nasty trap here. You can tell by reading the sentence that you are looking for answers that mean "unusual," but **(C)** *acquired* is not among the correct answers. The sentence's scope is clearly on just that the taste is different, not that it is good, bad, or requires any sort of culinary sophistication to be appreciated. Furthermore, the phrase "acquired taste" is without synonym among the other options, and you must reject **(C)** as a possible choice. As already mentioned, there is no specification as to how good or bad the taste is, so you can reject **(F)** *mediocre*. Nor does the sentence concern sophistication, so you can reject **(A)** *refined* and **(E)** *endowed* as well. This leaves **(B)** *idiosyncratic* and **(D)** *novel*, which both describe a taste that is unique but give no indication of personal opinion about it.

38. A, D
This sentence is pretty straightforward—because he does not want to donate to the charity, his image is reinforced. His image, then, is one of unwillingness to share or contribute; you can predict the answer will be a synonym of "stingy." **(A)** *Parsimonious* is a very promising choice, because it specifically means an unwillingness to part with one's goods. **(B)** *avaricious*, **(C)** *covetous*, and **(F)** *rapacious* all imply that he is not only careful to hold onto his own property but is also greedy for more. **(E)** *selfish* might be tempting because of

the possible meaning that it was selfish of him not to donate to the charity, but it lacks a synonym here. **(D)** *penurious* is a synonym of **(A)**, and both answers are further confirmed by the mention of his behavior being "penny-pinching."

39. B, D

This sentence describes a contrast created between the stories of abuse and the stories of the good Samaritans. You are told that the stories coming from areas hit by catastrophes are negative ones, but that it is important to *remember* the good stories as well—you can predict our answer thus. **(B)** *recall* and **(D)** *remember* are the obvious choices here, and you can discount all of the other options because they require more information than you are given. **(A)** *commend* is tempting, but there is not another answer choice that would give the completed sentence a similar meaning. **(C)** *expound* and **(E)** *pronounce* also imply further action—to speak of the good Samaritans—but the sentence does not contain enough information to infer a desired course of action. **(F)** *proscribe* might seem to be a similar concept (seeing the writing root "scribe" in the word), but the "pro-" prefix means to write against or condemn, which is definitely not what you are looking for.

40. D

The first thing you must always do is ask yourself what the topic and scope of the passage are. In this case, the topic is the development of the English language, and the scope is the effect of various ethnic groups on the development. You can see that the first highlighted phrase explicitly states the scope of the passage, which allows us to rapidly narrow down our answers, eliminating **(A)** as there are no defined arguments and counterarguments in this passage, **(B)** as it is not an example of the scope but the scope itself, and **(C)** and **(E)** as the first highlighted phrase is the scope not the topic. Now all that is left for us to do is determine whether the second half of **(D)** is correct. Considering the place of the second highlighted phrase, you can see that its relation to the scope of the passage (and hence the first highlighted section) is that it is an example of one of the effects that different ethnic groups had on the development of English. **(D)** is the correct answer.

41. A

Answering this question requires two steps: first, you must determine what part of speech the word "they" is—it is a pronoun. And secondly, you must read through the passage looking for clues as to from where pronouns are likely to be derived. In the final sentence you see that it explicitly states that English pronouns are of Germanic origin, so you can safely select **(A)** as your answer. Although Old English and Norse are related, choice **(C)** is meant as a distracter.

42. B

To answer this question, you are required to make a small inference from the text. The third sentence begins with a concession, "Although," which indicates that the immediately following clause is a fact—in this case that English is a part of the Germanic language family and that the rules governing its structure reflect this. From this you can infer that the structural rules of a language are significant in its classification, which tells us that answer **(B)** is correct. **(A)** is factually correct, but there is no indication that this is related to its current classification, so you cannot accept that as an explanation based on the passage. **(C)** concerns the balance of vocabulary origins between Germanic and Romance, but while the passage does speak of this at length, no mention of number of words as related to the classification of the language is made. **(D)** is not an option, as the Normans regarded English as lower class. **(E)** is incorrect, as the core of the language is noted to be Germanic. **(B)** is the correct choice.

43. A

As always, you must be careful with what you infer from a passage. Looking at answer A, you would need to find something in the text which would suggest that the shorter the word, the less likely it may be derived from Latin—which you can find in the final two sentences. There is no mention of the indigenous language before the arrival of the Germanic peoples, so you can dismiss **(B)**. **(C)** might seem tempting because the author notes that the words used for complex ideas today are primarily those used by the ruling class. However, while it might seem more likely to be the habit of those with leisure time and education, the passage does not specify anything that would allow us to draw this conclusion, and **(C)** must be rejected.

44. C

The difference between teleology and Teleology is mentioned in the first paragraph. To paraphrase, Teleology is idea that nature is progressing *towards* something, and teleology is the idea that nature progresses *by means of* something. From here you can begin to look at the options for answers. **(A)** *quality and quantity* do not make sense based on your predicted answer—there is no sense of amount in either concept. **(B)** *example and concept* and **(E)** *part and whole* are both inadequate—it may be tempting based on the phrase "teleology so conceived, though, mustn't be confused with," however this does not suggest that teleology is a type of Teleology. **(C)** *property and object* is a good choice—teleology is something possessed within nature and Teleology is its goal. **(D)** *cause and effect* also fails to properly describe the relation between the two, suggesting that teleology is a part of a larger Teleology. The passage describes the two as separate ideas, not one as a type of the other.

45. C

As always, you should begin our understanding of the passage through examining its topic and scope, the latter of which is the subject of this question. The passage discusses how evolutionary theory rejects the notion of Teleology, instead demonstrating the development of species through the process of natural selection. **(A)** and **(B)** both are part of the description of how evolutionary theory describes the biological history of the world, but are not the overall scope of the passage. **(C)** states that natural selection, a key part of evolutionary theory, obviates the need for Teleology—which is the focus, that is, the scope, of the passage. **(D)** is an end result, but not the overall main argument and thus is incorrect. **(E)** suggests that teleology and Teleology are nearly equivalent which, according to the passage, is incorrect.

46. A, B, C

With this sort of question, you must consider each of the listed statements. You can know that statement **(A)** is true because the passage describes the variety of species and fossils as a result of teleology and natural selection. Statements **(B)** and **(C)** are the focus of the third paragraph—how evolutionary theory can support the existence of increasingly complex and, finally, sentient beings. Thus, **(A)**, **(B)**, and **(C)** are all correct responses.

47. C

To answer this question, you must infer what the "mind-first" hypothesis is, even though it is not explicitly described in the passage. Based on the subject of the passage and its title, you can predict that the "mind-first" hypothesis will refer to the concept that mental existence preceded physical existence. Looking through the answers, you find our prediction in answer **(C)**. Answers **(A)** and **(B)** both would place mental existence after physical existence and can thus be rejected. **(D)** is unrelated to the question of the mind and sentience, and **(E)** is precisely what the passage repudiates—experiments, the author states, have proven the opposite of intelligent design.

48. B

This question is a simple test of our ability to paraphrase teleology and Teleology. As you have learned from the passage, teleology is a means *by which*, whereas Teleology is the reason *for which*. Even without prior knowledge of the term "Intelligent Design," by its components you can infer that it refers to "design with intent"—it is a matter of Teleology, answer **(B)**.

49. D

Remember, even in weighty passages like these, all the information that you need is apparent in the text. **(A)** *a physical object* cannot possibly be the right answer because the passage is talking about natural law and human behavior. You can also eliminate **(B)** *morally correct action as determined by God* because the passage specifies that "Finnis' theory does not require the presence of God." **(C)** *action which help us achieve a desireable, material end* can be rejected for the same reason as **(A)**. Furthermore, you are given an example of one basic human good, according to Finnis: curiosity about the nature of the universe. **(D)** *something self-evident which we ought to strive to embrace* is supported by the text both in the phrase "each good is self-evident" and his example of how something is made good by human participation. **(E)** *what is naturally occurring* could only be a reasonable possibility based on the repeated usage of the term "natural"; however, "natural law" is a metaphysical concept, and **(E)** is also incorrect.

50. B

The key to answering this question is to bear in mind Finnis' definition of "goods" that you concluded in the previous question. You can learn from the passage that they are self-evident and all equal, which immediately points us towards **(B)** *goods that demand opposing actions*—if they are all equally important, then how can you choose between actions that would allow us to pursue one good while distancing ourselves from the other? **(A)** *the study of the existence of God* is a poor choice, because while his argument does not rely on the existence of God as Aquinas' did, nowhere does the author imply that Finnis' theory hinged on the non-existence of God. **(C)** *the embracing of our natural desires* is likewise incorrect because of the emphasis on human volition and the notion that some actions are inherently "good" and others are not—to simply do as you will would not undermine his definition, but simply fail to follow his admonition. Finally, **(D)** *defining additional goods* would not necessarily weaken his definition so long as the new goods were not in opposition to his already established goods.

51. C

This is a fairly straightforward reading comprehension question. It does not require us to make any inferences from the text, just a careful reading to determine where each answer is referred to in the texts (and they all are). **(A)** and **(B)** are both listed explicitly under the adaptations he made to strengthen Aquinas' argument, so you can dismiss them. **(C)** is our only remaining option, and is correct, as its opposite is one of the adaptations.

52. E

To answer this question, you need to consider to which weakness in Finnis's argument the author is referring. His concern is about how natural law and our nature interact (or, according to Finnis, fail to). **(A)** you know to be incorrect, because the passage explicitly states that Finnis's argument does not rely on the existence of God, and that goods are determined by "human participation." You can eliminate **(D)** because the concept of "goods" is not the concern of the underlined passage. **(B)** might seem as if it is referring to the concern in how to evaluate goods and which are more important than others, but, again, that is clearly not the concern in the underlined passage. **(C)** suggests that our nature controls our behavior (such as participation in the goods), but earlier in the passage you are told that Finnis did allow for human volition, and so you cannot accept **(C)**, either. Thus, **(E)** is our answer.

53. C

This question asks you to examine the passage for the reasons it gives as to why it is difficult to determine the connection between the two poetic works and choose the answer that is *not*. Since you have no "none of the above" option, you know one must be missing from the passage, so it is a matter of closely reading the passage to find the missing option. The summary in the second paragraph mentions literary techniques and the placement in the poem, so you can dismiss **(A)** and **(D)**. Furthermore, you can see that **(B)** and **(D)** are both incorrect from the discussion in the first paragraph about the location of the poem and its related issues. Looking for mention of **(C)**, you find in the first sentence that Llywarch Hen *is* the narrator of the Llywarch Hen cycle, so you can know **(C)** to be the correct choice.

54. D

This question requires you to be a little careful in the wording; you have shades of meaning between a few of our choices. Based on the passage, the author seems to be saying that it is impossible to be certain of an original connection, but by the time the versions you have today were written the connection was intended to be made. Reading through our choices, you see that **(D)** matches our prediction. **(A)** *the connection is clear* is certainly untrue based on the passage, **(B)** *more likely than not* and **(E)** *possible but unlikely* possess the sense of uncertainty you are looking for but fail to properly match the author's meaning, and **(C)** *that it is fruitless* has too much personal opinion to be a good response for something written in an academic tone.

55. A

By the time you have gotten to the third question about the passage, you should have already figured out what the primary purpose of the passage is. In this case, you can see that the purpose of the passage is to describe the poem *Claf Abercuawg*. Be careful not to be tripped up by **(B)** *the origins of the poem* or **(D)** *the connection between* the works, which would be closer to the scope of the passage. Finally, **(C)** *Middle Welsh poetry* and **(E)** *all the Llywarch Hen poetry* are too broad even for the topic—the entirety of the passage is still limited by *Claf Abercuawg* as a piece.

56. C

The underlined passage uses the term "appellation" meaning that by which something is called—a name or title. With this in mind, you are looking for an answer that tells us that the title *Claf Abercuawg* was given to the poem only in modern times. **(A)** *the poem was recently rewritten* is clearly wrong, as is **(B)** *the poem originally had a different title* because the passage specifies it is without a title in the manuscript. **(D)** *the poem should not be called Claf Abercuawg* is too critical to make sense based on the phrase, but **(C)** *the poem was only given the title recently* matches our prediction and is the correct answer. Choice **(E)** *the poem has been heavily redacted* is too ambitious an assertion that goes beyond the scope of the argument and the date you are given.

57. B

The difference between the two kinds of societies, according to the author, is a matter of internal (guilt) and external (shame) motivators. What you must consider, then, is where a moral code might be placed. You are given one particularly useful clue in the phrase "internal guidelines," which even if it lacks the strength of a sense of moral right and wrong, still allows us to classify the society in the question as guilt-based. And furthermore, in the example at the end of the passage, it is suggested that "moral standards" are an example of a trait of a guilt-based society. The answer is **(B)**. Choice **(C)** is wrong; don't be distracted by the description at the end of the passage that describes how medieval Europe, a shame-based society, dealt with adultery. Choices **(D)** and **(E)** both go beyond the scope of the passage.

58. "IT WOULD SEEM THAT EARLY MEDIEVAL EUROPE WAS PRIMARILY A SHAME-BASED SOCIETY. . . ."

This sentence provides us with the particular focus of the passage, narrowed down from the scope of shame- and guilt-based societies.

59. A, B, C

You are looking for statements that go beyond what can reasonably be inferred from the passage. **(A)** is clearly a good choice, because while the passage mentions that it was "primarily a shame-based society," there is no mention of a lack of concern with moral codes; furthermore, the passage notes that neither classification of societies is without some influence of the other. **(B)** you can also see cannot be inferred from the sentence—in fact, it is clearly contradicted in the fourth sentence. While the passage mentions the complexity of the social guidelines of shame-based societies, and it might be inferred that there are many laws in such societies, there is no way you can infer from this that **(C)** guilt-based societies have few laws. All three of the answers are correct.

60. A

For this question you must consider the description of the society in the question compared to what you are given in the passage. Early in the passage, you see mention of dishonoring one's family as an example of a damaging effect on the social group. This is a clear enough indication that the society in the question would be a shame-based society as in the example in the passage, and the correct answer is thus **(A)**. This eliminates choice **(B)**. Choice **(C)** is wrong because there are certainly rules in a shame-based society. Similarly you can reject **(E)**. It goes beyond the scope of the passage, which does not offer evidence to suggest that individuals within a society that emphasizes social cohesion do not have an internally regulated morality. **(D)** is wrong because there is insufficient data to support such an assertion.

PART THREE

Quantitative Reasoning

CHAPTER 9

Introduction to Quantitative Reasoning

OVERVIEW

The Quantitative Reasoning section of the GRE is designed to place most of its emphasis on your ability to reason quantitatively—to read a math problem, understand what it's asking, and solve it. The mathematical concepts tested on the GRE are similar to those tested on the SAT. You will see questions related to arithmetic, algebra, geometry, and data interpretation. There is no trigonometry or calculus on the GRE. The emphasis in the Quantitative Reasoning section is on your ability to reason, using your knowledge of the various topics. The goal is to make the test an accurate indicator of your ability to apply given information, think logically, and draw conclusions. These are skills you will need at the graduate level of study.

In this section of the book, we'll take you through all the types of Quantitative Reasoning questions you'll see on the GRE and give you the strategies you need to answer them quickly and correctly. Also, all of the mathematical concepts you'll encounter on the test are included in the "Math Reference" Appendix at the back of this book. Think of the examples there as building blocks for the questions you will see on the test.

QUANTITATIVE REASONING QUESTION TYPES

The GRE contains two Quantitative Reasoning sections with approximately 20 questions each. Each section will last 35 minutes, and be composed of a selection of the following question types:

- Quantitative Comparison
- Problem Solving
- Data Interpretation

The Quantitative Reasoning portion of the GRE draws heavily upon your ability to combine your knowledge of mathematical concepts with your reasoning powers. Specifically, it evaluates your ability to:

- compare quantities using reasoning.
- solve word problems.
- interpret data presented in charts and graphs.

Within each section of Quantitative Reasoning questions on the GRE, you will see an assortment of question types.

PACING STRATEGY

As a multi-stage test, the GRE allows you to move freely within each section, which can be a big advantage on test day. If you get stuck on a particular question, you can tag it and come back to it later when you have time. You only score points for correct answers, so you don't want to get bogged down on one problem and lose time you could have used to answer several other questions correctly.

You will have 35 minutes to work on each Quantitative Reasoning section. The 20 questions in each section will be an assortment of Quantitative Comparison, Problem Solving, and Data Interpretation items. However, these types are not distributed equally. The chart below shows how many questions you can expect of each question type, as well as the average amount of time you should spend per question type.

	Quantitative Comparison	Problem Solving	Data Interpretation
Number of Questions	approx. 10	approx. 7	approx. 3
Time per Question	1.5 minutes	2 minutes	2 minutes

Try to keep these time estimates in mind as you prepare for the test. If you use them as you work the practice items, you will be comfortable keeping to the same amounts of time on test day. Additionally, you will be prepared to use the Mark and Review buttons to your advantage while taking the actual test.

TO CALCULATE OR NOT

An on-screen calculator will be available during the GRE, but there are several points to consider about its use. A calculator can be a time saver, and time is immensely important on a standardized test. But while calculators can speed up computations, they can also foster dependence, making it hard for you to spot the shortcuts in GRE questions. Using the calculator for a long, involved computation to answer a question will gobble up your allotted time for that question—and perhaps for several more. You may even make a mistake in your computation, leading to an incorrect answer. Remember, this is a reasoning test. The quantitative questions on the GRE are not designed to require lengthy computations.

If that is the case, why is a calculator provided? A calculator can be an asset for the occasional computation that a few questions require. It may prevent an error caused by a freehand calculation. The on-screen calculator provided is a simple, four-function calculator. An image of the calculator is provided below, showing the function keys, including the square root key and change of sign key.

By not relying on the calculator, you will be free to focus on interpreting numbers and data and using your critical thinking skills. This is the intention of the writers of the test. For example, Problem Solving questions will likely involve more algebra, and Quantitative Comparison questions will require more reasoning than calculating.

NAVIGATING THE QUANTITATIVE FOUNDATIONS AND CONTENT REVIEW SECTION

The chapter immediately following this one concerns Quantitative Foundations and Content Review and will review the classic math concepts and topics that you may encounter on the GRE. This section of the book also includes individual chapters on Quantitative Comparison, Problem Solving, and Data Interpretation questions. Each chapter includes an introduction and definition of the relevant question types, and a review and examples of the strategies to follow to answer those questions quickly and correctly. In addition, you'll find a practice set of questions with answers and explanations for each of the question types you'll encounter on the GRE.

Finally, at the end of this section, you'll find the Quantitative Reasoning Practice Sets, two sets of 60 Quantitative Reasoning questions along with answers and explanations. Use the Quantitative Practice Sets to test your skills and pinpoint areas for more focused study. When you are finished with this section of the book, you should be thoroughly prepared for any question you might encounter on the Quantitative Reasoning section of the GRE.

CHAPTER 10

Quantitative Foundations and Content Review

INTRODUCTION TO QUANTITATIVE FOUNDATIONS AND CONTENT REVIEW

The GRE tests a variety of math concepts that fall outside the range of straightforward algebra and arithmetic questions. These classic concepts are the foundation on which many other types of GRE questions are built. They include:

- Percentages
- Simultaneous Equations
- Symbolism
- Special Triangles
- Multiple and Oddball Figures
- Mean, Median, Mode, and Range
- Probability

This chapter will cover all these concepts, including specific strategies to conquer questions pertaining to each one.

THE KAPLAN APPROACH TO PERCENTAGES

A percent is really a comparison of a number to 100; 17% means 17 per 100, for example. Since a percent is a comparison, it can also be expressed as a fraction: $17\% = \frac{17}{100}$. And since the comparison is to 100, a percent can also be expressed as a decimal: $17\% = 0.17$. This ease of conversion between fractions, decimals, and percents leads to many uses for percents and many opportunities for problems involving them.

Most percent problems involve three quantities—whole, part, and percent. You are usually given two of the quantities and asked to find the third. First, recall the basic nature of a percent (a comparison of one number to another) and how to convert that ratio to a decimal and a percent.

To find a percent, find the ratio of the part to the whole, and then write that ratio in percent form.

Example: What percent of 60 is 45?

$$\text{Percent} = \frac{\text{Part}}{\text{Whole}}$$

$$\text{Percent} = \frac{45}{60} = \frac{3}{4} = \frac{75}{100} = 75\%$$

To find a part when you know the percent and the whole, multiply the whole by the decimal or fraction equivalent of the percent.

Example: What is 20% of $80?

$$\text{Part} = \text{Percent} \times \text{Whole}$$
$$\text{Part} = 20\% \times \$80 = 0.20 \times \$80 = \$16$$

The question below shows how percentages are applied to real situations.

Last year, Julie's startup company showed a profit of $20,000. This year, the same company showed a profit of $25,000. If her company shows the same percent increase in profit in the coming year, what will that profit be?

- Ⓐ $27,500
- Ⓑ $30,000
- Ⓒ $31,250
- Ⓓ $32,500
- Ⓔ $35,000

The problem about Julie's company asks us to calculate her profit next year—that is, her current profit plus an anticipated increase. Her previous increase was $25,000 − $20,000 = $5,000.

To express that increase as a percent, compare the amount, \$5,000, to the previous year's profit, \$20,000. That is, find what percent \$5,000 is of \$20,000.

$$\text{Percent} = \frac{\text{Part}}{\text{Whole}} = \frac{\$5,000}{\$20,000} = \frac{1}{4} = 25\%$$

Now you need to find the amount of the anticipated increase in profit for next year—so find 25% of \$25,000.

$$\text{Part} = \text{Percent} \times \text{Whole} = 25\% \times \$25,000 = \frac{1}{4} \times \$25,000 = \$6,250$$

Finally, add the amount of the anticipated increase to the current profit to find her next year's profit: \$25,000 + \$6,250 = \$31,250.

Choice **(C)** is correct.

A useful trick that sometimes saves a step is to add or subtract a given percent from 100%. For example, suppose an \$80 item is marked down 40%.

To find the new price, you can find 40% of \$80 and then subtract:

40% $\times$ \$80 = 0.40 $\times$ \$80 = \$32 and \$80 − \$32 = \$48

Or you can recognize that 100% − 40% = 60% and find 60% of \$80:

60% $\times$ \$80 = 0.60 $\times$ \$80 = \$48

As another example, suppose an \$80 item is marked up 20%. To find the new price, you can find 20% of \$80 and then add:

20% $\times$ \$80 = 0.20 $\times$ \$80 = \$16 and \$80 + \$16 = \$96

Or you can recognize that 100% + 20% = 120% and find 120% of \$80:

120% $\times$ \$80 = 1.20 $\times$ \$80 = \$96

KAPLAN STRATEGY

You can save a lot of time on test day by knowing the percent and decimal equivalents of the following commonly tested fractions.

$\frac{1}{8} = 12.5\% = 0.125$	$\frac{3}{8} = 37.5\% = 0.375$	$\frac{2}{3} = 66.\overline{6}\% = 0.\overline{6}$
$\frac{1}{6} = 16.\overline{6}\% = 0.1\overline{6}$	$\frac{2}{5} = 40\% = 0.4$	$\frac{3}{4} = 75\% = 0.75$
$\frac{1}{5} = 20\% = 0.2$	$\frac{1}{2} = 50\% = 0.5$	$\frac{4}{5} = 80\% = 0.8$
$\frac{1}{4} = 25\% = 0.25$	$\frac{3}{5} = 60\% = 0.6$	$\frac{5}{6} = 83.\overline{3}\% = 0.8\overline{3}$
$\frac{1}{3} = 33.\overline{3}\% = 0.\overline{3}$	$\frac{5}{8} = 62.5\% = 0.625$	$\frac{7}{8} = 87.5\% = 0.875$

PERCENTAGES PRACTICE SET

1. If a sweater sells for $48 after a 25% markdown, what was its original price?

   Ⓐ $56

   Ⓑ $60

   Ⓒ $64

   Ⓓ $68

   Ⓔ $72

2. A hardware store is selling a lawnmower for $300. If the store makes a 25% profit on the sale, what is the store's cost for the lawnmower?

   Ⓐ $210

   Ⓑ $225

   Ⓒ $240

   Ⓓ $250

   Ⓔ $275

3. A retailer marked up the cost of a coat by 20% when she first displayed it in her store. After several weeks, she reduced the selling price of the coat by 25%. If the retailer originally paid $50 for the coat, what will be her loss on the coat at the final price?

   Ⓐ $0

   Ⓑ $5

   Ⓒ $10

   Ⓓ $15

   Ⓔ $20

Percentages Practice Set Answers and Explanations follow on the next page.

PERCENTAGES PRACTICE SET ANSWERS AND EXPLANATIONS

1. C

The price after a 25% markdown is $48, so $48 is 75% of the original price.

$$\text{Percent} \times \text{Whole} = \text{Part}$$
$$75\% \times \text{Original Price} = \$48$$
$$0.75 \times \text{Original Price} = \$48$$
$$\text{Original Price} = \frac{\$48}{0.75}$$
$$\text{Original Price} = \$64$$

The original price was $64, which is choice **(C).**

2. C

The selling price of $300 represents 100% of the store's cost plus 25% of the store's cost. Use $0.25 \times \text{Cost}$ to represent the profit in an equation; solve for the cost.

$$\text{Selling price} = \text{Cost} + \text{Profit}$$
$$\text{Selling price} = 1 \times \text{Cost} + 0.25 \times \text{Cost}$$
$$\$300 = 1 \times \text{Cost} + 0.25 \times \text{Cost}$$
$$\$300 = 1.25 \times \text{Cost}$$
$$\frac{\$300}{1.25} = \text{Cost}$$
$$\$240 = \text{Cost}$$

The store's cost for the lawnmower was $240, choice **(C).**

3. B

The retailer first set the selling price of the coat at 120% of cost: $1.20 \times \$50 = \$60$. Later, she reduced the selling price 25%: $0.75 \times \$60 = \$45$. She will lose $5 selling the coat at that price. Choice **(B)** is correct.

THE KAPLAN APPROACH TO SIMULTANEOUS EQUATIONS

Solving a one-variable equation means finding the value of the variable that makes the equation true. But what about problems in which there are two equations with the same two variables in each equation? When there are two equations with two variables to be solved so that both equations are true simultaneously (at the same time), then those equations are sometimes called a system of simultaneous equations. Take a look at the simultaneous equations below.

If $p + 2q = 14$ and $3p + q = 12$, then $p =$

(A) -2

(B) -1

(C) 1

(D) 2

(E) 3

You could solve this problem with a method called *substitution*. Using that method, you solve one of the equations for one variable in terms of the other, and then substitute the resulting expression for the variable into the other equation. Then you have an equation with just one variable instead of two, and you solve for it.

But simultaneous equations on the GRE are often more easily solved by a method called *combination*, in which you add or subtract equations to eliminate one of the variables. The combination method is shown below.

For the simultaneous equations $p + 2q = 14$ and $3p + q = 12$, you cannot eliminate a variable by adding or subtracting the equations in their given form. The coefficients of the respective variables are not opposites of each other. But if you multiply both sides of an equation by a number that makes one set of coefficients opposites, then you have a way to solve the system. Here's how it works for this system of equations.

1. Write one equation under the other.

$p + 2q = 14$
$3p + q = 12$

2. Multiply the second equation by −2.

$p + 2q = 14$
$-2(3p + q) = -2(12)$

3. The sum of +2q and −2q is 0, so q will be eliminated when the equations are added.

$$p + 2q = 14$$
$$-6p - 2q = -24$$

4. Solve for p.

$$\begin{array}{r} p + 2q = 14 \\ + \quad -6p - 2q = -24 \\ \hline -5p = -10 \\ p = 2 \end{array}$$

Choice **(D)** is correct.

Now, if you also need to know the value of q, substitute 2 for p into either original equation.

Use the first equation:

$$p + 2q = 14 \rightarrow 2 + 2q = 14$$
$$2q = 12$$
$$q = 6$$

Or use the second equation:

$$3p + q = 12 \rightarrow 3(2) + q = 12$$
$$6 + q = 12$$
$$q = 6$$

In some cases there is no single value for each variable in a system of simultaneous equations. For example, consider this system.

$$4a + 2b = 10$$
$$12a + 6b = 30$$

When you try to solve this system, you find out that the equations are equivalent. If you try to eliminate one variable, you end up eliminating both variables.

1. Write one equation under the other.

$$4a + 2b = 10$$
$$12a + 6b = 30$$

2. Multiply the first equation by 3.

$$3(4a + 2b) = 3(10)$$
$$12a + 6b = 30$$

3. Notice that the equations are equivalent.

$$12a + 6b = 30$$
$$12a + 6b = 30$$

4. When the one equation is subtracted from the other, both variables are eliminated and a true statement remains.

$$\begin{array}{r} 12a + 6b = 30 \\ - \quad 12a + 6b = 30 \\ \hline 0 = 0 \end{array}$$

This means that there is no single value for each variable; there are an infinite number of possible sets of values for a and b.

SIMULTANEOUS EQUATIONS PRACTICE SET

1. If $x + y = 8$ and $y - x = -2$, then $y =$

   (A) -2

   (B) 3

   (C) 5

   (D) 8

   (E) 10

2. If $m - n = 5$ and $2m + 3n = 15$, then $m + n =$

   (A) 1

   (B) 6

   (C) 7

   (D) 10

   (E) 15

3. Which of the ordered pairs of numbers (c, d) satisfies the simultaneous equations shown?

   $$c + 2d = 6$$
   $$-3c - 6d = -18$$

   (A) $(-2, 4)$

   (B) $(-1, -3)$

   (C) $(0, 2)$

   (D) $(2, 1)$

   (E) $(3, -9)$

SIMULTANEOUS EQUATIONS PRACTICE SET ANSWERS AND EXPLANATIONS

1. B

When you add the two equations, the x's cancel out and you find that $2y = 6$, so $y = 3$, choice **(B)**.

2. C

Multiply the first equation by 2, and then subtract the first equation from the second to eliminate the m's and find that $5n = 5$, or $n = 1$.

Plugging this value for n into the first equation shows that $m = 6$, so $m + n = 7$. The correct answer is **(C)**.

3. A

If you multiply the first equation by -3, the result is $-3c - 6d = -18$. So the two equations are equivalent. To find a pair of numbers that satisfies the equations, solve one equation for d.

$$c + 2d = 6$$
$$2d = -c + 6$$
$$d = -\frac{1}{2}c + 3$$

The ordered pair (c, d) that satisfies the relationship is $(-2, 4)$. Choice **(A)** is correct.

THE KAPLAN APPROACH TO SYMBOLISM

You expect to see arithmetic symbols such as $+$, $-$, $\times$, $\div$, and % on the GRE, but you are likely to also encounter some very unusual symbols. You may be asked, for example, to find the value of 10 ✳ 2, 5 ✿ 7, or 65 ♥ 2.

Some GRE questions use unusual symbols as a way of testing your math and abstract reasoning ability. Such questions turn out to be not as difficult as they first appear; you simply need to substitute normal math symbols for the unusual ones and then perform the operations.

> If a ♦ $b = \sqrt{a + b}$ for all nonnegative numbers a and b, what is the value of 10 ♦ 6?
>
> (A) 0
>
> (B) 2
>
> (C) 4
>
> (D) 8
>
> (E) 16

To solve the problem, substitute 10 for a and 6 for b in the expression $\sqrt{a + b}$.

$$\sqrt{a + b} = \sqrt{10 + 6} = \sqrt{16} = 4$$

Choice **(C)** is correct.

Now take a look at a more involved symbolism question.

> If a ▲ means to multiply a by 3 and a ❖ means to divide a by -2, what is the value of ((8 ❖) ▲) ❖?
>
> (A) -6
>
> (B)   0
>
> (C)   2
>
> (D)   3
>
> (E)   6

This question seems to ask a lot, but don't be fooled. If you take it one step at a time, it's much easier to manage.

To solve this equation, we need to remember the order of operations. When an expression contains a set of parentheses nested inside another set of parentheses, begin with the innermost set first. The question stem tells us that a ❖ means to divide a by -2, so 8 ❖ means to divide 8 by -2.

$$8 \text{ ❖} = \frac{8}{-2} = -4$$

So replace (8 ❖) in the expression with -4, and the expression is now $(-4 \blacktriangle)$ ❖. And $-4 \blacktriangle$ means to multiply -4 by 3.

$$-4 \blacktriangle = -4 \times 3 = -12$$

Next, replace $(-4 \blacktriangle)$ with -12; the expression is now -12 ❖. And -12 ❖ means to divide -12 by -2.

$$-12 \text{ ❖} = \frac{-12}{-2} = 6$$

Even symbolism questions that appear to be difficult are manageable when you solve them one step at a time.

Choice **(E)** is correct.

SYMBOLISM PRACTICE SET

1. If $x \neq 0$, let ♠ x be defined by ♠ $x = x - \frac{1}{x}$. Then ♠ $(-3) =$

   (A) $-\frac{10}{3}$

   (B) $-\frac{8}{3}$

   (C) 0

   (D) $\frac{8}{3}$

   (E) $\frac{10}{3}$

2. If r ♥ $s = r(r - s)$ for all integers r and s, then 4 ♥ (3 ♥ 5) =

   (A) -8

   (B) -2

   (C) 2

   (D) 20

   (E) 40

3. If $c \clubsuit d = \dfrac{c - d}{c}$, where $c \neq 0$, what is the value of $12 \clubsuit 3$?

   (A) -3

   (B) $\dfrac{1}{4}$

   (C) $\dfrac{2}{3}$

   (D) $\dfrac{3}{4}$

   (E) 3

SYMBOLISM PRACTICE SET
ANSWERS AND EXPLANATIONS

1.   B

Substitute -3 for x: $\spadesuit\, x = \spadesuit\, (-3) = -3 - \dfrac{1}{-3} = -3 + \dfrac{1}{3} = -\dfrac{9}{3} + \dfrac{1}{3} = -\dfrac{8}{3}$

This is choice **(B)**.

2.   E

Start inside the parentheses.

$3 \heartsuit 5 = 3(3 - 5) = 3(-2) = -6$

Next, substitute -6 for $3 \heartsuit 5$ in the original expression.

$4 \heartsuit (3 \heartsuit 5) = 4 \heartsuit (-6) = 4[4 - (-6)] = 4[4 + 6] = 4[10] = 40$

The result is 40, and that's **(E)**.

3.   D

Substitute 12 for c and 3 for d.

$c \clubsuit d = \dfrac{c - d}{c}$

$12 \clubsuit 3 = \dfrac{12 - 3}{12} = \dfrac{9}{12} = \dfrac{3}{4}$

Choice **(D)** is correct.

THE KAPLAN APPROACH TO SPECIAL TRIANGLES

While geometry questions on the GRE use a variety of shapes and figures, knowing the properties of the most commonly tested figures prepares you to answer just about any geometry question you'll encounter. For example, the sum of the angle measures in a triangle is always 180 degrees. Special triangles are one of the most important categories of figures to master, since nearly every figure that isn't round will include one or more special triangles that you can use to your advantage. For instance, knowing the length of one side of a 30°-60°-90° triangle or 45°-45°-90° triangle enables you to find the lengths of the other sides. In some cases, you can use this knowledge to uncover more information about the original figure. For example:

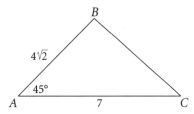

In the triangle above, what is the length of side *BC*?

- (A) 4
- (B) 5
- (C) $4\sqrt{2}$
- (D) 6
- (E) $5\sqrt{2}$

If you think the 45° angle might turn out to be useful, you are correct. But don't jump to any conclusion yet! The triangle may *look* like a right isosceles triangle (a 45°-45°-90° triangle), but remember, you can't always trust your first impressions of diagrams on the GRE. Use the information in the question stem instead.

The special triangles you should look for on the GRE are summarized below. Read about those triangles, and then you will be ready to return to the problem above.

EQUILATERAL TRIANGLES

All interior angles are 60° and all sides are the same length.

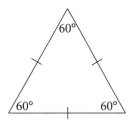

ISOSCELES TRIANGLES

Two sides are the same length, and the angles facing those sides are equal.

RIGHT TRIANGLES

Right triangles contain a 90° angle. The sides that form the 90° angle are the legs; the side facing the 90° angle is the hypotenuse. The sides are related by the Pythagorean theorem $a^2 + b^2 = c^2$, where a and b are the lengths of the legs, and c is the length of the hypotenuse.

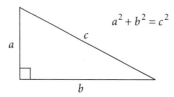

"SPECIAL" RIGHT TRIANGLES

Some triangles on the GRE are "special" right triangles—right triangles whose side lengths always come in predictable ratios. If you can spot them, you won't have to use the Pythagorean theorem to find a missing side length.

3:4:5 Right Triangles

These right triangles all have side lengths in the ratio 3:4:5. Be on the lookout for multiples. If you multiply 3, 4, and 5 each by the same number, you get a ratio equivalent to 3:4:5. For example, 6:8:10 is equivalent to 3:4:5 because 6, 8, and 10 are multiples of 3, 4, and 5, respectively, using the same multiplier, 2. So look for multiples—it will help you spot equivalent ratios.

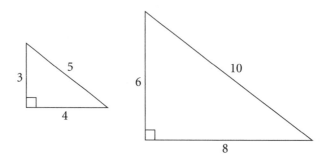

5:12:13 Triangles

Right triangles whose sides are in the ratio 5:12:13 also occur frequently in Quantitative Reasoning questions. You can verify that the three numbers 5, 12, and 13 form a Pythagorean triple by testing them in the Pythagorean theorem. If $a = 5$, $b = 12$, and $c = 13$, does $a^2 + b^2 = c^2$?

Yes, it does:

$$5^2 + 12^2 = 13^2$$
$$25 + 144 = 169$$
$$169 = 169$$

Keeping an eye out for the side lengths 5, 12, and 13—or multiples of those numbers—can help you apply your reasoning skills to a problem with one of these special triangles.

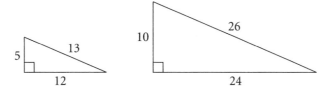

45°-45°-90° Right Triangles (Isosceles Right Triangles)

These triangles have side lengths in the ratio $1:1:\sqrt{2}$. Note that the legs have the same length. Again, be on the lookout for multiples. An isosceles right triangle is formed when a square is divided in half by one of its diagonals. This is often helpful in solving geometric questions.

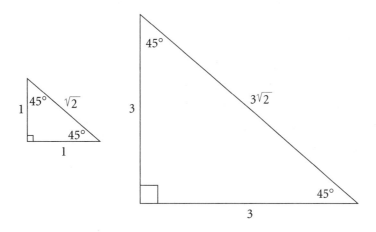

30°-60°-90° Right Triangles

These triangles have side lengths in the ratio $1:\sqrt{3}:2$. When an equilateral triangle is divided in half, the result is a 30°-60°-90° triangle.

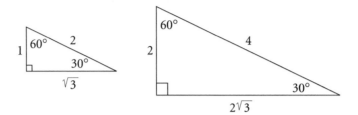

Now consider the example posed at the beginning of this section. You can draw a line segment from point B, perpendicular to side AC. This divides the triangle into two right triangles.

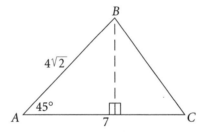

The triangle on the left has a 45° angle and a 90° angle. Since the sum of the angle measures in any triangle is 180°, the third angle is 45°. So the triangle is a 45°-45°-90° triangle. The hypotenuse is $4\sqrt{2}$, so the side lengths form the ratio $4:4:4\sqrt{2}$, which is equivalent to $1:1:\sqrt{2}$.

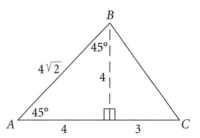

Notice that side AC, which you know is 7 units long, is now divided into two parts: 4 units long and 3 units long. The triangle on the right has a 90° angle and legs of lengths 3 and 4, so it is a $3:4:5$ right triangle, and the length of BC is 5.

Choice **(B)** is correct.

SPECIAL TRIANGLES PRACTICE SET

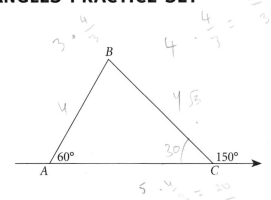

1. In triangle *ABC*, if *AB* = 4, then *AC* =

    Ⓐ   6

    Ⓑ   7

    Ⓒ   8

    Ⓓ   9

    Ⓔ   10

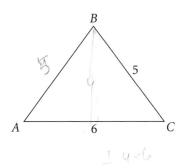

2. If the perimeter of triangle *ABC* above is 16, what is its area?

    Ⓐ   8

    Ⓑ   9

    Ⓒ   10

    Ⓓ   12

    Ⓔ   15

3. A ladder 20 feet long is placed against a wall. If the distance on the ground from the wall to the ladder is 12 feet, how many feet up the wall does the ladder reach?

- (A) 12
- (B) 15
- (C) 16
- (D) 21
- (E) 24

SPECIAL TRIANGLES PRACTICE SET ANSWERS AND EXPLANATIONS

1. C

Angle *BCA* is supplementary to the 150° angle, so angle *BCA* = 180° − 150° = 30°. The interior angles of a triangle have a sum of 180°, so angle *BAC* + angle *ABC* + angle *BCA* = 180°, and angle *ABC* = 180° − 60° − 30° = 90°. So triangle *ABC* is a 30-60-90 right triangle, and its sides are in the ratio 1 : $\sqrt{3}$: 2. You know that *AB* = 4, and *AB* is the shortest side because it is opposite the 30° angle. So the ratio of sides for this triangle is 4 : 4$\sqrt{3}$: 8, which is equivalent to 1 : $\sqrt{3}$: 2. And the hypotenuse *AC* = 8, which is choice **(C)**.

2. D

To find the area, you need to know the base and height. The perimeter is 16, so *AB* + *BC* + *AC* = 16; that is, *AB* = 16 − 5 − 6 = 5. Since *AB* = *BC*, this is an isosceles triangle. If you draw a line segment from vertex *B* perpendicular to *AC*, it will divide the base *AC* in half. This divides the triangle into two right triangles. The two right triangles each have one leg of 3 and a hypotenuse of 5, so they are 3 : 4 : 5 right triangles. So the length of the perpendicular line segment from *B* to *AC* (which is the height of triangle *ABC*) is 4. You know that *AC*, the base of triangle *ABC*, is 6, and you now know that the height is 4. So the area is $\frac{1}{2}$ × base × height = $\frac{1}{2}$ × 6 × 4 = 12, which is choice **(D)**.

3. C

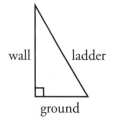

The wall forms a right angle with the ground, so the triangle is a right triangle. The length of the ladder is the hypotenuse of the triangle. Next, look at the numbers given in the problem and notice that 12 = 4 × 3 and 20 = 4 × 5. The lengths of the sides of this triangle are multiples of the basic 3 : 4 : 5 triangle. The missing length is 4 × 4 = 16, choice **(C)**.

THE KAPLAN APPROACH TO MULTIPLE AND ODDBALL FIGURES

You may see a combination of geometric shapes or an oddball figure on the GRE. While these problems may *look* difficult, you can often simplify them by first looking for familiar geometric shapes, such as special right triangles, squares, or circles. In a problem that combines figures, you have to look for relationships between the figures. For instance, if two figures share a side, information about that side will probably be the key to answering the question.

How could you approach the following question?

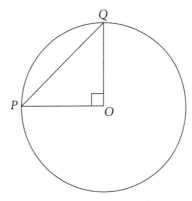

In the figure above, if the area of the circle with center O is 9π, what is the area of triangle POQ?

- Ⓐ 4.5
- Ⓑ 6
- Ⓒ 9
- Ⓓ 3.5π
- Ⓔ 4.5π

In this case the figures don't share a side, but each leg of the right triangle is also an important part of the circle—each leg, *OP* and *OQ*, is a radius of the circle, and therefore *OP* = *OQ*.

The area of a circle is πr^2. The area of circle O is 9π, so $r^2 = 9$ and $r = 3$. In this figure, 3 is both the radius of the circle and the length of each leg of the isosceles right triangle that is inscribed in the circle.

The area of a triangle is $\frac{1}{2} \times$ base $\times$ height. The legs of any right triangle can serve as the base and height of that triangle, so substitute 3 for both the base and the height. The area is $\frac{1}{2} \times 3 \times 3 = \frac{9}{2} = 4.5$. Choice **(A)** is correct.

But what if, instead of a figure made up of familiar shapes, you are given something like this?

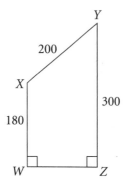

What is the perimeter of quadrilateral *WXYZ*?

(A) 680

(B) 760

(C) 840

(D) 920

(E) 1,000

Try breaking the unfamiliar shape into familiar shapes. Then use the same techniques as you would for multiple figures.

A figure's perimeter is the sum of the lengths of its sides, so you need to find the length of side *WZ*. Drawing a line segment from point *X* to side *YZ* divides the figure into a right triangle and a rectangle. Call the point of intersection *A*.

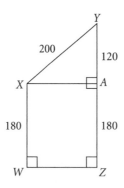

Since *WXAZ* is a rectangle, *WX* = *ZA* = 180. And since *ZA* = 180, you know that *AY* = 300 − 180 = 120. Looking at lengths *AY* and *XY*, you might recognize that the ratio 120 : 200 is equivalent to the ratio 3 : 5 (because 120 = 3 × 40 and 200 = 5 × 40). So triangle *XYA* is a 3:4:5 right triangle with side lengths of 40 times the lengths 3,

4, and 5. Therefore, $XA = 4 \times 40 = 160$. If you didn't realize that triangle XYA is a $3:4:5$ right triangle, you could have used the Pythagorean theorem, which applies to all right triangles, as follows:

$$a^2 + b^2 = c^2$$

$$120^2 + b^2 = 200^2$$

$$14{,}400 + b^2 = 40{,}000$$

$$b^2 = 25{,}600$$

$$b = 160$$

Now, knowing that $XA = 160$, you know that $WZ = 160$ also, because XA and WZ are opposite, equal sides of a rectangle. So the perimeter of the entire figure is $180 + 200 + 300 + 160 = 840$. Choice **(C)** is correct.

MULTIPLE AND ODDBALL FIGURES PRACTICE SET

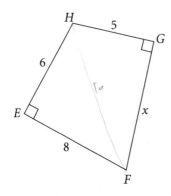

1. What is the value of x in the figure above?

    (A) 4

    (B) $3\sqrt{3}$

    (C) $3\sqrt{5}$

    (D) $5\sqrt{3}$

    (E) 9

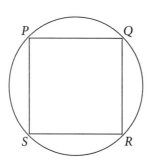

2. In the figure above, square *PQRS* is inscribed in a circle. If the area of square *PQRS* is 4, what is the radius of the circle?

    (A) 1

    (B) $\sqrt{2}$

    (C) 2

    (D) $2\sqrt{2}$

    (E) $4\sqrt{2}$

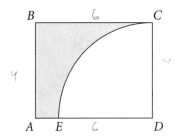

3. In the figure above, the quarter circle with center D has a radius of 4 and rectangle $ABCD$ has a perimeter of 20. What is the perimeter of the shaded region?

    (A) $20 - 8\pi$

    (B) $10 + 2\pi$

    (C) $12 + 2\pi$

    (D) $12 + 4\pi$

    (E) $4 + 8\pi$

MULTIPLE AND ODDBALL FIGURES PRACTICE SET ANSWERS AND EXPLANATIONS

1. D

Draw line segment *HF* to divide the figure into two right triangles.

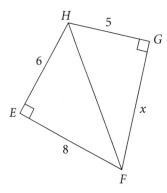

The symbol Δ can be used for the word "triangle." Δ*EFH* is a 3 : 4 : 5 triangle with side lengths 6, 8, and 10. So, *FH* = 10. Use the Pythagorean theorem in Δ*FHG* to find *x*.

$$x^2 + 5^2 = 10^2$$
$$x^2 + 25 = 100$$
$$x^2 = 75$$
$$x = \sqrt{75}$$
$$x = \sqrt{25}\sqrt{3}$$
$$x = 5\sqrt{3}$$

This value is choice **(D)**.

2. B

Draw diagonal *QS* and notice that it's also a diameter of the circle.

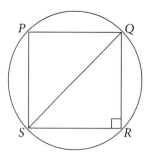

Each triangle formed is an isosceles (45-45-90) right triangle, so the sides of Δ*QRS* are in the ratio 1 : 1 : $\sqrt{2}$. The area of the square is 4, so each side of the square is 2, and the sides of Δ*QRS* are 2, 2, and 2$\sqrt{2}$. (Multiply all numbers in the ratio 1 : 1 : $\sqrt{2}$ by 2 to get the ratio 2 : 2 : 2$\sqrt{2}$.) So SQ = 2$\sqrt{2}$, and the radius is half that: $\frac{1}{2} \times 2\sqrt{2} = \sqrt{2}$. Choice **(B)** is correct.

3. C

You don't need to draw any new line segments for this question.

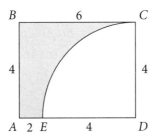

The perimeter of the shaded region is $BC + AB + AE +$ arc EC. The quarter circle has its center at D, and point C lies on the circle, so side DC is a radius of the quarter circle and has length 4. Opposite sides of a rectangle are equal, so $AB = 4$ also. The perimeter of the rectangle is 20, so BC and AD are each 6. Because $AD = 6$ and $ED = 4$, you know that $AE = 2$. The circumference of a full circle with radius r is $2\pi r$, so the length of a quarter circle arc is $\frac{1}{4} \times 2\pi r$. Arc EC is a quarter circle arc of a circle with radius 4, so its length is $\frac{1}{4} \times 2\pi(4) = \frac{1}{4} \times 8\pi = 2\pi$. So the perimeter of the shaded region is $6 + 4 + 2 + 2\pi = 12 + 2\pi$, choice **(C)**.

THE KAPLAN APPROACH TO MEAN, MEDIAN, MODE, AND RANGE

The mean of a set of numbers (sometimes called arithmetic mean) is simply the average of the numbers. The words *mean*, *arithmetic mean*, and *average* all have the same meaning. When a problem asks for the mean or arithmetic mean, you can use this formula:

$$\text{Average} = \frac{\text{Sum of Terms}}{\text{Number of Terms}}$$

For example, the average of the numbers 7, 5, and 12 is $\frac{7 + 5 + 12}{3} = \frac{24}{3} = 8$.

If you encounter a problem that is not quite so straightforward, it helps to remember that mean and sum are closely related. Look what happens when you rewrite the formula for the average:

$$\text{Average} = \frac{\text{Sum of Terms}}{\text{Number of Terms}} \longrightarrow \text{Number of Terms} \times \text{Average} = \text{Sum of Terms}$$

So, the sum is the product of the number of terms and the average. In the example above, $3 \times 8 = 24$. Consider how this relationship is used in the following problem.

Nancy shopped at four department stores and spent an average of $80 per store. If she wants to average no more than $70 per store over a total of six stores, what is the most she can average at the two remaining stores?

- (A) $40
- (B) $50
- (C) $55
- (D) $65
- (E) $70

This problem might be difficult if you try to approach it by looking for an average, but if you use the formula for the sum of terms, it is not difficult.

Nancy has spent an average of $80 per store at four stores, or a sum of 4 × $80 = $320. Her limit is an average of $70 per store at six stores, or a sum of 6 × $70 = $420. This means she can spend $100 at the two remaining stores, or an average of $\frac{\$100}{2} =$ $50 per store. Choice **(B)** is correct.

The median of a set is the middle term when all the terms in the set are listed in sequential order. When there is an even number of terms in a set, the median is the average of the two middle terms.

To find the median of the set {4, 7, 5, 23, 5, 67, 10}, first arrange the terms in order: {4, 5, 5, 7, 10, 23, 67}. The median is the middle term, 7. Now suppose the set contained one more term, say an 8. The set would be {4, 5, 5, 7, 8, 10, 23, 67}, and the median would be the average of the two middle terms, or $\dfrac{7+8}{2} = \dfrac{15}{2} = 7.5$.

The mode of a set is simply the term that occurs most frequently. For the set {4, 5, 5, 7, 10, 23, 67}, the mode is 5 because 5 occurs the greatest number of times. If one of the 5's were removed, the set would be {4, 5, 7, 10, 23, 67}, which has no mode. If another 10 were included in the original set, the set would be {4, 5, 5, 7, 10, 10, 23, 67}, and both 5 and 10 would be modes.

The range of a set is simply the difference between the greatest term and the least term. For the set {4, 5, 5, 7, 10, 23, 67}, the range is $67 - 4 = 63$.

MEAN, MEDIAN, MODE, AND RANGE PRACTICE SET

1. The only test scores for the students in a certain class are 44, 30, 42, 30, x, 44, and 30. If x equals one of the other scores and is a multiple of 5, what is the mode for the class?

    (A) 5
    (B) 6
    (C) 15
    (D) 30
    (E) 44

2. If half the range of the increasing sequence {11, A, 23, B, C, 68, 73} is equal to its median, what is the median of the sequence?

    (A) 23
    (B) 31
    (C) 33
    (D) 41
    (E) 62

3. If the average (arithmetic mean) of $x + 1$, $x + 2$, and $x + 3$ is 0, then $x =$

    (A) -2
    (B) -1
    (C) 0
    (D) 1
    (E) 2

MEAN, MEDIAN, MODE, AND RANGE PRACTICE SET ANSWERS AND EXPLANATIONS

1. D

Since x equals one of the other scores, it must be 30, 42, or 44. And since it is a multiple of 5, it must be 30. So 30 occurs four times—more than any other score, making 30 the mode. Choice **(D)** is correct.

2. B

Don't get confused by the variables. The terms of the sequence are in increasing order, so 11 is the least and 73 is the greatest, and the range is $73 - 11 = 62$. Half of 62 is 31, so the median is 31, which is choice **(B)**.

3. A

You can use the definition of the arithmetic mean to answer this question. Add the terms, divide by 3, and set the expression equal to 0:

$$\frac{x + 1 + x + 2 + x + 3}{3} = 0$$

$$\frac{3x + 6}{3} = 0$$

$$x + 2 = 0$$

$$x = -2$$

A quick check can be done by substituting -2 for x in each term to verify that the sum is 0, making the numerator of the fraction of the first equation equal to zero.

THE KAPLAN APPROACH TO PROBABILITY

Probability measures the likelihood of an event occurring. Probability can be represented as a fraction, decimal, or percent. For example, if rain today is just as likely as not, then the probability of rain today can be expressed as $\frac{1}{2}$, 0.5, or 50%. You may also see a probability expressed in everyday language: Saying "one chance in a hundred" means the probability is $\frac{1}{100}$.

To find the probability of something happening, use this formula:

$$\text{Probability} = \frac{\text{Number of Desired Outcomes}}{\text{Number of Possible Outcomes}}$$

For example: What is the probability of tossing a 4 if you toss a six-faced die? There is one desired outcome, 4, and six possible outcomes: 1, 2, 3, 4, 5, and 6. So the probability of tossing a 4 is $\frac{1}{6}$, and the probability of not tossing a 4 is $\frac{5}{6}$. Keep in mind that the probability of an event not happening is equal to 1 minus the probability of the event happening. This can be stated as: $P(\text{not event}) = 1 - P(\text{event})$.

Every probability is expressed as a number between 0 and 1 inclusive, with a probability of 0 meaning "no chance" and a probability of 1 meaning "guaranteed to happen." Remember, the higher the probability, the greater the chance that an event will occur. You can often eliminate answer choices on the GRE by having some idea of where the probability of an event falls between 0 and 1.

PROBABILITY PRACTICE SET

1. If 14 women and 10 men are employed in a certain office, what is the probability that one employee picked at random will be a woman?

    (A) $\frac{1}{14}$

    (B) $\frac{1}{6}$

    (C) $\frac{7}{12}$

    (D) 1

    (E) $\frac{7}{5}$

2. A bag contains 6 red, 6 green, 8 yellow, and 5 white marbles. You pick one marble at random from the bag. What the probability that the marble chosen is not green or yellow?

    (A) $\frac{14}{20}$

    (B) $\frac{16}{20}$

    (C) $\frac{11}{25}$

    (D) $\frac{14}{25}$

    (E) $\frac{11}{14}$

3. If Tom flips a fair coin twice, what is the probability that at least one head will occur?

    (A) $\frac{1}{4}$

    (B) $\frac{1}{3}$

    (C) $\frac{1}{2}$

    (D) $\frac{2}{3}$

    (E) $\frac{3}{4}$

Probability Practice Set Answers and Explanations follow on the next page.

PROBABILITY PRACTICE SET
ANSWERS AND EXPLANATIONS

1. C

$$\text{Probability} = \frac{\text{Number of Desired Outcomes}}{\text{Number of Possible Outcomes}} = \frac{\text{Number of Women Employees}}{\text{Number of Employees}}$$

$$= \frac{14}{24} = \frac{7}{12}$$

2. C

There are 25 marbles in the bag and 14 of them are either green or yellow. The probability that a marble chosen is *not* green or yellow is equal to 1 minus the probability that the marble chosen *is* green or yellow.

Probability of (not green or yellow) = 1 − Probability of (green or yellow)

$$= 1 - \frac{14}{25}$$

$$= \frac{11}{25}$$

Notice that this is also the probability of choosing a red or white marble; 11 of the 25 marbles are red or white. The correct answer is **(C)**.

3. E

An outcome in this situation is the result of two coin flips. For example, flipping a head and then a tail can be indicated by HT. There are four possible outcomes: HH, HT, TH, and TT. There are three desired outcomes: HH, HT, and TH. So the probability of at least one head is $\frac{3}{4}$.

In the chapters that follow this one, you will learn how to approach the three basic types of Quantitative Reasoning problems on the GRE. Although the format of these problems—Quantitative Comparison, Problem Solving, or Data Interpretation—varies from problem to problem, one thing is true: they are all built on the foundations you studied in this chapter.

CHAPTER 11

Quantitative Comparison

INTRODUCTION TO QUANTITATIVE COMPARISON

In each Quantitative Comparison question, you'll see two mathematical expressions. One is Quantity A, the other is Quantity B. You will be asked to compare them. Some questions include additional information about one or both quantities. This centered information applies to both quantities and is essential to making the comparison. Since this type of question is about the relationship between the two quantities, you usually won't need to calculate a specific value for either quantity. Therefore, you do not want to rely on the on-screen calculator to answer these questions.

The directions for a Quantitative Comparison question will look like this:

Directions: Select the correct answer.

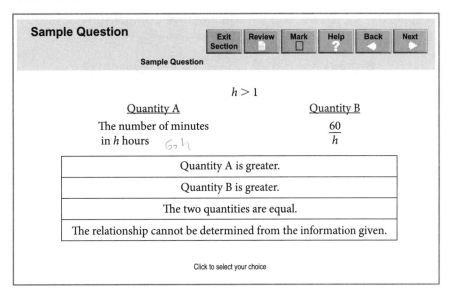

THE KAPLAN METHOD FOR QUANTITATIVE COMPARISON

STEP 1 Analyze the centered information and quantities.

STEP 2 Approach strategically.

HOW THE KAPLAN METHOD FOR QUANTITATIVE COMPARISON WORKS

Now let's discuss how the Kaplan Method for Quantitative Comparison works:

STEP 1
Analyze the centered information and the quantities.

Notice whether the quantities contain numbers, variables, or both. If there is centered information, decide how it affects the information given in the quantities. Note that a variable has the same value each time it appears within a question.

STEP 2
Approach strategically.

Think about a strategy you could use to compare the quantities now that you've reasoned out the information you have and the information you need. There are a variety of approaches to solving a Quantitative Comparison question, and the practice examples will take you through several of these.

HOW TO APPLY THE KAPLAN METHOD FOR QUANTITATIVE COMPARISON

Now let's apply the Kaplan Method to a Quantitative Comparison question:

Quantity A	Quantity B
$\frac{1}{4} + \frac{1}{5} + \frac{1}{6} + \frac{1}{7}$	$\dfrac{1}{\frac{1}{4} + \frac{1}{5} + \frac{1}{6} + \frac{1}{7}}$

   Ⓐ Quantity A is greater.

   Ⓑ Quantity B is greater.

   Ⓒ The two quantities are equal.

   Ⓓ The relationship cannot be determined from the information given.

STEP 1

Analyze the centered information and the columns.

This problem would be a nightmare to calculate under timed conditions. But the only thing you need to figure out is whether one quantity is greater than the other. One thing you might notice is that choice **(D)** is not an option here. Because both quantities contain only numbers, there is a definite value for each quantity, and a relationship can be determined.

What you do notice is that the quantity on the left is the same as the quantity in the denominator of the fraction on the right. You can think about this problem as a comparison of x and $\frac{1}{x}$ (or the reciprocal of x), where x has a definite value. Your job now is to figure out just how to compare them.

STEP 2

Approach strategically.

Before you start to do a long calculation, think about what you already know. While you may not know the sum of the four fractions in Quantity A, you do know two things: $\frac{1}{4} + \frac{1}{4} + \frac{1}{4} + \frac{1}{4} = 1$, and $\frac{1}{5}, \frac{1}{6}$, and $\frac{1}{7}$ are each less than $\frac{1}{4}$. This means that Quantity A is less than 1, and therefore its reciprocal in Quantity B is greater than 1. So choice **(B)** is correct. QCs rarely, if ever, ask for exact values, so don't waste time calculating them.

Now let's apply the Kaplan Method to a second Quantitative Comparison question:

$$w > x > 0 > y > z$$

Quantity A	Quantity B
$w + y$	$x + z$

    (A) Quantity A is greater.

    (B) Quantity B is greater.

    (C) The two quantities are equal.

    (D) The relationship cannot be determined from the information given.

STEP 1

Analyze the centered information and the quantities.

In this problem, there are four variables: w, x, y, and z. You are asked to compare the values of the sums of pairs of variables. You know the relative values of the different variables, but you don't know the actual amounts. You do know that two of the variables (w and x) must be positive and two of the variables (y and z) must be negative numbers.

⟩⟩ STEP 2
Approach strategically.

In this case, think about the different sums as pieces of the whole. If every "piece" in one quantity is greater than a corresponding "piece" in the other quantity, and the only operation involved is addition, then the quantity with the greater individual values will have the greater total value. From the given information, we know that:

- $w > x$
- $y > z$

The first term, w, in Quantity A is greater than the first term, x, in Quantity B. Similarly, the second term, y, in Quantity A is greater than the second term, z, in Quantity B. Because each piece in Quantity A is greater than the corresponding piece in Quantity B, Quantity A must be greater; the answer is **(A)**.

Now let's apply the Kaplan Method to a third Quantitative Comparison question:

The diameter of circle O is d, and the area is a.

Quantity A	Quantity B
$\dfrac{\pi d^2}{2}$	a

- Ⓐ Quantity A is greater.
- Ⓑ Quantity B is greater.
- Ⓒ The two quantities are equal.
- Ⓓ The relationship cannot be determined from the information given.

⟩⟩ STEP 1
Analyze the centered information and the quantities.

In this problem, you are given additional information: the sentence that tells you the diameter of circle O is d and the area is a. This is important information, and gives you a key to unlocking this question. Given that information, you can tell that you are comparing the area, a, of circle O and a quantity that includes the diameter of the same circle. If you're thinking about the formula for calculating area given the diameter, you're thinking right!

◆ STEP 2
Approach strategically

Make Quantity B look more like Quantity A by rewriting a, the area of the circle, in terms of the diameter, d. The area of any circle equals πr^2, where r is the radius. Because the radius is half the diameter, we can substitute $\frac{d}{2}$ for r in the area formula to get $a = \pi r^2 = \pi \left(\frac{d}{2}\right)^2$ in Quantity B. Simplifying, we get $\frac{\pi d^2}{4}$.

Because both quantities contain π, we could compare $\frac{d^2}{2}$ to $\frac{d^2}{4}$. But let's take it one step further. You know that d is a distance and must be a positive number. That makes it possible to divide both quantities, $\frac{d^2}{2}$ and $\frac{d^2}{4}$, by d^2 and then just compare $\frac{1}{2}$ to $\frac{1}{4}$. This makes it easy to see that Quantity A is always greater because $\frac{1}{2} > \frac{1}{4}$. Choice **(A)** is correct.

KAPLAN'S ADDITIONAL TIPS FOR QUANTITATIVE COMPARISON QUESTIONS

Memorize the Answer Choices.

While working through the chapter on Quantitative Comparison, it is a good idea to memorize what the answer choices mean. This is not as difficult as it sounds. Although the practice questions in this book are shown with the choices for each question, the choices are always the same. The wording and the order never vary. As you work the practice problems, the choices will become second nature to you, and you will get used to reacting to the questions without reading the four answer choices, thus saving you lots of time.

Try to Demonstrate Two Different Relationships Between Quantities.

Here's why demonstrating two different relationships between the quantities is an important strategy: If you can demonstrate two different relationships, then choice **(D)** is correct. There is no need to examine the question further.

But how can this be demonstration be done efficiently? A good suggestion is to look at the expression(s) containing a variable and notice the possible values of the variable given the mathematical operation involved. For example, if x can be any real number, and you need to compare $(x + 1)^2$ to $(x + 1)$, pick a value for x that will make $(x + 1)$ a fraction between 0 and 1, and then pick a value for x that will make $(x + 1)$ greater than 1. By choosing values for x in this way, you are basing your number choices on mathematical properties you already know: a positive fraction less than one becomes smaller when squared, but a number greater than one grows larger when squared.

Compare Quantities Piece by Piece.

Compare the value of each "piece" in each quantity. If every "piece" in one quantity is greater than a corresponding "piece" in the other quantity, and the operation involved is either addition or multiplication, then the quantity with the greater individual values will have the greater total value.

Make One Quantity Look Like the Other.

When the Quantities A and B are expressed differently, you can often make the comparison easier by changing the format of one quantity so that it looks like the other. This is a great approach when the quantities look so different that you can't compare them directly.

Do the Same Thing to Both Quantities.

If the quantities you are given seem too complex to compare immediately, look closely to see if there is an addition, subtraction, multiplication, or division you can perform on both quantities to make them simpler—provided you do not multiply or divide by zero or a negative number. For example, suppose you have the task of comparing $1 + \dfrac{w}{1+w}$ to $1 + \dfrac{1}{1+w}$, where w is greater than 0. To get to the heart of the comparison, subtract 1 from both quantities and you have $\dfrac{w}{1+w}$ compared to $\dfrac{1}{1+w}$. To simplify even further, multiply both quantities by $(1 + w)$ and then you can compare w to 1; much simpler.

Don't Be Tricked by Misleading Information.

To avoid Quantitative Comparison traps, stay alert and don't assume anything. If you are using a diagram to answer a question, use only information that is given or information that you know must be true based on properties or theorems. For instance, don't assume angles are equal or lines are parallel unless it is stated or can be deduced from other information given.

A common mistake is to assume that variables represent only positive integers. As you saw when using the Pick Numbers strategy, fractions or negative numbers often show a different relationship between the quantities.

Don't Forget to Consider Other Possibilities.

If an answer looks obvious, it may very well be a trap. Consider this situation: a question requires you to think of two integers whose product is 6. If you jump to the conclusion that 2 and 3 are the integers, you will miss several other possibilities. Not only are 1 and 6 possibilities, but there are also pairs of negative integers to consider: −2 and −3, −1 and −6!

Don't Fall for Look-alikes.

Even if two expressions look similar, they may be mathematically different. Be especially careful with expressions involving parentheses or radicals. If you were asked to compare $\sqrt{5x} + \sqrt{5x}$ to $\sqrt{10x}$, you would not want to fall into the trap of saying the two expressions were equal. Although time is an important factor in taking the GRE, don't rush to the extent that you do not apply your skills correctly. In this case, $\sqrt{5x} + \sqrt{5x} = 2\sqrt{5x}$, which is not the same as $\sqrt{10x}$ unless $x = 0$.

QUANTITATIVE COMPARISON PRACTICE SET

Try the following Quantitative Comparison questions using the Kaplan Method for Quantitative Comparison. If you're up to the challenge, time yourself; on test day, you'll want to spend only 1.5 minutes on each question.

	Quantity A	Quantity B
1.	$x^2 + 2x - 2$	$x^2 + 2x - 1$

- (A) Quantity A is greater.
- (B) Quantity B is greater.
- (C) The two quantities are equal.
- (D) The relationship cannot be determined from the information given.

$x = 2y$; y is a positive number.

	Quantity A	Quantity B
2.	4^{2y}	2^x

- (A) Quantity A is greater.
- (B) Quantity B is greater.
- (C) The two quantities are equal.
- (D) The relationship cannot be determined from the information given.

q, r, and s are positive numbers; $qrs > 12$.

	Quantity A	Quantity B
3.	$\dfrac{qr}{5}$	$\dfrac{3}{s}$

- (A) Quantity A is greater.
- (B) Quantity B is greater.
- (C) The two quantities are equal.
- (D) The relationship cannot be determined from the information given.

In triangle XYZ, the measure of angle X equals the measure of angle Y.

Quantity A	Quantity B

4.

The degree measure of angle Z — The degree measure of angle X plus the degree measure of angle Y

Ⓐ Quantity A is greater.

Ⓑ Quantity B is greater.

Ⓒ The two quantities are equal.

Ⓓ The relationship cannot be determined from the information given.

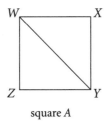 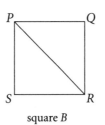

square A square B

Quantity A	Quantity B

5.

$$\dfrac{\text{Perimeter of square } A}{\text{Perimeter of square } B} \qquad \dfrac{\text{Length of } WY}{\text{Length of } PR}$$

Ⓐ Quantity A is greater.

Ⓑ Quantity B is greater.

Ⓒ The two quantities are equal.

Ⓓ The relationship cannot be determined from the information given.

QUANTITATIVE COMPARISON PRACTICE SET ANSWERS AND EXPLANATIONS

1. B

Comparing the two quantities piece by piece, you find that the only difference is the third piece: -2 in Quantity A and -1 in Quantity B. You don't know the value of x, but whatever it is, x^2 in Quantity A must have the same value as x^2 in Quantity B, and $2x$ in Quantity A must have the same value as $2x$ in Quantity B. Because any quantity minus 2 must be less than that quantity minus 1, Quantity B is greater than Quantity A. The answer is **(B)**.

2. A

Replacing the exponent x in Quantity B with the equivalent value given in the centered information, you're comparing 4^{2y} with 2^{2y}. Because y is a positive integer, raising 4 to the exponent $2y$ will result in a greater value than raising 2 to the exponent $2y$. The correct choice is **(A)**.

3. D

Do the same thing to both quantities to make them look like the centered information. When you multiply both quantities by $5s$, you get qrs in Quantity A and 15 in Quantity B. Because qrs could be any integer greater than 12, qrs could be greater than, equal to, or less than 15. Choice **(D)** is correct.

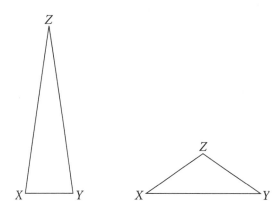

4. D

Because angle X = angle Y, at least two sides of the triangle are equal. You can draw two diagrams with X and Y as the base angles of a triangle. In one diagram, make the triangle tall and narrow, so that angle X and angle Y are very large and angle Z is very small. In this case, Quantity B is greater. In the second diagram, make the triangle short and wide, so that angle Z is much larger than angle X and angle Y. In this case, Quantity A is greater. Because more than one relationship between the quantities is possible, the correct answer is **(D)**.

5. C

You don't know the exact relationship between square *A* and square *B*, but it doesn't matter. The problem is actually just comparing the ratios of corresponding parts of two squares. The relationship between the specific side lengths of both squares will also exist between them for any other corresponding length. If a side of one square is twice the length of a side of the second square, the diagonal will also be twice as long. The ratio of the perimeters of the two squares is the same as the ratio of the diagonals. Therefore, the quantities are equal. Choice **(C)** is correct.

CHAPTER 12

Problem Solving

INTRODUCTION TO PROBLEM SOLVING

Problem Solving can be broken up into several general mathematics categories: algebra, arithmetic, number properties, and geometry.

In a Problem Solving question, you may be asked to solve a pure math problem or a word problem involving a real-world situation. You will be asked to enter your answer into an onscreen box, select one answer, or select one or more options that correctly answer the problem.

The directions for a Problem Solving question requiring a single answer will look like this:

Directions: Click to select your choice.

A Problem Solving question requiring you to select a single answer will look like this.

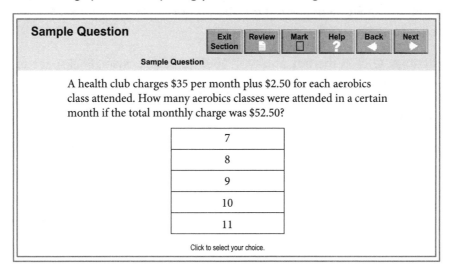

The directions for a Problem Solving question requiring you to select one or more answers will look like this:

Directions: Click to select your choice.

If a Problem Solving question asks you to select an exact number of choices, you must select that exact number of correct choices for the question to be counted as correct. Otherwise, you must select all the correct choices for the question to be counted as correct.

A Problem Solving question requiring you to select one or more answers will look like this.

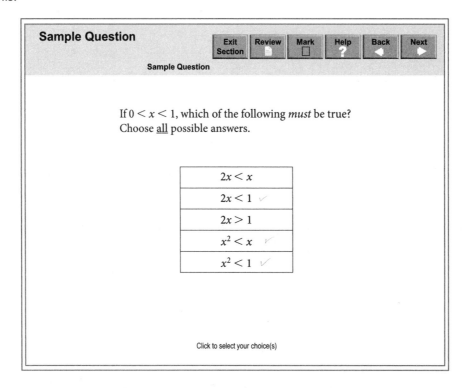

The directions for a Problem Solving question requiring you to make a Numeric Entry will look like this:

Directions: Click in the box and type your numeric answer. Backspace to erase.

Enter your answer as an integer or decimal if there is one box or as a fraction if there are two boxes.

To enter an integer or decimal, type directly in the box or use the Transfer Display button on the calculator.

- Use the backspace key to erase.
- Use a hyphen to enter a negative sign; type a hyphen a second time to remove it. The digits will remain.

- Use a period for a decimal point.
- The Transfer Display button will enter your answer directly from the calculator.
- Equivalent forms of decimals are all correct. (Example: 0.14 = 0.140)
- Enter the exact answer unless the question asks you to round your answer.

To enter a fraction, type the numerator and denominator in the appropriate boxes.

- Use a hyphen to enter a negative sign.
- The Transfer Display button does not work for fractions.
- Equivalent forms of fractions are all correct. (Example: $\frac{25}{15} = \frac{5}{3}$) If numbers are large, reduce fractions to fit in boxes.

A Problem Solving question with Numeric Entry will look like this.

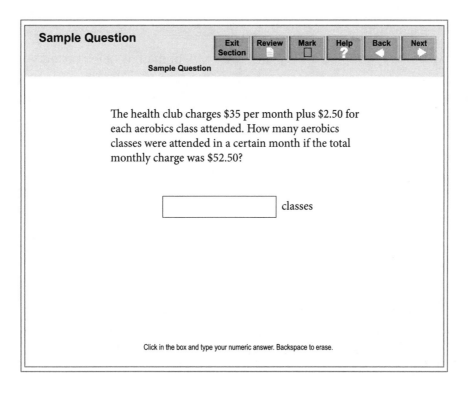

THE KAPLAN METHOD FOR PROBLEM SOLVING

STEP 1 Analyze the question.

STEP 2 Identify the task.

STEP 3 Approach strategically.

STEP 4 Confirm your answer.

HOW THE KAPLAN METHOD FOR PROBLEM SOLVING WORKS

Now let's discuss how the Kaplan Method for Problem Solving works:

STEP 1
Analyze the question.

Look at what the question is asking, and what area of math is being tested. Also note any particular trends in the answer choices: numbers v. variables, integers v. non-integers, and what information is being given. Unpack as much information as possible.

STEP 2
Identify the task.

Determine what question is being asked before solving the problem. Ask yourself, "What does the correct answer represent?" The GRE intentionally provides wrong answers for test takers who get the right answer to the wrong question.

STEP 3
Approach strategically.

Depending on the type of problem, you may use straightforward math—the textbook approach—to calculate your answer, or you may choose one of the following strategies: Picking Numbers, Backsolving, or Strategic Guessing.

When Picking Numbers to substitute for variables, chose numbers that are manageable and fit the description given in the problem. Backsolving is another form of Picking Numbers, where you'll start with one of the answer choices, and plug that choice back into the question. Lastly, Strategic Guessing can be a great time-saver on the GRE—being able to make a smart guess on a question is preferable to taking too much time and thus compromising your time and ability to answer other questions correctly.

STEP 4
Confirm your answer.

Check that your answer makes sense. Also check that you answered the question that was asked.

HOW TO APPLY THE KAPLAN METHOD FOR PROBLEM SOLVING

Now let's apply the Kaplan Method to a Problem Solving question:

> In a bag of candy, 7 of the candies are cherry-flavored, 8 are lemon, and 5 are grape. If a candy is chosen randomly from the bag, what is the probability that the candy is *not* lemon?

STEP 1
Analyze the question.

You are given the number of candies in a bag, and asked to identify the probability that a randomly selected candy is not lemon-flavored. You will have to type your answer into the box.

STEP 2
Identify the task.

The probability of an event is defined as $\frac{\text{Number of Favorable Outcomes}}{\text{Number of Possible Outcomes}}$. You will need to find the number of favorable outcomes (those in which you don't choose a lemon candy) and the total number of possible outcomes.

STEP 3
Approach strategically.

There are 20 candies in the bag, so there are 20 possible outcomes. Of all the candies, 12 are not lemon, so there are 12 favorable outcomes. So, the probability of *not* lemon is $\frac{12}{20}$. You should avoid reducing fractions for Numeric Entry questions, since all equivalent forms will be counted as correct. Save your time to use elsewhere, and limit your risk of committing an error in calculation.

◆ STEP 4

Confirm your answer.

Although it might be fun to get a bag of candies and check your answer in a real-world way, it's not practical, especially on test day. A more practical check would be to find the probability of choosing a lemon candy at random to be certain that: $P(\text{lemon}) = 1 - P(\text{not lemon})$. There are 8 lemon candies out of 20, so this check can be done easily.

$$P(\text{lemon}) \overset{?}{=} 1 - P(\text{not lemon})$$

$$\frac{8}{20} \overset{?}{=} 1 - \frac{12}{20}$$

$$\frac{8}{20} \overset{?}{=} \frac{20}{20} - \frac{12}{20}$$

$$\frac{8}{20} = \frac{8}{20}$$

This check is a way to confirm that the correct numbers have been used in the problem and the correct answer has been found.

Now let's apply the Kaplan Method to a second Problem Solving question:

> When n is divided by 14, the remainder is 10. What is the remainder when n is divided by 7?
>
> (A) 2
> (B) 3
> (C) 4
> (D) 5
> (E) 6

◆ STEP 1

Analyze the question.

In this question, you are asked to compare the relationship between the numbers 14 and 7 used as divisors. Be careful; you may be thinking of choosing $14 \div 7 = 2$ or $10 \div 2 = 5$. But these are both trap answer choices, because the question also involves using a remainder.

◆ STEP 2

Identify the task.

The task is to use the fact that division of a number, n, by 14 yields a remainder of 10 to identify the remainder when the same number is divided by 7.

STEP 3

Approach strategically.

A good strategy for this question is to pick a number for *n* that satisfies the condition for division by 14 and then see what happens when it is divided by 7.

Any number divided by itself will give a remainder of zero. So if we need a remainder of 10, we want a number that is 10 more than the number we are dividing by. 24 is a great number to pick here because when we try 24:

$$24 \div 14 = 1 \text{ Remainder } 10$$

Now that we've confirmed that 24 works, we answer the question that's being asked. Divide 24 by 7:

$$24 \div 7 = 3 \text{ Remainder } 3$$

Answer Choice **(B)** is the correct answer.

STEP 4

Confirm your answer.

You can quickly double-check your work, or try another number for *n* that results in a remainder of 10 when divided by 14:

$$38 \div 14 = 2 \text{ Remainder } 10, \text{ and } 38 \div 7 = 5 \text{ Remainder } 3$$

So the remainder is 3 in each case. The correct answer is **(B)**.

Now let's apply the Kaplan Method to a third Problem Solving question:

> The line $4x + 6y = 24$ passes through which of the following points?
> Indicate <u>all</u> possible answers.
>
> A (0, 4)
> B (2, 3)
> C (3, 2)
> D (5, 4)
> E (9, −1)

◈ STEP 1
Analyze the question.

This question is about a line on the coordinate plane. The equation is a function that represents a line. The numbers in the parentheses represent points (x, y) that are mentioned in the equation.

◈ STEP 2
Identify the task.

Your job is to identify which of the given points lie on the line. A line passes through a point if the coordinates of the point make the equation of the line true, so this is the same as saying that you need to find out which points, when plugged into the equation, make the equation true.

◈ STEP 3
Approach strategically.

You need to find all correct answers, so test all of them. Substitute the first coordinate for x and the second coordinate for y.

(A) Test (0, 4): $4x + 6y = 24 \rightarrow 4(0) + 6(4) = 0 + 24 = 24$. This works.

(B) Test (2, 3): $4x + 6y = 24 \rightarrow 4(2) + 6(3) = 8 + 18 \neq 24$. Eliminate.

(C) Test (3, 2): $4x + 6y = 24 \rightarrow 4(3) + 6(2) = 12 + 12 = 24$. This works.

(D) Test (5, 4): $4x + 6y = 24 \rightarrow 4(5) + 6(4) = 20 + 24 \neq 24$. Eliminate.

(E) Test (9, −1): $4x + 6y = 24 \rightarrow 4(9) + 6(-1) = 36 - 6 \neq 24$. Eliminate.

So, answer choices **(A)** and **(C)** are correct.

STEP 4
Confirm your answer.

Double-check your work to make sure you haven't made any careless errors, such as mistakenly plugging in a value for *x* when dealing with the variable *y*.

KAPLAN'S ADDITIONAL TIPS FOR PROBLEM SOLVING
Choose an Efficient Strategy

The GRE is not a traditional math test that requires that you show your work before you get credit, testing the process as well as the answer. The GRE tests only the answer—not how you found it. Because time is often your biggest concern on the GRE, the best way to each solution is often the quickest way, and the quickest way is often not straightforward math. Through practice, you'll become familiar with approaching each question in a more strategic way.

Rely on Kaplan Math Strategies

Kaplan strategies are a way to use reasoning in conjunction with mathematics to answer a question quickly. There may also be cases in which you can combine approaches: for example, using straightforward math to simplify an equation, then picking manageable numbers for the variables to solve that equation.

PICKING NUMBERS

Problems that seem difficult are good candidates for the Picking Numbers strategy. They include problems where either the question or the answer choices have variables; the problem tests a number property you don't recall; or the problem and the answer choices deal with percents or fractions, without using actual values.

BACKSOLVING

Backsolving is a similar strategy to Picking Numbers, except that you'll use one of the five answer choices as the number to pick. Remember, numerical answer choices are always in ascending or descending order. Use that information to your advantage when using Backsolving. Start with either **(B)** or **(D)** first, because you'll have a 40% chance that you can find the correct answer based on your first round of calculations. Then reason whether the choice you started with is correct, too large, or too small.

STRATEGIC GUESSING

This is a good strategy if you can eliminate choices by applying number-property rules or by estimating because gaps between answer choices are wide.

If some of the choices are out of the realm of possibility, eliminate them and move on.

PROBLEM SOLVING PRACTICE SET

Try the following Problem Solving questions using the Kaplan Method for Problem Solving. If you're up to the challenge, time yourself; on test day, you'll want to spend only about 2 minutes on each question.

1. If $r = 3s$, $s = 5t$, $t = 2u$, and $u \neq 0$, what is the value of $\frac{rst}{u^3}$?

   (A)   30

   (B)   60

   (C)   150

   (D)   300

   (E)   600 ✓

2. In the diagram, l_1 is parallel to l_2. The measure of angle q is 40 degrees. What is the sum of the measures of the acute angles shown in the diagram?

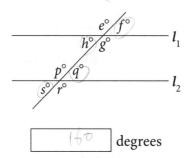

   [160] degrees

3. At Central Park Zoo, the ratio of sea lions to penguins is $4:11$. If there are 84 more penguins than sea lions, how many sea lions are there?

   (A)   24

   (B)   36

   (C)   48 ✓

   (D)   72

   (E)   121

4. Which of the following are prime numbers between $\frac{5}{2}$ and $\frac{43}{5}$? Indicate all possible answers.

   A 3

   B 4

   C 5

   D 7

   E 9

5. The figure above is made up of 3 squares having the same side length. If the perimeter of the figure is 40 units, what is the area in square units?

   A 50

   B 75

   C 120

   D 150

   E 200

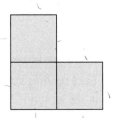

PROBLEM SOLVING PRACTICE SET ANSWERS AND EXPLANATIONS

1. E

The other variables all build upon u, so use the Picking Numbers strategy: pick a small number for u, and find the values for r, s, and t. For instance, if $u = 1$, then $t = 2u$, so $t = 2$; $s = 5t$, so $s = 10$; and $r = 3s$, so $r = 30$.

So, $\frac{rst}{u^3} = \frac{30 \times 10 \times 2}{1 \times 1 \times 1} = 600$. The correct answer is **(E)**.

2. 160

In the diagram, there are four acute angles and four obtuse angles created when the parallel lines are cut by the transversal. If angle q has a measure of 40°, then angles s, h, and f also have a measure of 40°. Therefore, the sum of their degree measures is **160**.

3. C

You need to find the number of sea lions, and there are fewer sea lions than penguins, so starting small is a good idea. You can use the Backsolving strategy; start with choice **(B)**, 36. If there are 36 sea lions, then there are $36 + 84 = 120$ penguins, and the ratio of sea lions to penguins is $\frac{36}{120} = \frac{3}{10}$. This ratio is less than $\frac{4}{11}$, so your answer must be larger. If we try **(D)**, there are 72 sea lions and there are $72 + 84 = 156$ penguins, and the ratio of sea lions to penguins is $\frac{72}{156} = \frac{6}{13}$. Since this ratio is too large, the correct answer must be **(C)**.

4. A, C, D

You need to find a range of values between two improper fractions. First, change the improper fractions to mixed numbers: $\frac{5}{2} = 2\frac{1}{2}$ and $\frac{43}{5} = 8\frac{3}{5}$. Now, a prime number is a positive integer with only two distinct factors, 1 and itself. The prime numbers in the answer choices are 3, 5, and 7, and they are all between $2\frac{1}{2}$ and $8\frac{3}{5}$. So the correct answers are **(A)**, **(C)**, and **(D)**.

5. B

There are 8 side lengths of the squares that make up the perimeter, which you are told is 40. So, each side of each square must be 5 units. The area of each square can found by squaring one side, so each square has an area of 25 square units. Since there are three squares, the total area of the figure is 75 square units. The correct answer is **(B)**.

CHAPTER 13

Data Interpretation

INTRODUCTION TO DATA INTERPRETATION QUESTIONS

Data Interpretation questions are based on information located in tables or graphs and are often statistics-oriented. The data may be located in one table or graph, but you might also need to extract data from two or more tables or graphs. There will be a set of questions for you to answer based on each data presentation.

You may be asked to choose one or more answers from a set of answer choices or to enter your answer in a Numeric Entry field.

The directions for Data Interpretation questions will look like this:

Questions 1–5 are based on the following table.

PERCENT OF SALES PER CLIENT
FOR CURTAIN FABRIC OVER THREE MONTHS

	May	June	July
The Home Touch	45%	25%	48%
Curtains Unlimited	30%	23%	33%
Max's Curtain Supply	9%	23%	22%
Valances by Val	13%	20%	10%
Wendy's Windows	3%	9%	7%

A Data Interpretation question that requires you to choose exactly one correct answer will look like this:

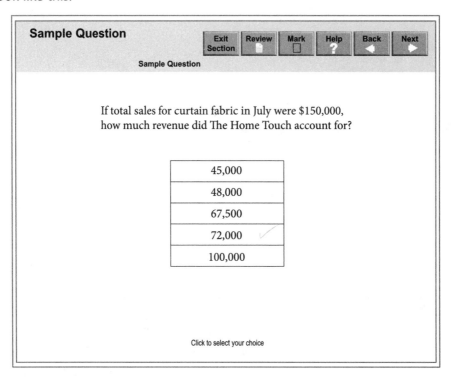

A Data Interpretation question that requires you to select all the answer choices that apply will look like this:

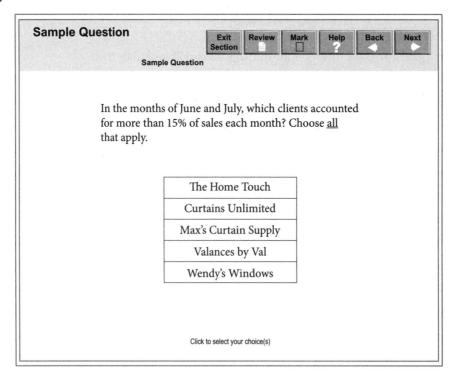

A Data Interpretation question that requires you to enter your numeric answer in a box will look like this:

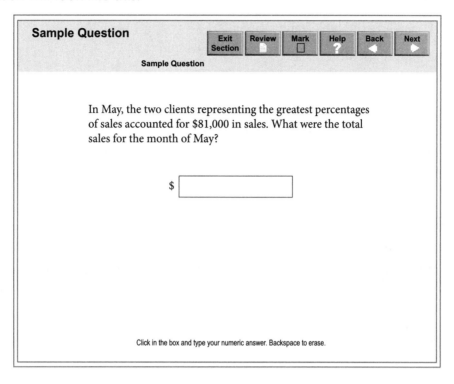

THE KAPLAN METHOD FOR DATA INTERPRETATION

STEP 1 **Analyze the tables and graphs.**

STEP 2 **Approach strategically.**

HOW THE KAPLAN METHOD FOR DATA INTERPRETATION WORKS

Now let's discuss how the Kaplan Method for Data Interpretation works.

⟫ STEP 1
Analyze the tables and graphs.

Tables, graphs, and charts often come in pairs that are linked in some way (for example: a manufacturer's total revenue and its revenue by product line). Familiarize yourself with the information in both graphs (or tables) and with how the two are related before attacking the questions. Scan the figures for these components:

- **Title**. Read the charts' titles to ensure you can get to the right chart or graph quickly.
- **Scale**. Check the units of measurement. Does the graph measure miles per minute or hour? Missing the units can drastically change your answer.
- **Notes**. Read any accompanying notes—the GRE will typically give you information only if it is helpful or even critical to getting the correct answer.
- **Key**. If there are multiple bars or lines on a graph, make sure you understand the key so you can match up the correct quantities with the correct items.

⟫ STEP 2
Approach strategically.

Data Interpretation questions are designed to test your understanding of fractions and percents and your attention to detail. Taking a split second to make sure you answered the right question can make the difference between a correct answer and a question answered wrong on a technicality.

Questions tend to become more complex as you move through a set. For instance, if a question set contains two graphs, the first question likely refers to just one graph. A later question will most often combine data from both graphs. If you don't use both graphs for this later question, the chances are good you have missed something.

No matter how difficult graph questions appear at first glance, you can usually simplify single-answer multiple-choice questions by taking advantage of their answer-choice format. By approximating the answer rather than calculating it wherever possible, you can quickly identify the right one. As we saw with Problem Solving, estimation is one of the fastest ways to solve math problems. Data Interpretation questions benefit from this strategy, as they tend to be the most time-consuming questions to answer.

HOW TO APPLY THE KAPLAN METHOD FOR DATA INTERPRETATION

Now let's apply the Kaplan Method to a Data Interpretation question:

Climograph of City S

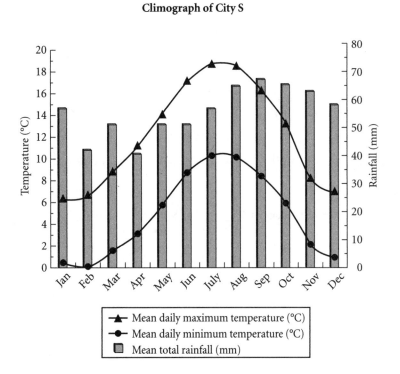

The Tourism Board of City S uses the information provided in the climograph to market the city as a tourist destination. One criterion is that the average monthly rainfall be less than 60 millimeters. What fraction of the months meets this criterion?

❯❯ STEP 1

Analyze the tables and graphs.

Take the analysis of the graph step-by-step. Start with the title of the graph to verify that the data given is for City S. Then take note of the scale for each type of information—degrees Celsius for temperature and millimeters for rainfall. There is data for each month of the year, which means you will not have to convert the units to answer the question that's being asked.

❯❯ STEP 2

Approach strategically.

The question asks only about rainfall; that data is given by the bars on the graph. According to the bars, rainfall is greater than 60 mm in Aug, Sep, Oct, and Nov. That's 4 of 12 months that *do not* meet the criteria, so 8 of 12 months *do* meet it. You may enter the fraction $\frac{8}{12}$ directly into the boxes, and your answer will be accepted. It is **not** required that you reduce it.

Now let's apply the Kaplan Method to a second Data Interpretation question:

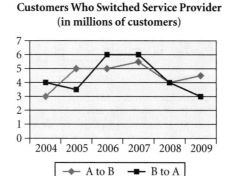

**Customers Who Switched Service Provider
(in millions of customers)**

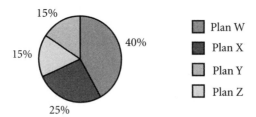

Company A Profit 2008

In 2008, Company A had a total profit of $220 million. If half of the customers who switched to Company A were responsible for half of the profit for Plan X, how much did those customers contribute per person towards Company A's profit for the year?

(A) $1.10

(B) $13.75

(C) $20.25

(D) $27.50

(E) $55.00

$$\frac{220 \times 0.25}{4}$$

STEP 1

Analyze the tables and graphs.

This question has information about numbers of customers switching service providers for various years. It also has information about one company's profit for the year 2008, so the data in the two graphs will be linked by the year 2008.

STEP 2

Approach strategically.

Approach the question methodically, starting with identifying the number of customers who switched to Company A. It indicates that 4 million customers switched to Company A. This is the only information needed from the top graph.

The pie chart shows the breakdown of profit from the various plans offered and indicates that 25% of the profit came from Plan X.

The other information you need to get to the correct answer is given in the question stem:

- Profit of $220 million
- Half of the customers who switched were responsible for half of Plan X's profits.

Now that your information is organized, all you need to do is the calculation. Plan X accounts for 25% of $220 million = $55 million. Half of $55 million is $27.5 million.

If 4 million people switched, then half of the people who switched would be 2 million.

The last step is to divide 27.5 by 2 (you can drop the zeroes in the millions because they will cancel out): $27.5 ÷ 2 = $13.75. The correct choice is **(B)**.

Now let's apply the Kaplan Method to a third Data Interpretation question:

**Customers Who Switched Service Provider
(in millions of customers)**

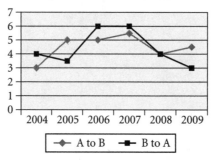

Company A Profit 2008

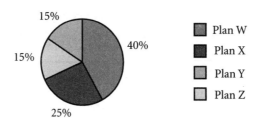

The management of Company B is most interested in the data for the years in which there were at least one million *more* customers who switched from Company A to Company B than switched from Company B to Company A. In which years did this happen?

Choose <u>all</u> that apply.

A 2005

B 2006

C 2007

D 2008

E 2009

❯ STEP 1

Analyze the tables and graphs.

This question asks for a comparison of facts between Company A and Company B. Take time to verify which line in the top graph represents customers switching to Company A and which line represents customers switching to Company B. Confirm that the title states that the data are given in millions and then look at the scale on the line graph.

❯ STEP 2

Approach strategically.

After examining the line graph carefully, you are ready to gather the information needed to answer the question. The years that satisfy the requirement are those years for which the line representing A to B is at least one full horizontal row above the line representing B to A. Read the graph carefully because you must identify all the correct choices to get credit for a correct answer.

When you are clear what to look for on the graph, start from the left and identify the years 2005 and 2009 as those in which at least one million more customers switched from A to B than switched from B to A. These are choices **(A)** and **(E)**.

KAPLAN'S ADDITIONAL TIPS FOR DATA INTERPRETATION QUESTIONS

Slow down

There's always a lot going on in Data Interpretation problems—both in the charts and in the questions themselves. If you slow down the first time through, you can avoid calculation errors and having to reread the questions and charts.

Pace Yourself Wisely

To ensure that you score as many points on the exam as possible, use the allotted time for a section wisely. Remember that each question type has the same value. If you must miss a few questions in a section, make them the ones that would take you the longest to answer, not the ones at the end of the section that you simply didn't get to, but could have answered correctly. Data Interpretation questions are generally some of the more time consuming ones to answer, and if answering them isn't one of your strong suits, save them for the end.

DATA INTERPRETATION PRACTICE SET

Try the following Data Interpretation questions using the Kaplan Method for Data Interpretation. If you're up to the challange, time yourself; on test day, you'll want to spend only about 2 minutes on each question.

Questions 1–5 are based on the following graphs.

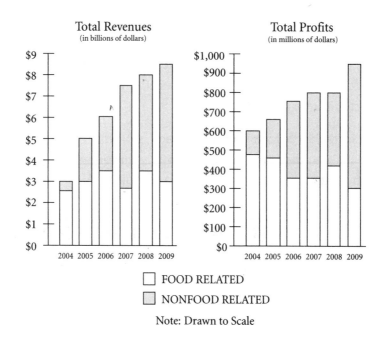

MEGACORP INC. REVENUE AND PROFIT DISTRIBUTION FOR FOOD AND NONFOOD RELATED OPERATIONS, 2004–2009

☐ FOOD RELATED
▨ NONFOOD RELATED

Note: Drawn to Scale

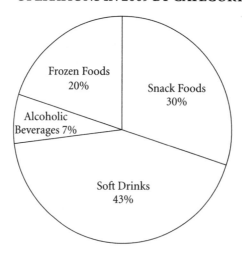

PERCENT OF REVENUES FROM FOOD–RELATED OPERATIONS IN 2009 BY CATEGORY

1. Approximately how much did total revenues increase from 2004 to 2007?

    Ⓐ $0.5 billion

    Ⓑ $1.5 billion

    Ⓒ $4 billion

    Ⓓ $4.5 billion

    Ⓔ $5 billion

2. For the year in which profits from food-related operations increased over the previous year, total revenues were approximately

    Ⓐ $3.5 billion.

    Ⓑ $4.5 billion.

    Ⓒ $5.7 billion.

    Ⓓ $6 billion.

    Ⓔ $8 billion.

3. In 2008, total profits represented approximately what percent of Megacorp's total revenues?

    Ⓐ 50%

    Ⓑ 20%

    Ⓒ 10%

    Ⓓ 5%

    Ⓔ 1%

4. For the first year in which revenues from nonfood-related operations surpassed $4.5 billion, total profits were approximately

    Ⓐ $250 million.

    Ⓑ $450 million.

    Ⓒ $550 million.

    Ⓓ $650 million.

    Ⓔ $800 million.

5. In 2009, how many millions of dollars were revenues from frozen food operations?

    | | millions of dollars

DATA INTERPRETATION PRACTICE SET ANSWERS AND EXPLANATIONS

1. D

This question asks about total revenues, so you should refer to the left bar graph. Each bar in the graph has two components, but you want to look at the total height of the bars for 2004 and 2007 because the question asks about total revenue. Total revenues for 2004 appear to be $3 billion, and for 2007 they appear to be about $7.5 billion. So the increase is roughly $7.5 billion − $3 billion = $4.5 billion. Answer choice **(D)** is correct.

2. E

You have to refer to both bar graphs to answer this question. First, refer to the right bar graph to find the lone year in which food-related profits increased over the previous year—the only year in which the unshaded portion of the bar increases in size is 2008. Now that you've zeroed in on the year, refer to the left bar graph to determine the total *revenues* for that year, which appear to be about $8 billion. Answer choice **(E)** is correct.

3. C

This is a percent question, so start with the bar graphs. You need the figures from both food-related and nonfood-related sources, so look at the total height of the bars. From the right bar graph, the total profits for 2008 appear to be $800 million; from the left bar graph, total revenues for that year appear to be $8 billion (i.e., $8,000 million). Now, convert the part/whole into a percent:

$$\frac{800 \text{ million}}{8 \text{ billion}} = \frac{800 \text{ million}}{8,000 \text{ million}} = \frac{1}{10} = 10\%$$

4. E

First, find the year for which revenues from nonfood-related operations surpassed $4.5 billion on the left bar graph. Finding the correct bar is made more difficult by the fact that you have to deal with the shaded portion, which is at the top of the bar, not at the bottom. Looking carefully, you should then see that 2007 is the year in question. The question asks for total *profits*, so once again refer to the right bar graph, and you'll see the profits for that year are around $800 million. This matches answer choice **(E)**.

5. 600

Finally, you have a question that refers to the pie chart. You are asked about revenues from frozen food operations, and the pie chart tells you that frozen foods represent 20 percent of all food-related revenues for 2009. To convert this into an amount, you need to locate the amount of food-related revenues for 2009. Once again, refer to the left bar graph, where you'll find that food-related revenues in 2009 were $3 billion, or $3,000 million. Then 20 percent of $3,000 million is **$600** million.

CHAPTER 14

Quantitative Reasoning Practice Set

In this section, you will take a practice test composed of 120 questions. This section has been divided into two parts to allow you to check your answers at the halfway mark. You will use a diagnostic tool at that point to help you learn from your mistakes and continue with more awareness of the traps you may encounter in the second set.

REVIEW OF THE KAPLAN METHOD FOR QUANTITATIVE REASONING QUESTION TYPES

Review the steps and strategies you have studied for answering each type of Quantitative Reasoning question quickly, efficiently, and correctly before starting your Practice Sets.

THE KAPLAN METHOD FOR QUANTITATIVE COMPARISONS

STEP 1   Analyze the centered information and quantities.

STEP 2   Approach strategically.

THE KAPLAN METHOD FOR PROBLEM SOLVING

STEP 1 Analyze the question.

STEP 2 Identify the task.

STEP 3 Approach strategically.

STEP 4 Confirm your answer.

THE KAPLAN METHOD FOR DATA INTERPRETATION

STEP 1 Analyze the tables and graphs.

STEP 2 Approach strategically.

QUANTITATIVE REASONING PRACTICE SET 1

NUMBERS

All numbers are real numbers.

FIGURES

The position of points, lines, angles, and so on may be assumed to be in the order shown; all lengths and angle measures may be assumed to be positive.

Lines shown as straight may be assumed to be straight.

Figures lie in the plane of the paper unless otherwise stated.

Figures that accompany questions are intended to provide useful information. However, unless a note states that a figure has been drawn to scale, you should solve the problems by using your knowledge of mathematics, not by estimation or measurement.

DIRECTIONS

Each of the following questions, 1–20, consists of two quantities, Quantity A and Quantity B. You are to compare the two quantities and choose

    Ⓐ if Quantity A is greater.

    Ⓑ if Quantity B is greater.

    Ⓒ if the two quantities are equal.

    Ⓓ if the relationship cannot be determined from the information given.

COMMON INFORMATION

In a question, information concerning one or both of the quantities to be compared is centered above the two quantities. A symbol that appears in both quantities represents the same thing in Quantity A as it does in Quantity B.

1. | Quantity A | Quantity B |

    The number of ways 6 people can be arranged in a line of 3 people where order matters.

    The number of ways 10 people can be arranged in a line of 3 people where order does not matter.

    Ⓐ Quantity A is greater.

    Ⓑ Quantity B is greater.

    Ⓒ The two quantities are equal.

    Ⓓ The relationship cannot be determined from the information given.

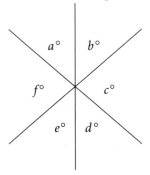

2. | Quantity A | Quantity B |
    | $a + c + e$ | $b + d + f$ |

    Ⓐ Quantity A is greater.

    Ⓑ Quantity B is greater.

    Ⓒ The two quantities are equal.

    Ⓓ The relationship cannot be determined from the information given.

$$7p + 3 = r$$
$$3p + 7 = s$$

3. | Quantity A | Quantity B |
    | r | s |

    Ⓐ Quantity A is greater.

    Ⓑ Quantity B is greater.

    Ⓒ The two quantities are equal.

    Ⓓ The relationship cannot be determined from the information given.

The original cost of a shirt is x dollars.

4. | Quantity A | Quantity B |
    | x | A 10% increase of x followed by a 10% decrease |

    Ⓐ Quantity A is greater.

    Ⓑ Quantity B is greater.

    Ⓒ The two quantities are equal.

    Ⓓ The relationship cannot be determined from the information given.

There are x dictionaries in a bookstore. After $\frac{1}{8}$ of them were purchased, 10 more dictionaries were shipped in, bringing the total number of dictionaries to 52.

5.
Quantity A	Quantity B
x	50

Ⓐ Quantity A is greater.

Ⓑ Quantity B is greater.

Ⓒ The two quantities are equal.

Ⓓ The relationship cannot be determined from the information given.

There are n people in a room. One third of them leave the room. Four people enter the room. There are now $\frac{5}{6}$ of the original number of people in the room.

6.
Quantity A	Quantity B
n	20

Ⓐ Quantity A is greater.

Ⓑ Quantity B is greater.

Ⓒ The two quantities are equal.

Ⓓ The relationship cannot be determined from the information given.

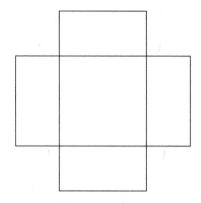

Two rectangles with dimensions 2 meters by 4 meters overlap to form the figure above. All the angles shown measure 90°.

7.
Quantity A	Quantity B
The perimeter of the figure, in meters	16

Ⓐ Quantity A is greater.

Ⓑ Quantity B is greater.

Ⓒ The two quantities are equal.

Ⓓ The relationship cannot be determined from the information given.

x is an integer.
$1 < x < 9$

8.
Quantity A	Quantity B
$(\sqrt{x} + \sqrt{x})^2$	$x + x\sqrt{x}$

Ⓐ Quantity A is greater.

Ⓑ Quantity B is greater.

Ⓒ The two quantities are equal.

Ⓓ The relationship cannot be determined from the information given.

9. | Quantity A | Quantity B |
    |---|---|
    | The average (arithmetic mean) of 100, 101, and 103 | The median of 100, 101, and 103 |

Ⓐ Quantity A is greater.

Ⓑ Quantity B is greater.

Ⓒ The two quantities are equal.

Ⓓ The relationship cannot be determined from the information given.

A and *B* are points on the circumference of the circle with center *O* (not shown). The length of chord *AB* is 15.

10. | Quantity A | Quantity B |
    |---|---|
    | Circumference of circle *O* | 12π |

Ⓐ Quantity A is greater.

Ⓑ Quantity B is greater.

Ⓒ The two quantities are equal.

Ⓓ The relationship cannot be determined from the information given.

$$x = \frac{4}{3} r^2 h^2$$

$$x = 1$$

r and *h* are positive.

11. | Quantity A | Quantity B |
    |---|---|
    | h | $\frac{\sqrt{3}}{2r}$ |

Ⓐ Quantity A is greater.

Ⓑ Quantity B is greater.

Ⓒ The two quantities are equal.

Ⓓ The relationship cannot be determined from the information given.

$\triangle ABC$ lies in the *xy*-plane with *C* at (0, 0), *B* at (6, 0), and *A* at (*x*, *y*), where *x* and *y* are positive. The area of $\triangle ABC$ is 18.

12. | Quantity A | Quantity B |
    |---|---|
    | y | 6 |

Ⓐ Quantity A is greater.

Ⓑ Quantity B is greater.

Ⓒ The two quantities are equal.

Ⓓ The relationship cannot be determined from the information given.

$$\text{For } x \neq y, \, x \, \Phi \, y = \frac{x + y}{x - y}$$
$$p > 0 > q$$

13. | Quantity A | Quantity B |
       |------------|------------|
       | $p \, \Phi \, q$ | $q \, \Phi \, p$ |

Ⓐ Quantity A is greater.

Ⓑ Quantity B is greater.

Ⓒ The two quantities
   are equal.

Ⓓ The relationship cannot
   be determined from the
   information given.

$$x \neq 0$$

14. | Quantity A | Quantity B |
       |------------|------------|
       | $\dfrac{1}{x} + \dfrac{1}{x}$ | $\dfrac{1}{x} \times \dfrac{1}{x}$ |

Ⓐ Quantity A is greater.

Ⓑ Quantity B is greater.

Ⓒ The two quantities
   are equal.

Ⓓ The relationship cannot
   be determined from the
   information given.

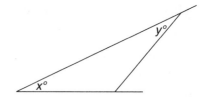

15. | Quantity A | Quantity B |
       |------------|------------|
       | $x + y$ | 180 |

Ⓐ Quantity A is greater.

Ⓑ Quantity B is greater.

Ⓒ The two quantities
   are equal.

Ⓓ The relationship cannot
   be determined from the
   information given.

$$4x - 5y = 10$$
$$-3x + 6y = 22$$

16. | Quantity A | Quantity B |
       |------------|------------|
       | 33 | $x + y$ |

Ⓐ Quantity A is greater.

Ⓑ Quantity B is greater.

Ⓒ The two quantities
   are equal.

Ⓓ The relationship cannot
   be determined from the
   information given.

The diameter of a circle is equal to a diagonal of a square with side 4.

17. | Quantity A | Quantity B |
The circumference of the circle | $20\sqrt{2}$

Ⓐ Quantity A is greater.

Ⓑ Quantity B is greater.

Ⓒ The two quantities are equal.

Ⓓ The relationship cannot be determined from the information given.

$$x < y < z$$
$$0 < z$$

18. | Quantity A | Quantity B |
x | 0

Ⓐ Quantity A is greater.

Ⓑ Quantity B is greater.

Ⓒ The two quantities are equal.

Ⓓ The relationship cannot be determined from the information given.

$$6(10)^n > 60,006$$

19. | Quantity A | Quantity B |
n | 6

Ⓐ Quantity A is greater.

Ⓑ Quantity B is greater.

Ⓒ The two quantities are equal.

Ⓓ The relationship cannot be determined from the information given.

In a three-digit positive integer y, the hundreds digit is three times the units digit.

20. | Quantity A | Quantity B |
The units digits of y | 4

Ⓐ Quantity A is greater.

Ⓑ Quantity B is greater.

Ⓒ The two quantities are equal.

Ⓓ The relationship cannot be determined from the information given.

21. What is the average (arithmetic mean) of $2x + 3$, $5x - 4$, $6x - 6$, and $3x - 1$?

Ⓐ $2x + 4$

Ⓑ $3x - 2$

Ⓒ $3x + 2$

Ⓓ $4x - 2$

Ⓔ $4x + 2$

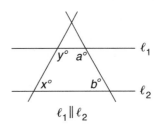

22. Which of the following statements must be true about the figure shown above?

Ⓐ $x = a$

Ⓑ $x = b$

Ⓒ $a = b$

Ⓓ $y = b$

Ⓔ $x + y = a + b$

23. If $\frac{x}{y} = \frac{2}{3}$ and $x + y = 5$, which of the following is greater than y?

    Indicate <u>all</u> possible choices.

    A $\sqrt{2}$

    B $\sqrt{10}$

    C $\sqrt{24}$

    D $\sqrt{35}$

    E $\sqrt{43}$

24. The product of two integers is 10. Which of the following could be the average (arithmetic mean) of the two numbers?

    Indicate <u>all</u> possible choices.

    A -5.5

    B -3.5

    C -1.5

    D 1.5

    E 3.5

25. Which number is greater than the sum of all the prime factors of 210?

    Indicate <u>all</u> possible choices.

    A 12

    B 17

    C 19

    D 21

    E 24

26. The average (arithmetic mean) bowling score of n bowlers is 160. The average of these n scores together with a score of 170 is 161. What is the number of bowlers, n?

    ☐ bowlers

27. Which of the following are even integers?

    Indicate <u>all</u> possible choices.

    A The sum of two odd integers

    B The product of two odd integers

    C The product of an even integer and an odd integer

    D The product of two even integers

    E The sum of an even integer and an odd integer

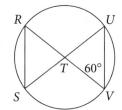

28. The circle shown has center T. The measure of angle TVU is 60°. If the circle has a radius of 3, what is the length of segment RS?

    Ⓐ 2

    Ⓑ $2\sqrt{2}$

    Ⓒ 3

    Ⓓ $3\sqrt{3}$

    Ⓔ $6\sqrt{2}$

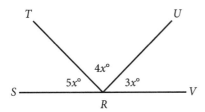

29. What is the degree measure of angle *TRV*?

   Ⓐ   45

   Ⓑ   60

   Ⓒ   75

   Ⓓ   105

   Ⓔ   135

30. There are at least 200 apples in a grocery store. The ratio of the number of oranges to the number of apples is 9 to 10. How many oranges could there be in the store?

Indicate <u>all</u> possible numbers.

   Ⓐ   171

   Ⓑ   180

   Ⓒ   216

   Ⓓ   252

   Ⓔ   315

31. What is the probability of rolling a 7 with a single roll of two fair dice?

   Ⓐ $\frac{1}{12}$

   Ⓑ $\frac{1}{6}$

   Ⓒ $\frac{2}{7}$

   Ⓓ $\frac{1}{3}$

   Ⓔ $\frac{1}{2}$

32. If it takes three days for 10 workers to finish building one house, how many days will it take 15 workers to finish four houses?

   ☐   days

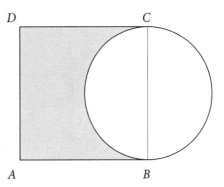

33. In the above square *ABCD*, the side *AB* has a length of 4. It is overlaid with a circle, with a diameter *BC*. Which of the following are greater than or equal to the area of the shaded region?

Indicate <u>all</u> such amounts.

   Ⓐ $16 - 16\pi$

   Ⓑ $16 - 4\pi$

   Ⓒ $16 - 2\pi$

   Ⓓ $16 + \pi$

   Ⓔ $16 + 4\pi$

34. If $A \blacklozenge B = \dfrac{A + B}{B}$, and $C \clubsuit = C + 3$, what is the value of $(9\clubsuit) \blacklozenge 3$?

   ☐

35. Rectangle *A* has a length of 12 inches and a width of 5 inches. Rectangle *B* has a length of 9 inches and a width of 10 inches. By what number must the area of rectangle *A* be multiplied in order to get the area of rectangle *B*?

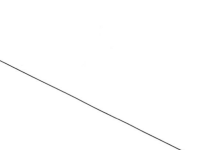

36. In right triangle *ABC* above, side *AB* has a length of 5, while side *BC* has a length of 13. What is the number of square units for the area of *ABC*?

square units

37. If the average test score of four students is 85, which of the following could the fifth student score in order to have the new average be greater than 84 and less than 86?

Indicate all such scores.

A   88
B   86
C   85
D   83
E   80

38. Meg is twice as old as Rolf, but three years ago, she was two years older than Rolf is now. How old is Rolf now?

years old

39. The cost, in cents, of manufacturing *x* crayons is 570 + 0.5*x*. The crayons sell for 10 cents each. What number of crayons would need to be sold so that the revenue received is at least equal to the manufacturing cost?

Indicate all such numbers.

A   50
B   57
C   60
D   61
E   95

40. If $xy \neq 0$, $\dfrac{1 - x}{xy} =$

Ⓐ $\dfrac{1}{xy} - \dfrac{1}{y}$

Ⓑ $\dfrac{x}{y} - \dfrac{1}{x}$

Ⓒ $\dfrac{1}{xy} - 1$

Ⓓ $\dfrac{1}{xy} - \dfrac{x^2}{y}$

Ⓔ $\dfrac{1}{x} - \dfrac{1}{y}$

Questions 41–45 are based on the following graphs.

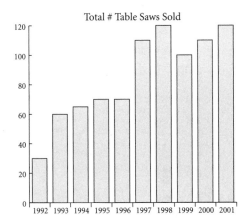

Total # Table Saws Sold

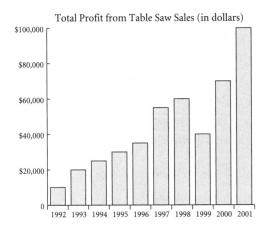

Total Profit from Table Saw Sales (in dollars)

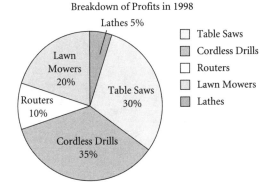

Breakdown of Profits in 1998

41. In 1998, what were the total profits from sales of all the hardware tools?

   $ [_____]

42. Which year had the greatest percentage increase in number of table saws sold from the previous year?

   (A) 1993

   (B) 1995

   (C) 1997

   (D) 2000

   (E) 2001

43. Of the following, what is the closest to the percentage change in profits from table saws between 1998 and 1999?

   (A) A 50% increase

   (B) A 33% increase

   (C) A 17% decrease

   (D) A 33% decrease

   (E) A 50% decrease

44. If the fixed cost of manufacturing table saws in 1993 was $22,000, how much did each table saw sell for?

   $ [_____]

45. In 1998, what were the approximate profits from the sales of cordless drills?

   (A) $50,000

   (B) $70,000

   (C) $80,000

   (D) $90,000

   (E) $100,000

Questions 46–49 are based on the following graph and table.

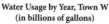

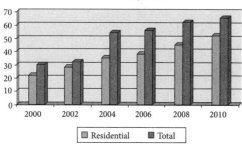

Water Usage by Year, Town W
(in billions of gallons)

□ Residential ■ Total

Daily Water Usage Statistics
(with Efficient Appliances and
Good Maintenance)

Use	Gallons per capita
Showers	9
Clothes Washers	10
Toilets	8
Leaks	4
Faucets	11
Other	4

46. Which best describes the range (in billions of gallons) for residential water consumption for the time period indicated?

   (A) 10

   (B) 20

   (C) 30

   (D) 40

   (E) 50

47. For the year in which total consumption exceeded residential consumption by the least number of gallons, approximately what percent did the residential usage comprise of the total usage?

   (A) 68%

   (B) 75%

   (C) 88%

   (D) 95%

   (E) 98%

48. In 2004, only 10,000 residents lived in homes with efficient appliances and good maintenance of the plumbing. How many gallons per day were used by these residents for the three purposes requiring the most water?

   (A) 110,000

   (B) 160,000

   (C) 270,000

   (D) 300,000

   (E) 460,000

49. Households with efficient appliances and good maintenance of plumbing fixtures can reduce water consumption by about 35%. If approximately half of the residential consumption in 2010 was by households with these characteristics, how many billions of gallons of water were saved that year?

   (A) 5
   (B) 14
   (C) 40
   (D) 52
   (E) 65

Questions 50–56 are based on the following graph.

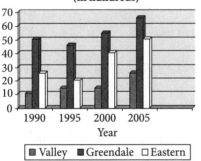

Enrollment at Three Community Colleges, 1990–2005 (in hundreds)

50. For the year in which the ratio was the highest, what was the ratio of the enrollment at Greendale to the enrollment at Valley?

   (A) 6:1
   (B) 5:1
   (C) 4:1
   (D) 3:1
   (E) 2:1

51. What was the total enrollment (in hundreds) for the three colleges in 2000?

   (A) 110
   (B) 125
   (C) 135
   (D) 140
   (E) 150

52. Which enrollment showed the greatest increase over the years shown?

   (A) Valley between 2000 and 2005
   (B) Greendale between 1995 and 2000
   (C) Greendale between 2000 and 2005
   (D) Eastern between 1995 and 2000
   (E) Eastern between 2000 and 2005

53. Expenses at the three colleges have shown the same percent increase between 2000 and 2005 as the percent increase in enrollment. Approximately what is that percent?

   (A) 10%
   (B) 21%
   (C) 27%
   (D) 36%
   (E) 40%

54. To the nearest hundred, what was the average (arithmetic mean) enrollment in 1995 at the three colleges?

  (A) 1,000
  (B) 1,500
  (C) 2,700
  (D) 80,000
  (E) 85,000

55. Valley and Greendale have plans to combine into one college in the future to make better use of their resources. If the 2005 combined student to faculty ratio of 9:1 remains the same, how many faculty members will be needed for the new college, based on current enrollment?

  [   ] faculty

56. The projected enrollment at Eastern in the next academic year is 6,200 students. What percent increase will that be over the enrollment in 2005?

  (A) 12%
  (B) 15%
  (C) 18%
  (D) 20%
  (E) 24%

Question 57–60 refer to the following graphs:

Team Revenues for 1997

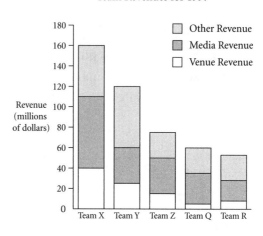

Percentages of Venue
Revenues for Team X, 1997

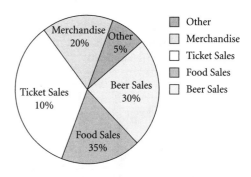

57. For the team with the median amount of venue revenue for 1997, media revenue represented approximately what percent of that team's total revenue for that year?

  (A) 25%
  (B) 30%
  (C) 40%
  (D) 55%
  (E) 60%

58. Of the following, which is greater than the amount of revenue, in millions of dollars, earned by Team *X* through food sales in 1997?

Indicate <u>all</u> such amounts.

[A]   7

[B]   10

[C]   14

[D]   18

[E]   22

59. In 1997, which teams had media revenues less than $25 million?

Indicate <u>all</u> such teams.

[A]   Team X

[B]   Team Y

[C]   Team Z

[D]   Team Q

[E]   Team R

60. If Team Y earned a total revenue of $150 million or greater in 1998, Team Y's total revenue increased by approximately what percent from 1997 to 1998?

Indicate <u>all</u> such percents.

[A]   20%

[B]   25%

[C]   30%

[D]   35%

[E]   40%

ANSWERS AND EXPLANATIONS

1. C	16. A	31. B	46. C
2. C	17. B	32. 8	47. C
3. D	18. D	33. C, D, E	48. D
4. A	19. D	34. 5	49. B
5. B	20. B	35. 1.5	50. B
6. A	21. D	36. 30	51. A
7. C	22. E	37. A, B, C, D	52. D
8. A	23. B, C, D, E	38. 5	53. C
9. A	24. A, B, E	39. C, D, E	54. C
10. A	25. C, D, E	40. A	55. 1000
11. C	26. 9	41. 200,000	56. E
12. C	27. A, C, D	42. A	57. C
13. D	28. C	43. D	58. D, E
14. D	29. D	44. 700	59 E
15. B	30. B, C, D, E	45. B	60. B, C, D, E

Diagnostic Tool

Tally up your score and write your results below.

Total

Total Correct: _____ out of 60 correct

By Question Type

Quantitative Comparisons (questions 1–20)_____ out of 20 correct
Problem Solving (questions 21–40) _____ out of 20 correct
Data Interpretations (questions 41–60)_____ out of 20 correct

DIAGNOSE YOUR RESULTS

Look back at the questions you got wrong and think about your experience answering them.

▶ STEP 1
Find the Road Blocks

If you struggled to answer some questions, to improve your score you need to pinpoint exactly what "road blocks" tripped you up. To do that, ask yourself the following two questions.

Am I weak in the skills being tested?

This will be very easy for you to judge. Maybe you've forgotten how to figure out the area of a triangle or what PEMDAS stands for. If you know you need to brush up on your math skills, try the *Kaplan GRE Exam Math Workbook*, which contains a focused review of all the fundamental math concepts tested on the GRE, as well as practice exercises to build speed and accuracy.

Was it the question types that threw me off?

Then you need to become more comfortable with them! Quantitative Comparisons have a unique format, and Data Interpretation questions can be daunting with their charts, graphs, and tables. If this was a problem for you, go back to the beginning of this chapter and review the Kaplan principles and methods for the question types you struggled with. Make sure you understand the principles and how to apply the methods. These strategies help to improve your speed and efficiency on test day. Remember, it's not a math test; it's a critical-reasoning test.

Also, get as much practice as you can so that you grow more at ease with the question formats. For even more practice, try the *Kaplan GRE Exam Math Workbook*, which includes practice sets for each question type.

STEP 2
Find the Blind Spots

Did you answer some questions quickly and confidently but get them wrong anyway?

When you come across wrong answers like these, you need to figure out what you thought you were doing right, what it turns out you were doing wrong, and why that happened. The best way to do that is to **read the answer explanations!**

The explanations give you a detailed breakdown of why the correct answer is correct and why all the other answers choices are wrong. This helps to reinforce the Kaplan principles and methods for each question type and helps you figure out what blind-sided you so it doesn't happen again. Also, just as with your "roadblocks," try to get in as much practice as you can.

STEP 3
Reinforce Your Strengths

Now read through all the answer explanations for the ones you got right. Again, this helps to reinforce the Kaplan principles and methods for each question type, which in turn helps you work more efficiently so you can get the score you want. Keep your skills sharp with more practice.

As soon as you are comfortable with all the GRE question types and Kaplan methods, complete a full-length practice test under timed conditions. Practice tests serve as milestones; they help you to chart your progress! So don't save them all for the final weeks before your test day. For even more practice, you can also try the Kaplan GRE Quiz Bank. You get more than 1,000 questions that you can access 24/7 from any Internet browser, each with comprehensive explanations. You can even customize your quizzes based on question type, content, and difficulty level. Take quizzes in Timed Mode to test your stamina or in Tutor Mode to see explanations as you work. Best of all, you also get detailed reports to track your progress.

Visit **kaplanGRE.com** for more details on our Quiz Bank and for more information on our other online and classroom-based options. If the Quantitative Reasoning section is where you need the most help, you should check out the new Kaplan course, GRE Math Advantage—Anywhere. It's available online anywhere you are, and you can get live instruction from an expert Kaplan GRE teacher.

1. C

Quantity A is a permutation because order matters. The number of ways 6 people can be arranged in a line of 3 people where order matters is $6 \times 5 \times 4 = 120$. Quantity B is a combination because order does not matter. The number of ways 10 people can be arranged in a line of 3 people where order does not matter is $_{10}C_3 = \dfrac{10!}{3!(10-3)!} = \dfrac{10 \times 9 \times 8}{3 \times 2 \times 1} = \dfrac{720}{6} = 120$. The two quantities are equal.

2. C

There are three sets of vertical angles in this diagram: (a, d), (b, e), and (c, f). In Quantity A, you can substitute b for e because they are vertical angles and therefore equal; this leaves the sum $a + b + c$ in Quantity A. Because these are the three angles on one side of a straight line, they sum to 180. Similarly, after substituting e for b in Quantity B, $b + d + f$ is the same thing as $d + e + f$, or also 180. The two quantities are equal.

3. D

Pick a value for p and see what effect it has on r and s. If $p = 1$, $r = (7 \times 1) + 3 = 10$, and $s = (3 \times 1) + 7 = 10$, and the two columns are equal. But if $p = 0$, $r = (7 \times 0) + 3 = 3$, and $s = (3 \times 0) + 7 = 7$, and Column A is less than Column B. Because there are at least two different possible relationships, the answer is **(D)**.

4. A

Use the Picking Numbers strategy to answer this question. Suppose the original selling price of the shirt, x, is $100. After a 10% increase in price, the shirt would sell for 110% of $100, which is $110. If there is a 10% decrease next, the shirt would sell for 90% of the current price. That would be 90% of $110: $0.9 \times \$110 = \$99$. This price is less than the original amount, x, so Quantity A is greater.

5. B

Try to set the quantities equal. If *x* is 50, then the bookstore started out with 50 dictionaries. Then $\frac{1}{8}$ of them were purchased. You can see already that the quantities can't be equal, because $\frac{1}{8}$ of 50 won't yield an integer. But go ahead and see whether the answer is **(A)** or **(B)**. Because $\frac{1}{8}$ of 50 is close to 6, after these dictionaries were purchased, the store would have been left with about 50 − 6 or 44 dictionaries. Then it received 10 more, giving a total of about 54 dictionaries. But this is more than the store actually ended up with; it only had 52. Therefore, it must have started with *fewer* than 50 dictionaries, and Quantity B is greater. (The last thing you care about is how many dictionaries it really had.)

6. A

There are *n* people in a room. One third of them leave the room. So, there are $n - \frac{1}{3}n$ people in the room. Four people enter the room, so you have $n - \frac{1}{3}n + 4$ people. There are now $\frac{5}{6}$ of the original number of people in the room, therefore $n - \frac{1}{3}n + 4 = \frac{5}{6}n$. Now solve for *n*.

$$n - \frac{1}{3}n + 4 = \frac{5}{6}n$$

$$\frac{2}{3}n + 4 = \frac{5}{6}n$$

$$4 = \frac{5}{6}n - \frac{2}{3}n$$

$$4 = \frac{5}{6}n - \frac{4}{6}n$$

$$4 = \frac{1}{6}n$$

$$n = 24$$

So, *n* = 24 and Quantity A is larger.

7. C

You may have thought this was a choice **(D)** question; after all, you don't know exactly where the boards overlap, whether in the middle of each board, as pictured, or near the end of one of the boards. But that doesn't matter; all you need to know is that they overlap and that all the angles are right angles. If the boards did not overlap, it would be easy to find the perimeter: 2 + 2 + 4 + 4 = 12 for each board, or 24 for both boards. Now, because the boards do overlap, the perimeter of the figure will be smaller than that, but how much smaller? It will be smaller by the amount of that "lost perimeter" in the middle; the perimeter of the square where the boards overlap. (You know it's a square, since all the angles are right angles.) The length of a side of that square is the shorter dimension of each of the boards: 2. Therefore, the perimeter of the square is 4 × 2 or 8. The perimeter of the figure, then, is 24 − 8 or 16. The two quantities are equal.

8. A

Start by simplifying the quantity in Quantity A: $(\sqrt{x}+\sqrt{x})^2$ is the same as $(2\sqrt{x})^2$, which is $4x$. Subtract x from both quantities, and you're left with $3x$ in Quantity A and $x\sqrt{x}$ in Quantity B. Now divide both sides by x, and you're left with 3 in Quantity A and $\sqrt{x}$ in Quantity B. Square both quantities, and you get 9 in Quantity A and x in Quantity B. Since x is an integer between 1 and 9, Quantity A is larger. If the algebra seems too abstract, go ahead and Pick a Number between 1 and 9. This will show that Quantity A is larger.

9. A

This question requires no computation but only a general understanding of how averages work and what the word *median* means. The median of a group of numbers is the "middle number"; it is the value above which half of the numbers in the group fall and below which the other half fall. If you have an even number of values, the median is the average of the two "middle" numbers; if you have an odd number of values, the median is one of the values. Here, in Quantity B, the median is 101. In Quantity A, if the numbers were 100, 101, and 102, then the average would also be 101, but because the third number, 103, is greater than 102, then the average must be greater than 101. Quantity A is greater than 101, and Quantity B equals 101; Quantity A is larger.

10. A

Start with the information you are given. You know that the length of the chord is 15. What does that mean? Well, because you don't know exactly where A and B are, that doesn't mean too much, but it does tell you that the distance between two points on the circle is 15. That tells you that the diameter must be at least 15. If the diameter were less than 15, then you couldn't have a chord that was equal to 15, because the diameter is always the longest chord in a circle. The diameter of the circle is 15 or greater, so the circumference must be at least 15π. That means that Quantity A must be larger than Quantity B.

11. C

This looks like a complex equation, but we'll take it one step at a time. Because Quantity A has only h in it, solve the equation for h, leaving h on one side of the equal sign and r on the other side. First substitute the value for x into the equation, then solve for h in terms of r.

$x = \frac{4}{3}r^2h^2$	Substitute 1 for x.
$1 = \frac{4}{3}r^2h^2$	Divide both sides by $\frac{4}{3}$.
$\frac{3}{4} = r^2h^2$	Take the positive square root of both sides, using the information that r and h are positive.
$\frac{\sqrt{3}}{2} = rh$	Divide both sides by r to get h alone.
$h = \frac{\sqrt{3}}{2r}$	The two quantities are equal.

12. C

Draw an *xy*-plane and label the points given to help solve this problem. You know where points *B* and *C* are; they're on the *x*-axis. You don't know where *A* is, however, which may make you think that the answer is choice **(D).** But you're given more information: you know that the triangle has an area of 18. The area of any triangle is one-half the product of the base and the height. Make side *BC* the base of the triangle; you know the coordinates of both points, so you can find their distance apart, which is the length of that side. *C* is at the origin, the point (0, 0); *B* is at the point (6, 0). The distance between them is the distance from 0 to 6 along the *x*-axis, or just 6. So that's the base. What about the height? Because you know that the area is 18, you can plug what you know into the area formula.

$$\text{Area} = \frac{1}{2} \times \text{base} \times \text{height}$$

$$18 = \frac{1}{2} \times 6 \times \text{height}$$

$$\text{height} = \frac{18}{3}$$

$$\text{height} = 6$$

That's the other dimension of the triangle. The height is the distance between the *x*-axis and point *A*. Now you know that *A* must be somewhere in the first quadrant, since both the *x*- and *y*-coordinates are positive. Don't worry about the *x*-coordinate of the point, because that's not what's being compared; you care only about the value of *y*. You know that the distance from the *x*-axis to the point is 6, because that's the height of the triangle, and that *y* must be positive. Therefore, the *y*-coordinate of the point must be 6. That's what the *y*-coordinate is: a measure of the point's vertical distance from the *x*-axis. (Note that if you hadn't been told that *y* was positive, there would be two possible values for *y*: 6 and −6. A point that's 6 units below the *x*-axis would also give a triangle with height 6.) You still don't know the *x*-coordinate of the point, and in fact you can't figure that out, but you don't care. You know that *y* is 6; therefore, the two quantities are equal.

13. D

With symbolism problems like this, it sometimes helps to put the definition of the symbol into words. For this symbol, you can say something like "*x* Φ *y* means take the sum of the two numbers and divide that by the difference of the two numbers." One good way to do this problem is to Pick Numbers. You know that *p* is positive and *q* is negative. So suppose *p* is 1 and *q* is −1. Figure out what *p* Φ *q* is first. You start by taking the sum of the numbers, or 1 + (−1) = 0. That's the numerator of the fraction, and you don't really need to go any further than that. Whatever their difference is, because the numerator is 0, the whole fraction must equal 0. (The difference can't be 0 also, since *p* ≠ *q*.) So that's *p* Φ *q*. Now what about *q* Φ *p*? Well, that's going to have the same numerator as *p* Φ *q*: 0. The only thing that changes when you reverse the order of the numbers is the denominator of the fraction. So *q* Φ *p* has a numerator of 0, and that fraction must equal 0 as well.

So you've found a case where the quantities are equal. Try another set of values and see whether the quantities are always equal. If $p = 1$ and $q = -2$, then the sum of the numbers is $1 + (-2)$ or -1. So that's the numerator of the fraction in each Quantity. Now for the denominator of $p \, \Phi \, q$, you need $p - q = 1 - (-2) = 1 + 2 = 3$. Then the value of $p \, \Phi \, q$ is $\frac{-1}{3}$. The denominator of $q \, \Phi \, p$ is $q - p = -2 - 1 = -3$. In that case, the value of $q \, \Phi \, p$ is $\frac{-1}{-3}$ or $\frac{1}{3}$. The quantities are different; therefore, the answer is **(D)**.

14. D
Picking Numbers will help you solve this problem. For $x = 1$, $\frac{1}{x} + \frac{1}{x} = \frac{1}{1} + \frac{1}{1} = 2$ and $\frac{1}{x} \times \frac{1}{x} = \frac{1}{1} \times \frac{1}{1} = 1$, so Quantity A is larger. For $x = -1$, $\frac{1}{x} + \frac{1}{x} = \frac{1}{-1} + \frac{1}{-1} = -2$ and $\frac{1}{x} \times \frac{1}{x} = \frac{1}{-1} \times \frac{1}{-1} = 1$, so Quantity B is larger. The quantities are different; therefore, the answer is **(D)**.

15. B

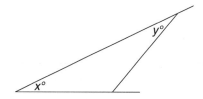

The sum of the three interior angles of a triangle is 180°. Because x and y are only two of the angles, their sum must be less than 180°. Quantity B is greater.

16. A
For the system of equations $4x - 5y = 10$ and $-3x + 6y = 22$, it is not necessary to solve for the values of x and y. Rather, you want to know about the sum of x and y. Notice what happens when you add the two equations.

$$4x - 5y = 10$$
$$\underline{-3x + 6y = 22}$$
$$x + y = 32$$

Because $x + y = 32$ and $33 > 32$, Quantity A is larger.

17. B
The diagonal of a square of side 4 is $4\sqrt{2}$. The circumference of a circle is π times the diameter. So, the circumference of this circle is $4\sqrt{2}\pi$. Now write Quantity B, $20\sqrt{2}$, as $4(5)\sqrt{2}$ and you can compare the quantities piece by piece. The factors of 4 and $\sqrt{2}$ are the same in both quantities, but π is less than 5. So, Quantity B is larger.

18. D
You could Pick Numbers here or else just use logic. You know that z is positive and that x and y are less than z. But does that mean that x or y must be negative? Not at all—they

could be, but they could also be positive. For instance, suppose $x = 1$, $y = 2$, and $z = 3$. Then Quantity A would be larger. However, if $x = -1$, $y = 0$, and $z = 1$, then Quantity B would be larger. You need more information to determine the relationship between the quantities. The answer is **(D)**.

19. D

Divide both sides of the inequality by 6. You're left with $(10)^n > 10,001$. 10,001 can also be written as $10^4 + 1$, so you know that $(10)^n > 10^4 + 1$. Therefore, Quantity A, n, must be 5 or greater. Quantity B is 6. Because n could be less than, equal to, or greater than 6, you need more information.

20. B

Try to set the quantities equal. Could the units digit of y be 4? If it is, and the hundreds digit is three times the units digit, then the hundreds' digit must be . . . 12? That can't be right. A digit must be one of the integers 0 through 9; 12 isn't a digit. Therefore, 4 is too big to be the units digit of y. You don't know what the units digit of y is, but you know that it must be less than 4. Quantity B is greater than Quantity A.

21. D

To find the average, add the quantities together and divide by 4. $(2x + 3) + (5x - 4)$ $+ (6x - 6) + (3x - 1) = 16x - 8$ and $\frac{16x - 8}{4} = 4x - 2$. The correct choice is **(D)**.

22. E

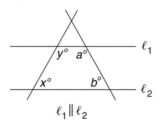

$\ell_1 \parallel \ell_2$

When a transversal cuts a pair of parallel lines, in this case ℓ_1 and ℓ_2, the angles are always supplementary and their sum is 180. So, the sum $(x + y)$ is equal to the sum $(a + b)$. The exact values of the individual angle measures cannot be determined from the figure. The answer is **(E)**.

23. B, C, D, E

If $\frac{x}{y} = \frac{2}{3}$, then $3x = 2y$ and $y = \frac{3x}{2}$. Substitute $y = \frac{3x}{2}$ into the equation $x + y = 5$. $x + \frac{3x}{2}$ $= 5$, $2x + 3x = 10$, $5x = 10$, $x = 2$. Then, $y = \frac{3x}{2} = \frac{3(2)}{3} = 3$ and $y^2 = 9$. So any number greater than 9 under the radical will be greater than y. Therefore, the correct choices are **(B)**, **(C)**, **(D)**, and **(E)**.

24. A, B, E

The best place to start here is with pairs of positive integers that have a product of 10. The numbers 5 and 2 have a product of 10, as do 10 and 1. But remember that integers may be negative, so −1 and −10 are possible, as well as −2 and −5. The mean of −1 and −10 is −5.5; the mean of −2 and −5 is −3.5. The mean of 2 and 5 is 3.5. The correct answers are **(A)**, **(B)**, and **(E)**.

25. C, D, E

The prime factorization of 210 is $2 \times 3 \times 5 \times 7$. The sum of the prime factors is $2 + 3 + 5 + 7 = 17$. So, the correct choices are **(C)**, **(D)**, and **(E)**.

26. 9

Use the definition of average to write the sum of the first n bowlers' scores:

$\dfrac{\text{sum of scores}}{n} = \text{average}$ and therefore, $n \times \text{average} = \text{sum of scores}$. Substitute the values given in the question and you have $160n = \text{sum of scores}$ for the initial set of bowlers. Now write the formula for the average again, using the additional score of 170. Now there are $n + 1$ bowlers.

$$\dfrac{\text{sum of scores}}{n} = \text{average}$$

$$\dfrac{160n + 170}{n + 1} = 161$$

Cross multiply and use algebra to solve for n.

$$160n + 170 = 161(n + 1)$$
$$160n + 170 = 161n + 161$$
$$170 - 161 = 161n - 160n$$
$$9 = n$$

There were **9** bowlers in the original group.

27. A, C, D

Test each answer choice by Picking Numbers; use 2 for the even number and 3 for the odd number. The results you get using these numbers will be representative of all integers.

Sum of two odd integers: $3 + 3 = 6$ (even)
Product of two odd integers: $3 \times 3 = 9$ (odd)
Product of an even integer and an odd integer: $2 \times 3 = 6$ (even)
Product of two even integers: $2 \times 2 = 4$ (even)
Sum of an even integer and an odd integer: $2 + 3 = 5$ (odd)
Choices **(A)**, **(C)**, and **(D)** are correct.

28. C

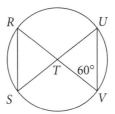

There are several steps involved with this problem, but none is too complicated. The circle has its center at point *T*. Start with the triangle on the right whose vertices are at *T* and two points on the circumference of the circle. This makes two of its sides radii of the circle. Because all radii must have equal length, this makes the triangle an isosceles triangle. In addition, you're told one of the base angles of this triangle has measure 60°. Thus, the other base angle must also have measure 60° (since the base angles in an isosceles triangle have equal measure). The sum of the two base angles is 120°, leaving 180 − 120 or 60° for the other angle, the one at point *T* (making △*TUV* an equilateral triangle).

Now, angle *RTS* is opposite this 60° angle; so, its measure must also be 60°. Therefore, △*RST* is another equilateral triangle, and its sides are 3. Therefore, the length of *RS* is 3, choice **(C)**.

29. D

First find the value of *x*, using the fact that there are 180° in a straight line. Set the sum of the angle measures equal to 180: $5x + 4x + 3x = 180$, $12x = 180$, and $x = 15$. Angle *TRV* equals $4x + 3x = 7x$, which is 105°. Choice **(D)** is correct.

30. B, C, D, E

You know that the ratio of oranges to apples is 9 to 10 and that there are at least 200 apples. The ratio tells you that there are more apples than oranges. At the minimum, there must be 180 oranges to satisfy the proportion $\frac{9}{10} = \frac{180}{200}$. There could be more than 200 apples, so any number of oranges greater than 180 for which the ratio 9:10 applies is correct. All of the choices are multiples of 9, so the correct choices are **(B)**, **(C)**, **(D)**, and **(E)**.

31. B

The probability formula is

$$\text{Probability} = \frac{\text{Number of desired outcomes}}{\text{Number of possible outcomes}}$$

When one die is rolled, there are six possible outcomes. When two dice are rolled, the number of possible outcomes is 6 × 6, or 36. Getting a total value of 7 can be achieved in the following ways: (1, 6), (2, 5), (3, 4), (4, 3), (5, 2), and (6, 1). There are six possible ways. So the probability of rolling a total of 7 is $\frac{6}{36}$, which can be reduced to $\frac{1}{6}$, choice **(B)**.

32. 8

In the first scenario, each day, $\frac{1 \text{ house}}{3 \text{ days}} = \frac{1}{3}$ of the house will be built. Because there are

10 workers, each person can build $\frac{1}{30}$ of a house each day. In the second scenario, there are 15 workers, so that means $15 \times \frac{1}{30} = \frac{1}{2}$ a house can be built each day. Four houses could, therefore, be built in 8 days: $\frac{4 \text{ houses}}{\frac{1}{2} \text{ house/day}} = 4 \times 2 = \mathbf{8}$ **days**.

33. C, D, E

The area of the shaded region is the area of the square minus the area of the portion of the circle that is inside the square. The area of a square is its side squared. The area of square *ABCD* is $4^2 = 4 \times 4$, which is 16. Now find the area of the portion of the circle that is inside the square. Because the diameter of the circle is a side of the square, you know that exactly one-half of the circle's area is inside the square. Because the diameter of the circle is twice the radius, the radius of the circle is $\frac{4}{2}$, or 2. The area of a circle with a radius *r* is πr^2. The area of the complete circle in this question is $\pi(2^2)$, which is 4π. So half the area of this circle is 2π. Thus, the area of the shaded region is $16 - 2\pi$.

That means that $16 - 4\pi$ and $16 - 16\pi$ are less than $16 - 2\pi$, so they cannot be correct choices. However, the sum of 16 and any positive number is greater than 16 and also greater than $16 - 2\pi$. So, the correct choices are **(C), (D)**, and **(E)**.

34. 5

Let's first find the value of 9♣. Then we'll find the value of (9♣) ♦ 3.

Since $C\clubsuit = C + 3, 9\clubsuit = 9 + 3 = 12$.
Then $(9\clubsuit) \blacklozenge 3 = 12 \blacklozenge 3$.
Since $A \blacklozenge B = \frac{A + B}{B}, 12 \blacklozenge 3 = \frac{12 + 3}{3} = \frac{15}{3}$
Thus, $(9\clubsuit) \blacklozenge 3 = 5$.

35. 1.5

The area of a rectangle is its length times its width.
The area of rectangle *A* is $12 \times 5 = 60$.
The area of rectangle *B* is $9 \times 10 = 90$.

So the area 60 of rectangle *A* must be multiplied by a number, which you can call *x*, to obtain the area 90 of rectangle *B*.

Then $60x = 90$. So $x = \frac{90}{60} = \frac{3}{2} = \mathbf{1.5}$.

36. 30

Here's a problem where it really pays to learn the special right triangles. Because one leg of the right triangle is 5 and the hypotenuse is 13, you have a special right triangle, the 5:12:13 right triangle. So the length of *AC* is 12.

The area of a triangle is $\frac{1}{2}$ of the base times the height. The area of a right triangle is $\frac{1}{2} \times$ (leg)$_1 \times$ (leg)$_2$, because one leg can be considered to be the base and the other leg can be considered to be the height. So the area of triangle *ABC* is $\frac{1}{2} \times (AC) \times (AB) = \frac{1}{2} \times 12 \times 5 = 6 \times 5 = 30$. The answer is **30**.

37. A, B, C, D

The average formula is as follows:

$$\text{Average} = \frac{\text{Sum of the terms}}{\text{Number of terms}}$$

Therefore,

$$\text{Sum of the terms} = \text{Average} \times \text{Number of terms}$$

The sum of the scores of the four students whose average was 85 is 85(4) = 340. Let's call the fifth student's score x. If the new average is to be greater than 84 and less than 86 and the sum of the scores of all five students is $340 + x$, then $84 < \frac{340 + x}{5} < 86$. If you multiply all parts of the inequality by 5, you get $420 < 340 + x < 430$. Subtracting 340 from all parts of the inequality, you get $80 < x < 90$, making **(A), (B), (C)**, and **(D)** the correct choices.

38. 5

This question can be broken into two equations with two unknowns, Meg's age now (M) and Rolf 's age now (R). Equation i shows the relationship now; equation ii shows the relationship 3 years ago.

$$\text{i. } M = 2 \times R \quad \text{ii. } M - 3 = R + 2$$

Substitute $2R$ for M in equation ii and solve for R:

$$M - 3 = R + 2$$
$$2R - 3 = R + 2$$
$$2R - R = 2 + 3$$
$$R = 5$$

Rolf is **5** years old now.

39. C, D, E

The cost of manufacturing x crayons is $(570 + 0.5x)$ cents. Because each crayon sells for 10 cents, x crayons will sell for $10x$ cents. You want the smallest value of x such that $10x$ cents is at least $570 + 0.5x$ cents. So you must solve the inequality $10x = 570 + 0.5x$ for the range of values that x can have.

$$10x \geq 570 + 0.5x$$
$$9.5x \geq 570$$
$$9.5x \geq 570$$
$$x \geq 60$$

The minimum number of crayons is 60. So, selling 60, 61, or 95 crayons would also make the revenue received at least equal to the manufacturing cost.

A great strategy to use here would be Backsolving, starting with either **(B)** or **(D)**.

40. A

You can write that $\dfrac{1-x}{xy} = \dfrac{1}{xy} - \dfrac{x}{xy}$. Canceling a factor of x from the numerator and

denominator of $\dfrac{x}{xy}$, you have $\dfrac{x}{xy} = \dfrac{1}{y}$.

So, $\dfrac{1-x}{xy} = \dfrac{1}{xy} - \dfrac{x}{xy} = \dfrac{1}{xy} - \dfrac{1}{y}$. The answer is **(A)**.

41. 200,000

From the second bar graph, the profits from table saws in 1998 were $60,000. From the pie chart, table saws were 30% of the total profits. Let's call the total profits T dollars. 30% of T dollars is $60,000. So $0.3T = 60,000$, and

$$T = \frac{60{,}000}{0.3} = \frac{60{,}000}{\frac{3}{10}} = \frac{10 \times 60{,}000}{3} = \frac{600{,}000}{3} = \mathbf{200{,}000}.$$

42. A

The year with the biggest percent increase over the previous year will be the year in which the increase is the biggest fraction of the amount from the previous year. Notice that in 1993, the increase from 1992 was approximately $60 - 30$, or 30. This is approximately a 100 percent increase, and it is the greatest percent increase over the previous year among all the years from 1993 through 2001. There was a greater increase in number of table saws from 1996 to 1997 than from 1992 to 1993, about $110 - 70 = 40$. However, the *percent* increase from 1996 to 1997 is approximately $\dfrac{40}{70} \times 100\%$, which is less than 100%, so choice **(A)** is correct.

43. D

In 1998, the profits from table saws were approximately $60,000. In 1999, the profits from table saws were approximately $40,000. From 1998 to 1999, there was a decrease in the profits from table saws. In general,

$$\text{Percent decrease} = \frac{\text{Original value} - \text{New value}}{\text{Original value}} \times 100\%$$

Here, the percent decrease is approximately

$$\frac{\$60{,}000 - \$40{,}000}{\$60{,}000} \times 100\% = \frac{\$20{,}000}{60{,}000} \times 100\% = \frac{1}{3} \times 100\% = 33\frac{1}{3}\%$$

A percent decrease of $33\frac{1}{3}\%$ is closest to **(D)**.

44. 700

In 1993, the profits were $20,000. Using the formula Profit = Revenue − Cost, you can write Revenue = Cost + Profit. The cost was $22,000. So the revenue was $22,000 + $20,000 = $42,000. Because in 1993, 60 table saws were sold, each table saw was sold for $\dfrac{\$42{,}000}{60}$, which is **$700**.

45. B

In 1998, the profits from table saws were about $60,000, and this profit was 30% of the total profits. Let's call the total profits T dollars. Then 30% of T dollars is $60,000. So $0.3T = 60,000$, and $T = \dfrac{60,000}{0.3} = 60,000 \times \dfrac{10}{3} = \dfrac{10 \times 60,000}{3} = \dfrac{600,000}{3} = 200,000$. The total profits in 1998 were approximately $200,000. The profits from cordless drills were 35% of the total. So the profits from cordless drills were approximately 0.35($200,000), which is $70,000 or answer **(B)**.

46. C

The residential usage (in billions) in 2000 was about 22; the usage was about 52 in 2010. The range is the difference because the residential usage increased over the time period. $52 - 22 = 30$, so the range is about 30 billion gallons. The correct answer is **(C)**.

47. C

The two amounts were closest to each other in 2002. The residential amount appears to be about 28; the total appears to be about 32: $28 \div 32 = 0.875$. Choice **(C)** is the closest.

48. D

The three usages with the greatest amounts per person are faucets, washers, and showers totaling 30 gallons per day. Multiply by 10,000 to get 300,000, choice **(D)**.

49. B

The residential consumption (in billions) in 2010 was approximately 52. Take half of that amount, 26, to represent the amount of water used by households with efficient appliances and plumbing. Let W represent the amount of water these households would have used otherwise.

Set up a percent equation to solve for W. Remember, the savings were 35%, so subtract 35 from 100 to find the amount that would have been used.

$$26 = (100\% - 35\%) \times W$$
$$26 = 65\% \times W$$
$$26 = 0.65 \times W$$
$$\frac{26}{0.65} = 40 = W$$

The savings in billions of gallons were $40 - 26 = 14$. The correct answer is **(B)**.

50. B

Compare the bar for Greendale to the bar for Valley for each year shown. The greatest difference occurred in 1990. Write the ratio 50:10 and reduce to 5:1. The correct answer is **(B)**.

51. A

Combine the three values shown for the year 2000: $15 + 55 + 40 = 110$. Choice **(A)** is correct.

52. D

Check each option carefully, being sure to look at the correct bar and the correct time frame. This is the most efficient way to answer the question. Except for choice **(D)**, each increase was 1,000 students. The correct answer is **(D)** because there was an increase of 2,000 students in that time frame.

53. C

To find the percent increase, first find the total enrollment in 2000 and the total enrollment in 2005. Don't worry about the hundreds; just use the numbers from the graph. For 2000, this number is 110. For 2005, this number is 140. To find the percent increase, compare the amount of increase, 30, to the original amount, 110. The closest answer is **(C)**.

54. C

The three enrollment figures for 1995 are 1,500 + 4,500 + 2,000 = 8,000. Divide by 3 to find the average: 8,000 ÷ 3 ≈ 2,667. The closest answer choice is **(C)**, 2,700.

55. 1000

There were 2,500 + 6,500 = 9,000 students enrolled in 2005. To maintain the 9:1 ratio, **1,000** faculty will be needed.

56. E

The enrollment at Eastern in 2005 was 5,000, so an increase of 1,200 students is expected. Compare 1,200 to 5,000 or simply compare 12 to 50. 12 is to 50 as 24 is to 100, so the percent increase is 24%. The correct answer is **(E)**.

57. C

Before you answer any graph question, begin by examining the graphs. Here you have two graphs, a segmented bar graph representing team revenue breakdowns for five teams and a pie chart showing the distribution of venue revenues for Team X. You're now ready to attack the question, which asks you to find the team with the median venue revenue for 1997 and to determine what percent of that team's total revenue is media revenue. This question must refer to the first graph, and the first part of the question—finding the team with the median venue revenue—is a simple matter. *Median* refers to the number in the middle. Looking at the white portions of the bars in the top graph, you see that Team Z has the median venue revenue. The fastest approach to the answer here (and throughout graph questions generally) is to approximate. The downside to bar graphs is that it's often very hard to get a read on the values. The upside is that if you approximate, often you don't have to read the values. Here you need to determine what percent of Team Z's bar is represented by media revenue (the segment in the middle—always be especially careful to isolate the correct piece of data). By approximating, you should be able to see that the middle segment is more than a third and less than a half of the entire bar. Thus the correct answer has to be between 33% and 50%. The only answer that works is **(C)**, 40%.

58. D, E

The key to this question is that it involves *both* graphs. The question asks for the amount Team X earned through food sales, which takes you first to the pie chart, where you see that food sales accounted for 35% of the venue revenues for Team X. But to convert that to a dollar amount, you need a figure for the amount earned in venue revenues by Team X in 1997. According to the bar graph, this is somewhere around $40 million. Now, take 35% of $40 million: $0.35 \times 40 = 14$, so the answer is any amount greater than 14. The answers are **(D)** and **(E)**.

59. E

Look at the graph; team Q had media revenue of $35 - 5 = 30$ million, and teams X, Y, and Z had media revenues greater than team Q. Team R had media revenue of $30 - 10 = 20$ million. The only correct choice is **(E)**.

60. B, C, D, E

Percent change problems are extremely popular graph questions, and as long as you set them up correctly, they're generally no problem. This question asks for the approximate percent increase in Team Y's total revenue from 1997 to 1998, so you need to figure out (roughly) the amount of increase, place that over the original (or smaller) amount, then convert the fraction into a percent. You are given the total revenue for 1998 as $150 million or greater, so you need to locate the total revenue for 1997 from the bar graph. It looks to be approximately $120 million, so the amount of increase is $30 million, and the original (or smaller) amount is $120 million. Now let's apply the formula:

$$\text{Percent Increase} = \frac{\$30 \text{ million}}{\$120 \text{ million}} \times 100\%$$

$$= \frac{1}{4} \times 100\%$$

$$= 25\%$$

So, any percent greater than or equal to 25% is the answer. The answers are **(B)**, **(C)**, **(D)**, and **(E)**.

QUANTITATIVE REASONING PRACTICE SET 2

NUMBERS

All numbers are real numbers.

FIGURES

The position of points, lines, angles, and so on, may be assumed to be in the order shown; all lengths and angle measures may be assumed to be positive.

Lines shown as straight may be assumed to be straight.

Figures lie in the plane of the paper unless otherwise stated.

Figures that accompany questions are intended to provide useful information. However, unless a note states that a figure has been drawn to scale, you should solve the problems by using your knowledge of mathematics, not by estimation or measurement.

DIRECTIONS

Each of the following questions, 1–20, consists of two quantities, Quantity A and Quantity B. You are to compare the two quantities and choose

- (A) if Quantity A is greater;
- (B) if Quantity B is greater;
- (C) if the two quantities are equal; or
- (D) if the relationship cannot be determined from the information given.

COMMON INFORMATION

In a question, information concerning one or both of the quantities to be compared is centered above the two quantities. A symbol that appears in both quantities represents the same thing in Quantity A as it does in Quantity B.

1. **Quantity A**   **Quantity B**

   The number of positive integer factors of 96

   The number of positive integer factors of 72

   - (A) Quantity A is greater.
   - (B) Quantity B is greater.
   - (C) The two quantities are equal.
   - (D) The relationship cannot be determined from the information given.

$$x > 0$$

2. **Quantity A**   **Quantity B**

   $$\dfrac{x+1}{x} \qquad \dfrac{x}{x+1}$$

   - (A) Quantity A is greater.
   - (B) Quantity B is greater.
   - (C) The two quantities are equal.
   - (D) The relationship cannot be determined from the information given.

$$2^p = 4^q$$

3. <u>Quantity A</u>   <u>Quantity B</u>

    p $2q$

    (A) Quantity A is greater.

    (B) Quantity B is greater.

    (C) The two quantities are equal.

    (D) The relationship cannot be determined from the information given.

4. <u>Quantity A</u>   <u>Quantity B</u>

    The number   The number
    of seconds in   of hours in
    7 hours   52 weeks

    (A) Quantity A is greater.

    (B) Quantity B is greater.

    (C) The two quantities are equal.

    (D) The relationship cannot be determined from the information given.

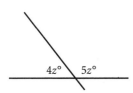

5. <u>Quantity A</u>   <u>Quantity B</u>

    z 20

    (A) Quantity A is greater.

    (B) Quantity B is greater.

    (C) The two quantities are equal.

    (D) The relationship cannot be determined from the information given.

$$x > 2$$

6. <u>Quantity A</u>   <u>Quantity B</u>

    x^3 $4x$

    (A) Quantity A is greater.

    (B) Quantity B is greater.

    (C) The two quantities are equal.

    (D) The relationship cannot be determined from the information given.

7. <u>Quantity A</u>   <u>Quantity B</u>

    $(a + 2)(a - 2)$ $(a + 1)(a - 1)$

    (A) Quantity A is greater.

    (B) Quantity B is greater.

    (C) The two quantities are equal.

    (D) The relationship cannot be determined from the information given.

8. <u>Quantity A</u>   <u>Quantity B</u>

    The area of a   Twice the area
    square with   of a square with
    perimeter 16   perimeter 8

    (A) Quantity A is greater.

    (B) Quantity B is greater.

    (C) The two quantities are equal.

    (D) The relationship cannot be determined from the information given.

The area of one face of a cube is 35.

9. Quantity A   Quantity B

   The total   The total
   surface area   volume of the
   of the cube.   cube.

   Ⓐ Quantity A is greater.
   Ⓑ Quantity B is greater.
   Ⓒ The two quantities are equal.
   Ⓓ The relationship cannot
       be determined from the
       information given.

$$\sqrt{x} = \sqrt{x + 6}$$
$$\sqrt{3y} = \sqrt{y + 4}$$

10. Quantity A   Quantity B
        y x

    Ⓐ Quantity A is greater.
    Ⓑ Quantity B is greater.
    Ⓒ The two quantities
        are equal.
    Ⓓ The relationship cannot
        be determined from the
        information given.

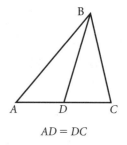

$AD = DC$

11. Quantity A   Quantity B

    The area of   The area of
    $\triangle BAD$ $\triangle BCD$

    Ⓐ Quantity A is greater.
    Ⓑ Quantity B is greater.
    Ⓒ The two quantities
        are equal.
    Ⓓ The relationship cannot
        be determined from the
        information given.

12. Quantity A   Quantity B
    $[x + (x + 1)]^2$ $x^2 + (x + 1)^2$

    Ⓐ Quantity A is greater.
    Ⓑ Quantity B is greater.
    Ⓒ The two quantities
        are equal.
    Ⓓ The relationship cannot
        be determined from the
        information given.

A circle with radius *r* is inscribed in a square. *r* is greater than or equal to 1.

13. Quantity A | Quantity B

    The area of   *r*
    the square
    <u>not</u> in the
    circle

    Ⓐ Quantity A is greater.

    Ⓑ Quantity B is greater.

    Ⓒ The two quantities
        are equal.

    Ⓓ The relationship cannot
        be determined from the
        information given.

Eight points lie on a circle.

14. Quantity A | Quantity B

    The number | The number
    of triangles | of pentagons
    you can | you can make
    make using | using 5 points
    3 points as | as vertices
    vertices

    Ⓐ Quantity A is greater.

    Ⓑ Quantity B is greater.

    Ⓒ The two quantities
        are equal.

    Ⓓ The relationship cannot
        be determined from the
        information given.

Two die are rolled.

15. Quantity A | Quantity B

    The number | The number of
    of different | different ways
    ways to get a | to get a sum
    sum of 5 | of 9

    Ⓐ Quantity A is greater.

    Ⓑ Quantity B is greater.

    Ⓒ The two quantities
        are equal.

    Ⓓ The relationship cannot
        be determined from the
        information given.

16. Quantity A | Quantity B

    The number | The number of
    of different | different ways
    ways to | to arrange the
    arrange the | letters in the
    letters in the | word *circle*
    word *square*

    Ⓐ Quantity A is greater.

    Ⓑ Quantity B is greater.

    Ⓒ The two quantities
        are equal.

    Ⓓ The relationship cannot
        be determined from the
        information given.

17. **Quantity A**   **Quantity B**

    The sum of   The sum of
    the prime   the prime
    factors of 36   factors of 22

    Ⓐ Quantity A is greater.

    Ⓑ Quantity B is greater.

    Ⓒ The two quantities
    are equal.

    Ⓓ The relationship cannot
    be determined from the
    information given.

18. **Quantity A**   **Quantity B**

    $(x - 1)^2$ $(x - 1)^3$

    Ⓐ Quantity A is greater.

    Ⓑ Quantity B is greater.

    Ⓒ The two quantities
    are equal.

    Ⓓ The relationship cannot
    be determined from the
    information given.

    The perimeter of a square equals
    the perimeter of a rectangle that is
    not a square.

19. **Quantity A**   **Quantity B**

    The area of   The area of
    the square   the rectangle

    Ⓐ Quantity A is greater.

    Ⓑ Quantity B is greater.

    Ⓒ The two quantities
    are equal.

    Ⓓ The relationship cannot
    be determined from the
    information given.

$x \neq 0$

Quantity A   **Quantity B**

20. $\dfrac{|x|}{x}$ -1

    Ⓐ Quantity A is greater.

    Ⓑ Quantity B is greater.

    Ⓒ The two quantities
    are equal.

    Ⓓ The relationship cannot
    be determined from the
    information given.

21. A 7 by 24 rectangle is inscribed
    in a circle. What is the
    circumference of the circle?

    Ⓐ 7π

    Ⓑ 12.5π

    Ⓒ 24π

    Ⓓ 25π

    Ⓔ 31π

22. If $a < 0$ and $b < 0$, what are the
    possible values for $\dfrac{a + b}{ab}$?
    Indicate <u>all</u> that apply.

    Ⓐ 2

    Ⓑ 1

    Ⓒ 0

    Ⓓ -1

    Ⓔ -2

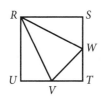

23. In the figure, *RSTU* is a square with side 4. Points *V* and *W* are the midpoints of sides $\overline{UT}$ and $\overline{ST}$, respectively. Which is the area of △*RWV*?

 Ⓐ 5

 Ⓑ 6

 Ⓒ 7

 Ⓓ 8

 Ⓔ 9

24. What is the solution of the system of equations shown below?

$$6x - 3y = 9$$
$$4x - 3y = 5$$

 Ⓐ (2, 2)

 Ⓑ (2, 1)

 Ⓒ (1, 2)

 Ⓓ (−1, 2)

 Ⓔ (−1, −1)

25. If $x \neq 0$, which of the following must be greater than *x*?

 Indicate <u>all</u> possible choices.

 Ⓐ x^2

 Ⓑ $x - 2$

 Ⓒ $x + 2$

 Ⓓ $(x - 2)^2$

 Ⓔ $(x + 2)^2$

26. A rectangle has a perimeter of 24. Which of the following could be its area?

 Indicate <u>all</u> possible choices.

 Ⓐ 28

 Ⓑ 32

 Ⓒ 35

 Ⓓ 36

 Ⓔ 40

27. A square has the same area as a rectangle whose length is 2 more that its width. If the perimeter of the rectangle is 12, what is the perimeter of the square?

 Ⓐ 6

 Ⓑ $6\sqrt{2}$

 Ⓒ 8

 Ⓓ $8\sqrt{2}$

 Ⓔ 10

28. A cube with an edge of 3 units sits inside a cube with an edge of 5 units. How many cubic units of space are there between the smaller cube and the larger cube?

 ☐ cubic units

29. What is the area of a rectangle with a side of 5 and a diagonal of 13?

 ☐ square units

30. What is the sum of the reciprocal of x, the reciprocal of y, and the reciprocal of xy?

    (A) $\dfrac{x + y - 1}{xy}$

    (B) $\dfrac{x + y}{xy}$

    (C) $\dfrac{xy}{x + y + 1}$

    (D) $\dfrac{x + y + 1}{xy}$

    (E) $\dfrac{xy}{x + y - 1}$

31. If a fair coin is flipped four times, what is the probability that it will land with the "head" side up precisely twice?

    (A) $\dfrac{1}{16}$

    (B) $\dfrac{1}{4}$

    (C) $\dfrac{3}{8}$

    (D) $\dfrac{13}{32}$

    (E) $\dfrac{1}{2}$

32. Find the 50th term of the arithmetic sequence 13, 4, −5, −14,...

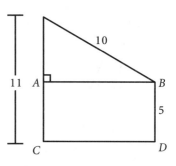

33. In the figure above, what is the area of rectangle *ABCD*?

    (A) 25

    (B) 30

    (C) 40

    (D) 50

    (E) 55

34. The symbol ☺ represents one of the four operations of addition, subtraction, multiplication, and division, and 12 ☺ (6 ☺ 2) = 4. What is the value of 24 ☺ 8 ☺ 3?

35. There will be 291 people attending a wedding. If the caterer can seat 12 people at each table, how many tables should be set up and used at the wedding?

    tables

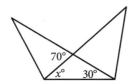

36. In the figure above, what is the value of *x*?

37. What is the least common multiple of 48 and 64?

   Ⓐ 96
   Ⓑ 128
   Ⓒ 152
   Ⓓ 178
   Ⓔ 192

38. Find the 12th term of the geometric sequence 1, −2, 4, −8,…

39. The length of a rectangle is 3 times the width. If the length is 90, what is the perimeter of the rectangle?

   Ⓐ 120
   Ⓑ 240
   Ⓒ 480
   Ⓓ 560
   Ⓔ 720

40. How many different 3-digit numbers can be formed if no digit is used more than once?

   Ⓐ   504
   Ⓑ   648
   Ⓒ   729
   Ⓓ   900
   Ⓔ 1,000

Questions 41–45 are based on the following graph.

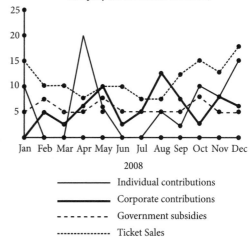

Income sources for the Victor Le Havre Dance Company (in Thousands of Dollars)

41. For how many months in 2008 were government subsidies less than any other source of income indicated?

   ☐ months

42. Approximately how much greater were corporate contributions than individual contributions in August?

   Ⓐ $3,000
   Ⓑ $5,000
   Ⓒ $5,500
   Ⓓ $6,000
   Ⓔ $7,500

43. In which of the following months were ticket sales approximately double government subsidies?

   Ⓐ January
   Ⓑ February
   Ⓒ March
   Ⓓ August
   Ⓔ September

44. What was the approximate increase in government subsidies from August to October as a percent of the increase in ticket sales over the same period?

- (A) 25%
- (B) $33\frac{1}{3}$%
- (C) 100%
- (D) 200%
- (E) 300%

45. If government subsidies to all dance companies totaled $5,000,000 in 2008, approximately what percent of this amount went to the Victor Le Havre Dance Company?

- (A) 0.07%
- (B) 0.14%
- (C) 1.4%
- (D) 7%
- (E) 14%

Questions 46–48 are based on the following graph.

Fresh-Fruit Stand

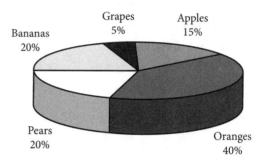

46. The pie chart shows the relative quantities of five types of fruit sold at a market stand. If the total revenue for all the fruit sold one season was $7,520, how much more revenue was collected for pears than for apples?

- (A) $113
- (B) $200
- (C) $376
- (D) $752
- (E) $1,128

47. The markup on oranges sold at the stand is 20%. What was the original cost of all the oranges sold at the stand, based on total revenue of $7,520?

- (A) $601.60
- (B) $2,148.57
- (C) $2,406.40
- (D) $2,506.67
- (E) $3,760.00

48. Due to spoilage, there was a loss on the sale of bananas. Although the cost of the bananas was $2,005, only $1,504 was realized in sales. What was the percent loss on the sale of bananas?

   (A) 5%

   (B) 10%

   (C) 15%

   (D) 20%

   (E) 25%

Questions 49–53 are based on the following graphs.

SALES AND NET INCOME FOR
COMPANIES *A* AND *B*
(in Millions of Dollars)

Sales
Company *A* vs. Company *B*

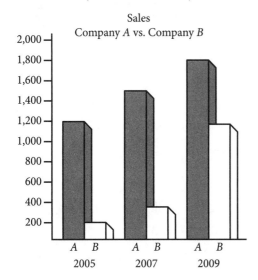

NET INCOME
(in Millions of Dollars)

Company *A* vs. Company *B*
for the years 2005, 2007, 2009

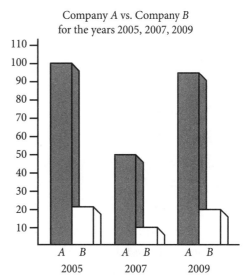

49. What were Company *A*'s average sales, in millions of dollars, for the three years shown?

   ☐ millions of dollars

50. Sales of Company *B* in 2009 were approximately how many times as great as its sales in 2005?

   (A) 3.5

   (B) 4.5

   (C) 5.5

   (D) 6.0

   (E) 6.5

51. From 2007 to 2009, Company
    A's increase in net income was
    approximately how many more
    millions of dollars than the increase
    in net income of Company *B*?

    Ⓐ   9

    Ⓑ   18

    Ⓒ   36

    Ⓓ   40

    Ⓔ   45

52. In 2009, which of the following
    ratios was the lowest?

    Ⓐ   Company *A*'s sales to
        Company *A*'s net income

    Ⓑ   Company *B*'s sales to
        Company *B*'s net income

    Ⓒ   Company *A*'s sales to
        Company *B*'s net income

    Ⓓ   Company *B*'s sales to
        Company *A*'s net income

    Ⓔ   The sum of Company *A*'s
        and Company *B*'s sales
        to the sum of Company
        A's and company *B*'s net
        income.

53. For what company in which year
    was net income at least 10 percent
    of sales?

    Ⓐ   Company *A* in 2005

    Ⓑ   Company *B* in 2005

    Ⓒ   Company *A* in 2007

    Ⓓ   Company *B* in 2007

    Ⓔ   Company *A* in 2009

**Questions 54–56 are based on the
following graphs**.

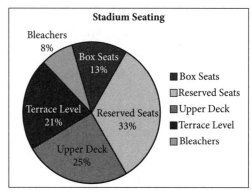

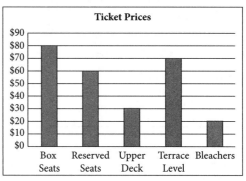

The stadium has 50,000 seats.

54. How many seats are either box
    seats or reserved seats?

    Ⓐ   6,500

    Ⓑ   10,500

    Ⓒ   12,500

    Ⓓ   16,500

    Ⓔ   23,000

55. If the stadium is sold out, what is the gross income on the sale of all the upper deck tickets?

   (A) $300,000

   (B) $350,000

   (C) $375,000

   (D) $400,000

   (E) $425,000

56. If the stadium is sold out, what type of ticket generates the greatest gross income?

   (A) Box Seats

   (B) Reserved Seats

   (C) Upper Deck

   (D) Terrace Level

   (E) Bleachers

Question 57–60 refer to the following tables:

BASEBALL STANDINGS

EAST DIVISION

TEAM	W	L	PCT	GB	HOME	ROAD
A	87	53	0.621	–	49-25	38-28
B	84	55	0.604	2.5	43-26	41-29
C	78	62	0.557	9.0	42-30	36-32
D	72	68	0.514	15.0	37-29	35-39
E	53	87	0.379	34.0	30-41	23-46

WEST DIVISION

TEAM	W	L	PCT	GB	HOME	ROAD
W	77	63	0.550	–	43-26	34-37
X	69	70	0.496	7.5	42-29	27-41
Y	67	73	0.479	10.0	35-34	32-39
Z	55	85	0.393	22.0	33-38	22-47

W – Wins, L – Losses, GB – Games Behind, PCT – Winning Percentage, HOME – Won-Loss record for home games, ROAD – Won-Loss record for away games

57. Games Behind (GB) is the average of the differences between the leading team wins and the trailing team wins, and the trailing team losses and leading team losses. If Team W were in the East Division, how many games would it be behind Team A?

   (A) 8

   (B) 8.5

   (C) 9

   (D) 9.5

   (E) 10

58. The Elimination Number for any team is determined by adding its number of losses to the number of wins for the team leading the division, and subtracting that total from 163. If the Elimination Number is less than or equal to 0, a team is eliminated. Which team has an elimination number less than 5?

Indicate <u>all</u> possible choices.

- [A] Team C
- [B] Team D
- [C] Team E
- [D] Team Y
- [E] Team Z

59. If Team W were in the East Division, which place would it be in?

- (A) First
- (B) Second
- (C) Third
- (D) Fourth
- (E) Fifth

60. Which team has the best won-loss percentage for road games?

- (A) Team A
- (B) Team B
- (C) Team C
- (D) Team W
- (E) Team X

ANSWERS AND EXPLANATIONS

1. C	16. A	31. C	46. C
2. A	17. B	32. −428	47. D
3. C	18. D	33. C	48. E
4. A	19. A	34. 1	49. 1500
5. C	20. D	35. 25	50. C
6. A	21. D	36. 40	51. C
7. B	22. D, E	37. E	52. D
8. A	23. B	38. −2048	53. B
9. A	24. B	39. B	54. E
10. B	25. C, E	40. B	55. C
11. C	26. B, C, D	41. 3	56. B
12. D	27. D	42. E	57. E
13. D	28. 98	43. C	58. C, E
14. C	29. 60	44. B	59. D
15. C	30. D	45. C	60. B

Diagnostic Tool

Tally up your score and write your results below.

Total

Total Correct: _____ out of 60 correct

By Question Type

Quantitative Comparisons (questions 1–20) _____ out of 20 correct
Problem Solving (questions 21–40) _____ out of 20 correct
Data Interpretations (questions 41–60) _____ out of 20 correct

DIAGNOSE YOUR RESULTS

Look back at the questions you got wrong and think about your experience answering them. Refer back to the Steps given at the end of Practice Set 1 to pinpoint the trouble and make use of the suggestions given there.

1. C

There are 12 positive integer factors of 96: 1, 2, 3, 4, 6, 8, 12, 16, 24, 32, 48, and 96. There are 12 positive integer factors of 72: 1, 2, 3, 4, 6, 8, 9, 12, 18, 24, 36, and 72. The two quantities are equal.

2. A

If $x > 0$, then $\frac{x+1}{x}$, which also equals $1 + \frac{1}{x}$, must be greater than 1. On the other hand, $\frac{x}{x+1}$ must be less than 1. This is because when $x > 0$, the numerator x is smaller than the denominator, so the ratio $\frac{x}{x+1} < 1$. Therefore, $\frac{x+1}{x} > \frac{x}{x+1}$ when $x > 0$, and Quantity A is greater.

3. C

For this question, notice the relationship between the bases, 2 and 4. When comparing exponents, it's easiest to work with equal bases.

You know that $4 = 2^2$. Therefore, $4^q = (2^2)^q = 2^{2q}$. The quantities are equal, choice **(C)**.

4. A

Before you go to the trouble of multiplying the terms, let's see if there's a shortcut. For the GRE, make sure you know the common unit conversions for time. There are 60 seconds in a minute and 60 minutes in an hour, so there are $7 \times 60 \times 60$ seconds in 7 hours. There are 24 hours in a day and 7 days in a week, so there are $7 \times 24 \times 52$ hours in 52 weeks. Let's rewrite the quantities:

Quantity A	Quantity B
$7 \times 60 \times 60$	$7 \times 24 \times 52$

Taking away the common values gives you:

Quantity A	Quantity B
60×60	24×52

You still shouldn't do the math, however. The best strategy is to compare piece by piece, which shows that Quantity A is larger than Quantity B.

5. C

The sum of the measures of the angles on one side of a straight line is 180°. Therefore, $4z + 5z = 180$, so $9z = 180$. Divide both sides by 9 to find $z = 20$. **(C)** is the answer.

6. A

Since $x > 2$, you know $x > 0$ and you can divide both quantities by x without changing their relationship. Quantity A is then x^2 and Quantity B is 4. Since $x > 2$, the least value for x^2 is greater than $2^2 = 4$. You can also use the Picking Numbers strategy, starting with $x = 2$. If $x = 2$, then $x^3 = 8$, and $4x = 8$ also. However, $x > 2$, so x^3 must actually be larger than 8. Therefore, **(A)** is right.

7. B

You might recognize these expressions as part of the Difference of Squares equation. Here's what that equation looks like (remember, in math, "difference" means "subtraction"):

$$a^2 - b^2 = (a + b)(a - b) \text{ or } (a - b)(a - b)$$

This would give you $a^2 - 4$ for Quantity A and $a^2 - 1$ for Quantity B, making Quantity B larger.

Alternatively, you could apply the distributive law (FOIL) to multiply the terms out:

$$(a + 2)(a - 2) = \qquad\qquad (a + 1)(a - 1) =$$
$$a^2 - 2a + 2a - 4 = \qquad\qquad a^2 - a + a - 1 =$$
$$a^2 - 4 \qquad\qquad\qquad\qquad a^2 - 1$$

Therefore, $a^2 - 4 < a^2 - 1$, and **(B)** is the greater quantity.

8. A

The area of a square is equal to the square of the length of one of its sides. A square with a perimeter of 16 must have sides each equal to 4 (since $4 + 4 + 4 + 4 = 16$). Therefore, its area must be 4^2, which also equals 16. Likewise, a square with a perimeter of 8 must have sides equal to 2. That means the area of this square is given by $2^2 = 4$, and twice 4 is 8. Since $16 > 8$, **(A)** is the answer.

9. A

A cube has 6 identical square faces. Since each side has an area of 35, the total surface area is 6×35. This gives you Quantity A.

The volume of a cube is equal to the cube of the length of one side, s: Volume of a cube $= s^3$.

Now you need to find the length of a side of the cube. You know that each side of a cube is a square, and that the area of a square is equal to the length of one of its sides squared. You also know that the area of each square side of this cube is 35. Since the area of a square equals the length of one of its sides squared, the square root of the area equals the length of a side. Therefore, the length of a side of this cube is $\sqrt{35}$. So the volume of the cube, which is the cube of the length of a side, is $\sqrt{35} \times \sqrt{35} \times \sqrt{35} = \sqrt{35} \times 35$.

If you divide both Quantity A and Quantity B by 35, you're left with 6 in Quantity A and $\sqrt{35}$ in Quantity B. Since $6 = \sqrt{36}$, Quantity A is greater than Quantity B.

10. B

For Quantity A, square both sides of $\sqrt{3y} = \sqrt{y + 4}$ and simplify. The result is $3y = y + 4$, $2y = 4$, $y = 2$. For Quantity B, square both sides of $\sqrt{3x} = \sqrt{x + 6}$ and simplify. The result is $3x = x + 6$, $2x = 6$, $x = 3$. Quantity B is larger.

11. C

The area of a triangle is given by $A = \frac{1}{2}$ base $\times$ height.

You're given that $\triangle BAD$ and $\triangle BDC$ have equal bases AD and DC, respectively. Therefore, you only need to compare their heights in order to compare their areas. To determine the height of $\triangle BAD$, start at point B and draw a vertical line perpendicular to the base. You'll have to extend base AD past point D in order to intersect. Do the same for $\triangle BDC$, and you should find that the two triangles have the same height. This is because their bases are on the same line and the upper vertex of each triangle is at the same point, B. Therefore, the area of $\triangle BAD$ equals the area of $\triangle BDC$, and **(C)** is correct.

12. D

Use the Picking Numbers strategy. Let $x = 1$.
Quantity A: $[x + (x + 1)]^2 = [(1 + (1 + 1)]^2 = 3^2 = 9$.
Quantity B: $x^2 + (x + 1)^2 = 1^2 + (1 + 1)^2 = 1 + 2^2 = 5$. So, Quantity A is larger.
Let $x = -1$.
Quantity A: $[x + (x + 1)]^2 = [(-1 + (-1 + 1)]^2 = (-1)^2 = 1$.
Quantity B: $x^2 + (x + 1)^2 = (-1)^2 + (-1 + 1)^2 = 1 + 0^2 = 1$.

So, the quantities are equal. Since two different outcomes can be found, the correct answer is **(D)**.

13. D

If a circle of radius r is inscribed in a square, a side of the square is $2r$. The area of the square is $(2r)^2 = 4r^2$. The area of the circle is πr^2. The area of the square *not* in the circle is $4r^2 - \pi r^2 = (4 - \pi)r^2$. Try several values for r keeping in mind that $(4 - \pi)$ is less than 1, approximately 0.86. Start with $r = 1$. In this case, $(4 - \pi)r^2$ is less than r. Now try a greater number, say $r = 10$. Without calculating, you can see that $(4 - \pi)r^2$ is greater than $r = 10$. Therefore, the correct answer is **(D)**.

14. C

The number of triangles you can make using 3 points as vertices is the same as $_8C_3$ $= \dfrac{8!}{3!(8 - 3)!} = \dfrac{8!}{3!5!}$. The number of pentagons you can make using 5 points as vertices is the same as $_8C_5 = \dfrac{8!}{5!(8 - 5)!} = \dfrac{8!}{5!3!}$. The columns are equal; **(C)** is the correct answer.

15. C

When two die are rolled, you can get a sum of 5 by rolling (4, 1), (3, 2), (2, 3) or (1, 4). You can get a sum of 9 by rolling (6, 3), (5, 4), (4, 5), and (3, 6). So, (C) is the correct answer.

16. A

There are $6! = 720$ ways to arrange the letters *square*. The letters *circle* have the letter c repeated. Because there are two cs, divide 6! by 2 to find the number of possible arrangements. There are $\dfrac{6!}{2!} = \dfrac{720}{2} = 360$ ways to arrange the letters *circle*. So, the correct answer is **(A)**.

17. B

The sum of the prime factors of 36 is $2 + 2 + 3 + 3 = 10$. The sum of the prime factors of 22 is $2 + 11 = 13$. So, the correct answer is **(B)**.

18. D

Use the Picking Numbers strategy. Let $x = 3$. Quantity A is $(3 - 1)^2 = 4$. Quantity B is $(3 - 1)^3 = 8$. Let $x = -1$. Quantity A is $(-1 - 1)^2 = 4$. Quantity B is $(-1 - 1)^3 = -8$. So, the correct answer is **(D)**.

19. A

Let $4x$ equal the perimeter of both figures. A side of the square is x. The area of the square is x^2. One side of the rectangle must be greater than x and the other side less than x in order for the perimeters to be equal. Let the longer side be $x + a$. The other side is $x - a$ where $x > a > 0$. The area of the rectangle is $(x + a)(x - a) = x^2 - a^2$. Because a^2 is positive, the area of the rectangle is less than the area of the square. The correct answer is **(A)**.

20. D

Use the Picking Numbers strategy. If $x = 1$, $\dfrac{|x|}{x} = \dfrac{|1|}{1} = 1$. If $x = -1$, $\dfrac{|x|}{x} = \dfrac{|-1|}{-1} = -1$. So, the correct answer is **(D)**.

21. D

All the angles of a rectangle are $90°$. If a rectangle is inscribed in a circle, each angle subtends a $180°$ arc. So, a diagonal of the rectangle is a diameter of the circle. By the Pythagorean Theorem, the diagonal, and thus the diameter $= \sqrt{7^2 + 24^2} = \sqrt{49 + 576} = \sqrt{625} = 25$. The circumference of a circle is π times the diameter. The correct answer is **(D)**.

22. D, E

Because $a < 0$ and $b < 0$, the product $ab > 0$ and the sum $a + b < 0$. Therefore, $\dfrac{a + b}{ab} < 0$ and the correct answers are **(D)**, **(E)**.

23. B

The square is divided up into 3 right triangles and $\triangle RWV$.

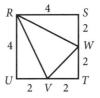

The area of the square is $4 \times 4 = 16$. The area of $\triangle RWV$ is the area of the square minus the area of the 3 right triangles.

The area of $\triangle RUV = \dfrac{1}{2}(4)(2) = 4$.

The area of $\triangle RSW = \dfrac{1}{2}(4)(2) = 4$.

The area of $\triangle WTV = \dfrac{1}{2}(2)(2) = 2$.

The area of $\triangle RWV = 16 - (4 + 4 + 2) = 16 - 10 = 6$.

The correct answer is **(B)**.

24. B

Solve the system of equations by subtracting the second equation from the first. The result is $2x = 4$ and $x = 2$. Substitute $x = 2$ into the second equation: $4(2) - 3y = 5$, $8 - 3y = 5$, $-3y = -3$, $y = 1$. The solution is the ordered pair $(2, 1)$ and the correct answer is **(B)**.

25. C, E

For choice **(A)**, let $x = \frac{1}{2}$. $x^2 = \frac{1}{4}$. So, $x > x^2$. Eliminate **(A)**.

For choice **(B)**, you know that $x - 2$ cannot be greater than x. Eliminate **(B)**.

For choice **(C)**, you know that $x + 2$ is always greater than x. Choice **(C)** works!

Choice **(D)** is not going to work because there are x values that will make $x - 2$ a fraction and the square of a fraction is less than x.

If choice **(C)** is correct, then choice **(E)** must also be correct. The correct answers are **(C)** and **(E)**.

26. B, C, D

The perimeter of a rectangle is 2 times the length l plus 2 times the width w: $2l + 2w = 24$. Divide both sides of the equation by 2: $l + w = 12$. The area of a rectangle is lw. So, you want 2 numbers l and w whose sum is 12 and whose product lw is the area. Consider the factors of each answer choice to see if you can form two numbers whose sum is 12.

$28 = 2 \times 2 \times 7$, so 28 does not work.
$32 = 2 \times 2 \times 2 \times 2 \times 2 = 4 \times 8$ and $4 + 8 = 12$.
$35 = 5 \times 7$ and $5 + 7 = 12$.
$36 = 2 \times 2 \times 3 \times 3 = 6 \times 6$ and $6 + 6 = 12$.
$40 = 2 \times 2 \times 5$, so 40 does not work.

The correct answers are **(B)**, **(C)**, and **(D)**.

27. D

If x is the width of the rectangle, the length is $x + 2$. The perimeter of the rectangle would be $x + x + 2 + x + x + 2 = 4x + 4$. Since the perimeter of the rectangle is 12, $4x + 4 = 12$. $4x = 8$ and $x = 2$. The area of the rectangle is $x(x + 2) = 2 \times 4 = 8$. The area of the square is 8 because the area of the rectangle is equal to the area of the square. So, a side of the square equals $\sqrt{8} = \sqrt{(4)(2)} = 2\sqrt{2}$. The perimeter of the square is $4(2\sqrt{2}) = 8\sqrt{2}$. The correct answer is **(D)**.

28. 98

The volume of a cube with edge e is $V = e^3$. If the edge is 5, the volume is $V = 5^3 = 125$. If the edge is 3, the volume is $V = 3^3 = 27$. The difference between the two values is $125 - 27 = 98$. So, the correct answer is **98**.

29. 60

The diagonal of a rectangle is the hypotenuse of a right triangle with legs equal to the sides of the rectangle. A triangle with one leg equal to 5 and hypotenuse equal to 13 is a 5:12:13 triangle. So, the length and width of the rectangle are 12 and 5. The area of the rectangle is $5 \times 12 = $ **60**.

30. D

The sum of the reciprocal of x, the reciprocal of y, and the reciprocal of xy is $\dfrac{1}{x} + \dfrac{1}{y}$ $+ \dfrac{1}{xy} = \dfrac{y}{xy} + \dfrac{x}{xy} + \dfrac{1}{xy} = \dfrac{y + x + 1}{xy} = \dfrac{x + y + 1}{xy}$. Choice **(D)** is correct.

31. C

To find the probability of any event occurring, use the formula for probability:

$$\text{Probability} = \frac{\text{Number of desired outcomes}}{\text{Number of possible outcomes}}$$

For each flip of a coin, the possible outcomes are heads or tails. In a sequence of four flips, the possible outcomes are the different possible sequences of heads and tails over the course of the four flips. This problem asks you for the probability that heads will result exactly twice during the course of those four flips.

Because the equation for probability requires you to know the total number of possible outcomes, you have to figure the denominator in the equation above.

But don't fall for this question's trap: The numerator in the equation above is *not* the number of *times* you want heads to show up, 2. It's the number of different *ways* in which this can occur in four flips.

Let's work on the denominator first. For each flip of the coin, there are two possible outcomes, heads or tails. So the number of possible outcomes in four flips of the coin is $2 \times 2 \times 2 \times 2 = 2^4 = 16$.

In general, you can find the total number of outcomes in a repeated process (like flipping a coin) by raising the number of possible outcomes for *each* part of the process to an exponent that equals the *total* number of repetitions in the process. In this case, you have two possible outcomes per flip, and you repeat the process—the flip of the coin—four times. So there are $2^4 = 16$ total possible outcomes.

To calculate the numerator, you can use the combination formula to get the result: $_nC_k = \dfrac{n!}{k!(n-k)!}$ gives the number of ways of choosing k items from a group of n different items. What you need is the number of times two items (two heads) will occur in a set of 4 flips. The set of n objects in this case is four flips—the total number of times you're flipping the coin. You're looking for the number of times the four flips will have heads exactly twice, so $k = 2$. Putting these numbers into the formula, you get:

$$\frac{4!}{2!(4-2)!}$$
$$\frac{(4)(3)(2)(1)}{(2)(2)}$$
$$\frac{24}{4} = 6$$

Now you can calculate the probability of getting exactly 2 heads in four flips. The number of desired outcomes is 6 and the total number of outcomes is 16, so the probability is $\dfrac{6}{16} = \dfrac{3}{8}$. Choice **(C)** is correct.

32. −428

You could write out 50 more terms to solve this problem, but there's a shortcut. You're told that this is an arithmetic sequence, and the value of the nth term in an arithmetic sequence is the first term in the sequence (a_1) added to the value of the common difference between each successive pair of terms (d) multiplied by 1 less than n.

Here, the common difference in −9. So:

$$a_n = a_1 + (n - 1) \times d$$
$$a_{50} = 13 + (50 - 1) \times (-9)$$
$$a_{50} = 13 + 49 \times (-9)$$
$$a_{50} = 13 + (-441)$$
$$a_{50} = -428$$

You don't want to fall for the trap in this question by forgetting to follow the order of operations; be sure to multiply 49 by −9 before you add. An easy way to remember the order of operations is with the mnemonic *Please Excuse My Dear Aunt Sally*: Parentheses, Exponents, Multiplication and Division, Addition and Subtraction.
The correct answer is **−428**.

33. C

The area of a rectangle is length $\times$ width. You are given the width, 5, but you need the length. You know that $AC = 5$, since the opposite sides of rectangles are equal. So the length of the shorter leg of the triangle is $11 - 5 = 6$. The triangle has one leg of 6, and a hypotenuse of 10. This is a multiple of the 3:4:5 right triangle; in this case, it's a 6:8:10 right triangle. $AB = 8$, so the area of $ABCD$ is $8 \times 5 = 40$, choice (**C**).

34. 1

Since ☺ could be addition, subtraction, multiplication, or division, let's begin by testing 12 ☺ (6 ☺ 2) = 4 with each operation to determine which can true.
Addition: 12 + (6 + 2) = 12 + 8 ≠ 4 so ☺ cannot represent addition.
Subtraction: 12 – (6 – 2) = 12 − 4 ≠ 4 so ☺ cannot represent subtraction.
Multiplication: 12 × (6 × 2) = 12 × 12 ≠ 4 so ☺ cannot represent multiplication.
Division: 12 ÷ (6 ÷ 2) = 12 ÷ 3 = 4 so ☺ can represent division.
Thus, ☺ can only represent division.
$$24 ☺ 8 ☺ 3 = 24 ÷ 8 ÷ 3 = 3 ÷ 3 = \mathbf{1}$$

35. 25

To solve the problem, first divide the total number of people at the wedding by the maximum number of people that can be seated at a table.

$$\frac{291}{12} = 24\frac{1}{4}$$

This isn't the right answer, however—you can't have $\frac{1}{4}$ of a person at a table. You can't round the number down to 24, because that would leave three people standing. The correct answer is to round up our result to 25—the caterer must set up **25** tables. He'll have nine seats left over, but all the attendees will be seated.

36. 40

To find x, look at the triangle that includes $x°$ and 30°. If you can get the third angle of that triangle, you can solve for x. The missing angle is the angle adjacent and supplementary to the angle marked 70°. It equals $180° − 70° = 110°$. Therefore, the triangle has angles of $x°$, 30°, and 110°, and $x = 180 − (110 + 30) = \mathbf{40}$.

37. E

Multiples of 48 are 48, 96, 144, 192,… Multiples of 64 are 64, 128, 192,… The least common multiple is 192. So, the correct answer is **(E)**.

38. −2048

The nth term of a geometric sequence is $a_n = a_1 r^{(n − 1)}$, where a_1 is the first term and r is the common ratio. Because $\frac{-2}{1} = \frac{4}{-2} = -2$, the common ratio $r = -2$. The first term is 1, so $a_1 = 1$. Then, $a_{12} = 1(-2)^{(12 − 1)} = (-2)^{(11)} = \mathbf{-2048}$.

39. B

The length of the rectangle is 3 times the width w and the length is 90. So, $3w = 90$, $w = 30$. The perimeter is $90 + 30 + 90 + 30 = 240$. Choice **(B)** is correct.

40. B

In a 3-digit number, there are 9 choices for the first digit (1, 2, 3, 4, 5, 6, 7, 8, 9). If no digit can be used more than once, there are 9 choices for the second digit (the 8 digits left from the digits from 1 thru 9 and 0). Then there are 8 digits left for the third digit. That means that there are $9 \times 9 \times 8 = 648$ different 3-digit numbers. So, the correct answer is **(B)**.

41. 3

First, find the line style for government subsidies from the legend. Then follow the line for government subsidies from January to December, and note each time it is lower than the other three lines. For the months of April, November, and December, government subsidies were less than the other three forms of income. Be careful not to include August, when government subsidies were equal to individual contributions. The total is **3** months.

42. E

Start by finding August on the horizontal axis. Next, find the values for corporate contributions and individual contributions and take the difference. Be sure to identify the correct line styles from the legend. Corporate contributions were about 12.5 (in thousands of dollars), and individual contributions were about 5 (also in thousands of dollars). So the difference is 7.5, which represents $7,500, choice **(E)**.

43. C

Begin by finding the line styles for ticket sales and government subsidies from the legend. Next, look at the ratio of ticket sales to government subsidies for the ratio closest to 2:1. You don't have to include the multiple of 1,000 dollars since it will cancel in the ratio. In January, ticket sales were 15 and government subsidies were 5, giving a ratio of 15:5. You can reduce ratios the same way you reduce fractions, so 15:5 is the same as 3:1, and choice **(A)** is out. As for February, ticket sales were about 10 and government subsidies about 7.5, giving a ratio of 10:7.5. After dividing the left and right sides by 2.5, this ratio equals 4:3, and **(B)** is also no good. In March, ticket sales were about 10, and government subsidies were about 5, giving a ratio of 10:5. This is the same as 2:1, and **(C)** is the correct answer. For completeness, here are the results for the remaining choices: In August, you get 7.5:5, which equals 3:2. In September, you get 12.5:5, which equals 5:2.

44. B

Start by finding the respective increases in government subsidies and ticket sales from August to October. Next, take the increase in government subsidies as a percent of the increase in ticket sales. In other words, divide the increase in government subsidies by the increase in ticket sales, and convert that number to a percent. Government subsidies (in thousands of dollars) were about 5 in August and about 7.5 in October, resulting in an increase of 2.5. Ticket sales (in thousands of dollars) were about 7.5 in August and about 15 in October, resulting in an increase of 7.5. Therefore, the increase in government subsidies divided by the increase in ticket sales equals $\frac{2.5}{7.5} = \frac{1}{3}$.

To convert $\frac{1}{3}$ to a percent, multiply it by 100 to get $\frac{100}{3}\% = 33\frac{1}{3}\%$. The answer is **(B)**.

45. C

First, express the $5,000,000 as 5,000 thousand dollars so you can easily compare it to the values on the *y*-axis of the graph. Next, the straightforward thing to do is add up the different amounts of government subsidies for each month to get the total amount for the Victor Le Havre Dance Company (VLHDC) in 2008. Divide this value by 5,000, then multiply the result by 100% to get the percent. You must be careful to identify the correct line style for government subsidies.

The sum for the 12 months is

$5 + 7.5 + 5 + 5 + 7.5 + 5 + 5 + 5 + 5 + 7.5 + 5 + 5 = 9 \times 5 + 3 \times 7.5$.

This equals $45 + 22.5 = 67.5$.

The percent of government subsidies for VLHDC is therefore $\frac{67.5}{5,000} \times 100\%$, which equals $\frac{675}{500}\%$. This is a little less than $\frac{750}{500}\% = 1.5\%$ and the closest answer choice is **(C)**.

46. C

The question asks for the difference between the revenue collected for two types of fruit. To find the answer quickly, subtract the percents given, 20% for pears and 15% for apples, 20% − 15% = 5%. Multiply the total amount by 0.05: 0.05 × $7,520 = $376. Alternatively, take 10% of $7,520 by moving the decimal point one place to the left and then divide the result by 2. The correct answer is **(C)**.

47. D

Find the amount of revenue from the sale of oranges first: 40% × $7,520 = 0.4 × $7,520 = $3,008. Since the markup was 20%, this amount represents 120% of the original cost, c, of the oranges and $3,008 = 120% of c. Divide $3,008 by 1.2: $3,008 ÷ 1.2 = $2,506.67, choice **(D)**.

48. E

The key thing to remember is that percent gain or loss is always calculated based on the original cost. So find the amount of the loss and compare it to the cost of the bananas, not the revenue from them. Step 1: $2,005 − $1,504 = $501; Step 2: $501 ÷ $2,005 ≈ 0.25. The loss on the sale of bananas was about 25%, choice **(E)**.

49. 1500

Gather the data for Company A first. Its sales for the three years were 1,200, 1,500, and 1,800. To get the average, notice that the sum of these three numbers is the same as 1,500 + 1,500 + 1,500. Without any calculation, you find that the average is **1,500**.

50. C

Start by finding the sales of Company B in 2005 and 2009 from the graph. Sales in 2009 were approximately 1,100 and sales in 2005 were approximately 200. Divide 1,100 by 200 to see that sales in 2009 were about 5.5 times as great as sales in 2005: 1,100 ÷ 200 = 5.5. Choice **(C)** is correct.

51. C

It is best to line up the tops of the bars for net income with the amounts on the vertical axis. First, calculate the increase in net income from 2007 to 2009 for Company A and Company B. Then take the difference: Company A's increase minus Company B's increase. This value tells you (in millions of dollars) how much greater Company A's increase in net income was than Company B's increase. In 2007, Company A's net income (in millions of dollars) was 50. In 2009, the net income was about 95, so the increase for Company A is 95 − 50 = 45. Company B's net income in 2007 was about 10, and the net income in 2009 was about 20. So the increase for Company B is 20 − 10 = 10. Therefore, Company A's increase is about 45 − 10 = 35 million dollars more than Company B's increase. The closest choice is 36, so **(C)** is correct.

52. D

Ratios can be written as fractions, and it is usually easier to deal with them in fraction form. The lesser the fraction, the lower the ratio, so find the fractions and compare them as efficiently as possible. The information that is needed is:

Company *A*'s sales: 1,800
Company *B*'s sales: 1,100
Company *A*'s net income: 95
Company *B*'s net income: 20

The value for each answer choice in fractional form is:

(A) $\dfrac{1,800}{95}$ (B) $\dfrac{1,100}{20}$ (C) $\dfrac{1,100}{20}$ (D) $\dfrac{1,100}{95}$ (E) $\dfrac{1,800 + 1,100}{95 + 20} = \dfrac{2,900}{115}$

Choices **(A)** and **(D)** have the same denominator, but **(A)** is larger and can be eliminated because its numerator is greater. Choices **(B)** and **(D)** have the same numerator, but **(B)** is larger and can be eliminated because its denominator is less. Likewise, **(C)** can be eliminated. That leaves **(D)** and **(E)** to be compared. Remember that answer choices on Data Interpretation questions tend to be far apart and that is the case with choices **(D)** and **(E)**. Notice that the denominators are relatively close, 95 compared to 115. But the numerators are far apart, making choice **(E)** much greater. Therefore, the smallest ratio is choice **(D)**.

53. B

You'll need to compare the net income to the sales for each answer choice. If the ratio of net income to sales is at least $\dfrac{1}{10}$, then net income was at least 10% of sales. For choice **(A)**, the ratio is $\dfrac{100}{1200} = \dfrac{1}{12}$, which is too small. For choice **(B)**, the ratio is $\dfrac{22}{200} > \dfrac{1}{10}$. There is no need to continue; only one correct choice is indicated. The correct answer is **(B)**.

54. E

Out of the 50,000 seats, 13% are box seats and 33% are reserved seats. So, 13% + 33% = 46% of the seats are box seats or reserved seats. 46% of 50,000 = 0.46 × 50,000 = 23,000 and the answer is **(E)**.

55. C

Twenty-five percent of the 50,000 seats are upper deck seats. From the second graph, upper deck seats cost $30 each. So, the gross income is 0.25 × 50,000 × $30 = $375,000. The answer is **(C)**.

56. B

The gross income is the percent of the total number of seats times 50,000 times the cost of the ticket.

Box Seats: 13% × 50,000 × $80
Reserved Seats: 33% × 50,000 × $60
Upper Deck: 25% × 50,000 × $30
Terrace Level: 21% × 50,000 × $70
Bleachers: 8% × 50,000 × $20

Drop all the percent signs, the dollar sign, the 0 in the last factor, and the factor $50,000 because they are common to all amounts.
That gives you:

Box Seats: 13 × 8
Reserved Seats: 33 × 6
Upper Deck: 25 × 3
Terrace Level: 21 × 7
Bleachers: 8 × 2

The Upper Deck and Bleacher products are clearly less than the other products, so forget about them.
Rewrite the rest of the products as follows:

Box Seats: 13 × 8 = 13 × 4 × 2 = 26 × 2 = 26 + 26
Reserved Seats: 33 × 6 = 11 × 3 × 6 = 66 × 3 = 66 + 66 + 66
Terrace Level: 21 × 7 = 3 × 7 × 7 = 3 × 49 = 49 + 49 + 49

So, the Reserved Seats generate the greatest gross income. Choice **(B)** is correct.

57. E

Team A has won 87 and lost 53. Team W has won 77 and lost 63. The difference in wins is 87 − 77 = 10. The difference in losses is 63 − 53 = 10. The average of 10 and 10 is $\frac{10 + 10}{2} = \frac{20}{2} = 10$. So, the correct choice is **(E)**.

58. C, E

In the East Division, start with Team E. Team E has 87 losses. Team A has 87 wins. 87 + 87 = 174 and 163 − 174 = −11. Team D has 68 losses. Team A has 87 wins. 68 + 87 = 155 and 163 − 155 = 8. The elimination number is greater than 5. Teams B and C have better records than Team D, so they have larger elimination numbers.

In the West Division, start with Team Z. Team Z has 85 losses. Team W has 77 wins. 85 + 77 = 162 and 163 − 162 = 1. Team Y has 73 losses. Team Z has 77 wins. 73 + 77 = 150 and $163 - 150 = 13$. The elimination number is greater than 5. Team X has a better record than Team Z, so it has a larger elimination number.

The answers are **(C)** and **(E)**.

59.   D
The winning percentage for Team W is 0.550, which is less than Team C (0.557) and greater than Team D (0.514). So, the team would be in fourth place. The correct choice is **(D)**.

60.   B
Find the difference between the road wins and losses. By inspection, you call tell that Teams D, E, W, X, Y, and Z have negative differences. The difference for Team C is 4, for Team A 10, and for Team B 20. So, Team B has the best winning percentage for road games. The correct choice is **(B)**.

PART FOUR

Analytical Writing

CHAPTER 15

Introduction to Analytical Writing

OVERVIEW

The Analytical Writing section assesses not only how well you write, but also the thought processes you employ to formulate and articulate a position. Your analytical and critical thinking skills will be tested by questions that ask you to evaluate complex arguments and form an argument of your own. The goal of the Analytical Writing section is to make the test an accurate indicator of your ability to understand and formulate an argument, and to assess your analytical reasoning skills. These skills are exactly those you will need to perform well as a student at the graduate level.

In this section of the book, we'll take you through all the Analytical Writing Essay types you'll see on the GRE and give you the strategies you need to compose a well-written essay quickly and correctly. Also, all of the writing skills you'll need to perform well on the test are reviewed in the Writing Foundations and Content Review chapter.

ANALYTICAL WRITING ESSAY TYPES

The Analytical Writing Section of the GRE contains two different essay types. You'll be given 30 minutes for each essay. You'll be writing essays according to two different tasks:

- The Issue Task will provide a brief quotation on an issue of general interest and instructions on how to respond to the issue. You can discuss the issue from any perspective, making use of your own educational and personal background, examples from current or historical events, things you've read, or even relevant hypothetical situations. In this task, you will be developing your own argument.
- The Argument Task will contain a short argument that may or may not be complete, and specific instructions on how to respond to the argument. You will assess the cogency of the argument, analyzing the author's chain of reasoning and evaluating her or his use of evidence. In this task you do not develop your own argument, but instead critique the argument presented in the prompt.

For each task, you'll be given one topic, rather than a choice of several topics.

The Analytical Writing section will allow the graders to evaluate your ability to plan and compose a logical, well-reasoned essay under timed conditions. The essays are written on the computer, using a simple word processing program. Only a score report is sent to the schools to which you apply.

The Analytical Writing portion of the GRE draws heavily upon your critical thinking abilities and your facility for understanding and analyzing written material. Specifically, it evaluates your ability to:

- articulate and defend a position
- deconstruct and evaluate a complex argument
- develop a cogent argument
- assess the fundamental soundness of an argument
- recognize major, minor, and irrelevant points
- provide evidence and support for an argument
- detect the flaws in an unsound argument
- write articulately and effectively at a high level

How the Computer-Based Essays Are Administered

You can (and should) outline your essays on scratch paper, but your final answer must be typed into the computer before the end of the timed segment in order to receive a grade for your work. At the start of the first Analytical Writing section, you will be given a brief tutorial on how to use the word processing program. Don't worry. The GRE's word processor is simple and easy to use; the only functions you'll be able to use are *insert text*, *delete text*, *cut and paste*, and *undo*. You'll be well acquainted with these commands by the time you start writing. When practicing writing essays, turn off any auto-edit function your word processor has. The GRE's word processor doesn't have this function, so do your practice essays without it.

PACING STRATEGY

You'll have a limited amount of time to show the essay graders that you can think logically, analyze critically, and express yourself in clearly written English. Consequently, you'll need to know ahead of time how you're going to approach each essay. The Kaplan Method for Analytical Writing will help you plan and execute a clear, organized essay in the amount of time allotted. Note that the timing guidelines below are suggestions for how you should most effectively divide the 30 minutes you'll have for each of the essays. Different writers go through the different steps at their own pace, so don't feel chained to the breakdown below. As you practice, you will get a better sense of the amount of time you need to spend on each step to produce the best essay possible.

	Analyze an Issue	Analyze an Argument
Number of Questions	1	1
Time per Question	30 minutes	30 minutes

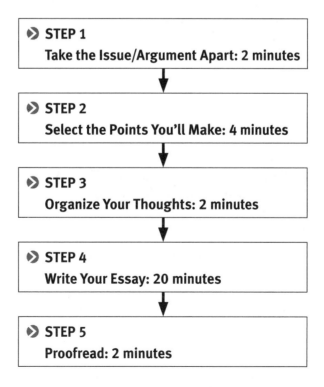

> **STEP 1**
> **Take the Issue/Argument Apart: 2 minutes**

> **STEP 2**
> **Select the Points You'll Make: 4 minutes**

> **STEP 3**
> **Organize Your Thoughts: 2 minutes**

> **STEP 4**
> **Write Your Essay: 20 minutes**

> **STEP 5**
> **Proofread: 2 minutes**

Try to keep these estimates in mind as you prepare for the test. If you use them as you work the practice items, you will be comfortable keeping to the same amounts of time on test day.

SCORING

The essay scoring for the Analytical Writing sections is *holistic*, which means that the graders base your score on their overall impression of your essay, rather than deducting specific point values for errors. A holistic score emphasizes the interrelationship of content, organization, and syntax and denotes the unified effect of these combined elements.

The scoring scale is from 0 to 6, with 6 being the highest score. Two graders will read and score each essay. If their scores differ by more than one point, a third reader will also score the essay.

Although the Analytical Writing section comprises two separate essays, ETS reports a single score that represents the average of your scores for the two essays, rounded up to the nearest half-point.

You will receive your essay score, along with your official score report, within 10–15 days of your test date.

THE SCORING RUBRIC

Each of the two essays requires different reasoning and presentation, so each has slightly different grading criteria. However, the following rubric will give you a general idea of the guidelines graders have in mind when they score Analytical Writing essays.

6: "Outstanding" Essay

- Insightfully presents and convincingly supports an opinion on the issue or a critique of the argument
- Communicates ideas clearly and is generally well-organized; connections are logical
- Demonstrates superior control of language: grammar, stylistic variety, and accepted conventions of writing; minor flaws may occur

5: "Strong" Essay

- Presents well-chosen examples and strongly supports an opinion on the issue or a critique of the argument
- Communicates ideas clearly and is generally well-organized; connections are logical
- Demonstrates solid control of language: grammar, stylistic variety, and accepted conventions of writing; minor flaws may occur

4: "Adequate" Essay

- Presents and adequately supports an opinion on the issue or a critique of the argument
- Communicates ideas fairly clearly and is adequately organized; logical connections are satisfactory
- Demonstrates satisfactory control of language: grammar, stylistic variety, and accepted conventions of writing; some flaws may occur

3: "Limited" Essay

- Succeeds only partially in presenting and supporting an opinion on the issue or a critique of the argument
- Communicates ideas unclearly and is poorly organized
- Demonstrates less than satisfactory control of language: contains significant mistakes in grammar, usage, and sentence structure

2: "Weak" Essay

- Shows little success in presenting and supporting an opinion on the issue or a critique of the argument
- Struggles to communicate ideas; essay shows a lack of clarity and organization
- Meaning is impeded by many serious mistakes in grammar, usage, and sentence structure

1: "Fundamentally Deficient" Essay

- Fails to present a coherent opinion and/or evidence on the issue or a critique of the argument
- Fails to communicate ideas; essay is seriously unclear and disorganized
- Lacks meaning due to widespread and severe mistakes in grammar, usage, and sentence structure

0: "Unscorable" Essay

- Completely ignores topic
- Attempts to copy the task
- Written in a language other than English or contains undecipherable text

NAVIGATING THE ANALYTICAL WRITING FOUNDATIONS AND CONTENT REVIEW SECTION

The chapter immediately following this one is on Writing Foundations and Content and will review the classic writing techniques, concepts, and topics that you may encounter on the GRE. This section of the book also includes individual chapters on the Issue essay and the Argument essay questions. Each chapter includes an introduction and definition of the different tasks, and a review and examples of the strategies to follow to answer those questions quickly and correctly.

Finally, at the end of this section, you'll find the Analytical Writing Practice. This will consist of two Issue essay prompts and two Argument essay prompts. At the end will be sample essays for each of the prompts. Use the Practice Prompts to test your writing skills and pinpoint areas for more focused study. When you are finished with this section of the book, you should be thoroughly prepared for any task you might encounter on the Analytical Writing section of the GRE. In addition, you'll find a practice set of essay prompts with sample essays and assessments of each sample essay.

CHAPTER 16

Analytical Writing Foundations and Content Review

INTRODUCTION TO ANALYTICAL WRITING FOUNDATIONS AND CONTENT REVIEW

The GRE tests your ability to construct a coherent, logical, and well-developed response to a writing prompt. This requires a mastery of grammatical, syntactical, and language concepts, as well as an awareness of audience and command of the writing process. These concepts include:

- Streamlining wordy phrases
- Eliminating redundancy
- Avoiding excessive qualification
- Removing unnecessary sentences
- Avoiding needless self-reference
- Using active rather than passive voice
- Including strong openings
- Avoiding needlessly vague language
- Rewording clichés
- Avoiding jargon
- Ensuring subject-verb agreement
- Avoiding faulty modification
- Avoiding unclear pronoun reference
- Including parallelism
- Using a consistent narrative voice
- Avoiding slang and colloquialisms
- Avoiding sentence fragments and run-ons
- Correctly using commas
- Correctly using semicolons
- Correctly using colons
- Correctly using hyphens and dashes
- Correctly using apostrophes

This chapter will cover all these grammatical and writing concepts and provide practice sets to help you conquer the writing task using the clearest, strongest language possible.

THE KAPLAN APPROACH TO STREAMLINING WORDY PHRASES

Why use several words when one will do? Many people make the mistake of writing phrases such as *at the present time* or *at this point in time* instead of the simpler *now*, or *take into consideration* instead of simply *consider*, in an attempt to make their prose seem more scholarly or more formal. It doesn't work. Instead, their prose ends up seeming inflated and pretentious. Don't waste your words or your time.

> WORDY: I am of the opinion that the aforementioned managers should be advised that they will be evaluated with regard to the utilization of responsive organizational software for the purpose of devising a responsive network of customers.

> CONCISE: We should tell the managers that we will evaluate their use of flexible computerized databases to develop a customer network.

STREAMLINING WORDY PHRASES PRACTICE SET

Read the following sentences and revise the wordy phrases.

1. Government funding cripples the natural relationship of arts enthusiasts and artists by subsidizing work and makes artists less creative and forces the taxpayer to take on the burden of paying for art they don't like.

   _____

   _____

2. There are many reasons why some may believe that the services of one real estate agent are superior in quality to the services of another competing real estate agent or group of agents, including the personal service, care and quality of the work they do, and the communication lines they set up and keep open.

   _____

   _____

STREAMLINING WORDY PHRASES PRACTICE SET ANSWERS AND EXPLANATIONS

Examples of the revised sentences with explanations:

1. The government should not subsidize artists because it will make them less creative and force taxpayers to pay for art they may not like.

The original sentence contained unnecessary repetition. The original sentence does not need to include both "funding" and "subsidizing," as both words refer to the same thing. The clause about "crippling the natural relationship" is also redundant, as that is implied by listing the negative effects government funding will have on both artists and the taxpayers.

2. Some of the reasons for choosing one real estate agent over another include personal service, care, communication, and quality of work.

The revised sentence condenses the two main clauses, i.e. the main idea (choosing one real estate agent over another) and the subsequent list. It also pares down the unnecessary repetition. There is no need to explain that communication lines are set up and kept open, for example.

THE KAPLAN APPROACH TO ELIMINATING REDUNDANCY

Redundancy means that the writer needlessly repeats an idea. For example, it's redundant to speak of *a beginner lacking experience*. The word *beginner* implies lack of experience by itself. You can eliminate redundant words or phrases without changing the meaning of the sentence.

Here are some common redundancies:

REDUNDANT	CONCISE
refer back	refer
few in number	few
small-sized	small
grouped together	grouped
in my own personal opinion	in my opinion
end result	result
serious crisis	crisis
new initiatives	initiatives

REDUNDANT: It is always wise to plan ahead for unexpected problems.

CONCISE: It is always wise to plan for unexpected problems.

In this example, "plan ahead" is redundant. In what situation would you "plan behind?" "Unexpected problems" is acceptable because, while some problems are unexpected, there are those that are readily anticipated.

REDUNDANCY PRACTICE SET

Read the following sentences and revise to eliminate redundancy.

1. All of these problems have combined together to create a serious crisis.

   _____

   _____

2. That monument continues to remain a significant tourist attraction.

   _____

   _____

REDUNDANCY PRACTICE SET ANSWERS AND EXPLANATIONS

Examples of the revised sentences with explanations:

1. All of these problems have combined to create a crisis.

Crises are inherently serious, and things cannot combine apart. The adjectives are redundant.

2. That monument remains a significant tourist attraction.

There is no need to reinforce remain with "continues." The verb "remain" implies that.

THE KAPLAN APPROACH TO AVOIDING EXCESSIVE QUALIFICATION

Because the object of your essay is to convince your reader of your point of view, you will want to adopt a reasonable tone. There will likely be no single, clear-cut "answer" to the essay topic, so don't overstate your case. Occasional use of such qualifiers as *fairly*, *rather*, *somewhat*, and *relatively* and of such expressions as *seems to be*, *a little*, and a *certain amount of* will let the reader know you are reasonable, but overusing such modifiers weakens your argument. Excessive qualification makes you sound hesitant. Like wordy phrases, qualifiers can add bulk without adding substance.

WORDY: This rather serious breach of etiquette may possibly shake the very foundations of the corporate world.

CONCISE: This serious breach of etiquette may shake the foundations of the corporate world.

Just as bad is the overuse of the word *very*. Some writers use this intensifying adverb before almost every adjective in an attempt to be more forceful. If you need to add emphasis, look for a stronger adjective or adverb.

WEAK: Adelaide is a very good flautist.

STRONG: Adelaide is a virtuoso flautist.

OR

Adelaide plays beautifully.

And don't try to qualify words that are already absolute.

WRONG	CORRECT
more unique	unique
the very worst	the worst
completely full	full

EXCESSIVE QUALIFICATION PRACTICE SET

Read the following sentences and revise the excessive qualification(s).

1. She is a fairly excellent teacher.

   _____

   _____

2. In my experience, a book is best enjoyed with a hot cup of coffee and a cool breeze, which just makes the day perfect and allows you to relax and enjoy the story.

   _____

   _____

EXCESSIVE QUALIFICATION PRACTICE SET ANSWERS AND EXPLANATIONS

Examples of the revised sentences with explanations:

1. She is an excellent teacher.

The use of the adverb "fairly" unnecessarily weakens the point of the sentence.

2. A book is best enjoyed with a cup of coffee and a cool breeze, which makes for a perfectly relaxing day to enjoy a story.

The first part of the sentence is unnecessary, and the second clause is unnecessarily cumbersome.

THE KAPLAN APPROACH TO REMOVING UNNECESSARY SENTENCES

Brevity is crucial for success on a timed test that emphasizes content over form. Remember, the essays on this test will force you to economize your expression. This principle suggests several things:

- Don't write a sentence that strays from the thesis.
- Don't ask a question only to answer it; rhetorical questions are a no-no.
- Don't merely copy the essay's prompt.
- Don't write a whole sentence only to announce that you're changing the subject.

If you have something to say, say it without preamble. If you need to smooth over a change of subject, do so with a transitional word or phrase rather than with a meaningless sentence.

WORDY: Which idea of the author's is more in line with what I believe? This is a very interesting question.
CONCISE: The author's beliefs are similar to mine.

The author of the wordy example above is just wasting words and time. Get to the point quickly and stay there.

UNNECESSARY SENTENCES PRACTICE SET

Read the sentences and rewrite them as one concise statement.

1. What's the purpose of getting rid of the chemical pollutants in water? People cannot safely consume water that contains chemical pollutants.

_____

_____

2. I do not believe it is necessary to include the telemetry data. The telemetry data adds little of value to the study of stellar drift.

_____

_____

UNNECESSARY SENTENCES PRACTICE SET ANSWERS AND EXPLANATIONS

Examples of the revised sentences with explanations:

1.   People cannot safely consume water that contains chemical pollutants.
The first sentence is an unnecessary rhetorical question.

2.   It is not necessary to include the telemetry data, as it adds little of value to the study of stellar drift.
In this situation, there are two different but related thoughts: the author's assessment of the merits of the data, and her or his opinion of whether or not to include it. It is therefore best to combine the sentences, which can be done elegantly and without destroying the flow of the passage.

THE KAPLAN APPROACH TO AVOIDING NEEDLESS SELF-REFERENCE

Avoid such unnecessary phrases as _I believe_, _I feel_, and _in my opinion_. There is no need to remind your reader that what you are writing is your opinion. Self-reference is another—very obvious—form of qualifying what you say.

WEAK: I am of the opinion that air pollution is a more serious problem than most people realize.
FORCEFUL: Air pollution is a more serious problem than most people realize.

NEEDLESS SELF-REFERENCE PRACTICE SET

Eliminate needless self-references in these sentences.

1. I am studying in a biotechnology program, but if it wasn't for the painting and drawing classes I took in high school, I would have never made it through.

   _____

   _____

2. The author, in my personal opinion, is stuck in the past.

   _____

   _____

NEEDLESS SELF-REFERENCE PRACTICE SET ANSWERS AND EXPLANATIONS

Examples of the revised sentences with explanations:

1. Getting through a biotechnology program would not have been possible without the painting and drawing classes I took in high school.
It is not necessary to remind the reader that you are recounting a personal anecdote by using the pronoun "I" three times in one sentence.

2. The author is stuck in the past.
Unless specified otherwise, your writing will always express your opinion.

THE KAPLAN APPROACH TO USING ACTIVE VOICE RATHER THAN PASSIVE VOICE

Using the passive voice is a way to avoid accountability (it's often referred to as the "politician's voice"). Put verbs in the active voice whenever possible. In the active voice, the subject performs the action (e.g., we write essays). In the passive voice, the subject is the receiver of the action and is often only implied (e.g., essays are written by us).

PASSIVE: The estimate of this year's tax revenues was prepared by the General Accounting Office.
ACTIVE: The General Accounting Office prepared the estimate of this year's tax revenues.

The passive voice creates weak sentences and is usually the product of writing before you think. Avoid this by organizing your thoughts before you begin writing. Take a few minutes to find out what you want to say before you say it. To change from the passive to the active voice, ask yourself WHO or WHAT is performing the action. In the sentence above, the General Accounting Office is performing the action; therefore, the General Accounting Office should be the subject of the sentence.

You should avoid the passive voice EXCEPT in the following cases:

- When you do not know who performed the action: *The letter was opened before I received it.*
- When you prefer not to refer directly to the person who performs the action: *An error has been made in computing this data.*

It is rare to have a good reason to use passive voice in either of the Analytical Writing essays on the GRE.

ACTIVE VOICE PRACTICE SET

Replace passive voice with active wherever possible.

1. One situation in which ignoring negative actions is problematic is when damage is caused to someone or something.

   _____

   _____

2. The Spanish-American War was fought by brave but misguided men.

   _____

   _____

ACTIVE VOICE PRACTICE SET ANSWERS AND EXPLANATIONS

Examples of the revised sentences with explanations:

1.   It is problematic to ignore negative actions when damage to someone or something is involved.

The original sentence is clunky and not particularly forceful. The revision is both more concise and stronger.

2.   Brave but misguided men fought the Spanish-American War.

There is no need for the passive in this situation, as it is absolutely clear who did the fighting.

THE KAPLAN APPROACH TO INCLUDING STRONG OPENINGS

Try not to begin a sentence with *there is, there are*, or *it is*. These roundabout expressions usually indicate that you are trying to distance yourself from the position you are taking. Again, weak openings usually result from writing before you think.

STRONG OPENINGS PRACTICE SET

Read the following sentences and revise to improve the opening.

1. I believe there isn't much wilderness left so we should protect what we have.

   _____

   _____

2. There are several reasons why this plane is obsolete.

   _____

   _____

STRONG OPENINGS PRACTICE SET ANSWERS AND EXPLANATIONS

Examples of the revised sentences with explanations:

1. We should protect what little wilderness we have left.
Notice how this opening statement takes a forceful position right away. Our expectation is that the writer will now go on to defend her position, explaining what makes these spaces precious and the critical steps we must take to preserve the land.

2. This plane is obsolete for several reasons.
The revised sentence is less timid and states its purpose in a stronger tone.

THE KAPLAN APPROACH TO AVOIDING NEEDLESSLY VAGUE LANGUAGE

Don't just ramble on when writing your GRE essays. Choose specific, descriptive words. Vague language weakens your writing because it forces the reader to guess what you mean instead of concentrating fully on your ideas and style. The essay topics you'll be given aren't going to be obscure. You will be able to come up with specific examples and concrete information about the topics. Your argument will be more forceful if you stick to this approach.

WEAK: Ms. Brown is highly educated.
FORCEFUL: Ms. Brown has a master's degree in business administration.

WEAK: She is a great communicator.
FORCEFUL: She speaks persuasively.

Notice that sometimes, to be more specific and concrete, you will have to use more words than you might with vague language. This principle is not in conflict with the general objective of concision. Being concise may mean eliminating unnecessary words. Avoiding vagueness may mean adding necessary words.

NEEDLESSLY VAGUE LANGUAGE PRACTICE SET

Rewrite these sentences to replace vague language with specific, concrete language.

1. There are no boundaries to the age of people who enjoy books, and the inclusion of a café is a scheme that potentially has ill effects where young readers are concerned.

   _____

   _____

2. Water is transformed into steam when the former is heated up to 100°C.

   _____

   _____

NEEDLESSLY VAGUE LANGUAGE PRACTICE SET ANSWERS AND EXPLANATIONS

Examples of the revised sentences with explanations:

1. The inclusion of a café is unwise, as it has potentially ill effects for young readers, and there are no boundaries to the age of people who enjoy books.

In the original sentence, the purpose of the introductory phrase was obscure. This is best clarified by making sure the sentence asserts that the café is going be in an area with young readers.

2. Water heated to 100° C is transformed into steam.

The use of the "former" to refer to water is ambiguous and easily clarified by rewording the sentence.

THE KAPLAN APPROACH TO REWORDING CLICHÉS

Clichés are overused expressions that may once have seemed colorful and powerful, but are now dull and worn out. Time, pressure, and anxiety may make you lose focus; that's when clichés may slip into your writing. A reliance on clichés will suggest you are a lazy thinker. Keep them out of your essay.

WEAK: Performance in a crisis is the acid test for a leader.
FORCEFUL: Performance in a crisis is the best indicator of a leader's abilities.

Putting a cliché in quotation marks to indicate your distance from the cliché does not strengthen the sentence. If anything, it just makes weak writing more noticeable. If you notice any clichés in your writing, ask yourself if you could replace them with more specific language.

REWORDING CLICHÉS PRACTICE SET

Read the following sentences and remove any clichés.

1. Be positive is my motto!

_____

_____

2. Beyond the shadow of a doubt, Jefferson was a great leader.

_____

_____

REWORDING CLICHÉS PRACTICE SET
ANSWERS AND EXPLANATIONS

Examples of the revised sentences with explanations:

1. **It is more effective to praise positive actions than to dwell on negative ones.**

The unrevised sentence is a particularly hackneyed cliché that is irritatingly saccharine as well. The revised sentence is forceful and direct, which will serve you far better in writing an analytical essay.

2. **Jefferson was a great leader.**

The revised sentence makes an equally strong assertion, but has a less histrionic tone.

THE KAPLAN APPROACH TO AVOIDING JARGON

Jargon includes two categories of words that you should avoid. First is the specialized vocabulary of a group, such as that used by doctors, lawyers, or baseball coaches. Second is the overly inflated and complex language that burdens many students' essays. You will not impress anyone with big words that do not fit the tone or context of your essay, especially if you misuse them. If you are not certain of a word's meaning or appropriateness, leave it out. An appropriate word, even a simple one, will add clarity to your argument. As you come across words you are unsure of, ask yourself, "Would a reader in a different field be able to understand exactly what I mean from the words I've chosen? Is there any way I can say the same thing more simply?"

WEAK: The company is not able to bankroll the project.
FORCEFUL: The company is not able to finance the project.

The following are commonly used jargon words:

assistance	downside	optimize
ballpark	face time	originate
bandwidth	facilitate	parameter
blindside	finalize	prioritize
bottom line	input/output	target
conceptualize	maximize	time frame
cookie-cutter	mutually beneficial	user-friendly
designate	ongoing	utilize

JARGON PRACTICE SET

Revise the following sentences to remove the jargon.

1. When a parent attempts to correct the bad behavior of a child by positively reinforcing good behavior, this classical conditioning can become ineffective due to extinction.

   _____

   _____

2. Foreign diplomats should always interface with local leaders.

   _____

   _____

JARGON PRACTICE SET
ANSWERS AND EXPLANATIONS

Examples of the revised sentences with explanations:

1. **Attempting to correct a child's bad behavior by rewarding good behavior can become ineffective when the reward is withdrawn.**

The first sentence was loaded with jargon not readily understood by the average reader. The revised sentence expresses the exact same thought, but in less technically opaque language.

2. **Foreign diplomats should always talk to local leaders.**

The verb "interface" is most appropriately used in a technical context. It sounds jarring and pretentious in the unrevised sentence.

THE KAPLAN APPROACH TO ENSURING
SUBJECT-VERB AGREEMENT

A verb must agree with its subject regardless of intervening phrases. Do not let the words that come between the subject and the verb confuse you as to the number (singular or plural) of the subject. Usually one word can be pinpointed as the grammatical subject of the sentence. Find the verb, no matter how far removed, and make sure that it agrees with that subject in number.

INCORRECT: The joys of climbing mountains, especially if one is a novice climber without the proper equipment, escapes me.
CORRECT: The *joys* of climbing mountains, especially if one is a novice climber without the proper equipment, *escape* me.

Watch out for collective nouns like *group, audience, committee,* or *majority*. These take a singular noun unless you are emphasizing the individuals forming the group.

CORRECT: A *majority* of the committee *have signed* their names to the report. (The individual members of the committee are being emphasized.)
CORRECT: A *majority* of the jury *thinks* that the defendant is guilty. (The collective is being emphasized.)

A subject that consists of two or more nouns connected by the conjunction *and* takes the plural form of the verb.

CORRECT: *Karl*, an expert in cooking Hunan chicken, *and George*, an expert in preparing Hunan spicy duck, *have combined* their expertise to start a new restaurant.

However, when the subject consists of two or more nouns connected by *or* or *nor*, the verb agrees with the CLOSEST noun.

CORRECT: Either the senators or the *president is* misinformed.
CORRECT: Either the president or the *senators are* misinformed.

Some connecting phrases look as though they should make a group of words into a plural but actually do not. The only connecting word that can make a series of singular nouns into a plural subject is *and*. In particular, the following connecting words and phrases do NOT result in a plural subject:

along with, as well as, besides, in addition to, together with

INCORRECT: The president, along with the secretary of state and the director of the CIA, are misinformed.
CORRECT: The *president*, along with the secretary of state and the director of the CIA, *is* misinformed.

You can usually trust your ear to give you the correct verb form. However, subject-verb agreement can be tricky in the following instances:

- When the subject and verb are separated
- When the subject is an indefinite pronoun
- When the subject consists of more than one noun

If a sentence that is grammatically correct still sounds awkward, you should probably rephrase your thought.

SUBJECT-VERB AGREEMENT PRACTICE SET

Read the sentences below and revise to ensure subject-verb agreement.

1. The arts is a very important topic to discuss at this point in our history.

   _____

   _____

2. The majority of the organization's members is over 60 years old.

   _____

   _____

SUBJECT-VERB AGREEMENT PRACTICE SET ANSWERS AND EXPLANATIONS

Examples of the revised sentences with explanations:

1. The arts are very important topics to discuss at this point in our history.

The verb is plural because the sentence is referring to more than one type of art.

2. The majority of the organization's members are over 60 years old.

The verb must be pluralized because the subject is more than one member.

THE KAPLAN APPROACH TO AVOIDING FAULTY MODIFICATION

Modifiers should be placed as close as possible to what they modify. In English, the position of the word within a sentence often establishes the word's relationship to other words in the sentence. If a modifier is placed too far from the word it modifies, the meaning may be lost or obscured. Notice, in the following sentences, the ambiguity that results when the modifying phrases are misplaced.

UNCLEAR: Gary and Martha sat talking about the problem in the office.
CLEAR: Gary and Martha sat in the office talking about the problem.

UNCLEAR: He only threw the ball eight yards.
CLEAR: He threw the ball only eight yards.

In addition to misplaced modifiers, watch for dangling modifiers: modifiers whose intended referents are not even present.

INCORRECT: Coming out of context, Peter was startled by Julia's perceptiveness.
CORRECT: Julia's remark, coming out of context, startled Peter with its perceptiveness.

FAULTY MODIFICATION PRACTICE SET

Read the following sentences and revise the faulty modification.

1. Without government funding, you would see the arts die out in a matter of years.

_____

_____

2. Having been an avid reader all my life, a bookstore with a café seems like heaven on earth to me.

_____

_____

FAULTY MODIFICATION PRACTICE SET ANSWERS AND EXPLANATIONS

Examples of the revised sentences with explanations:

1. You would see the arts die out in a matter of years if government funding did not support them.

The revised sentence clears away the ambiguity introduced by the phrase "Without government funding." In the unrevised sentence, it is unclear if only you would see the arts die out, or if the effect would be universal.

2. A bookstore with a café seems like heaven on earth to a life-long reader like me.

In the unrevised sentence it is unclear whether it is the author or the bookstore that has been a life-long avid reader.

THE KAPLAN APPROACH TO AVOIDING UNCLEAR PRONOUN REFERENCE

A pronoun is a word that replaces a noun in a sentence. Every time you write a pronoun—_he, him, his, she, her, it, its, they, their, that,_ or _which_—be sure there can be absolutely no doubt what its antecedent is. (An antecedent is the particular noun to which a pronoun refers.) Careless use of pronouns can obscure your intended meaning.

UNCLEAR: The teacher told the student he was talented. (Does _he_ refer to _teacher_ or _student_?)
CLEAR: The student was talented, and the teacher told him so.
CLEAR: The teacher considered himself talented and told the student so.

UNCLEAR: Sara knows more about history than Irina because she learned it from her father.
(Does _she_ refer to _Sara_ or _Irina_?) You can usually rearrange a sentence to avoid ambiguous pronoun references.
CLEAR: Because Sara learned history from her father, she knows more than Irina does.

CLEAR: Because Irina learned history from her father, she knows less about it than Sara does.

If you are worried that a pronoun reference will be ambiguous, rewrite the sentence so that there is no doubt. Don't be afraid to repeat the antecedent if necessary.

UNCLEAR: I would rather settle in Phoenix than in Albuquerque, although it lacks wonderful restaurants.
CLEAR: I would rather settle in Phoenix than in Albuquerque, although Phoenix lacks wonderful restaurants.

A reader must be able to pinpoint the pronoun's antecedent. Even if you think the reader will know what you mean, do not use a pronoun without a clear and appropriate antecedent.

INCORRECT: When you are painting, be sure not to get it on the floor.
(*It* could only refer to the noun *paint*. But do you see the noun *paint* anywhere in the sentence? Pronouns cannot refer to implied nouns.)
CORRECT: When you are painting, be sure not to get any paint on the floor.

UNCLEAR PRONOUN REFERENCE PRACTICE SET

Revise the following sentences to correct unclear pronouns.

1. Sports enthusiasts' desires should not trump the needs of the river and the quiet enjoyment of the people who live near the river. Their opinions should be taken into account.

   _____

   _____

2. Caroline telephoned her friends in California before going home for the night, which she had not done for weeks.

   _____

   _____

UNCLEAR PRONOUN REFERENCE PRACTICE SET ANSWERS AND EXPLANATIONS

Examples of the revised sentences with explanations:

1. Sports enthusiasts' desires should not trump the needs of the river and the quiet enjoyment of the people who live near the river, whose opinions should be taken into account.

In the original sentences, it is unclear if the pronoun "their" refers the people who live near the river, or the needs of the river. Replacing "their" with "whose" clarifies matters.

2. Because she had not telephoned her California friends in weeks, Caroline called them before she went home for the night.

We do not know whether Caroline had not spent the night at home in weeks or whether she had not telephoned her friends in weeks.

THE KAPLAN APPROACH TO INCLUDING PARALLELISM

It can be rhetorically effective to use a particular construction several times in succession to provide emphasis. The technique is called parallel construction, and it is effective only when used sparingly.

EXAMPLE: *As a* leader, Lincoln inspired a nation to throw off the chains of slavery; *as a* philosopher, he proclaimed the greatness of the little man; *as a* human being, he served as a timeless example of humility.

The repetition of the italicized construction provides a strong sense of rhythm and organization to the sentence and alerts the reader to the multiple aspects of Lincoln's character. Matching constructions must be expressed in parallel form. Writers often use a parallel structure incorrectly for dissimilar items.

INCORRECT: They are sturdy, attractive, and cost only a dollar each. (The phrase *They are* makes sense preceding the adjectives *sturdy* and *attractive*, but cannot be understood before *cost only a dollar each*.)
CORRECT: They are sturdy and attractive, and they cost only a dollar each.

Parallel constructions must be expressed in parallel grammatical form: all nouns, all infinitives, all gerunds, all prepositional phrases, or all clauses.

INCORRECT: All business students should learn word processing, accounting, and how to program computers.
CORRECT: All business students should learn word processing, accounting, and computer programming.

This principle applies to any words that might precede items in a series: either repeat the word before every element in a series or include it only before the first item. (In effect, your treatment of the second element of the series determines the form of all subsequent elements.)

INCORRECT: He invested his money in stocks, in real estate, and a home for retired performers.
CORRECT: He invested his money in stocks, in real estate, and in a home for retired performers.
CORRECT: He invested his money in stocks, real estate, and a home for retired performers.

A number of constructions always call for you to express ideas in parallel form. These constructions include the following:

X is as _____ as Y.
X is more _____ than Y.
X is less _____ than Y.
Both X and Y ...
Either X or Y ...
Neither X nor Y ...
Not only X but also Y ...

X and Y can stand for as little as one word or as much as a whole clause, but in any case, the grammatical structure of X and Y must be identical.

INCORRECT: The view from this apartment is as spectacular as from that mountain lodge.
CORRECT: The view from this apartment is as spectacular as the view from that mountain lodge.

PARALLELISM PRACTICE SET

Read these sentences and revise to correct parallelism.

1. Homes sell faster or slowly for all types of reasons.

   _____

   _____

2. The grocery baggers were ready, able, and were quite determined to do a great job.

   _____

   _____

PARALLELISM PRACTICE SET ANSWERS AND EXPLANATIONS

Examples of the revised sentences with explanations:

1. Homes sell faster or slower for all types of reasons.

In order for the parallel construction to work in this sentence, the two thoughts must have identical grammatical form. Therefore, "slower" is correct because it is gramatically similar to "faster."

2. The grocery baggers were ready, able, and quite determined to do a great job.

In this example, there is no need to repeat the verb; the phrase "quite determined to do a great job" can be treated as the final object in the series of terms.

THE KAPLAN APPROACH TO USING A CONSISTENT NARRATIVE VOICE

True, we have advised you to avoid needless self-reference. But an occasional self-reference may be appropriate in your GRE essays. You may even call yourself *I* if you want, as long as you keep the number of first-person pronouns to a minimum. Less egocentric ways of referring to the narrator include *we* and *one*. If these more formal ways of writing seem stilted, stay with *I*.

- In my lifetime, I have seen many challenges to the principle of free speech.
- We can see how a free society can get too complacent when free speech is taken for granted.
- One must admit that one should not over-generalize.

The method of self-reference you select is called the narrative voice of your essay. Any of the previous narrative voices are acceptable. Nevertheless, whichever you choose, you must be careful not to shift narrative voice in your essay. If you use *I* in the first sentence, for example, do not use *we* in a later sentence. You can shift narrative voice when presenting someone else's point of view, or when speaking hypothetically, but your authorial voice should always be consistent.

INCORRECT: In my lifetime, *I* have seen many challenges to the principle of free speech. *We* can see how a free society can get too complacent when free speech is taken for granted.

It is likewise wrong to shift from *you* to *one*:

INCORRECT: Just by following the news, *you* can readily see how politicians have a vested interest in pleasing powerful interest groups. But *one* should not generalize about this tendency.

USING A CONSISTENT NARRATIVE VOICE PRACTICE SET

Read the sentences below and revise the narrative voice to make it consistent.

1. Not all wilderness areas are similar to the glorious Ansel Adams landscapes that we all imagine. If you've seen pictures of ANWAR, one would be unimpressed by the "natural beauty" of that massive swamp.

    _____

    _____

2. I am disgusted with the waste we tolerate in this country. One cannot simply stand by without adding to such waste: living here makes you wasteful.

    _____

    _____

USING A CONSISTENT NARRATIVE VOICE PRACTICE SET ANSWERS AND EXPLANATIONS

Examples of the revised sentences with explanations:

1. Not all wilderness areas are similar to the glorious Ansel Adams landscapes that you might imagine. If you were to see pictures of ANWAR, you would be unimpressed by the "natural beauty" of that massive swamp.

The narrative voice of most of the passage is personal and first-person, and does not justify a switch to the more formal third person "one" in the second sentence.

2. I am disgusted with the waste we tolerate in this country. We cannot simply stand by without adding to such waste: living here makes us wasteful.

Similarly, in this passage the tone and narrative is impassioned and therefore emphatically first person. The author relies on addressing the reader directly for the emotional thrust of his or her argument. Therefore, it should retain both the singular and plural forms of the first person pronoun.

THE KAPLAN APPROACH TO AVOIDING SLANG AND COLLOQUIALISMS

Conversational speech is filled with slang and colloquial expressions. But you should avoid slang on the GRE. Slang terms and colloquialisms, or overly casual sayings, can be confusing to the reader, since these expressions are not universally understood. Even worse, such informal writing may give readers the impression that you are poorly educated or arrogant. Always bear in mind the audience for whom your writing is intended. Finally, remember that contractions are not commonly used in formal writing, so try to avoid them altogether in your essays. You should be fine if you keep in mind the differences between *written* and *spoken* English.

INAPPROPRIATE: He is really into gardening.
CORRECT: He is an avid gardener.
INAPPROPRIATE: She plays a wicked game of tennis.
CORRECT: She excels at tennis.
INAPPROPRIATE: Myra has got to go to Memphis for a week.
CORRECT: Myra must go to Memphis for a week.
INAPPROPRIATE: Joan's been doing science for eight years now.
CORRECT: Joan has been a scientist for eight years now.

SLANG AND COLLOQUIALISM PRACTICE SET

Read the sentences below and revise the tone to eliminate slang and jargon.

1. Gertrude has been rockin' the sales floor for almost thirty years now.

   _____

   _____

2. Normal human beings can't cope with repeated humiliation.

   _____

   _____

SLANG AND COLLOQUIALISM PRACTICE SET ANSWERS AND EXPLANATIONS

Examples of the revised sentences with explanations:

1. **Gertrude has excelled as a salesperson for almost thirty years.**

Not only is the tone in the unrevised sentence too informal, you should not try to make your writing sound like spoken language. The spoken and written registers are very different, and on the GRE writing sections you will always want to spell out words in their entirety, and avoid contractions when possible.

2. **Normal human beings cannot tolerate repeated humiliation.**

Again, avoid contractions wherever possible.

THE KAPLAN APPROACH TO AVOIDING SENTENCE FRAGMENTS AND RUN-ONS

Every sentence in formal expository writing must have an independent clause: a clause that contains a subject and a predicate. A sentence fragment has no independent clause; a run-on sentence has two or more independent clauses that are improperly connected. As you edit your practice essays, check your sentence constructions, noting any tendency toward fragments or run-on sentences.

FRAGMENT: Global warming. That is what the scientists and journalists are worried about this month.
CORRECT: Global warming is the cause of concern for scientists and journalists this month.

FRAGMENT: Seattle is a wonderful place to live. Mountains, ocean, and forests, all within easy driving distance. If you can ignore the rain.
CORRECT: Seattle is a wonderful place to live, with mountains, ocean, and forests all within easy driving distance. However, it certainly does rain often.

FRAGMENT: Why is the author's position preposterous? Because he makes generalizations that are untrue.
CORRECT: The author's position is preposterous because he makes generalizations that are untrue.

Beginning single-clause sentences with coordinate conjunctions—*and, but, or, nor*, and *for*—is acceptable in moderation (although some readers still object to beginning a sentence with *and*).

CORRECT: Most people would agree that indigent patients should receive wonderful health care. But every treatment has its price.

Time pressure may also cause you to write two or more sentences as one. When you proofread your essays, watch out for independent clauses that are not joined with any punctuation at all or are only joined with a comma.

RUN-ON: Current insurance practices are unfair they discriminate against the people who need insurance most.

You can repair run-on sentences in any one of three ways. First, you could use a period to make separate sentences of the independent clauses.

CORRECT: Current insurance practices are unfair. They discriminate against the people who need insurance most.

You could also use a semicolon. A semicolon is a weak period. It separates independent clauses but signals to the reader that the ideas in the clauses are related.

CORRECT: Current insurance practices are unfair; they discriminate against the people who need insurance most.

The third method of repairing a run-on sentence is usually the most effective. Use a conjunction to turn an independent clause into a dependent one and to make explicit how the clauses are related. A comma is also called for when using one of the FANBOYS (**F**or, **A**nd, **N**or, **B**ut, **O**r, **Y**et, **S**o) coordinating conjunctions. You should insert a comma before one of these conjunctions when it separates two independent clauses.

CORRECT: Current insurance practices are unfair because they discriminate against the people who need insurance most.

CORRECT: Current insurance practices are unfair, for they discriminate against the people who need insurance most.

A common cause of run-on sentences is the misuse of adverbs like *however, nevertheless, furthermore, likewise,* and *therefore.*

RUN-ON: Current insurance practices are discriminatory, furthermore they make insurance too expensive for the poor.
CORRECT: Current insurance practices are discriminatory. Furthermore, they make insurance too expensive for the poor.

SENTENCE FRAGMENTS AND RUN-ONS PRACTICE SET

Read the sentences below and revise the fragment/run on sentence.

1. The writer of this letter lays out a very cogent argument about why Adams Realty is superior it is organized, has strong points with clear examples, and is convincing.

   _____

   _____

2. Leadership ability. That is the elusive quality that our current government employees have yet to capture.

   _____

   _____

SENTENCE FRAGMENTS AND RUN-ONS PRACTICE SET ANSWERS AND EXPLANATIONS

Examples of the revised sentences with explanations:

1. The writer of this letter lays out a very cogent, organized, and convincing argument with clear examples and strong points to illustrate the superiority of Adams Realty.

The unrevised sentence was turgid and unruly. We have two choices: condense the series of nouns and adjectives, or break it into two different sentences. We've gone with concision for this example. By deleting the "it is," which really should indicate the start of a new sentence, we have put the adjectives describing the argument in a series with commas, and put the nouns into a prepositional phrase at the end of the sentence.

2. Leadership ability is the elusive quality that our current government employees have yet to capture.

This pair of sentences is fairly easy to revise. The first is a fragment that can easily be incorporated into the second, as the pronoun "that" is referring back to "Leadership ability."

THE KAPLAN APPROACH TO CORRECTLY USING COMMAS

Commas are one of the trickier points of style and usage. Different editors have different preferences and conventions for how and when they should be used. The guidelines below are ideally suited for use in terse, analytical essays, such as those found on the GRE Analytical Writing sections.

Use commas to separate items in a series. If more than two items are listed in a series, they should be separated by commas. The final comma—the one that precedes the word *and*—is optional (but be consistent throughout your essays).

CORRECT: My recipe for buttermilk biscuits contains flour, baking soda, salt, shortening and buttermilk.
CORRECT: My recipe for buttermilk biscuits contains flour, baking soda, salt, shortening, and buttermilk.

Don't place commas before the first element of a series or after the last element.

INCORRECT: My investment advisor recommended that I construct a portfolio of, stocks, bonds, commodities futures, and precious metals.
INCORRECT: The elephants, tigers, and dancing bears, were the highlights of the circus.

Use commas to separate two or more adjectives before a noun, but don't use a comma after the last adjective in the series.

INCORRECT: The manatee is a round, blubbery, bewhiskered, creature whose continued presence in American waters is endangered by careless boaters.
CORRECT: The manatee is a round, blubbery, bewhiskered creature whose continued presence in American waters is endangered by careless boaters.

Use commas to set off parenthetical clauses and phrases. (A parenthetical expression is one that is not necessary to the main idea of the sentence.)

CORRECT: Gordon, who is a writer by profession, bakes an excellent cheesecake.

The main idea is that Gordon bakes an excellent cheesecake. The intervening clause merely serves to identify Gordon; thus, it should be set off with commas.

Use commas after introductory, participial, or prepositional phrases.

CORRECT: Having watered his petunias every day during the drought, Harold was very disappointed when his garden was destroyed by insects.
CORRECT: After the banquet, Harold and Martha went dancing.

Use commas to separate independent clauses (clauses that could stand alone as complete sentences) connected by coordinating conjunctions such as *and, but, yet,* and so on.

INCORRECT: Susan's old car has been belching blue smoke from the tailpipe for two weeks, but has not broken down yet.

CORRECT: Susan's old car has been belching blue smoke from the tailpipe for two weeks, but it has not broken down yet.

INCORRECT: Zachariah's pet frog eats 50 flies a day, and never gets indigestion.

CORRECT: Zachariah's pet frog eats 50 flies a day, yet it has never gotten indigestion.

COMMAS PRACTICE SET

Correct the punctuation errors in the following sentences.

1. Teaching, is not a popularity contest!

   _____

   _____

2. Pushing through the panicked crowd the security guards frantically searched for the suspect.

   _____

   _____

COMMAS PRACTICE SET
ANSWERS AND EXPLANATIONS

Examples of the revised sentences with explanations:

1. Teaching is not a popularity contest!

The gerund "Teaching" functions as the subject of the main clause, and therefore cannot be set off by a comma.

2. Pushing through the panicked crowd, the security guards frantically searched for the suspect.

The participial phrase "Pushing through the panicked crowd," is not necessary to the main idea of the sentence, and must therefore be set off with a comma.

THE KAPLAN APPROACH TO CORRECTLY USING SEMICOLONS

Use a semicolon instead of a coordinating conjunction (such as *and, or,* or *but*) to link two closely related independent clauses. Additionally, use semicolons to separate items in a series in which the items contain commas. Be certain that there are complete sentences on both sides of a semicolon unless you are using it to separate items in a series.

INCORRECT: Whooping cranes are an endangered species; and they are unlikely to survive if we continue to pollute.
CORRECT: Whooping cranes are an endangered species; there are only 50 whooping cranes in New Jersey today.
CORRECT: Three important dates in the history of the company are December 16, 1999; April 4, 2003; and June 30, 2007.

Use a semicolon between independent clauses connected by words like *therefore, nevertheless,* and *moreover.*

CORRECT: The staff meeting has been postponed until next Thursday; therefore, I will be unable to get approval for my project until then.
CORRECT: Farm prices have been falling rapidly for two years; nevertheless, the traditional American farm is not in danger of disappearing.

SEMICOLONS PRACTICE SET

Correct the punctuation errors in the following sentences.

1. Very few students wanted to take the class in physics, only the professor's kindness kept it from being canceled.

   _____

   _____

2. Marcus has five years' experience in karate; but Tyler has even more.

   _____

   _____

SEMICOLONS PRACTICE SET ANSWERS AND EXPLANATIONS

Examples of the revised sentences with explanations:

1. Very few students wanted to take the class in physics; only the professor's kindness kept it from being canceled.

The two independent clauses in the sentence have to be separated by a semicolon or a coordinating conjunction. Since "only" does not function as that type of conjunction, a semicolon is required for the sentence to be grammatically correct.

2. Marcus has five years' experience in karate, but Tyler has even more.

There is no need to separate the two clauses with a semicolon because of the use of the coordinating conjunction "but."

THE KAPLAN APPROACH TO CORRECTLY USING COLONS

In formal writing, the colon is used only as a means of signaling that what follows is a list, definition, explanation, or concise summary of what has gone before. The colon usually follows an independent clause, and it will frequently be accompanied by a reinforcing expression like *the following, as follows*, or *namely* or by an explicit demonstrative pronoun like *this*.

CORRECT: Your instructions are as follows: read the passage carefully, answer the questions on the last page, and turn over your answer sheet.
CORRECT: This is what I found in the refrigerator: a moldy lime, half a bottle of stale soda, and a jar of peanut butter.

Be careful not to put a colon between a verb and its direct object.

INCORRECT: I want: a slice of pizza and a small green salad.
CORRECT: This is what I want: a slice of pizza and a small green salad. (The colon serves to announce that a list is forthcoming.)
CORRECT: I don't want much for lunch: just a slice of pizza and a small green salad. (Here what follows the colon defines what *don't want much* means.)

Context will occasionally make clear that a second independent clause is closely linked to its predecessor, even without an explicit expression like those used above. Here, too, a colon is appropriate, although a period will always be correct too.

CORRECT: We were aghast: the "charming country inn" that had been advertised in such glowing terms proved to be a leaking cabin full of mosquitoes.

COLONS PRACTICE SET

Correct the punctuation errors in the following sentences.

1. The residents of Mason City do not just enjoy: swimming, boating, and fishing.

_____

_____

2. The chef has created a masterpiece, the pasta is delicate yet firm, the mustard greens are fresh, and the medallions of veal are melting in my mouth.

_____

_____

COLONS PRACTICE SET ANSWERS AND EXPLANATIONS

Examples of the revised sentences with explanations:

1. The residents of Mason City do not just enjoy swimming, boating, and fishing.

The use of a colon is inappropriate in this situation because colons should not separate a verb and its direct object, such as "enjoy" and "swimming."

2. The chef has created a masterpiece: the pasta is delicate yet firm, the mustard greens are fresh, and the medallions of veal are melting in my mouth.

A colon should follow the word "masterpiece" in order to signal that list is coming (note that the list does not have to be single words; it can be composed of independent clauses).

THE KAPLAN APPROACH TO CORRECTLY USING HYPHENS AND DASHES

Use a hyphen with the compound numbers twenty-one through ninety-nine and with fractions used as adjectives.

CORRECT: Sixty-five students constituted a majority.
CORRECT: A two-thirds vote was necessary to carry the measure.

Use a hyphen with the prefixes _ex-_, _all-_, and _self-_ and with the suffix _-elect_.

CORRECT: The constitution protects against self-incrimination.
CORRECT: The president-elect was invited to chair the meeting.

Use a hyphen with a compound adjective when it comes before the word it modifies but not when it comes after the word it modifies.

CORRECT: The no-holds-barred argument continued into the night.
CORRECT: The argument continued with no holds barred.

Use a hyphen with any prefix used before a proper noun or adjective.

CORRECT: His pro-African sentiments were heartily applauded.
CORRECT: They believed that his accent was un-Australian.

Use a hyphen to separate component parts of a word to avoid confusion with other words or to avoid the use of a double vowel.

CORRECT: The sculptor was able to re-form the clay after the dog knocked over the bust.
CORRECT: The family re-entered their house after the fire marshal departed.

Use a dash to indicate an abrupt change of thought.

CORRECT: The inheritance must cover the entire cost of the proposal—Gail has no other money to invest.
CORRECT: To get a high score—and who doesn't want to get a high score?— you need to devote yourself to prolonged and concentrated study.

HYPHENS AND DASHES PRACTICE SET

Correct the punctuation errors in the following sentences.

1. The synopsis must cover elements of the plot—such as—story, character, and plot outline.

   _____

   _____

2. John and his ex wife remained on friendly terms.

   _____

   _____

HYPHENS AND DASHES PRACTICE SET ANSWERS AND EXPLANATIONS

Examples of the revised sentences with explanations:

1. The synopsis must cover elements of the plot such as story, character, and plot outline.

The use of a dash is unnecessary as you are introducing a list, not radically changing your thought.

2. John and his ex-wife remained on friendly terms.

The prefix "ex" modifies the word "wife," and thus requires a hyphen.

THE KAPLAN APPROACH TO CORRECTLY USING APOSTROPHES

Use an apostrophe in a contraction to indicate that one or more letters have been eliminated. But try to avoid using contractions altogether on the GRE: using the full form of a verb is more appropriate in formal writing.

CONTRACTED: We'd intended to address the question of equal rights, but it's too late to begin the discussion now.
FULL FORM: We had intended to address the question of equal rights, but it is too late to begin the discussion now.

One of the most common errors involving the apostrophe is using it in the contraction *you're* or *it's* to indicate the possessive form of *you* or *it*. When you write *you're*, ask yourself whether you mean *you are*. If not, the correct word is *your*. Similarly, are you sure you mean *it is*? If not, use the possessive form *its*.

INCORRECT: You're chest of drawers is ugly.
CORRECT: *Your* chest of drawers is ugly.

INCORRECT: The dog hurt it's paw.
CORRECT: The dog hurt *its* paw.

Use the apostrophe to indicate the possessive form of a noun.

NOUN	POSSESSIVE
the boy	the boy's
Harry	Harry's
the children	the children's
the boys	the boys'
the bass	the bass's

NOTE: Possessive forms can sometimes look like contractions. The word *boy's*, for example, could have one of three meanings:

- The boy's an expert at chess. (contraction: the boy is . . .)
- The boy's left for the day. (contraction: the boy has . . .)
- The boy's face was covered with pie. (possessive: the face of the boy)

The word boys' can have only one meaning: a plural possessive (the ___ of the boys).

CORRECT: Ms. Fox's office is on the first floor. (One person possesses the office.)
CORRECT: The Foxes' apartment has a wonderful view. (There are several people named Fox living in the same apartment. First you must form the plural; then add the apostrophe to indicate possession.)

Possessive pronouns do not use an apostrophe (with the exception of the neutral *one*, which forms its possessive by adding *'s*).

INCORRECT: The tiny cabin had been our's for many years.
CORRECT: The tiny cabin had been *ours* for many years.

APOSTROPHES PRACTICE SET

Read the sentences below and revise for appropriate apostrophe use.

1. Private investors should pay for what they like, and people should be allowed to keep their own money and use it for the thing's they want. The government has no business paying for art.

    _____

    _____

2. The young men were students at the Boy's Latin School.

    _____

    _____

APOSTROPHES PRACTICE SET
ANSWERS AND EXPLANATIONS

Examples of the revised sentences with explanations:

1. Private investors should pay for what they like, and people should be allowed to keep their own money and use it for the things they want. The government has no business paying for art.

The word "things" in this sentence is used as a direct object and not as a possessive. There is no need for an apostrophe, as the 's' is simply pluralizing it.

2. The young men were students at the Boys' Latin School.

The comma should follow the 's' in 'Boys,' as the term is referring to more than one boy.

In the chapters that follow, you will learn how to approach the two basic types of Analytical Writing Reasoning tasks on the GRE. The Argument task will ask you to analyze an incomplete argument, while the Issue task will oblige you to come up with own of your own. Although each type of task requires you to approach an argument in distinctly different ways, one thing is true: both are built on the foundations you studied in this chapter.

CHAPTER 17

The Issue Essay

INTRODUCTION TO THE ISSUE ESSAY

The first of the Analytical Writing essay tasks is the Issue essay. On the Issue essay, you will be given a point of view about which you'll have to form an opinion and then provide a well-supported and justifiable case for that opinion.

The Issue essay requires you to construct your own argument by making claims and providing evidence to support your position on a given issue. The directions will ask you to take a position on the issue and instruct you to explain your position convincingly, using reasons and/or examples to back up your assertions.

For the assignment topic, expect about one to two sentences that discuss a broad, general issue, sometimes presenting only one point of view, sometimes presenting two conflicting points. Either way, the test will present a statement that could reasonably be either supported or argued against. Your job is to form an opinion on the topic and make a case for that opinion.

The directions for Issue essays will look like this:

> You have 30 minutes to plan and compose a response in which you evaluate the argument passage that appears below. A response to any other argument will receive a score of zero. Make sure that you respond according to the specific instructions and support your evaluation with relevant reasons and/or examples.

An Issue essay will always begin with a statement. It will look something like this:

> *The drawbacks to the use of nuclear power mean that it is not a long-term solution to the problem of meeting ever-increasing energy needs.*

The second part of the directions, the prompt, will give specific directions for how to approach the essay. An Issue essay prompt will look something like this:

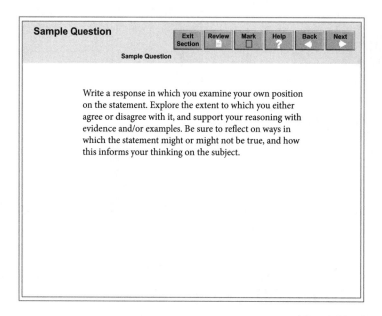

The Issue essay prompt may vary. Other prompts you may see for the Issue essay will look like this:

- Write a response in which you examine your own position on the statement. Explore the extent to which you either agree or disagree with it, and support your reasoning with evidence and/or examples. Be sure to reflect on ways in which the statement might or might not be true, and how this informs your thinking on the subject.

- Write your own response to the recommendation in which you discuss why you either agree or disagree with it. Support your response with evidence and/or examples. Use a hypothetical set of circumstances to illustrate the consequences of accepting or rejecting the recommendation, and explain how this informs your thinking.

- Develop a response to the claim in which you discuss whether or not you agree with it. Focus specifically on the most powerful or compelling examples that could be used to refute your position.

- Write a response in which you determine which view bears the closest resemblance to your own. In justifying your reasoning and supporting your position, be sure to include your reaction to both of the views presented.

- Develop a response to the claim in which you discuss whether or not you agree with it. Focus specifically on whether or not you agree with the reason upon which the claim is based.

- Write a response discussing your reaction to the policy stated above. Justify your reasoning for the position you take. Explain the potential consequences or implications for implementing such a policy and how this informs your position.

THE KAPLAN METHOD FOR ANALYTICAL WRITING

STEP 1 **Take the issue/argument apart.**

STEP 2 **Select the points you will make.**

STEP 3 **Organize, using Kaplan's essay templates.**

STEP 4 **Type your essay.**

STEP 5 **Proofread your work.**

HOW THE KAPLAN METHOD FOR ANALYTICAL WRITING WORKS

Now let's discuss how the Kaplan Method for Analytical Writing works for the Issue essay:

STEP 1
Take the issue apart.

Read the assignment and consider both sides of the issue. Use your scratch paper throughout Steps 1–3. Restate the issue in your own words. Consider the other side of the issue, and put that into your own words as well.

STEP 2
Select the points you will make.

After you consider what both sides of the issue mean, think of reasons and examples for both sides and make a decision as to which side you will support or the extent to which you agree with the stated position.

STEP 3
Organize, using Kaplan's essay templates.

Organize your thoughts by outlining what you want to say, so that you will be able to approach the actual writing process confidently and focus on expressing your ideas clearly. In the introduction, restate the prompt in your own words and then state whether you agree or disagree, and give a preview of the supporting points you plan to make. In the middle paragraphs give your points of agreement (or disagreement) and provide support. Determine what evidence you will use to support each point. Be sure to lead with your best argument. Think about how the essay as a whole will flow. Conclude by summing up your position on the issue.

STEP 4
Type your essay.

You shouldn't proceed with this step until you've completed the three preceding ones. Graders have a limited amount of time in which to read your essay, so start out and conclude with strong statements. Be emphatic and concise with your prose, and link related ideas with transitions. This will help your writing flow and make things easier on the grader. Furthermore, you'll save time and energy by preparing your essay before you start typing it.

STEP 5
Proofread your work.

Save enough time to read quickly through the entire essay. Look for errors you can address quickly: capitalization, paragraph divisions, double-typed words, general typos and small grammatical errors.

HOW TO APPLY THE KAPLAN METHOD FOR ANALYTICAL WRITING TO THE ISSUE ESSAY

Now let's apply the Kaplan Method for Analytical Writing to an Issue prompt:

> The drawbacks to the use of nuclear power mean that it is not a long-term solution to the problem of meeting ever-increasing energy needs.

Write a response in which you examine your own position on the statement. Explore the extent to which you either agree or disagree with it, and support your reasoning with evidence and/or examples. Be sure to reflect on ways in which the statement might or might not be true and how this informs your thinking on the subject.

STEP 1
Take the issue apart.

Your first step is to dissect the issue. Take notes on your scratch paper. Start by restating the issue in your own words: "Although we have a need for alternate sources of energy, we cannot count nuclear energy as a solution because of the major drawbacks."

Now, consider the other side of the issue—in your own words, what is it: "Nuclear power is safe and effective and does not have such intense drawbacks as this statement would make it seem."

STEP 2

Select the points you will make.

Your job, as stated in the directions, is to decide whether or not you agree with the statement and then to explain your decision. Some would argue that the use of nuclear power is too dangerous, while others would say that we can't afford not to use it. Which side do you take?

Remember, this isn't about showing the graders what your deep-seated beliefs about the environment are—it's about showing that you can formulate an argument and communicate it clearly. The position you choose to take for the Issue essay does not have to be one you actually believe in.

Quickly jot down on your scratch paper the pros and cons of each side, and choose the side for which you have the most relevant things to say. For this topic, that process might go something like this:

Arguments *for* the use of nuclear power:

- It is inexpensive compared to other forms of energy.
- Fossil fuels will eventually be depleted.
- Solar power is still too problematic and expensive.

Arguments *against* the use of nuclear power:

- It is harmful to the environment.
- It is dangerous to mankind.
- Safer alternatives already exist.
- Better alternatives may lie undiscovered.

Again, it doesn't matter which side you take. Strictly speaking, there is no *right* answer, as far as ETS is concerned. Let's say that in this case you decide to argue against nuclear power. Remember, the prompt asks you to argue why the cons of nuclear power outweigh the pros—the inadequacy of this power source is the end towards which you're arguing, so don't list it as a supporting argument.

STEP 3

Organize, using Kaplan's essay templates.

You should have already begun to think out your arguments—that's how you picked the side you did in the first place. Now's the time to write your arguments out, including those that weaken the opposing side. This step involves your own note taking, so feel free to use abbreviations.

Paragraph 1: Nuclear power is not a viable alternative to other energy sources.

Paragraph 2: Nuclear power creates radioactive waste.

Paragraph 3: Nuclear energy is an industry with related costs to consumers.

Paragraph 4: There are other, more environmentally-friendly energy sources.

Paragraph 5: Further investment in nuclear power would be a waste of time and money.

STEP 4

Type your essay.

Remember, open up with a general statement indicating that you understand the issue and then assert your position. From there, make your main points. Note: As a basis for comparison, we've included one outstanding essay that deserves a score of 6. The second prompt will include one adequate essay that deserves a score of 4.

Sample Issue Essay 1

Proponents of nuclear energy as "the power source for the future" have long touted its relative economy, "clean-burning" technology, and virtually inexhaustible fuel supply. However, a close examination of the issue reveals that nuclear energy proves more problematic and dangerous than other forms of energy production and thus is not an acceptable solution to the problem of meeting ever-increasing energy needs.

First and foremost, nuclear power production presents the problem of radioactive waste storage. Fuel byproducts from nuclear fission remain toxic for thousands of years, and the spills and leaks from existing storage sites have been hazardous and costly to clean up. This remains true despite careful regulation and even under the best of circumstances. Even more appalling is the looming threat of accidents at the reactor itself: Incidents at the Three Mile Island and Chernobyl power plants and at other production sites have warned us that the consequences of a nuclear meltdown can be catastrophic and felt worldwide.

But beyond the enormous long-term environmental problems and short-term health risks, the bottom-line issue for the production of energy is one of economics. Power production in our society is a business just like any other, and the large companies that produce this country's electricity and gas claim they are unable to make alternatives such as solar power affordable. Yet—largely due to incentives from the federal government—there already exist homes heated by solar power and cars fueled by the sun. If the limited resources devoted to date to such energy alternatives have already produced working models, a more intensive, broadly based and supported effort is likely to make those alternatives less expensive and problematic.

Besides the benefits in terms of both cost and safety, renewable resources such as solar and hydroelectric power represent far better options in the long run for development: These options require money only for the materials needed to harvest the renewable resources. While sunlight and water are free, the innovative technologies and industrial strategies devised to harness them have created a geometric progression of spin-offs affecting fields as diverse as agriculture, real estate, space exploration, and social policy. These options also repeatedly produced secondary economic and social benefits, such as the large recreational and irrigation reservoirs created in the American Southwest behind large hydroelectric dams like the Hoover and Grand Coulee.

While it may now be clear that the drawbacks to the use of nuclear power are too great, it should also be apparent that the long-term benefits of renewable resources would reward investment. If these alternatives are explored more seriously than they have been in the past, safer and less expensive sources of power will undoubtedly live up to their promise. With limited resources at our disposal and a burgeoning global population to consider, further investment in nuclear power would mark an unconscionable and unnecessary waste of time and money.

STEP 5
Proofread your work.

Be sure to allot a few minutes after you have finished writing to review your essay. Though you do not have to write a grammatically flawless essay to score well, you will want to review so that you can catch some of the standout mistakes. You can practice your writing skills in Chapter 16: Writing Foundations and Content Review.

ASSESSMENT OF SAMPLE ISSUE ESSAY 1: "OUTSTANDING," SCORE OF 6

Now we'll look at how this essay would have been scored on the actual GRE Analytical Writing Section:

This essay is carefully constructed throughout, enabling the reader to move effortlessly from point to point as the writer examines the multifaceted implications of the issue. The writer begins by acknowledging arguments for the opposing side, and then uses his thesis statement ("a close examination of the issue reveals that nuclear energy proves more problematic and dangerous than other forms of energy production") to explain his own position on the issue. He proceeds to provide compelling reasons and examples to support the premise, and then takes the argument to an effective conclusion. The writing is clean, concise, and error-free. Sentence structure is varied, and diction and vocabulary are strong and expressive.

How to Apply the Kaplan Method for Analytical Writing to Another Issue Essay

Now let's apply the Kaplan Method for Analytical Writing to a second Issue prompt:

People who hold high expectations for others are rewarded with high performance and respect.

Develop a response to the claim in which you provide specific reasons whether or not you agree with it. Focus specifically on the most powerful or compelling examples that could be used to support your position.

❯ STEP 1
Take the issue apart.

Begin by putting the issue in your own words, "If you expect people to do well, they will, and they will respect you for it." Next, consider the other side of the issue, and do the same: "If you expect too much of people, they may get frustrated and perform lower or you may compromise their respect."

❯ STEP 2
Select the points you will make.

Your job, as stated in the directions, is to decide whether or not you agree with the statement and then to explain your decision. Some would argue that high expectations yield high results, while others may think that unrealistic high expectations may destroy confidence. Which side do you take?

Quickly think through the pros and cons of each side, and choose the side for which you have the most relevant things to say. For this topic, that process might go something like this:

Arguments *for* holding people to high expectations:

- Without expectations, people don't know how they will be measured or to what level they should perform.
- High expectations convey confidence and trust.
- Higher performance improves people's skills and confidence once they meet the expectations.

Arguments *against* holding people to high expectations:

- People could give up or lose confidence if they are unable to meet the expectations.
- You may be thought of as someone who is unyielding or only concerned with performance.

Remember, it doesn't matter which side you take. Strictly speaking, there is no *right* answer.

◆ STEP 3

Organize, using Kaplan's essay templates.

Now's the time to write those arguments out, including counterarguments that weaken the opposing side.

Paragraph 1:
High expectations yield high performance and respect in every case, whether the expectations are met or unmet.

Paragraph 2:
Without expectations, people don't know how they will be measured or to what level they should perform. 2nd graders design skyscrapers; retirees train for Olympics.

Paragraph 3:
Challenges from teachers: high expectations convey confidence and trust.

Paragraph 4:
Higher performance improves people's skills and confidence once they meet the expectations. (Challenge office interns example)

Paragraph 5: (opposition)
People fail because others do not value them enough and believe they are capable of less than they actually are.

Paragraph 6: In all cases, high expectations are worth the risk.

◆ STEP 4

Type your essay.

Sample Issue Essay 2

High expectations yield high performance and respect in every case, whether the expectations are met or unmet. Setting expectations allows people to know how they will be measured and to what level they should perform. They also convey confidence and a sense of trust. Once the expectations are met, people feel bolstered by their achievement and have a much stronger sense of self-confidence, leading to even higher performance. These results hold up in a variety of contexts, including in educational, business, and political realms.

The purpose of expectations is often lost in the assignment of a task. The expectations themselves may take the form of the actual tasks to be done, but really, the expectation is the ownership, resourcefulness, and skill of the person assigned the task. Expecting someone to do something overly challenging, such as asking second-graders to design a skyscraper or challenging a retiree to train for the Olympics, may seem egregious, but the stories that intrigue us most are usually about people rising to the challenge. Our own expectations are recalibrated when we learn of people exceeding the expectations we set ourselves to. We look to where the bar is set to see how we measure up. Given a bar, people will usually do what it takes to measure up.

Good teachers are often described as "hard, but fair." This is a good description of someone who holds high expectations for his or her students, and is rewarded by that assessment. A hard but fair teacher is one who challenges the students to exceed their own expectations of themselves, and often others' expectations of them. These are the teachers who assign fourth grade students research papers or ask eighth graders to take a 100 question math test in 100 minutes. Students take up the challenge because it feels good to succeed. They gain confidence and look at tasks unrelated to the classroom in new ways.

High performance breeds higher performance. Once someone has been resourceful or learned a new skill to achieve a task, the person feels empowered to be similarly resourceful achieving different tasks. In fact, a high performer may take on more challenges without prompting. This bears out in business: the neophyte office intern who pulls together a critical report through resourcefulness, skill, and a little luck is a familiar story, but for good reason. This intern with his or her fresh ideas stands out among the drones and is challenged further, rocketing to the proverbial top of the company. If the same expectations were put on the rest of the workforce, would other employees be as resourceful to achieve the expectations? Most likely, as long as the employee is motivated enough by the challenge.

Some people may be frustrated by high expectations, and some may simply ignore those expectations, but being presented with a challenge ultimately builds a person's confidence. No one ever failed because he or she was fairly challenged by a daunting task and supported while tackling it. People fail because others do not value them enough and believe they are capable of less than they actually are. In fact, just being challenged is often enough to shake up people's self-expectations and make them reconsider what they are actually capable of.

In all cases, high expectations are worth the risk. The challenge bolsters self-esteem and self-confidence, and yields high performance. It improves performance in classrooms, on the job, and in other areas where challenges present themselves.

❯❯ STEP 5
Proofread your work.

Take the last couple of minutes to catch any glaring errors.

ASSESSMENT OF SAMPLE ISSUE ESSAY 2: "ADEQUATE," SCORE OF 4

Now we'll look at how this essay would have been scored on the actual GRE Analytical Writing Section:

This essay is, on the whole, well constructed and laid out. The reader can systematically move from point to point as the writer examines the implications of the issue. The writer begins by agreeing with the statement and presenting specific reasons for agreeing. She gives examples to illustrate her point and organizes her essay according to the Kaplan template. The author's analysis is generally cogent. She asks the reader to take a bit of a leap with some of her claims. For example, claiming that "people will usually do what it takes to measure up" when given a bar is a conclusion not really supported by the paragraph leading us to that conclusion. She asserts, without really justifying, that people are inherently encouraged, rather than discouraged, by daunting challenges. However, the writing is clean, concise, and error-free. Sentence structure is varied, and the author's diction is strong and expressive. For all these reasons, this essay receives a score of 4.

KAPLAN'S ADDITIONAL TIPS FOR THE ISSUE ESSAY

Don't overcomplicate your prose

The types of issues that the essays use as their subject aren't supposed to be too abstruse or esoteric. Don't worry if you're not extremely familiar with a subject. Similarly, your responses shouldn't be too convoluted. Try to be as clear and linear in your writing as possible when supporting an argument. Bombastic flourishes of rhetoric may seem impressive when you first write them, but the point here is to assert and defend a position, not impress the graders with your vocabulary or wit. Substance will easily outweigh style.

Don't worry about whether or not your position is "correct"

The purpose of the Issue essay is to develop an argument and defend it. You're going to be scored on how well supported your position is, not on whether or not it is the "right answer." Indeed, by design most of the topics chosen for this task are not black-and-white issues; they can be argued successfully from very different points of view.

Think about the issue from different perspectives

An important skill you'll need in graduate school (as in life) is the ability to understand an issue or problem from someone else's point of view. Removing your own personal biases from the equation can be a great help, as it will force you to think about an issue logically, and not just go with your gut reaction.

ISSUE ESSAY PRACTICE SET

ISSUE ESSAY 1

Time: 30 minutes
Length: 1 essay

Directions: You will be given a statement that presents an issue you need to respond to, along with detailed instructions on how to respond to the statement. You have 30 minutes to plan and compose a response in which you develop an argument according to the instructions. A response to any other issue results in a score of zero.

"The perceived greatness of any political leader has more to do with the challenges faced by that leader than with any of his or her inherent skills and abilities."

Write a response in which you examine your own position on the statement. Explore the extent to which you either agree or disagree with it, and support your reasoning with evidence and/or examples. Be sure to reflect on ways in which the statement might or might not be true, and how this informs your thinking on the subject.

ISSUE ESSAY 2

Time: 30 minutes

Length: 1 essay

Directions: You will be given a statement that presents an issue you need to respond to, along with detailed instructions on how to respond to the statement. You have 30 minutes to plan and compose a response in which you develop an argument according to the instructions. A response to any other issue results in a score of zero.

"Progress should be the aim of any great society. People too often cling unnecessarily to obsolete ways of thinking and acting because of both a high comfort level and a fear of the unknown."

Write a response in which you examine your own position on the statement. Explore the extent to which you either agree or disagree with it, and support your reasoning with evidence or examples. Be sure to reflect on ways in which the statement might or might not be true, and how this informs your thinking on the subject.

ISSUE ESSAY SAMPLE ESSAYS AND ASSESSMENTS

What follows are top-scoring sample essays for each of the practice prompts. Note how the authors adhere to the Kaplan Method for Analytical Writing.

ISSUE ESSAY 1: "OUTSTANDING," SCORE OF 6

Perceptions of greatness in national and political leaders are largely determined by the seriousness of the problems that they face during their terms in office. Most national histories principally highlight individuals in the context of significant events in which the leaders played important roles. Most political leaders need to have large stores of inherent skill and ability just in order to become a political leader. However, history remembers those who lived in great times more fondly than those who did not. Examples of this are numerous and include the histories of Abraham Lincoln, Woodrow Wilson, and Winston Churchill—all men who are perceived as great leaders largely because of the times in which they lived.

Abraham Lincoln is often considered the greatest of all the American Presidents. He graces two units of the currency and has one of the largest monuments built in his honor in Washington D.C. However, Lincoln is considered great largely because he faced a great challenge—the civil war between the North and the South in the 1860s. Lincoln led the United States to victory over the rebels and reunited the country and is therefore considered great. This is not to say that Lincoln was not skilled. Many know that he was born in a log cabin and progressed to law school and eventually to the presidency. He was also a skilled orator. However another man, James Buchanan, also was born in a log cabin, went to law school, gave good speeches and ascended to the presidency. However there are no monuments to Buchanan in the capital or pictures of his face on the five-dollar bill.

Woodrow Wilson was another talented man who ascended to the presidency of the United States. However his talents are not what make his perceived greatness. In this age, few remember if Wilson was particularly smart, a very good speechmaker, or a good arbitrator. Most remember that he led the United States to victory in the first World War and therefore perceive him as great. At the time, however, Wilson was rather unpopular. In fact, he had so little sway with Congress that he was unable to get the United States to join the League of Nations—a fact that many claim helped lead to the second World War.

Winston Churchill was another man that history views favorably because of the incredible challenges that he faced. However, Churchill was not very popular before the war. When Franklin Roosevelt first met Churchill before either was the leader of his respective country, Roosevelt wrote in his diary that Churchill was full of himself and far too talkative. Early in his term as Prime Minister, Churchill even faced a no-confidence vote in Parliament. However, the events of World War II accorded him the perception of greatness in the eyes of history.

Many might argue that these men and other men and women were already great before history gave them great challenges. While it is impossible to definitely disprove this assertion and it may be true that they had great skill and ability, otherwise they would not have been political leaders, most examples point to the fact that the times make the man or woman. If the presidencies of Buchanan and Lincoln were switched, we would very likely have the Buchanan memorial instead. In summary, it is true that the perceived greatness of a political leader is more due to great challenges than great inherent ability. The historical examples of Lincoln, Wilson, and Churchill bear this out. All were talented, but so too are all political leaders. Only the leaders that live in eventful times are remembered as great.

ASSESSMENT OF ESSAY 1

This essay is particularly well-constructed; the author begins by acknowledging the arguments for how famous historical leaders should be judged. He asserts his position, "men are perceived as great leaders largely because of the times in which they lived" clearly and effectively. He proceeds to support his position with compelling evidence, drawing on his knowledge of three historical figures who are, by consensus, regarded as great. He contrasts the example of Lincoln with that of Buchanan, who had a similar background but lived under less trying circumstances. The writing is largely clear and direct, with skillful use of diction. For all these reasons, this essay receives a score of 6.

ISSUE ESSAY 2: "OUTSTANDING," SCORE OF 6

Keeping up with global progress is, doubtless, a desirable attribute of any society. However, to purport that the reasons certain societies may not progress at the same rate as "great" societies are their reluctance to break from their comfort zones and a fear of the unknown is to present an overly simplistic view. Such a view does not take into consideration the set of economic, political, and cultural constraints that affect every society's ability to progress on a global scale.

Before exploring these constraints, it would be useful to examine the use of the word "great" in the above context. The concept of what makes a society great is highly subjective; some may equate greatness with military might or economic dominance, while others would emphasize cultural achievement or progress in care for less privileged citizens. Whatever one's definition of greatness, however, it is ludicrous to suggest that any society actively rejects the desire to be great. Many societies face the seemingly insurmountable struggle to maintain societal structure in the face of economic need and/or political upheaval; the desire for greatness can only come when a society's basic structure is intact.

Societies facing severe economic challenges are virtually unable to progress in areas like medicine, militia, and agriculture even if they want to do so. Countries like Bolivia use a majority of their limited resources to maintain an agricultural status quo. Bolivian farmers are not afraid of the unknown or passively content with their current situation, but are using all of their resources to maintain a functional economic climate and structure. Given this situation, the luxury of advancements in medicine, economics and military power is simply not possible.

Also, societies embroiled in political upheaval, such as Bangladesh, are unable to send its young and talented members to university where they can spearhead progress; the most viable sectors of the population are required to serve in the military and/or to care for their families through difficult economic and political times. Maintaining a societal structure amid chaotic conditions engenders a lack of globally accepted progress, but as we have seen throughout time, episodes of great drama in any given society can yield important works of art, one such example being Albert Camus' *The Stranger*, written during the French Resistance.

Another point to consider is that, in some cases, an entire society's cultural history, including its artistic contributions, is preserved only through its living members' rich oral tradition and their active rejecting of progress in the worlds of technology, medicine, and science. This is evident when considering such so-called "primitive" societies as the African Masai or certain Native American tribes. The introduction of technology into the world of the Masai would inarguably lead to the demise of the entire society.

In conclusion, to devalue a society that isn't among the most progressive in the world is to discount the contributions a so-called "unprogressive" society can provide, such as artistic and cultural phenomena unique to a given society. Progress is a valuable tool for the advancement of a society, but blindly reaching for greatness can lead to a society's downfall just as much as ignoring it altogether can. The balance between accepting a society's constraints and highlighting its strengths is what will ultimately lead to a society's greatness.

ASSESSMENT OF ESSAY 2

This is a particularly insightful essay. The author goes deeper with her argument than you might expect based on the prompt. The argument developed in this essay asks the reader to question his or her presuppositions and preconceived notions about what constitutes "greatness" as the term is applied to a society. Instead of merely answering the question of whether or not the progress of society is hindered by clinging to traditional views and obsolete ways of thinking, the reader is forced to reconsider what progress actually entails. This elicits the cultural bias of the readers, and forces them to confront it. The author challenges the received notions of "great" and "progress" as "an overly simplistic view." From there, she proceeds to defend her position. She examines different cultural contexts, and how we might understand "greatness" within those contexts. The essay is well constructed; the author begins by providing examples of how greatness must be understood contextually. She then adds several examples, such as the publication of Camus' *The Stranger*, to illustrate greatness produced under conditions we might think of as making progress impossible. The writing is clear, direct, and error-free, and reveals skillful use of diction. For all these reasons, this essay receives a score of 6.

CHAPTER 18

The Argument Essay

INTRODUCTION TO THE ARGUMENT ESSAY

The second type of Analytical Writing essay type you have to contend with is the Argument essay. This time you're given an expressed point of view—an "argument"—that contains a conclusion and supporting evidence. Here the writer tries to persuade you of something (her conclusion) by citing some evidence. You should read the "argument" with a critical eye. Be on the lookout for *assumptions* in the way the writer moves from evidence to conclusion. You aren't being asked to agree or disagree with the author's *position* or *conclusion*; instead, you must analyze the *chain of reasoning* used in the argument.

The screen directions ask you to decide how convincing you find the argument. Know that every argument presented for this essay on the GRE will be flawed. To make your case, first analyze the argument itself and evaluate its use of evidence; second, explain how a different approach or more information would make the argument better (or possibly worse).

The directions for an Argument essay will look like this:

> You have 30 minutes to plan and compose a response in which you evaluate the argument passage that appears below. A response to any other argument will receive a score of zero. Make sure that you respond according to the specific instructions and support your evaluation with relevant reasons and/or examples.

An Argument task will always begin with a passage containing an author's argument or position that she or he is advocating. It will look like this:

> The following is a memorandum from the business manager of a television station:

> Over the past year, our late night news program has devoted increased time to national news and less time to weather and local news. During this time period, most of the complaints received from viewers were concerned with our station's coverage of weather and local news. In addition, local businesses that used to advertise during our late-night news program have just canceled their advertising contracts with us. Therefore, in order to attract more viewers to the program and to avoid losing any further advertising revenues, we should restore the time devoted to weather and local news to its former level.

The second part of the directions, the prompt, will give specific directions for how to approach the essay. An Argument essay prompt will look like this:

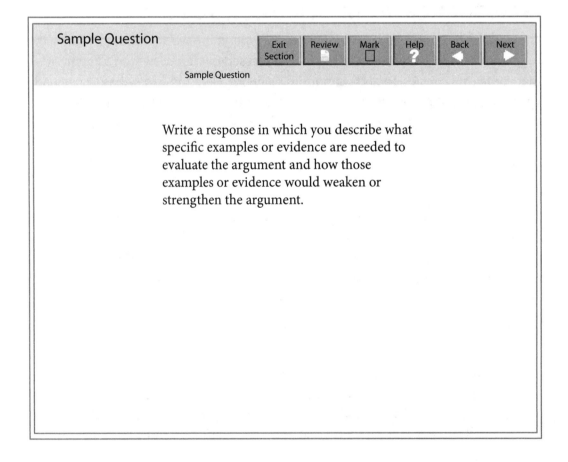

Write a response in which you describe what specific examples or evidence are needed to evaluate the argument and how those examples or evidence would weaken or strengthen the argument.

The Argument essay prompt may vary. Other Argument essay prompts will look like this:

- Write a response in which you explore the assumptions, both implicit and explicit, in the author's argument. Explain how the argument hinges on these assumptions and what the implications are if the assumptions prove unfounded.

- Write a response in which you explain what information would be necessary in order to decide whether the recommendation and the argument on which it is based are reasonable. Be sure to explain how the answers to these questions or pieces of information would help to evaluate the recommendation.

- Write a response in which you discuss what questions would need to be answered to decide how likely the stated recommendation is to yield the predicted result. Be sure to explain how the answers to these questions would help to evaluate the recommendation.

- Write a response in which you discuss what questions would need to be answered in order to assess the reasonableness of both the prediction and the argument upon which it is based. Be sure to explain how the answers to these questions would help to evaluate the prediction.

- Write a response in which you discuss one or more viable alternatives to the proposed explanation. Justify, with support, why your explanation could rival the proposed explanation and explain how your explanation(s) can plausibly account for the facts presented in the argument.

THE KAPLAN METHOD FOR ANALYTICAL WRITING

STEP 1   Take the issue/argument apart.

STEP 2   Select the points you will make.

STEP 3   Organize, using Kaplan's essay templates.

STEP 4   Type your essay.

STEP 5   Proofread your work.

How the Kaplan Method for Analytical Writing Works

Now let's discuss how the Kaplan Method for Analytical Writing works for the Argument Essay:

STEP 1

Take the argument apart.

The first step to deconstructing an argument is to identify the conclusion, that is, the main point the author is trying to make. After you've nailed down the conclusion, your next step is to locate the evidence used to support the conclusion. Lastly, identify the unstated assumptions (pieces of evidence that are not explicitly stated but that must be true in order for the argument to be convincing). Note any terms that are ambiguous and need defining.

STEP 2

Select the points you will make.

Identify all the important assumptions between the evidence and the conclusion. Think of additional evidence that might be found that could strengthen or weaken those assumptions.

STEP 3

Organize, using Kaplan's essay templates.

Organize your thoughts by outlining what you want to say. Think about how the essay as a whole will flow. In the introduction, show that you understand the argument by putting it into your own words. Point out the author's conclusion and the evidence used to support that conclusion. In each of the middle paragraphs, identify a flaw in the author's reasoning. Find the unstated assumption(s), and explain how the argument could be logically invalid if the assumptions proved unfounded. In your second to last paragraph, address a way to strengthen the argument and provide examples of evidence that would confirm the unstated assumption(s). Conclude by saying that, without such evidence, you are not persuaded.

STEP 4

Type your essay.

You shouldn't proceed with this step until you've completed the three preceding ones. Graders also have a limited amount of time to work with, so start out and conclude with strong statements. Be emphatic and concise with your prose, and make transitions link related ideas. This will help your writing flow and make things easier on the grader.

STEP 5

Proofread your work.

Save enough time to read through your response in its entirety. As you do so, have a sense of the errors you are liable to make.

Now let's see how these steps work with an Argument assignment by applying the Kaplan Method to the example prompt question provided.

HOW TO APPLY THE KAPLAN METHOD FOR ANALYTICAL WRITING TO THE ARGUMENT ESSAY

Now let's apply the Kaplan Method for Analytical Writing to a sample Argument prompt:

> "The problem of poor teacher performance that has plagued the state public school system is bound to become a good deal less serious in the future. The state has initiated comprehensive guidelines that oblige state teachers to complete a number of required credits in education and educational psychology at the graduate level before being certified."

Write a response that examines this argument's unstated assumptions.

Make sure you explain how this argument depends on those assumptions and what the implications are if the assumptions are wrong.

STEP 1

Take the argument apart.

Conclusion (the point the argument is trying to make): The problem of poorly trained teachers that has plagued the state public school system is bound to become a good deal less serious in the future.

Evidence (basis offered to support the conclusion): The state has initiated comprehensive guidelines that oblige state teachers to complete a number of required credits in education and educational psychology at the graduate level before being certified.

Assumptions (unspoken conditions or beliefs necessary for the conclusion to make sense in light of the evidence):

- Credits in education will improve teachers' classroom performance.
- Current bad teachers haven't already met this standard of training.
- Current bad teachers will not still be teaching in the future, or will have to be trained, too.

STEP 2

Select the points you will make.

Analyze the use of evidence in the argument. Determine whether there's anything relevant that's not discussed.

- Whether the training will actually address the cause of the problems
- What "poorly performing" means
- How to either improve or remove the bad teachers now teaching

Also determine what types of evidence would make the argument stronger or more logically sound. In this case, we need some new evidence to support the assumptions.

- Evidence verifying that this training will make better teachers
- Evidence making it clear those current bad teachers haven't already had this training
- Evidence suggesting why all or many bad teachers won't still be teaching in the future (or why they'll be better trained)

STEP 3

Organize, using Kaplan's essay templates.

For an essay on this topic, your opening sentence might look like this:

The argument that improved academic training, ensured by requiring credits in education and psychology, will substantially alleviate the current problem of poorly trained teachers may seem logical at first glance.

> Paragraph 1: The argument is that improved academic training, ensured by requiring credits in education and psychology, will substantially alleviate the current problem of poorly trained teachers.

Paragraph 2: Will training address the cause of the problem?

Paragraph 3: "Poorly performing" is not precisely defined.

Paragraph 4: Has a similar state instituted similar guidelines and seen results?

Paragraph 5: The author has not presented well-defined terms and relies upon unproven assumptions; for these reasons it is not convincing.

Then use your notes as a working outline. In Argument essays, you'll primarily address the ways in which the assumptions seem unsupported. You might also recommend new evidence you'd like to see and explain why. Remember to lead with your best arguments.

STEP 4

Type your essay.

Begin writing your essay now. Your essay for this assignment might look like one of the following sample essays. Note: As a basis for comparison, we've included one outstanding essay that deserves a score of 6, and one adequate essay that deserves a score of 4.

Sample Argument Essay 1

The argument that improved academic training, ensured by requiring credits in education and psychology, will substantially alleviate the current problem of poorly performing teachers may seem logical at first glance. The author makes a valid argument, one that would be correct if its premises were true. However, his conclusion relies on assumptions for which there is no clear evidence, and it uses terms that lack definition.

First, the writer assumes that the required courses will produce better teachers. In fact, the courses might be entirely irrelevant to the teachers' failings. Suppose, for example, that the main problem lies in cultural and linguistic gaps between teachers and students; graduate level courses that do not address these issues would be of little use in bridging these gaps and improving educational outcomes. Furthermore, the writer assumes that poorly performing teachers lack this standard of training. In fact, the writer makes no useful correlation between classroom performance and level of training.

Additionally, the writer provides no evidence that poorly performing teachers who are already certified will either stop teaching in the near future or will undergo additional training. In its current form, the argument implies that only teachers seeking certification will receive the specified training. If this is the case, the bright future the writer envisions may be decades away. The argument's conclusion requires the support of evidence demonstrating that all teachers in the system who are identified as having "poor performance" will receive the remedial training and will then change their teaching methods accordingly.

The notion that the coursework will provide better teachers would be strengthened by a clear definition of "poor performance" in the classroom and by additional evidence that the training will address the relevant issues. The author's argument would be strengthened considerably if he provided evidence of a direct relationship between teachers' effectiveness in the classroom and their educational backgrounds.

In conclusion, the writer would not necessarily be wrong to assert that the state's comprehensive guidelines will potentially lead to some improvement in the educational environment in public schools. After all, the additional training will certainly not adversely affect classroom performance. But to support the current conclusion that the guidelines will effectively solve the state's problem, the writer must first define the scope of the problem more clearly and submit more conclusive evidence that the new requirements will, in fact, improve overall teaching performance.

❯❯ STEP 5

Proofread your work.

Be sure to allot some time after you have finished writing to review your essay. While a few grammatical errors here and there won't harm your score, having enough of them will affect the overall clarity of your essay and that certainly won't look good. You want to make sure the graders are as favorably disposed to you as possible, and a well-written essay makes their job a bit less tedious.

ASSESSMENT OF SAMPLE ARGUMENT ESSAY 1: "OUTSTANDING," SCORE OF 6

Now we'll look at how these essays would have been scored on the actual GRE Analytical Writing Section:

This outstanding response demonstrates the writer's insightful analytical skills. The introduction notes the prompt's specious reasoning occasioned by unsupported assumptions and a lack of definition and evidence. The writer follows this up with a one-paragraph examination of each of the root flaws in the argument. Specifically, the author exposes these points undermining the argument:

- The assumption that the required courses will produce better teachers
- The assumption that poorly performing teachers currently in the schools have not already had the proposed training
- The complete lack of evidence that ineffective teachers currently working will either stop teaching in the future or will successfully adapt the required training to their classroom work

Each point receives thorough and cogent development (given the time constraints) in a smooth and logically organized discourse. This essay is succinct, economical, and error-free, with sentences that vary in length and complexity, while the diction and vocabulary stand out as both precise and expressive.

HOW TO APPLY THE KAPLAN METHOD FOR ANALYTICAL WRITING TO ANOTHER ARGUMENT ESSAY

Now let's apply the Kaplan Method for Analytical Writing to a second Argument prompt:

"The commercial airline industry in the country of Freedonia has experienced impressive growth in the past three years. This trend will surely continue in the years to come, since the airline industry will benefit from recent changes in Freedonian society: incomes are rising, most employees now receive more vacation time, and interest in travel is rising, as shown by an increase in media attention devoted to foreign cultures and tourist attractions."

Write a response that examines this argument's unstated assumptions. Make sure you explain how this argument depends on those assumptions and what the implications are if the assumptions are wrong.

STEP 1
Take the argument apart.

Conclusion (the point the argument's trying to make): The upward trend of growth in Freedonia's airline industry will continue due to recent changes in Freedonian society.

Evidence (basis offered to support the conclusion): The airline industry has grown in the past three years. Recent changes in Freedonian society will allow this to continue. These changes include rising incomes, more vacation time for employees, interest in travel is rising.

Assumptions (unspoken conditions or beliefs necessary for the conclusion to make sense in light of the evidence):

- Incomes will continue to rise in the future.
- Employees will want to spend their vacation time abroad and not at home.
- Those who do wish to travel will want to go somewhere requiring air travel.
- The increased media attention on foreign cultures and tourist attractions is due to public interest in travel.
- The airline industry will directly benefit from these changes.

STEP 2

Select the points you will make.

Analyze the use of evidence in the argument. Determine whether there's anything relevant that's not discussed, such as:

- What actually caused the growth in the airline industry?
- The fact that employees may want to spend their increased disposable income and vacation time doing other things.
- Whether the increased media attention on foreign cultures is due to other factors besides increased public interest in travel.

Also determine what types of evidence would make the argument stronger or more logically sound. In this case, we need some new evidence to support the assumptions.

- Evidence verifying that the positive economic changes in Feeedonian society will continue.
- Evidence suggesting the cause of the increased media coverage of foreign cultures is in fact due to an interest in travel.

STEP 3

Organize, using Kaplan's essay templates.

For an essay on this topic, your opening sentence might look like this:

"The argument that the recent growth in Freedonia's commercial airline industry will continue for years to come may seem logical at first glance."

Paragraph 1: The argument is that the positive growth in Freedonia's commercial airline industry will continue.

Paragraph 2: The author assumes that the favorable economic conditions will continue. However, the cause of these conditions is not explained, and neither is the economy's relation to the airline industry.

Paragraph 3: The argument would be strengthened if we knew what caused the media attention and growth in the commercial airline industry.

Paragraph 4: What is the source of the economic conditions, and how do they relate to the airline industry?

Paragraph 5: The argument the author makes, if wrong, means that Freedonia's airline industry might experience trouble in the future.

Then use your notes as a working outline. In Argument essays, you'll primarily address the ways in which the assumptions seem unsupported. You might also recommend new evidence you'd like to see and explain why. Remember to lead with your best arguments.

❱ STEP 4
Type your essay.

Sample Argument Essay 2

The argument that the positive growth in Freedonia's commercial airline industry will continue for years to come may seem tenable at first glance. However, the conclusion relies on assumptions for which there is no clear evidence and on terms that lack definition.

First, the writer assumes that the favorable economic conditions in Freedonia will continue. It is entirely possible that they will not, and that employees will have neither the money nor the vacation time necessary to pay for expensive foreign vacations. Suppose, for example, that incomes do not continue to rise. People would not have the money to spend on expensive vacation. Secondly, do we really know that the citizens of Freedonia will *want* to spend their money on vacations? Also, how do we know they will want to visit places that necessitate air travel?

His argument would be strengthened considerably if he provided evidence of a direct relationship between the increased media attention on foreign cultures and tourist attractions and the genuine desire to spend disposable income and vacation time traveling. The author does not explain where this interest comes from. Also, even if people are interested, it does not necessarily follow that they will be either willing or able to indulge that interest with extravagant holidays.

Furthermore, the writer does not explain the source of these economic conditions, nor what relation, if any, they have to the airline industry. What if the changes in Freedonian society that have led to higher incomes and more vacation time do not help the airline industry? Perhaps the economic changes are the result of protective tariffs and trade policies that make it harder for Freedonians to conduct business internationally. Perhaps the government is limiting imports and exports. These possibilities could shrink the growth of the airline industry.

If the writer is wrong about the assumptions he has made regarding Freedonian society, the implications for the commercial airline industry in Freedonia are less rosy. It would mean that there will be less income and no less interest in foreign travel.

◆ STEP 5
Proofread your work.

Take the last couple of minutes to catch any glaring errors.

ASSESSMENT OF SAMPLE ARGUMENT ESSAY 2: "ADEQUATE," SCORE OF 4

Now we'll look at how this essay would have been scored on the actual GRE Analytical Writing Section:

This essay is reasonably well constructed throughout, enabling the reader to move from point to point as the writer examines the multifaceted implications of the issue. He correctly identifies and articulates several assumptions that the argument makes but does not justify. The author does an adequate job of pointing out how the argument depends upon those assumptions for its cogency. The essay suffers because the writer jumps around a little bit. The paragraph explaining how the argument could be strengthened should be the second-to-last paragraph, not mixed into the body of the essay. Also, the explication of the economic climate of Freedonia, and its implications for foreign travel, is slight. Finally, the author's conclusion does not do a particularly good job of restating the author's position effectively. The writing itself is direct and relatively error-free. Sentence structure is not particularly varied, and the word choice and vocabulary are adequate. For these reasons, the essay earns an "Adequate" score of 4.

KAPLAN'S ADDITIONAL TIPS FOR THE ARGUMENT ESSAY

Try to Keep Things Simple

These essays aren't supposed to be so opaque in their logic that they can't be unpacked on test day. Similarly, your responses don't have to abstruse or convoluted (and shouldn't be!). Try to be as clear and linear in your writing as possible when dissecting an argument.

Don't Worry about Agreeing or Disagreeing with the Argument

This is important. You don't have to agree or disagree with the argument itself. What you (and the graders) are interested in is your ability to *reason*. That means you have to understand the argument and grasp it well enough to be able to point out its assumptions (i.e. where the author takes a leap in logic by assuming, rather than proving, a point). You should not dispute the conclusion or the evidence, only the assumptions. Do not spend any time at all on your personal opinion about the conclusion.

Paraphrase Long or Complex Sentences

You may encounter a sentence that, because of its length or structure, is hard to get a handle on. When faced with a complex sentence, put it into your own words; this will make the argument itself much easier to decipher and wrestle with.

ARGUMENT ESSAY PRACTICE SET

ARGUMENT ESSAY 1

Time: 30 minutes

Length: 1 essay

Directions: You will be given a brief passage that presents an argument, or an argument you need to complete, along with detailed instructions on how to respond to the passage. You have 30 minutes to plan and compose a response in which you analyze the passage according to the instructions. A response to any other argument results in a score of zero.

Note: You are not being asked to present your opinions on the subject. Make sure you respond to the instructions and support your analysis with pertinent reasons and/or examples.

Feel free to take a few minutes to consider the argument and instructions, and to plan your response, before you begin to write. Be certain your analysis is fully developed and logically organized, and make sure you leave enough time to review and revise what you've written.

The following appeared in the City Council Proceedings section of the local newspaper in Smithville:

"The city council of Smithville has instituted changes to police procedures to improve the visibility of the police force. These changes require that the town hire more police officers, budget more funds for police overtime, and direct officers to patrol significantly more often on foot rather than from their patrol cars. These improvements in visibility will significantly lower the crime rate in Smithville and make its citizens feel safer."

Write a response in which you discuss what questions would need to be answered to decide how likely the stated recommendation is to yield the predicted result. Be sure to explain how the answers to these questions would help to evaluate the recommendation.

ARGUMENT ESSAY 2

Time: 30 minutes

Length: 1 essay

Directions: You will be given a brief passage that presents an argument, or an argument you need to complete, along with detailed instructions on how to respond to the passage. You have 30 minutes to plan and compose a response in which you analyze the passage according to the instructions. A response to any other argument results in a score of zero.

Note: You are *not* being asked to present your opinions on the subject. Make sure you respond to the instructions and support your analysis with pertinent reasons and/or examples.

Feel free to take a few minutes to consider the argument and instructions, and to plan your response, before you begin to write. Be certain your analysis is fully developed and logically organized, and make sure you leave enough time to review and revise what you've written.

"Tusk University should build a new recreational facility, both to attract new students and to better serve the needs of our current student body. Tusk projects that enrollment will double over the next 10 years, based on current trends. The new student body is expected to reflect a much higher percentage of commuter students than we currently enroll. This will make the existing facilities inadequate. Moreover, the cost of health and recreation club membership in our community has increased rapidly in recent years. Thus, students will find it much more advantageous to make use of the facilities on campus. Finally, an attractive new recreation center would make prospective students, especially athletically gifted ones, more likely to enroll at Tusk."

Write a response that examines this argument's unstated assumptions. Make sure you explain how this argument depends on those assumptions and what the implications are if the assumptions are wrong.

ARGUMENT ESSAY SAMPLE ESSAYS AND ASSESSMENTS

What follows are top-scoring sample essays for each of the practice prompts. Note how the authors adhere to the Kaplan Method for Analytical Writing.

ARGUMENT ESSAY 1 : "OUTSTANDING," SCORE OF 6

The city council of Smithville believes that increasing the visibility of its police force will reduce crime and increase the safety of its citizens. However, the memo provides no evidence to support this argument, and the city council may not be taking other variables, alternative solutions, or the citizens' desires into consideration.

The Smithville city council assumes that crime persists because the city's police force has too low a profile, but the memo never cites evidence to support this position. The council could do something as simple yet effective as asking the town librarian to review published studies to see if a parallel exists between a high police presence and reduced crime rates. It could also hire an independent research firm to see if a correlation exists between Smithville crime scenes and a lack of police activity.

The council should consider other factors that might account for the current crime rate. The police force may be under-trained or poorly managed. If so, adding more officers or encouraging officers to work longer hours could actually compound the problem. Here again, research could be a vital ally in the council's case: What have other towns with similar problems identified as causal factors? What training do their police forces receive? How are they deployed, on foot or in patrol cars? Answering question like these might help clarify a solution to the town's problem. The council should also research historic solutions to the problem: How have towns like theirs reduced a growing crime rate? This research could bolster the council's position or provide alternative, less costly solutions that have successfully fought crime.

The council also assumes that a higher police presence automatically reduces citizen concerns over crime, but it doesn't take into consideration the relationship between the residents and the police. Some communities regard police officers with a great deal of distrust, and that attitude may be pronounced in a community where the police force is perceived as unable to cope with crime. Has the community itself, through its elected leaders, the police chief, op-ed pieces in the newspaper, or community groups, expressed a need for a stronger police force? The memo never says.

As it currently stands, the Smithville city council's memo announces a decision that appears to have been made in a vacuum. To convince citizens that bolstering the police force and changing patrol procedures is the way to fight crime, the memo needs to state how the council arrived at this decision. Only then can citizens feel that the council is taking the right course of action.

ASSESSMENT OF ESSAY 1

The author successfully identifies and analyzes this argument's recommendation: that the way for Smithville to lower its crime rate and improve citizen safety is to increase police visibility.

In the opening paragraph, the essay restates the argument, and then cites its unsupported assumptions. In the following four paragraphs, the author insightfully identifies flaws in the assumptions and perceptively suggests what would need to be known to make such a recommendation, and how knowing this information would help in evaluating this recommendation.

Specifically, the author cites these points undermining the argument:

1. The assumption that a higher police profile will lower the crime rate
2. The assumption that no other cause exists for the high crime rate but low police visibility
3. The lack of research into historically successful alternative solutions
4. The assumption that the town's citizens will agree that the council's solution is the right one

Throughout the essay, the author uses well-organized paragraphs—each starts with a broad statement followed by supporting statements—and her ideas logically flow from one sentence to the next. She uses succinct, economical diction and rotates complex and simple sentences.

The essay concludes strongly by summarizing the evidence necessary for the council to recommend that higher police visibility will reduce crime and increase citizen safety. The essay remains focused and clear throughout, earning a score of 6.

ARGUMENT ESSAY 2 : "STRONG," SCORE OF 5

The author contends that Tusk University should build a new recreational facility to attract new students, and to better serve the needs of its current students. The argument also asserts that this will lead to greater enrollment over the next ten years. While it may prove to be a worthy project, the argument appears to rely on assumptions that lack conclusive supporting evidence. The writer would be well advised to address these issues to make the point of the argument more cogent and convincing.

First and foremost, the writer assumes, without providing any evidence, that recreational facilities will be a significant factor in attracting and serving students interested in Tusk.

This begs the question of the role of recreation and/or athletic facilities in the matriculation and retention of students in institutions of higher learning. In the absence of any reference to the academic mission of the University, or even of the role that the facility might have in attracting, retaining, or helping to fund areas more central to that mission, the writer's conclusion appears unsupported.

Secondly, the writer assumes, again without citing specific evidence, that the projected doubling of enrollment will by itself lead to an increase in demand for the new recreational facilities proposed. Even if the facilities would indeed be attractive relative to those available off campus, the author has provided no proof that a substantial part of the increased or even current enrollment would be inclined to consider the new facilities an asset to their education. Suppose for a moment that this enlarged commuter-based enrollment turns out to be largely made up of part-time students with jobs and family demands away from the campus. Would such a student body see the new facility as a priority? Would the schedules of such students allow them to take advantage of the improvement?

Finally, the author fails to describe what specific services, programs, and amenities the proposed new facility will provide, how and at what cost relative to facilities available elsewhere these will be made available to the university community, and how the financial burden of both building and operating the new center will be offset. Beyond these issues endemic to the campus setting, the writer presents no overview of the environmental, social, and public relations aspects of the project in a larger context, either intra- or extra-collegiate.

The issues raised here could easily be addressed by providing evidence that backs up the author's claim. By assembling sufficient and specific demographic and economic evidence to support the argument's questionable assumptions, the writer may not only be able to overcome the limitations of the current argument, but provide a rationale for the proposal beyond the terms offered here.

ASSESSMENT OF ESSAY 2

This essay adequately targets the argument's unstated assumptions and inadequate evidence. The essay identifies and critiques the gaps in the author's chain of logic reasoning that results from assuming:

- That recreational facilities will be a significant factor in attracting and serving students interested in Tusk.
- That doubling of enrollment will by itself lead to an increase in demand and presumably in use for the new recreational facilities

The writer clearly grasps the argument's central weaknesses. But although the ideas are clear, the essay lacks transitional phrases and is not well organized. The writing feels rushed and lacks proofreading. While the writer demonstrates a better-than-adequate control of language and ably conforms to the conventions of written English, this 5 essay suffers from turgid prose and a lack of the more thorough development of a typical 6 response.

CHAPTER 19

Analytical Writing Practice Set

In this section, you will take a practice test made of four analytical writing questions, two Analyze an Issue tasks and two Analyze an Argument tasks. When you complete the set, read the sample essays and analysis to gauge whether your essays are similarly strong and whether they would earn a high score.

REVIEW OF THE KAPLAN METHOD FOR ANALYTICAL WRITING

Before starting your Practice Sets review the steps and strategies you have studied for answering each type of analytical writing task quickly, thoughtfully, and cohesively.

> **STEP 1** Take the issue/argument apart.
>
> **STEP 2** Select the points you will make.
>
> **STEP 3** Organize, using Kaplan's essay templates.
>
> **STEP 4** Type your essay.
>
> **STEP 5** Proofread your work.

ANALYTICAL WRITING PRACTICE PROMPTS

ANALYZE AN ISSUE PRACTICE

You will be given a brief quotation that states or implies an issue of general interest, along with explicit instructions on how to respond to that topic. You have 30 minutes to plan and write an essay that communicates your perspective on the issue according to the instructions.

Respond to the instructions and support your position with relevant reasoning drawn from your academic studies, reading, observation, and/or experience.

Feel free to consider the issue for a few minutes before you begin to write. Be certain your ideas are fully developed and logically organized, and make sure you leave enough time to review and revise what you've written.

Issue Essay 1 Prompt

"Because people increasingly eat at restaurants, all restaurants should be required to display nutritional information about the meals they serve. This knowledge makes it easier for diners to make healthy choices and reduces the risk of diet-related health problems."

Write an essay in which you take a position on the statement above. In developing and supporting your viewpoint, consider ways in which the statement might or might not hold true. (Use a separate sheet of paper or computer to write your essay.)

Issue Essay 2 Prompt

"All results of publicly funded scientific studies should be made available to the general public free of charge. Scientific journals that charge a subscription or newsstand price are profiting unfairly."

Write an essay in which you take a position on the statement above. In developing and supporting your viewpoint, consider ways in which the statement might or might not hold true. (Use a separate sheet of paper or computer to write your essay.)

ANALYZE AN ARGUMENT PRACTICE

You will be given a brief passage that presents an argument, or an argument you need to complete, along with detailed instructions on how to respond to the passage. You have 30 minutes to plan and compose a response in which you analyze the passage according to the instructions. A response to any other argument results in a score of zero.

Note: You are not being asked to present your opinions on the subject. Make sure you respond to the instructions and support your analysis with pertinent reasons and/or examples.

Feel free to take a few minutes to consider the argument and instructions, and to plan your response, before you begin to write. Be certain your analysis is fully developed and logically organized, and make sure you leave enough time to review and revise what you've written.

Argument Essay 1 Prompt

The following appeared as part of a promotional campaign to sell advertising on channels provided by the local cable television company:

> "Advertising with Cable Communications Corp. is a great way to increase your profits. Recently the Adams Car Dealership began advertising with Cable Communications and over the last 30 days, sales are up 15% over the previous month. Let us increase your profits, just as we did for Adams Cars!"

Write a response that examines this argument's unstated assumptions. Make sure you explain how this argument depends on those assumptions and what the implications are if the assumptions are wrong. (Use a separate sheet of paper or computer to write your essay.)

Argument Essay 2 Prompt

The following appeared in the *Ram*, the Altamonte High School student newspaper:

> "Of Altamonte students polled, 65 percent say they participate in either an intramural, varsity, or community sports team. Being a member of a sports team keeps one fit and healthy and promotes an active lifestyle. Since the majority of students are taking care of their physical fitness after or outside of school, Altamonte High should eliminate all physical education classes and put more resources into the development of the intramural and varsity sports teams."

Write a response in which you explain specific evidence needed to evaluate the argument and discuss how the evidence might weaken or strengthen the argument. (Use a separate sheet of paper or computer to write your essay.)

ANALYTICAL WRITING SAMPLE ESSAYS AND ASSESSMENTS

ISSUE ESSAY 1

"Outstanding" Essay (score of 6)

Requiring restaurants to publish the fat and calorie content of their meals has its detractors; they say that disclosing the makeup of meals will alarm diners, driving them away and reducing the restaurants' income. They also balk at the cost of determining these figures in the first place. But the benefits of such a program far outweigh its drawbacks. Disclosure lets people make informed eating choices, an important consideration given what we know about unhealthy diets. In addition, disclosure may end up benefiting the restaurants, both in terms of revenue and public relations.

People are eating in restaurants with increasing frequency, and we know that a healthy diet contributes to better overall health; studies show, for example, that a healthy diet lowers cholesterol and reduces the risk of heart disease. By contrast, a poor diet, one rich in fat and calories, contributes to obesity and diabetes, both of which are on the rise in the United States.

For these reasons, we should require that restaurants post nutritional information on the meals they serve. That way, people can choose the meals they want to eat, whether their desire is to eat healthily or not.

Restaurant owners are understandably concerned that disclosing information perceived as negative could scare people off, but if all restaurants have to comply, no single business should suffer. In addition, disclosure may encourage restaurants to find healthier ways to prepare their meals, which would benefit everyone.

Determining the fat and calorie content of meals will cost restaurants money initially, but such disclosure can benefit them overall; people will appreciate the openness of the disclosure and feel confident that they're in charge of their fat and calorie intake, instilling in them a sense of comfort and control, and making them more likely, rather than less so, to eat at a restaurant that lists fat and calorie contents.

Requiring restaurants to post nutrition information can benefit both owners and patrons. It can have immediate and lasting positive effects on diners who choose to eat healthily, and it can instill a sense of control and confidence in diners who appreciate knowing what they're eating, making them more likely to continue the trend of dining out.

Analyze an Issue Essay 1 Assessment

This essay is well constructed; the author begins by recognizing arguments against restaurant disclosure, and then states his opinion ("disclosure lets people make informed eating choices, an important consideration given what we know about unhealthy diets"). He proceeds to support his position with compelling evidence, about health studies, medical trends, business operations, and public relations. The writing is clear and direct, and reveals skillful use of diction. For all these reasons, this essay receives a score of 6.

Issue Essay 2

"Outstanding" Essay (score of 6)

Scientific journals that charge a subscription or newsstand price should amend this practice to avail the public of results of publicly funded research. The reasoning here is twofold: first, the public's taxes have paid for all or a part of the research, and second, scientific results should always be readily accessible to all interested parties.

A publicly funded project means, in effect, that the taxpayers own the research and have a right to the results free of charge. Granted, many research projects are funded by a combination of private contributions, institutional grants, and public funding. Even when this is the case, the public should not be punished for being one part of a coalition that may include profit-making groups. Perhaps the research committee will need to include in its duties finding venues to make research results readily available at no charge. The mere fact of public financial support of research, in whole or in part, entitles taxpayers to have access to the fruits of that research.

Another reason to let the public see results at no charge (besides being totally or partially financially responsible for such research) is that from a larger philosophical standpoint, people should be allowed access to scientific information. Innovation in the private sector and the market necessitate access to the latest research and developments. The result of making such research widely available is that the process becomes self-sustaining. New discoveries feed new developments in the private or industrial sector, which in turn fuel further research. Publishers of scientific journals may respond to such an argument by saying that they need to make a profit in order to cover their expenses of reporting, printing, handling, and mailing research results. With that said, shouldn't the government and private sponsors of a project cover these expenses and include them in their overhead, in the same proportion as their support of the research? Additionally, popular science magazines, using their revenues from advertisers and subscribers, might pay journals to reprint research in their magazines. This practice could also provide funds for making the information available for free to parties not interested in an entire slick magazine with multiple subjects.

It is supposed that some scientists and government officials will refuse to allow sensitive or secret scientific information to be available to the public for free. Governments should not disseminate sensitive or secret research publicly, but the scope of research we are talking about is what is already published in scientific journals and available for public consumption. It's also probably true that more transparency will promote more international research and more freedom to experiment. Soviet scientists in the former Soviet Union were not allowed to read about scientific endeavors outside of the USSR. This led to decades of wasted money, effort, and time; errors made that shouldn't have been; and a lot of reinventing of the wheel. Furthermore, other scientists, pharmacists, and pharmaceutical companies need access to professional journals to keep up on the cutting-edge information released post-research. Ethically speaking, they are charged with nurturing scientific debate and keeping the public safe and informed.

In conclusion, scientific journals that charge a subscription or newsstand price are profiting unfairly when they publish wholly or partially publicly funded research results. These journals need to adjust this practice for the benefit of the public and other professionals. The public's taxes have paid for all or a part of the research, and for ethical reasons, research results must always be readily accessible to all interested parties.

ANALYZE AN ISSUE ESSAY 2 ASSESSMENT

From the very beginning, the author takes a specific position on the issue and supports it using strong examples and reasons. The author includes counterarguments, such as the potential cost of publication that the scientific journals must foot, but provides clear rebuttals with powerful supporting evidence. His inclusion of the Soviet example gives a vivid illustration of the consequences of not freely sharing information, and appeals to the reader's sense of public justice and safety. The writing is solid, well-developed, and error-free, and the writer demonstrates a mastery of rhetorical language. For all these reasons, this essay receives a score of 6.

ARGUMENT ESSAY 1

"Outstanding" Essay (score of 6)

The promotional campaign by Cable Communications Corporation argues that all businesses would benefit from advertising with the cable television company in the form of increased profitability. As evidence to back up this assertion, the promotional campaign notes the experience of the Adams Car Dealership, a recent advertiser with Cable Communications Corporation. Over the last 30 days, Adams Cars has seen a 15% increase in sales over the previous month. The argument as it now stands is unconvincing because it is missing evidence that would make the argument more well reasoned. It also suffers from poorly defined vocabulary, which makes the argument less easy to understand.

The argument presupposes that the example of the Adams Car Dealership is relevant for other businesses. It could be that there is a particular advantage from advertising for car dealerships because car buyers are willing to travel around to buy a car. The same may not be said, for example, of a dry cleaner. In general, people will take their dry cleaning business to the closest dry cleaner because it is a commodity service and a relatively small expenditure. Thus, advertising would be much more effective for a car dealership than a dry cleaner. The statement also presupposes that business owners do not have a better option for advertising. A company may get a higher increase in profits by advertising in print media or online. For business owners to make an informed decision regarding their advertising expenditures, they need to see a comparison between Cable Communication's offering and the offerings of other advertising outlets.

The argument suffers from poorly defined vocabulary. The first piece of such vocabulary is the word "recently." From just this word, it is impossible to tell when the advertising began. If Adams' advertising began three months ago, it would not be very impressive that sales increased 15% between month two and month three of the advertising campaign. Why would there not have been a boost before the most recent month? If the promotional campaign told business owners exactly when Adams began advertising, the owners would have a better ability to evaluate the argument's conclusion. The author should also clarify the phrase "increase your profits." The promotional campaign's argument gives no details on the fees associated with advertising with Cable Communications. If Adams Cars had to develop an ad and pay large sums to Cable Communications to run the ad, the total cost of advertising with the cable company very well may have exceeded the additional profits derived from increased sales. Without additional information in this regard, business owners cannot possibly evaluate the argument's conclusion.

To convince business owners that they should advertise with Cable Communications, the promotional campaign should show additional evidence from a wide variety of business that have benefited by advertising with the company. The argument presupposes that the 15% increase in sales at Adams Car Dealership is a direct result of the recent advertising campaign with Cable Communications Corporation. It could be that the dealership had announced a sale for this month or that the previous month's sales were seasonably low—for example sales in March might always be better than sales in February due to some exogenous factor. In order to better believe that Adams benefited from the advertising campaign with Cable Communications, business owners need evidence that there was not some other factor causing the 15% increase. Perhaps evidence could be shown comparing the last 30 days sales with the same period in the previous year, or the last time the dealership was running the same promotions.

To conclude, the promotional campaign by Cable Communications suffers from poorly defined vocabulary and lack of strong evidence. It turns upon unstated presuppositions, such as assuming that business owners do not have a better alternative for advertising. To better convince business owners of the benefits of advertising with Cable Communications, the company should provide additional details regarding the relevance of cable advertising to multiple business types, the exact nature of Adams' increase in sales, the ability of cable advertising to outperform other forms of advertising, and the true costs of advertising with Cable Communications. With this additional information, the promotional campaign would be much more convincing when it concludes that advertising with Cable Communications is a great way to increase a business's profits.

ANALYZE AN ARGUMENT ESSAY 1 ASSESSMENT

The author successfully identifies and analyzes this argument's main contention: that advertising with Cable Communications will increase the profits of every business.

In the opening paragraph, the essay restates the argument, then cites its unsupported assumptions. In the following four paragraphs, the author insightfully identifies flaws in the assumptions and perceptively suggests ways to clarify them.

Specifically, the author cites these points undermining the argument:

1. The one-size-fits-all fallacy of the argument that all businesses would benefit from the exposure
2. The example of 15% profit increase is misleading—not all potential profits would be similar

3. The argument that cable advertising is the best possible option for businesses
4. Vague and misleading language, and not defining key terms

Throughout the essay, the author uses well-organized paragraphs—each starts with a broad statement followed by supporting statements—and her ideas logically flow from one sentence to the next. She uses succinct, economical diction and rotates complex and simple sentences.

The essay concludes strongly by making specific suggestions that would improve the essay's arguments. The essay remains focused and clear throughout, earning it a score of 6.

ARGUMENT ESSAY 2

"Outstanding" Essay (score of 6)

The Ram article falls short of presenting a convincing and logical argument for eliminating all physical education classes at Altamonte High School and putting more resources into the development of intramural and varsity sports. First, the article's statistics are unclear and poorly labeled; they lead to a faulty conclusion. Second, among other things, the article draws conclusions that go beyond what is supported by the evidence, concluding in the drastic recommendation that "Altamonte High should eliminate all physical education classes."

The statistics in the article are not properly labeled and, therefore, have the potential to be misleading: "…65 percent of Altamonte students polled." However, maybe only 100 out of 2,400 students were polled, which is not a legitimate sampling. Maybe only athletes were polled. Maybe only seniors, who tend to have more intramural and varsity members than freshmen, were polled.

The author also overlooks the extent to which the 65 percent of polled students participate in the intramural, varsity, and community teams—some students might be on multiple teams, but others might barely be involved. In any case, this part of the argument is an appeal-to-the-majority fallacy: "A majority of people do such-and-such, so it must automatically be the best way to go." Even if 65% is a completely legitimate statistic, this may not be enough of a majority when one is making decisions about the health and future of all our youth

In addition, the Ram article draws conclusions beyond what the data supports: "Being a member of a sports team keeps one fit and healthy and promotes an active lifestyle." Just because some members of sports teams are fit and healthy does not logically mean that all are. Or maybe not all sports participants are sufficiently active. For example, perhaps some outfielders of the community sports team rarely get to run, catch, or throw and are never selected by their competitive coach for more challenging positions such as pitcher or catcher. Additionally, the author fails to note if any of these out-of-school activities teach nutrition, how to make healthy choices, how to avoid drug abuse and eating disorders, and other physical education goals beyond competition and teamwork.

In conclusion, the Ram article would be more convincing if the statistics were properly identified and labeled. In addition to data that is properly contextualized and understood, more precise and specific details would bolster the conclusion, such as how active the members of the intramural, varsity, and community teams are ("They stretch for 15 minutes and run for 30 minutes during warm-up"). With such details, the author could support all of the generalizations the article puts forth. Finally, the author of the article needs to justify why 65 percent, if indeed a legitimate sampling, is a sufficient majority for such a major change in school curriculum.

ANALYZE AN ARGUMENT ESSAY 2 ASSESSMENT

The author successfully addresses several flaws of the argument in this response, including the potentially faulty or misunderstood statistics and classical reasoning errors, such as the appeal-to-the-majority fallacy and the hasty generalization fallacy.

The author cites this evidence as potentially flawed:

1. The polled students may reflect a sample size or makeup that is skewed, and the inclusion of better labeled or explained statistics would help support the argument.
2. The illogical conclusion that what is good for a majority of students would be good for all the students.
3. The hasty generalization that students who participate in sports teams are healthier and fitter than those who don't.

Throughout the essay, the paragraphs are well constructed and follow the blueprint of the thesis statement. Every claim is supported by evidence.

The essay concludes by suggesting ways to improve the article, which is what the prompt asks the writer to do. The suggestions are good ones that would definitely strengthen the article writer's argument. The essay remains focused and clear throughout, earning it a score of 6.

PART FIVE

Practice Test

How to Take the Practice Test

Before taking this Practice Test, find a quiet place where you can work without interruption for 3 hours and 45 minutes. Make sure you have a comfortable desk, several pencils, and scrap paper. Time yourself according to the time limits shown at the beginning of each section. For the most accurate results, you should go through all five sections in one sitting. Mark your answers to the multiple-choice sections in the book or on scrap paper. You'll find the answer key and explanations in the next chapter. Good luck!

Note that the time limits and section lengths for this paper-based practice GRE are the same as those for the computer-based GRE. On the actual test, you will have the capability to mark questions within a section to return to them later if time allows. It would be a good idea to use that same approach as you take the practice test. Also, write your essay if you're going to take paper-based GRE and type it if you plan to take the computer-based GRE to better simulate the test day experience. You should type it with spell-check and grammar-check off.

Analytical Writing 1
Analyze an Issue

Directions: You will be given a brief quotation that states or implies a topic of general interest, along with explicit instructions on how to respond to that topic. Your response will be evaluated according to how well you:

- Respond to the specific directions the task gives you.
- Reflect on the complexities of the issue.
- Organize and develop your thoughts.
- Support your reasoning with relevant examples.
- Express yourself in standard written English.

"Scientific theories, which most people consider as 'fact,' almost invariably prove to be inaccurate. Thus, one should look upon any information described as 'factual' with skepticism since it may well be proven false in the future."

Write an essay in which you take a position on the statement above. In developing and supporting your viewpoint, consider ways in which the statement might or might not hold true.

Analytical Writing 2
Analyze an Argument

Directions: You will be presented with a short passage that asserts an argument or position, along with explicit instructions on how to respond to the passage. Your response will be evaluated according to how well you:

- Respond to the specific directions the task gives you.
- Analyze and interpret important elements of the passage.
- Organize and develop your analysis.
- Support your reasoning with relevant examples.
- Express yourself in standard written English.

The following appeared in a memorandum from the owner of the Juniper Café, a small, local coffee shop in the downtown area of a small American city:

"We must reduce overhead here at the café. Instead of opening at 6 a.m. weekdays, we will now open at 8 a.m. On weekends, we will only be open from 9 a.m. until 4 p.m. The decrease in hours of operations will help save money because we won't be paying for utilities, employee wages, or other operating costs during the hours we are closed. This is the best strategy for us to save money and remain in business without having to eliminate jobs."

Write a response in which you discuss what questions would need to be answered in order to assess the reasonableness of both the prediction and the argument upon which it is based. Be sure to explain how the answers to these questions would help to evaluate the prediction.

You have finished this section and now will begin the next section.

Verbal Reasoning

20 Questions
30 Minutes

Directions: For each item, select the best answer choice using the directions given.

If a question has answer choices with **ovals**, then the correct answer will be a single choice. If a question's answer choices have **squares**, the correct answer may have more than one choice. Be sure to read all directions carefully.

Verbal Reasoning Section 1

> Select one answer choice for the blank. Fill in the blank in such a way
> that it best completes the text.

1. Known for their devotion to their masters, dogs were often used as symbols of
   _____ in Medieval and Renaissance paintings.

   (A) treachery

   (B) opulence

   (C) fidelity

   (D) antiquity

   (E) valor

2. By nature _____, the poet Philip Larkin nonetheless maintained a
   spirited correspondence with a wide circle of friends.

   (A) voluble

   (B) reclusive

   (C) prolific

   (D) gregarious

   (E) pensive

> For each blank select an answer choice from the corresponding column of
> choices. Fill all blanks in such a way that it best completes the text.

3. Because the decision-making process was entirely (i) _____, there
   was no way to predict its outcome. The process was (ii) _____ rolling
   dice, where there are a finite number of possibilities but no way to accurately
   predict which two numbers will come up.

Blank (i)		Blank (ii)	
A	arbitrary	D	likened to
B	regimented	E	belittled by
C	unilateral	F	dissimilar to

4. Although the heralded "variance in taxation bill" at first received much
   (i) _____ it has had a (ii) _____ impact on the majority of
   the middle-class population, whose burden lies in the relatively unvarying
   property tax.

Blank (i)		Blank (ii)	
A	commotion	D	negligible
B	acclaim	E	necessary
C	hullabaloo	F	detrimental

5. It is easiest for critics to make allusions to other earlier work when reviewing a
   new piece; however, this is detrimental to the person reading the review prior
   to seeing the piece, as any (i) _____ viewpoint toward the referenced
   earlier piece will inevitably (ii) _____ the opinion of the unseen piece,
   potentially not allowing for (iii) _____ viewing of the new piece.

Blank (i)		Blank (ii)		Blank (iii)	
A	established	D	rebuke	G	biased
B	inaccurate	E	skew	H	impartial
C	virulent	F	complete	I	enjoyable

6. The shift away from fossil fuels as the world's primary energy source
   is not sufficient to stabilize or reduce emissions, and therefore carbon
   (i) _____ technologies are implemented to (ii) _____ and
   store carbon waste.

Blank (i)		Blank (ii)	
A	sequestration	D	incarcerate
B	reduction	E	capture
C	diminution	F	liberate

> For the following questions, select the **two** answer choices that, when inserted
> into the sentence, fit the meaning of the sentence as a whole **and** yield
> complete sentences that are similar in meaning.

7. W.C. Handy's self-conferred sobriquet, "The Father of the Blues" is widely
   _____; although he composed and published the first written blues
   song, other musicians had been playing the blues for several years.

   A professed

   B deconstructed

   C disputed

   D proven

   E contested

   F demonstrated

8. The expectation of instant gratification engendered by the ease and speed
   of modern communication can set one up for _____ in personal
   relationships that rely on e-mail or text messages, especially if they're not
   returned immediately.

   A chagrin

   B endearment

   C recompense

   D vexation

   E elation

   F pacifism

9. Anticipating the arrival of the baby panda, zookeepers _____ the
   panda exhibit to handle the influx of visitors, scientists, and veterinarians.

   A abridged

   B emended

   C meliorated

   D maintained

   E truncated

   F neglected

10. Some scientists _____ that by sensing a change in barometric pressure or electricity, certain species of fish may be able to portend seismic events; just before a recent earthquake, several fish were observed leaping into the air from the ocean.

    A repudiate

    B authorize

    C foresee

    D hypothesize

    E question

    F contend

Questions 11 and 12 are based on the passage below.

Modern entomologists are primarily engaged in the research of insects that provide a direct benefit, or cause direct harm, to human interests. The benefits of researching and protecting insect life may be immediate, such as using an insect presence to control pests or diseases, or long-term, such as protecting native species from unnecessary human intercession in order to maintain a balanced ecosystem. Research on harmful insect life endeavors to produce methods of insect control that are reliable and effective, while minimizing the effect of the control on other species. Although most insect orders include both pests and beneficial species, a few orders, such as lice and fleas, provide no benefits to humans and are said to be entirely parasitic.

> Consider each of the following choices separately and select all that apply.

11. Which of the following statements is supported by the passage?

    A The majority of insect orders are capable of both advancing and inhibiting human interests.

    B An effective insect control method will never cause side effects to insect or animal life outside the targeted order.

    C Entomological research has facilitated the development of insect species that are considered parasitic.

12. In the context in which it appears, "intercession" most nearly means

   Ⓐ obliteration.

   Ⓑ competition.

   Ⓒ alliance.

   Ⓓ intrusion.

   Ⓔ heterogeneity.

Question 13 is based on the passage below.

Instigated primarily by the Irish Republican Brotherhood, the Easter Rising of 1916 was a landmark event in the battle against English rule. Armed members of the Brotherhood, in concert with the Irish Volunteers, seized control of several government buildings in the capital city of Dublin and issued the Easter Proclamation, a proclamation of Irish independence. However, the rebels were outnumbered by British forces, which had greater access to weapons and ammunition.

The siege ended with the unconditional surrender of the militant forces, and sixteen of their leaders were subsequently executed for their roles in the uprising. Those who survived, however, went on with renewed fervor to lobby for Ireland's independence, and the public nature of the uprising changed popular sentiment about British rule. **While the Easter Rising was a failure by military and tactical standards, it is viewed as an important milestone in the 1919 establishment of the Republic of Ireland.**

13. In the argument given, the two portions in boldface above play which of the following roles?

   Ⓐ The first states the conclusion of the argument as a whole; the second provides support for part of that conclusion.

   Ⓑ The first provides support for the conclusion of the argument as a whole; the second provides evidence that supports an objection to that conclusion.

   Ⓒ The first provides support for part of the conclusion of the argument as a whole; the second states the argument's conclusion.

   Ⓓ The first provides support for an intermediate conclusion that supports a further conclusion stated in the argument; the second states that intermediate conclusion.

   Ⓔ The first states an outside position that the argument as a whole supports; the second states the conclusion of the argument.

Questions 14 through 16 are based on the passage below.

Many Iranian Americans, whether they are immigrants or American-born, identify themselves as being of Persian heritage. This descriptor is a frequent cause for confusion among non-Persians who know the country as Iran and understand Persia as an antiquated name for the empire that encompassed part of Iran as well as parts of modern-day Pakistan and Afghanistan. Opponents of the term argue that because some Afghani and Pakistani groups refer to themselves as being of Persian heritage, the term loses meaning as a signifier of nationality. However, critics argue that just as the English language recognizes "Spain" rather than "Espana," English speakers should refer to the country as Persia, and not as Iran, which is the Persian translation of the country's name.

14. The author is primarily concerned with

   Ⓐ arguing that English usage of descriptors of nationality should reflect usage within the native languages of the countries in question.

   Ⓑ clarifying how the fall of the Persian Empire has influenced the terminology that modern citizens of Iran use to define their nationality.

   Ⓒ distinguishing among three groups that use the same term to describe their national identities.

   Ⓓ explaining two opposing positions in an argument about the use of a descriptor of national identity.

   Ⓔ persuading readers that in order for the term Persian to have a clear relationship to nationality, only Iranians, not Afghanis or Pakistanis, should use the term.

   > Consider each of the following choices separately
   > and select all that apply.

15. Based on the information in the passage, which of the following individuals might describe themselves as Persian?

   Ⓐ an Afghani-born woman who is a naturalized citizen of Iran

   Ⓑ an American man born in the United States to Iranian immigrant parents

   Ⓒ an American woman of English descent who has worked in Pakistan for 15 years

16. According to the passage, the ancient Persian Empire

    (A) covered parts of modern-day Pakistan and Iran, and all of modern-day Afghanistan.

    (B) covered the entirety of the modern-day nations of Afghanistan, Pakistan, and Iran.

    (C) covered parts of modern-day Afghanistan and Pakistan, and all of modern-day Iran.

    (D) covered all of modern-day Iran and Afghanistan, and parts of modern-day Pakistan.

    (E) covered parts of the modern-day nations of Afghanistan, Pakistan, and Iran.

Questions 17 through 19 are based on the passage below.

In Greco-Roman societies, women applied white lead and chalk to their faces to attract attention. Ancient Egyptians wore light foundation to gild their skin, while their kohl eyeliner was only slightly heavier than the eye makeup popular in the mid-1960s. Persians believed that henna dyes, used to stain hair and faces dark, enabled them to summon the majesty of the earth. The European Middle Ages followed the Greco-Roman trend of pale faces. Those rich enough not to work outdoors and acquire a suntan wanted to flaunt their affluence by being pale. **To look feminine, fashionable sixth-century women would achieve the same ideal by bleeding themselves.** While pale of skin, regal 13th-century Italian women wore bright pink lipstick, showing they could afford synthetic makeup.

17. The author would probably consider which of the following statements to be most similar in meaning to the highlighted sentence?

    (A) Contrary to common opinion, zebras are dark animals, with white stripes where the pigmentation is inhibited.

    (B) The frog's brown and yellow coloring, as well as its rough texture, allows it to blend in with tree trunks.

    (C) The short-tailed cricket is known to eat its own wings to survive.

    (D) To look masculine, birds called budgerigars display naturally occurring yellow fluorescent plumage on their crowns.

    (E) The male blue-tailed iguana will chew down some of its spines to appear more masculine.

> Consider each of the following choices separately
> and select all that apply.

18. Which of the following statements is supported by this passage?

    A   The lightening of women's skin has often, but not always, been preferred.

    B   A woman's social position could be revealed by her makeup.

    C   The practice of lightening the skin originated in Greco-Roman societies.

19. The passage cites each of the following reasons for some cultures' preferring artificially pale skin EXCEPT

    A   to flaunt affluence

    B   to look golden

    C   to call up the splendor of the earth

    D   to attract attention

    E   to look feminine

Question 20 is based on the passage below.

Solipsism is the belief that only oneself and one's own experiences are real, while anything else—a physical object or another person—is nothing more than an object of one's consciousness. Thus, in a sense, solipsism is the concept that nothing 'exists' outside of one's own mind. As a philosophical position, solipsism is usually the unintended consequence of an overemphasis on the reliability of internal mental states, which provide no evidence for the existence of external referents.

20. In this passage, the author is primarily concerned with

    A   discussing the importance of a phenomenon.

    B   refuting a hypothesis advanced by philosophers.

    C   contrasting two schools of thought.

    D   presenting the definition of a concept.

    E   comparing a physical object to a person.

You have finished this section and now will begin the next section.

Quantitative Reasoning 1

20 Questions
35 Minutes

Directions: For each question, indicate the best answer, using the directions given.

You may use a calculator for all the questions in this section.

If a question has answer choices with **ovals,** then the correct answer is a single choice. If a question has answer choices with **squares,** then the correct answer consists of one or more answer choices. Read each question carefully.

Important Facts:
All numbers used are real numbers.

All figures lie in a plane unless otherwise noted.

Geometric figures, such as lines, circles, triangles, and quadrilaterals **may or may not be** drawn to scale. That is, you should not assume that quantities such as lengths and angle measures are as they appear in a drawing. But you can assume that lines shown as straight are indeed straight, points on a line are in the order shown, and all geometric objects are in the relative positions shown. For questions involving drawn figures, base your answers on geometric reasoning, rather than on estimation, measurement, or comparison by sight.

Coordinate systems, such as *xy*-planes and number lines, **are** drawn to scale. Therefore, you may read, estimate, and compare quantities in these figures by sight or by measurement.

Graphical data presentations, such as bar graphs, line graphs, and pie charts, **are** drawn to scale. Therefore, you may read, estimate, and compare data values by sight or by measurement.

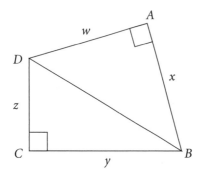

$\triangle ABD$ and $\triangle CDB$ are right triangles.

1.

Quantity A	Quantity B
$w^2 + x^2$	$y^2 + z^2$

Ⓐ Quantity A is greater.

Ⓑ Quantity B is greater.

Ⓒ The two quantities are equal.

Ⓓ The relationship cannot be determined from the information given.

$$x + 4y = 6$$
$$x = 2y$$

2.

Quantity A	Quantity B
x	y

Ⓐ Quantity A is greater.

Ⓑ Quantity B is greater.

Ⓒ The two quantities are equal.

Ⓓ The relationship cannot be determined from the information given.

In a certain accounting firm, there are exactly three types of employees: managerial, technical, and clerical. The firm has 120 employees, of which 25 percent are managerial.

3.

Quantity A	Quantity B
The number of managerial employees	Two-thirds of the number of clerical employees

Ⓐ Quantity A is greater.

Ⓑ Quantity B is greater.

Ⓒ The two quantities are equal.

Ⓓ The relationship cannot be determined from the information given.

4.

Quantity A	Quantity B
$(a + 1)(b + 1)$	$ab + 1$

Ⓐ Quantity A is greater.

Ⓑ Quantity B is greater.

Ⓒ The two quantities are equal.

Ⓓ The relationship cannot be determined from the information given.

In the two-digit number *jk*, the value of the digit *j* is twice the value of the digit *k*.

5. | Quantity A | Quantity B |
    |:---:|:---:|
    | *k* | 6 |

    Ⓐ Quantity A is greater.

    Ⓑ Quantity B is greater.

    Ⓒ The two quantities are equal.

    Ⓓ The relationship cannot be determined from the information given.

Henry purchased *x* apples, and Jack purchased 10 apples fewer than one-third of the number of apples Henry purchased.

6. | Quantity A | Quantity B |
    |:---:|:---:|
    | The number of apples Jack purchased | $\dfrac{x - 30}{3}$ |

    Ⓐ Quantity A is greater.

    Ⓑ Quantity B is greater.

    Ⓒ The two quantities are equal.

    Ⓓ The relationship cannot be determined from the information given.

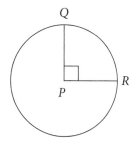

P is the center of the circle, and the area of sector *PQR* is 4.

7. | Quantity A | Quantity B |
    |:---:|:---:|
    | The area of circle P | 4π |

    Ⓐ Quantity A is greater.

    Ⓑ Quantity B is greater.

    Ⓒ The two quantities are equal.

    Ⓓ The relationship cannot be determined from the information given.

8. | Quantity A | Quantity B |
    |:---:|:---:|
    | The volume of a rectangular solid with a length of 5 feet, a width of 4 feet, and a height of *x* feet | The volume of a rectangular solid with a length of 10 feet, a width of 8 feet, and a height of *y* feet |

    Ⓐ Quantity A is greater.

    Ⓑ Quantity B is greater.

    Ⓒ The two quantities are equal.

    Ⓓ The relationship cannot be determined from the information given.

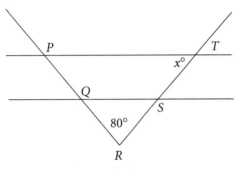

$$PQ = ST$$
$$QR = RS$$

9. In the figure shown above, what is x?

    (A) 40

    (B) 50

    (C) 60

    (D) 70

    (E) 80

10. A producer must select a duo, consisting of one lead actor and one supporting actor, from six candidates. What is the number of possible duos the producer could select?

    [   ] possible duos

11. Jane must select three different items for each dinner she will serve. The items are to be chosen from among five different vegetarian and four different meat selections. If at least one of the selections must be vegetarian, how many different dinners could Jane create?

    (A) 30

    (B) 40

    (C) 60

    (D) 70

    (E) 80

12. A computer can perform 30 identical tasks in six hours. At that rate, what is the minimum number of computers that should be assigned to complete 80 tasks within three hours?

    [   ] computers

13. Given an integer c, how many integers are greater than c and less than $2c$?

    (A) $\frac{c}{2}$

    (B) c

    (C) $c - 1$

    (D) $c - 2$

    (E) $c + 1$

14. If the ratio of $2a$ to b is 8 times the ratio of b to a, then $\frac{b}{a}$ could be

Indicate <u>all</u> possible choices.

- [A] -2
- [B] $-\frac{1}{2}$
- [C] $\frac{1}{4}$
- [D] $\frac{1}{2}$
- [E] 2

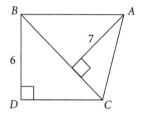

15. In the figure above, the area of $\triangle ABC$ is 35. What is the length of DC?

16. If $3^m = 81$, then $m^3 =$

- (A) 9
- (B) 16
- (C) 27
- (D) 54
- (E) 64

17. If $0 < x < 1$, which of the following must be true? Choose all possible choices.

Indicate <u>all</u> possible choices.

- [A] $2x < x$
- [B] $2x < 1$
- [C] $2x > 1$
- [D] $x^2 < x$
- [E] $x^2 < 1$

Questions 18–20 are based on the following graphs.

ENERGY USE BY YEAR, COUNTRY Y, 1980–2010
(in millions of kilowatt-hours)

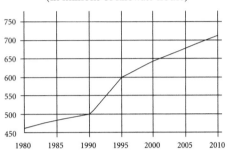

ENERGY USE BY TYPE, COUNTRY Y

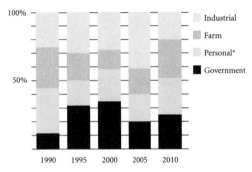

*Total personal use = population × per capita personal use

18. In 1995, how many of the categories shown had energy use greater than 150 million kilowatt-hours?

    (A) None

    (B) One

    (C) Two

    (D) Three

    (E) Four

19. If the population of Country Y increased by 20 percent from 1990 to 1995, approximately what was the percent decrease in the per capita personal use of energy between those two years?

    (A) 0%

    (B) 17%

    (C) 25%

    (D) 35%

    (E) 50%

20. Which of the following can be inferred from the graphs? Choose all that apply.

    [A] Farm use of energy increased between 1990 and 2010.

    [B] In 2010, industrial use of energy was greater than industrial use of energy in 1995.

    [C] More people were employed by the government of Country Y in 2010 than in 1990.

    [D] About twice as many kilowatt hours of energy were used for farm purposes in 2005 than in 2000.

    [E] The energy usage by type was most equally distributed over the four categories in 1990.

You have finished this section and now will begin the next section.

Verbal Reasoning Section 2

20 Questions
30 Minutes

Directions: For each item, select the best answer choice using the directions given.

If a question has answer choices with **ovals,** then the correct answer will be a single choice. If a question's answer choices have **squares**, the correct answer may be more than one choice. Be sure to read all directions carefully.

Select one answer choice for the blank. Fill in the blank in such a way
that it best completes the text.

---

1. The current need for diversification does not mean the organization should
   be diverted from its earlier and historical purpose; instead, this diversification
   should be construed as a means of _____ that purpose.

   (A) undermining

   (B) furthering

   (C) retracting

   (D) classifying

   (E) deterring

For each blank select an answer choice from the corresponding column of
choices. Fill all blanks in such a way that it best completes the text.

---

2. Researchers have decoded the DNA of the honeybee. They discovered
   that bees' keen sense of smell enables them to (i) _____ kin from
   foe. Genes that regulate vulnerability to (ii) _____, however, are
   surprisingly deficient. Scientists speculate that the observed extensive
   grooming among hive mates (iii) _____ from various diseases, thus
   protecting the colony.

Blank (i)		Blank (ii)		Blank (iii)	
A	promulgate	D	pathogens	G	minimizes incursions
B	discern	E	cold	H	implicates replication
C	arbitrate	F	poison	I	simulates action

3. A United Nations working group issued a report describing a
   (i) _____ need to draw up valid plans for dealing with the global
   water crisis. The report emphasizes the critical necessity of galvanizing
   political efforts to (ii) _____ resources and (iii) _____
   international attention on both water and sanitation.

Blank (i)		Blank (ii)		Blank (iii)	
A	exigent	D	produce ineffable	G	request
B	leviathan	E	retain abundant	H	focus
C	specious	F	mobilize limited	I	require

Select one answer choice for the blank. Fill in the blank in such a way
that it best completes the text.

---

4. Although the French general Henri Philippe Petain was greatly honored
   for his role as military leader of France during World War I, he incurred
   _____ for his collaboration during the German occupation of World
   War II.

   (A) status
   (B) reputation
   (C) kudos
   (D) recompense
   (E) obloquy

For each blank select an answer choice from the corresponding column of choices. Fill all blanks in such a way that it best completes the text.

5. Although cellophane is not immediately thought of as a paper product, it is, in fact, just that. Implausibly, this (i) _____ material is made from the same components as the everyday brown paper bag. Its inventor, Jacques E. Brandenberger, originally wanted to plastic-coat fabric to prevent stains, but the overwhelming usefulness of just the clear plastic film became (ii) _____ and (iii) _____ product was born.

Blank (i)		Blank (ii)		Blank (iii)	
A	diaphanous	D	unjustifiably marketable	G	an amorphous
B	standardized	E	immediately apparent	H	an ingenuous
C	opaque	F	outrageously fashionable	I	a ubiquitous

Select one answer choice for the blank. Fill in the blank in such a way that it best completes the text.

6. Unlike most other philosophers, who try to determine whether an objective reality exists, David Hume felt that the issue was _____.

- (A) pragmatic
- (B) challenging
- (C) theoretical
- (D) insoluble
- (E) esoteric

For the following questions, select the two answer choices that, when inserted into the sentence, fit the meaning of the sentence as a whole and yield complete sentences that are similar in meaning.

7. Although a plethora of evidence exists to the contrary, a portion of the population still disregards warnings about the _____ effects of nicotine and continues to smoke, believing no harm is done to their health.

   A deleterious

   B addictive

   C inimical

   D antagonistic

   E benign

   F pernicious

8. To the public's great shock, the group recently voted into power on a platform of peaceable reform conducted _____ acts against existing branches of government as soon as the election was over.

   A contumacious

   B endemic

   C erratic

   D estimable

   E irresolute

   F seditious

9. Photo retouching and inflated claims are so well concealed in most advertising campaigns that consumers are unaware of the _____ being employed.

   A cabal

   B artifice

   C hegemony

   D chicanery

   E dominance

   F imprecation

10. The performers agreed that the topic of marriage was an excellent theme for their upcoming performance at a conservative organization's charity event; however, the audience was unreceptive to the _____ jokes made during the show.

   A plucky

   B ribald

   C coarse

   D traitorous

   E politic

   F treacherous

Question 11 is based on the passage below.

Although sharks are classified as fish, not mammals, they differ significantly in several respects from other freshwater and saltwater fish. Most significantly, a shark's skeleton is composed of lightweight, flexible cartilage, providing an advantage in hunting other marine life; other superclasses of fish have stable calcified skeletons. **Additionally, sharks possess no swim bladder, the small organ that allows most fish to control their buoyancy; instead, a substantial liver filled with oil works to keep the sharks afloat.**

11. In the argument given, the two portions in boldface play which of the following roles?

   (A) The first supports the conclusion of the argument; the second summarizes a position that is in opposition to that conclusion.

   (B) The first provides support for the conclusion of the argument as a whole; the second provides that conclusion.

   (C) The first states the position that the argument as a whole opposes; the second states an intermediate conclusion that provides support for the argument as a whole.

   (D) The first serves as an intermediate conclusion; the second states the conclusion of the argument as a whole.

   (E) The first states the conclusion of the argument as a whole; the second provides support for that conclusion.

Question 12 is based on the passage below.

The Dewey Decimal System provided the first standardized, easily understood method of classifying the items in a library's collection. Classification, in combination with the process of cataloging, meant that patrons could easily identify and locate for themselves items that had a certain title, were written by a certain author, or related to a given subject. Because the system was adopted at most libraries, patrons who learned the system could use it at any library.

12. Based on the information of the passage it is probably true that prior to the implementation of the Dewey Decimal System,

  (A) libraries were generally small enough that no classification system was needed.

  (B) libraries refused to share make public the systems they used to classify books.

  (C) patrons relied heavily on library staff to identify and locate the materials they sought.

  (D) more people worked as librarians than after its use became widespread.

  (E) library patrons were never able to understand the order in which books were shelved.

Questions 13 and 14 are based on the passage below.

The first smallpox prevention methods were inoculations, intentional infections with active diseased matter that typically caused a mild illness, and would later result in immunity. Modern epidemiologists believe that inoculated patients were less likely to contract a fatal case of tuberculosis because they contracted the disease through skin contact, not inhalation. However, due to extreme disparities in the type and amount of virus used, health practitioners could offer no real prediction of how severe a case a given patient might contract after being inoculated. Inoculation differs from vaccination, which uses a standard dose of dead or weakened virus culture and therefore poses a much lower risk of fatal infection. After a smallpox vaccine was developed in the 1790s, inoculation gradually fell from favor and was eventually banned in numerous jurisdictions.

Consider each of the following choices separately
and select all that apply.

13. Which of the following statements is supported by the passage?

   A Vaccination replaced inoculation because it was a safer method of
      protecting against disease.

   B Two random doses of a vaccine were likely to be more similar than two
      random doses of an inoculum.

   C Prior to the 1790s, live virus cultures were often used in tuberculosis
      inoculations.

14. In the context in which it appears, "disparities" most nearly means which of
    the following?

   Ⓐ incapacities

   Ⓑ vulnerabilities

   Ⓒ inconsistencies

   Ⓓ resemblances

   Ⓔ ineffectiveness

Questions 15 through 20 are based on the passage below

Surveying paradigmatic works of tragic literature from antiquity to the present
alongside the immense and ever-growing body of secondary literature on the
subject, the literary critic Terry Eagleton arrived at the pat judgment that not
only had no satisfactory definition of tragedy been offered to date, but also
that none besides the admittedly vacuous "very sad" could ever be offered.
Overly broad definitions, which for all intents and purposes equate the tragic
with seriousness, lead invariably to Scylla; overly narrow ones, such as the
Renaissance-inspired struggle theory, to Charybdis. Notwithstanding this
definitional dilemma, Eagleton's conclusion, as clear a case of defeatism as
any heretofore advanced, leaves much to be desired.

In *A Definition of Tragedy*, Oscar Mandel, who is decidedly more sanguine
than Eagleton on this score, discerns in Aristotle's *De Poetica* the rudiments
of a substantive definition of the tragic. Following the spirit, albeit not the

letter, of Aristotle's text, Mandel sets forth three requirements for any work to be counted as tragic, the third weighing most heavily in his account. First, it must have a protagonist whom we highly (or at least moderately) esteem. Second, it must show how the protagonist comes to suffer greatly. And, third, it must reveal how the protagonist's downfall was inevitably but unwittingly brought about by his own action. It is plain to see that, of the three requirements, the third (call this the *inevitability requirement*) is beyond question the most contentious as well as the most dubious. The truth is that the inevitability requirement is entirely too stringent. While it may be a sufficient condition, it is not, Mandel's assertions notwithstanding, the *sin qua non* of tragic literature.

One need look no further than Anton Chekhov's *Three Sisters*, a quintessential work of modern tragedy, to see why this is so. In a provincial capital quite remote from cosmopolitan Moscow, the well-educated, tireless, but spiritually drained sisters are ground down by the inexorable forces of time and fortune. Their failure to leave for Moscow, the childhood home they yearn for, can be understood as their failure to extricate themselves from the tedious and insufferable life brought on by their workaday habits. This suggests a certain acknowledgement on their part of their powerlessness to defy the hands of fate. In the final analysis, the question of whether the protagonist's fate is sealed in consequence of tragic action, as in Greek and Renaissance tragic dramas, or of inaction, as with modern tragedies, has very little to do with one of the absolutely essential ingredients of tragic literature. That, of course, is the profound sense of insurmountable powerlessness that yields an unnamable, implacable feeling expressing alienation from life itself.

15. In the middle of his discussion of Terry Eagleton's work, the author alludes to Scylla and Charybdis in order to

   (A) point out the principal faults with Eagleton's ideas about tragedy.

   (B) argue for the importance of understanding myths in our investigation into the nature of tragedy.

   (C) establish that a dilemma pertaining to the essence of tragedy has its origin in myth.

   (D) illustrate how a dilemma common to other intellectual inquiries also applies to our understanding of tragedy.

   (E) delineate the potential problems that lie in wait for anyone who wishes to define tragedy.

16. The primary purpose of the passage is to

　Ⓐ　criticize Eagleton's view that the most adequate definition of tragedy is very sad.

　Ⓑ　cast doubt on Eagleton's and Mandel's views of tragic literature for failing to enumerate all the necessary conditions for tragedy.

　Ⓒ　conclude, after analyzing the views of two tragic theorists, that tragedy cannot be defined adequately.

　Ⓓ　criticize Eagleton's view that tragedy cannot be adequately defined and Mandel's view that tragedy requires tragic action and to offer up another condition indispensible for tragedy.

　Ⓔ　find fault with Eagleton's view that tragedy amounts to what is "very sad" and Mandel's view that tragedy requires great suffering in order to advance a new definition of tragedy in their place.

17. The author's attitude toward the protagonists in *Three Sisters* can best be characterized as

　Ⓐ　laudatory.

　Ⓑ　conciliatory.

　Ⓒ　despondent.

　Ⓓ　myopic.

　Ⓔ　diffident.

18. It can reasonably be inferred from the author's assessments of Eagleton's and Mandel's views of tragedy that

　Ⓐ　Mandel's and Eagleton's conceptions of tragedy can ultimately be dismissed.

　Ⓑ　both theorists fall short of the mark of what constitutes tragedy, but for different reasons.

　Ⓒ　the tragic has as much to do with what is very sad as it has to do with the inevitability requirement.

　Ⓓ　the fact that tragic heroes undergo great suffering is at the center of both accounts.

　Ⓔ　tragic literature is most fully understood when it combines the insights of many different thinkers.

19. The author voices dissatisfaction with the present conception of tragedy in paragraph 3 by

    A) describing in some detail how a particular genre influences the way we think about tragic literature more generally.

    B) analyzing a work of literature in order to help us better appreciate its supreme aesthetic value.

    C) raising a pointed objection to Mandel's definition of tragedy and supporting the objection with a counterexample.

    D) quibbling with the main criteria in Mandel's definition, none of which is applicable to a particular work of literature.

    E) cogently defending conclusions about works of tragedy that, on pain of contradiction, Mandel cannot accept.

20. Regarding the passage as a whole, the author's opinion of the first and second requirements spelled out in Mandel's definition of tragedy is most likely that

    A) neither the first nor the second requirement fits very easily with the condition of powerlessness that he defends in the final paragraph.

    B) the first but not the second requirement is essentially at odds with his claim that Chekhov's *Three Sisters* is a work that exemplifies the condition of powerlessness.

    C) the second but not the first requirement would have to be rejected on the grounds that it is ostensibly the case that the sisters in *Three Sisters* do not undergo great suffering.

    D) in light of the condition of powerlessness that he endorses, it can be concluded that both requirements should not figure prominently in any account of tragedy.

    E) neither the first nor the second requirement should be necessarily ruled out in our attempt to grasp the essence of tragedy, provided that neither is antithetical to the condition of powerlessness.

You have finished this section and now will begin the next section.

Quantitative Reasoning 2

20 questions
35 minutes

Directions:

For each question, indicate the best answer, using the directions given.

You may use a calculator for all the questions in this section.

If a question has answer choices with **ovals**, then the correct answer is a single choice. If a question has answer choices with **squares**, then the correct answer consists of one or more answer choices. Read each question carefully.

Important Facts:

All numbers used are real numbers.

All figures lie in a plane unless otherwise noted.

Geometric figures, such as lines, circles, triangles, and quadrilaterals **may or may not be** drawn to scale. That is, you should not assume that quantities such as lengths and angle measures are as they appear in a drawing. But you can assume that lines shown as straight are indeed straight, points on a line are in the order shown, and all geometric objects are in the relative positions shown. For questions involving drawn figures, base your answers on geometric reasoning, rather than on estimation, measurement, or comparison by sight.

Coordinate systems, such as *xy*-planes and number lines, **are** drawn to scale. Therefore, you may read, estimate, and compare quantities in these figures by sight or by measurement.

Graphical data presentations, such as bar graphs, line graphs, and pie charts, **are** drawn to scale. Therefore, you may read, estimate, and compare data values by sight or by measurement.

The perimeter of isosceles $\triangle ABC$ is 40 and the length of side BC is 12.

1. | Quantity A | Quantity B |
    |---|---|
    | The length of side AB | 14 |

   (A) Quantity A is greater.

   (B) Quantity B is greater.

   (C) The two quantities are equal.

   (D) The relationship cannot be determined from the information given.

$$y = (x + 3)^2$$

2. | Quantity A | Quantity B |
    |---|---|
    | The value of y when $x = 1$ | 9 |

   (A) Quantity A is greater.

   (B) Quantity B is greater.

   (C) The two quantities are equal.

   (D) The relationship cannot be determined from the information given.

3. | Quantity A | Quantity B |
    |---|---|
    | The number of miles traveled by a car that traveled for four hours at an average speed of 40 miles per hour | The number of miles traveled by a train that traveled for two and a half hours at an average speed of 70 miles per hour |

   (A) Quantity A is greater.

   (B) Quantity B is greater.

   (C) The two quantities are equal.

   (D) The relationship cannot be determined from the information given.

4. | Quantity A | Quantity B |
    |---|---|
    | The number of cookies in a bag that weighs 3 kilograms | The number of grapes in a bag that weighs 2 kilograms |

   (A) Quantity A is greater.

   (B) Quantity B is greater.

   (C) The two quantities are equal.

   (D) The relationship cannot be determined from the information given.

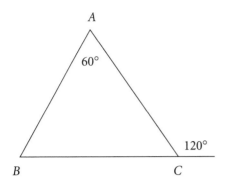

5.   Quantity A   Quantity B

       AB BC

   Ⓐ   Quantity A is greater.

   Ⓑ   Quantity B is greater.

   Ⓒ   The two quantities are equal.

   Ⓓ   The relationship cannot be determined from the information given.

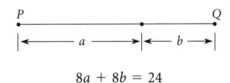

$$8a + 8b = 24$$

6.   Quantity A   Quantity B

    The length of   2
segment PQ

   Ⓐ   Quantity A is greater.

   Ⓑ   Quantity B is greater.

   Ⓒ   The two quantities are equal.

   Ⓓ   The relationship cannot be determined from the information given.

$$x < y$$

7.   Quantity A   Quantity B

      $y - x$ $x - y$

   Ⓐ   Quantity A is greater.

   Ⓑ   Quantity B is greater.

   Ⓒ   The two quantities are equal.

   Ⓓ   The relationship cannot be determined from the information given.

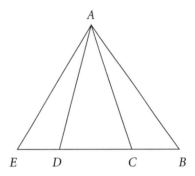

The area of triangular region ABE is 75.

8.   Quantity A   Quantity B

    The area of   The area of
$\triangle ABC$ $\triangle ADE$

   Ⓐ   Quantity A is greater.

   Ⓑ   Quantity B is greater.

   Ⓒ   The two quantities are equal.

   Ⓓ   The relationship cannot be determined from the information given.

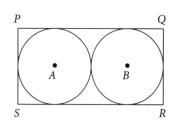

9. The two circles with centers A and B have the same radius, r. If $r = 3$, what is the perimeter of rectangle $PQRS$?

  (A) 12
  (B) 18
  (C) 24
  (D) 36
  (E) 48

10. What is the least value of x for which $1 - \left(\frac{1}{4}\right)^x$ is greater than 0?

  (A) -2
  (B) -1
  (C) 0
  (D) 1
  (E) 2

11. If $\dfrac{p - q}{p} = \dfrac{2}{7}$, then $\dfrac{q}{p} =$

  (A) $\frac{2}{5}$
  (B) $\frac{5}{7}$
  (C) 1
  (D) $\frac{7}{5}$
  (E) $\frac{7}{2}$

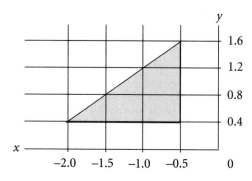

12. What is the area of the shaded region in the figure above?

  [   ] square units

13. Which of the following is 850 percent greater than 8×10^3?

  (A) 8.5×10^3
  (B) 6.4×10^4
  (C) 6.8×10^4
  (D) 7.6×10^4
  (E) 1.6×10^5

14. Which of the following has/have *exactly* 4 positive integer factors?

    Indicate all possible numbers.

    A 4
    B 6
    C 8
    D 12
    E 14

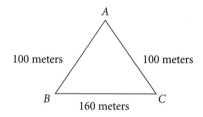

A

100 meters   100 meters

B   160 meters   *C*

15. The figure above represents a triangular field. What is the minimum distance, in meters, that a person would have to walk to go from point *A* to a point on side *BC*?

    _____ meters

16. If the average of two numbers is $3y$ and one of the numbers is $y - z$, what is the other number, in terms of y and z?

    Ⓐ $y + z$
    Ⓑ $3y + z$
    Ⓒ $4y - z$
    Ⓓ $5y - z$
    Ⓔ $5y + z$

17. Which points lie on the graph of
    $$y = \frac{x^2}{x + 1}?$$

    Indicate all possible choices.

    A $(-3, -5)$
    B $(-2, -4)$
    C $(-1, -3)$
    D $\left(1, \frac{1}{2}\right)$
    E $\left(3, 2\frac{1}{2}\right)$

Questions 18–20 refer to the charts below.

U.S. PHYSICIANS IN SELECTED SPECIALTIES BY GENDER, 1986

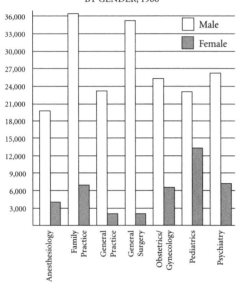

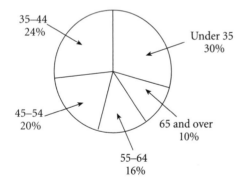

GENERAL SURGERY PHYSICIANS BY AGE, 1986

18. Which of the following physician specialties had the lowest ratio of males to females in 1986?

   Ⓐ Family practice

   Ⓑ General surgery

   Ⓒ Obstetrics/gynecology

   Ⓓ Pediatrics

   Ⓔ Psychiatry

19. If the number of female general surgeon physicians in the under-35 category represented 3.5 percent of all the general surgeon physicians, approximately how many male general surgeon physicians were under 35 years?

   Ⓐ 9,200

   Ⓑ 9,800

   Ⓒ 10,750

   Ⓓ 11,260

   Ⓔ 11,980

20. Approximately what percent of all general practice physicians in 1986 were male?

   Ⓐ 23%

   Ⓑ 50%

   Ⓒ 75%

   Ⓓ 82%

   Ⓔ 90%

Your Practice Test is now complete.

CHAPTER 21

Practice Test Answers

ANSWER KEY

VERBAL REASONING SECTION 1 ANSWER KEY

1. C
2. B
3. A, D
4. B, D
5. A, E, H
6. A, E
7. C, E
8. A, D
9. B, C
10. D, F
11. A
12. D
13. C
14. D
15. A, B
16. E
17. E
18. A, B
19. C
20. D

QUANTITATIVE REASONING SECTION 1 ANSWER KEY

1. C
2. A
3. D
4. D
5. B
6. C
7. A
8. D
9. B
10. 30
11. E
12. 6
13. C
14. B, D
15. 8
16. E
17. D, E
18. C
19. D
20. A, D

Verbal Reasoning Section 2 Answer Key

1. B
2. B, D, G
3. A, F, I
4. E
5. A, E, I
6. D
7. A, F
8. A, F
9. B, D
10. B, C
11. E
12. C
13. A, B
14. C
15. E
16. D
17. A
18. B
19. C
20. E

Quantitative Reasoning Section 2 Answer Key

1. D
2. A
3. B
4. D
5. C
6. A
7. A
8. D
9. D
10. D
11. B
12. 0.9
13. D
14. B, C, E
15. 60
16. E
17. B, D
18. D
19. B
20. E

Diagnostic Tool

Tally up your score and write the results below.

Total

Total Correct: _____ out of 80

By Section

Verbal Reasoning _____ out of 40
Quantitative Reasoning _____ out of 40

ANSWERS AND EXPLANATIONS

VERBAL REASONING SECTION 1 EXPLANATIONS

1. C

This particular sentence has no detour road signs. Here the key phrase is "known for their devotion to their masters," so you might predict that the missing word means something like "loyalty" or "devotedness." The correct answer, *fidelity*, is a close match for this prediction.

2. B

This sentence contains a detour road sign, "nonetheless," so you can expect the first part of the sentence to contrast with the fact that he "maintained a spirited correspondence with a wide circle of friends." So you might predict that the missing word means something like "withdrawn" or "shy." Choice **(B)** matches this prediction: "By nature *reclusive*, Philip Larkin nonetheless maintained a spirited correspondence with a wide circle of friends." That makes perfect sense.

3. A, D

The road sign "because" in the first half of this sentence tells you that the second half will continue the thought of the first. The second half indicates that there was "no way to predict" the decision-making process's outcome, so a description of the process as "random" makes sense. The prediction matches **(A)**, *arbitrary*. Choice **(B)**, *regimented*, "rigidly organized," means the opposite of what the sentence requires. Choice **(C)**, *unilateral*, is also incorrect—although the decision-making process may have been entirely in the hands of one person that's not the same thing as having "no way to predict its outcome." The best way to complete the second blank, with its multi-word answer choices, is to try each one in place

and see which works best. The sentence compares the decision-making process to throwing dice, so making decisions was *likened to* **(D)** a roll of the dice, the correct answer. Choice **(E)**, *belittled by*, doesn't make sense in context, and **(F)**, *dissimilar to*, means the opposite of what the sentence requires.

4. B, D

Look at blank (ii) first. The tax burden of most of the citizens comes from an "unvarying" tax, so the legislation mentioned earlier in the sentence had a *minor* effect on the middle class. **(D)** *negligible* matches that perfectly. The word "although" indicates contrast, so the bill that produced "negligible" results was expected not only to have a significant effect, but a positive one. A prediction is "optimism" or "praise." **(B)** *acclaim* works best. **(C)** *hullabaloo* and **(A)** *commotion* are tempting choices, but do not have sufficiently strong positive connotations, particularly as the bill is described as having been "heralded."

5. A, E, H

The three blanks are related in this sentence: Blank (i) causes blank (ii) and prevents blank (iii). In the first two blanks, **(A)** *established* and **(B)** *inaccurate* could potentially **(E)** *skew* the opinion, but only **(A)** *established*, would logically exclude **(H)** *impartial* for the last blank. With the information given, only *established*, *skew*, and *impartial* logically follow each other.

6. A, E

This is a high-difficulty sentence, but elimination and prediction will help you out a great deal. The first clause and then the road sign "therefore" suggest that the clause with the blanks will provide an alternative to the fact that you cannot "stabilize emissions" with current technologies. Blank (ii) has a meaning similar to "store", so eliminate **(F)** *liberate*. **(D)** *incarcerate* looks like incinerate, but to incarcerate means to put in prison. **(E)** *capture* matches. For blank (i), notice that the technologies must also be for storing carbon waste. Choices **(B)** *reduction* and **(C)** *diminution* can be eliminated and **(A)** *sequestration* matches the prediction of "storing".

7. C, E

To figure out what fits in the blank, note the detour road sign "although" between the first and second halves of the sentence. This tells you that what came before will be contradicted by what comes after. The first clause tells us that Handy's nickname is "self-conferred," so you can speculate that not everyone shares Handy's self assessment. You could paraphrase the sentence this way to predict the blank: "Handy feels he's the father of the blues, but other musicians 'disagree.'" You're looking for a synonym for "disagree." You can eliminate choices **(A)**, **(D)**, and **(F)**, which say that Handy's moniker was *professed*, *proven*, or *demonstrated*—they mean the opposite of what you want. Choice **(B)**, which states that Handy's nickname was widely *deconstructed*, or "examined," *could* be right since other musicians came up with a different opinion, so keep it as a possibility. Choice **(C)**, *disputed*, has exactly the meaning you need, so keep this, too. That leaves choice **(E)**, *contested*, another exact fit for the prediction, and a better fit than **(B)** given the context of the sentence, so this becomes your second answer.

8. A, D

In this sentence, which has no road signs, read for key words and what's implied (i.e., for logic). When an "expectation of instant gratification" isn't fulfilled, a feeling of disappointment would ensue. So the answer choices have to mean "disappointment." You can eliminate choices **(B)** and **(E)**, *endearment* and *elation*, right away since they have the opposite meaning. Choice **(F)**, *pacifism*, "an opposition to war of any kind," isn't right for this sentence— an unreturned message would cause *conflict* in a relationship, rather than promote peace. That leaves **(A)** and **(D)**, *chagrin* and *vexation*, both of which match the prediction and have the right meaning for the sentence.

9. B, C

This is an intriguing sentence since the answer choices include two arcane words, *emended* and *meliorated*. A good strategy for questions like this is to use the process of elimination on the answer choices. First, look at what the sentence implies, paraphrase it, and predict the answer: "The zookeepers are 'changing' the exhibit to handle more visitors." All the answer choices except **(D)** and **(F)**, *maintained* and *neglected*, express change, so eliminate those two. Of the remaining choices, **(A)** and **(E)**, *abridged* and *truncated*, mean "to make shorter," which, when applied to the sentence, wouldn't help the exhibit accommodate more traffic. The final choices are **(B)** and **(C)**, which are two high-level vocabulary words (meaning "changed" and "improved" respectively) and the correct answers.

10. D, F

Without structural road signs, you need to see if paraphrasing or key words can help you find synonyms. Scientists have observed odd behavior in fish that precedes seismic events— the fish jump out of the water. Your paraphrase and prediction would look something like this: "Scientists 'theorize' that fish respond to physical precursors of seismic events." Both choices **(D)** and **(F)**, *hypothesize* and *contend*, fit this definition, and are therefore the correct answers. Choice **(A)**, *repudiate*, means to reject an idea, not present one. Scientists don't *authorize* information, so choice **(B)** is also incorrect. Choice **(C)**, *foresee*, does imply prediction, but one based on intuition, not on observed behavior. Finally, it wouldn't make sense for scientists to *question*, **(E)**, their own prediction in this context.

11. A

You're asked to find the statement or statements that have direct support in the passage. The last sentence in the passage states that most orders are not exclusively beneficial of exclusively parasitic, but include species with both characteristics, choice **(A)**. Choice **(B)** is too extreme, since the author speaks of minimizing harm to other species, not eliminating it. Choice **(C)** presents a scenario that's the opposite of what the passage expresses: facilitating the development of parasitic insects isn't in line with the goal of controlling pest species.

12. D

The key phrases "protecting native species" and "maintaining a balanced ecosystem" suggest that entomologists are trying to prevent humans from changing the existing environment. *Intrusion*, choice **(D)**, is a good description of what they're trying to avoid. *Obliteration*, **(A)**, means extinction, and is too extreme in this context. There's no suggestion that humans are fighting against or collaborating with insects, so rule out **(B)** and **(C)**, respectively. Choice **(E)** refers to diversity, which is the entomologists' goal and therefore could not be described as "unnecessary."

13. C

In this Sentence Function question, you have to characterize the relationship between the two highlighted sentences. While it may be a bit hard to determine the function of the first sentence right away, the wording of the second sentence makes it clear that this is

the passage's conclusion. You can paraphrase it this way: "The Easter Rising is viewed as a milestone in establishing the Republic of Ireland." Looking at the second phrase in each answer choice, you can see that only **(C)** and **(E)** correctly describe the second sentence. The passage describes no outside position, so you can rule out **(E)**, making **(C)** the correct choice. Choice **(A)** includes the correct roles for the sentences, but associates each role with the wrong sentence. The author doesn't present an objection to the passage's conclusion, eliminating **(B)**. Choice **(D)** is incorrect because the second sentence expresses the main conclusion, not an intermediate conclusion.

14. D

This Global question asks you to sum up the passage's purpose. The author's tone is one of explanation rather than argument, so you can rule out **(A)** (*arguing that…*) and **(E)** (*persuading readers…*) right away. Choice **(A)** also expresses only one of the two viewpoints the author includes in this passage. The passage explains how the terms Persian and Iranian intersect and provides two perspectives on why one term might be preferable to the other, **(D)**. The author mentions the Persian Empire to explain why some people may be confused by the word "Persian," choice **(B)**, but doesn't discuss its fall. Although three groups are mentioned, the author doesn't focus on differentiating among them, so **(C)** isn't the best summary of the passage.

15. A, B

To select the correct choices, you must identify the groups to whom the term "Persian" applies, according to the passage. Since both Iranian and Afghani people may use the descriptor, the woman in **(A)** could be described as Persian. The first sentence says that both Iranian immigrants and U.S.-born Iranian Americans identify as Persian, so the man in **(B)** also fits the criteria. However, it is clear that the term refers to heritage or citizenship or both, so it would not be accurate to describe someone of English descent who is an American citizen, choice **(C)**, as Persian.

16. E

This Detail question references a detail from the passage directly: that the Persian Empire covered "part of Iran and parts of… Pakistan and Afghanistan." That's choice **(E)**. The Persian Empire isn't said to have covered the entirety of any of the countries in question, so we can eliminate choices **(A)**, **(B)**, **(C)**, and **(D)**.

17. E

The question asks which choice is most similar in meaning to the boldfaced sentence, "To look feminine, fashionable sixth-century women would achieve the same ideal by bleeding themselves." All the choices are about animals, not people, but only **(E)** contains a similar meaning: self-destructive physical harm to (allegedly) produce a more alluring image to the opposite sex. Choice **(A)** mentions light and dark coloring, which the passage does discuss, but it's not similar to the boldfaced sentence in meaning. The second choice **(B)** concerns camouflage only. While **(C)** includes self-destructive physical harm, it isn't as complete a choice as **(E)**. The opening phrase of **(D)** sounds like the boldfaced sentence, but the meaning of the remainder of the sentence is too far removed.

18. A, B

The author describes **(A)**, several societies where women lightened their skin as the fashion of the time, but also cites a culture where darker colors were preferred (Persians with henna dye). The passage states that in 13th-century Italy, the use of makeup was a sign of social status **(B)**. The passage begins with the Greco-Roman societies, but doesn't say whether they originated the practice **(C)**.

19. C

For varied reasons—*to flaunt affluence* **(A)**, *to attract attention* **(D)**, and *to look feminine* **(E)**—most of the societies described in the passage preferred white color or paleness on women's faces. The Egyptians preferred a light foundation also, but of a *golden* hue **(B)**. In this passage, only the Persians went for a darker look with henna dye in their hair and on their skin to call up the splendor of the earth **(C)**.

20. D

The passage discusses a particular "ism" (a theory or concept) called solipsism, which is the view that self is the only object of real knowledge or that nothing but self exists. The best answer to the question, then, is **(D)**, *presenting the definition of a concept*. Choice **(A)** is close, except that solipsism is a belief, not a *phenomenon*, which is an observable fact or event that can be scientifically described. Although a "philosophical position" is mentioned, no philosophers are describing or refuting a *hypothesis* (theory) in this passage **(B)**. Also, there are no key words, such as "conversely" or "on the other hand" to indicate contrasting *two schools of thought* **(C)**. The phrase "a physical object to a person" describes what the author meant by "anything else," and isn't used for *comparing a physical object to a person* **(E)**; and there are no key words indicating comparison, such as "like," "similar to" or "analogous to."

QUANTITATIVE REASONING SECTION 1 EXPLANATIONS

1. C

Right triangles *ABD* and *CDB* share a hypotenuse, segment *DB*. The shared hypotenuse should clue you to use the Pythagorean theorem. See that *w* and *x* are lengths of the legs of right triangle *ABD*; side *AD* has length *w*, side *AB* has length *x*. Also, *y* and *z* are lengths of the legs of right triangle *CDB*; side *CD* has length *z*, side *CB* has length *y*. Where *a* and *b* are lengths of the legs of a right triangle, and *c* is the length of the hypotenuse, $a^2 + b^2 = c^2$. So here $w^2 + x^2 = $ length BD^2; $y^2 + z^2$ also equals length BD^2. The quantities are equal, and the answer is **(C)**.

2. A

You have $x + 4y = 6$ and $x = 2y$, and you want to compare *x* and *y*. Let's start by finding *y*. Substitute 2*y* for *x* in the first equation and get $2y + 4y = 6$ or $6y = 6$. Divide both sides by 6 and get $y = 1$. If $y = 1$ and $x = 2y$, as the second equation states, *x* must equal 2. Because 2 is greater than 1, Quantity A is greater.

3. D

Quantity A asks for the number of managerial employees—that number can be found. There are 120 employees in the firm, and 25 percent of them are managerial. One-fourth of 120 is 30, the value of Quantity A. Quantity B asks for two-thirds of the clerical employees. But there is no information given about the number of clerical workers, so you can't find two-thirds of that number. You can't determine a relationship, and the answer is choice **(D)**.

4. D

To make the quantities look as much alike as you can, use FOIL to multiply out Quantity A.

You'll multiply $a \times b$, $1 \times b$, $1 \times a$, and 1×1 and get $ab + a + b + 1$. Quantity B also has $ab + 1$. Quantity A has the additional terms *a* and *b*. There is no information given about possible values for *a* or *b*. Because $a + b$ could be positive, negative, or zero, a relationship cannot be determined and the answer is **(D)**.

You can also use Picking Numbers; let $a = 1$ and $b = 2$. Then Quantity A is $(1 + 1)(2 + 1) = 6$ and Quantity B is $(1 \times 2) + 1 = 3$. In this case, Quantity A is greater. But if you let $a = -1$ and $b = -2$, you have Quantity A $= (-1 + 1)(-2 + 1) = 0$ and Quantity B $= (-1 \times -2) + 1 = 3$. In this case, Quantity B is greater. You have demonstrated that a definite relationship cannot be determined, leading to answer choice **(D)**.

5. B

In the two-digit number *jk*, the value of digit *j* is twice the value of digit *k*. You have to compare the value of *k* in Quantity A with 6 in Quantity B. If you plug in 6 for *k*, it is not possible to enter "twice the value of the digit *k*" for the digit *j*. That is because *j* can only be a single digit; it cannot be 12. In other words, *k* has to be something less than 6, so the answer must be **(B)**. The value in Quantity B is greater.

6. C

Henry purchased *x* apples, and Jack purchased 10 apples less than one-third the number of apples Henry purchased. *One-third of* means the same as *one-third times*, and the number of apples Henry purchased is *x*. Thus, this boils down to $J = \frac{1}{3}x - 10$. You can plug this in for Quantity A. We have $\frac{1}{3}x - 10$ in Quantity A and $\frac{x - 30}{3}$ in Quantity B. Now you can clear the fraction in Quantity B. Let's split Quantity B into two fractions. $\frac{x}{3} - \frac{30}{3}$. Leave the $\frac{x}{3}$ alone and cancel the factor of 3 from the numerator and denominator of $\frac{30}{3}$ and you're left with $\frac{x}{3} - 10$. What's $\frac{x}{3}$? It's one-third of x. So Quantity A equals $\frac{1}{3}x - 10$, while Quantity B also equals $\frac{1}{3}x - 10$, and the answer is **(C)**.

7. A

The figure shows a circle with right angle QPR as a central angle. The area of sector PQR is 4, and you're asked to compare the area of the circle with 4π. There's a shortcut—the right angle defines the sector, and you have the area of that sector. A 90° angle cuts off one-fourth of the circle. Therefore, if you multiply the area of the sector by 4, you have the area of the circle. So in Quantity A you have 4×4, and in Quantity B you have 4π. You know that π is about 3.14, and 4 is greater than that, so Quantity A, 4×4, must be greater than 4π, and the answer is **(A)**.

8. D

You can suspect **(D)** because there are unrestricted variables. In Quantity A, you have the volume of a rectangular solid with length 5 feet, width 4 feet, and height x feet. The formula is length times width times height, so the volume is 5 times 4 times x, or $20x$. In Quantity B, you have the volume of rectangular solid with length 10 feet, width 8 feet, and height y feet: 10 times 8 times y gives you a volume of $80y$. There is no information given about the values for x and y; they could be any positive numbers. You can Pick Numbers to test the relationship. If $x = 5$ and $y = 1$, Quantity A is greater. If you reverse the values—let $x = 1$ and $y = 5$—then Quantity B is greater. So, the correct answer is **(D)**.

9. B

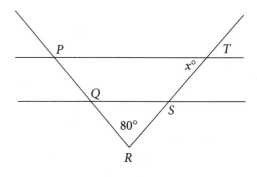

$$PQ = ST$$
$$QR = RS$$

The goal is to find x, the measure of one of the angles formed by the intersection of ST and PT. Now angle QRS is labeled 80°. You also know PQ and ST have the same length and QR and RS have the same length. If you add PQ and QR, you get PR. If you add ST and RS, you get RT. If you add equals to equals, you get equals, so $PQ + QR$ must be the same as $ST + RS$, which means that PR and RT are the same. You have isosceles triangle PRT, and you're given one angle that has measure 80 and a second angle that has measure x. The angle measuring x is opposite equal side PR. That means the other angle must have the same measure. The sum of the interior angles in a triangle always equals 180°. Thus, $x + x + 80$ must equal 180, $2x = 100$, and $x = 50$. The answer is **(B)**.

10. 30

This is a permutation problem because the order in which the duo is chosen matters. The producer has two slots to fill. For the lead role, there are 6 people to choose from. For the supporting role, there will be 5 people to choose from. So the number of possible duos is $6 \times 5 = $ **30**.

11. E

The question asks for the number of different dinners Jane could make. Since the order of the selections in the dinner doesn't matter, this is a combination problem. But it involves three possible combination types: Veg, Meat, Meat; Veg, Veg, Meat; or Veg, Veg, Veg. We must calculate the possibilities for each type of combination and then add the results to find the total number of different combinations possible.

Let V represent vegetarian and M represent meat.

Then with V, M, M, she has 5 choices for the vegetarian (she must choose 1) $\times$ 4 choices for meat (she must choose 2).

For V, V, M, she will choose 2 from among 5 for the vegetarian and 1 among 4 for the meat.

If she goes with V, V, V, the all-vegetarian menu, she will choose a subgroup of 3 from among 5 vegetarian choices.

If n and k are positive integers where $n = k$, then the number of different subgroups consisting of k objects that can be selected from a group consisting of n different objects, denoted by $_nC_k$, is given by the formula

$$_nC_k = \frac{n!}{k!(n-k)!}$$

Here the total number of different possible servings for a plate is $(_5C_1)(_4C_2) + (_5C_2)(_4C_1) + (_5C_3)$.

Now $_5C_1$ represents choosing 1 type of vegetable selection from 5 different types, so $_5C_1 = 5$. (The formula also gives this result.) Now we use the formula to find the next two variables:

$$_4C_2 = \frac{4!}{2!(4-2)!} = \frac{4!}{2! \times 2!} = \frac{4 \times 3 \times 2 \times 1}{2 \times 1 \times 2 \times 1} = 6$$

$$_5C_2 = \frac{5!}{2!(5-2)!} = \frac{5!}{2! \times 3!} =$$

$$\frac{5 \times 4 \times 3 \times 2 \times 1}{2 \times 1 \times 3 \times 2 \times 1} =$$

$$\frac{5 \times \cancel{4}^2 \times \cancel{3} \times \cancel{2} \times \cancel{1}}{\cancel{2} \times 1 \times \cancel{3} \times \cancel{2} \times \cancel{1}} = 10$$

Here $_4C_1$ corresponds to choosing 1 type of meat selection from 4 different types, so $_4C_1 = 4$. Then we use the formula again:

$$_5C_3 = \frac{5!}{3!(5-3)!} = \frac{5!}{3! \times 2} =$$

$$\frac{5 \times 4 \times 3 \times 2 \times 1}{3 \times 2 \times 1 \times 2 \times 1} = 10$$

So the number of different possible servings that can be made for a plate is $5 \times 6 + 10 \times 4 + 10 = 80$, choice **(E)**.

12. 6

You could find the number of tasks per hour from one computer, but that would add extra steps, because you want to find out how many computers you need to do a certain number of tasks in three hours. Well, if the computer can do 30 tasks in six hours, it can do 15 tasks in three hours. So, two computers could complete 30 tasks in that time. Three computers could do 45; four could do 60; five could do 75; six could do 90. You can't get by with five computers because you have to get 80 tasks done, so you'll need **6** computers.

13. C

To make the number of integers easier to count, note that the number of integers between c and $2c$ is equal to the number of integers between 0 and c. For example, there are 4 integers between 5 and 10, and there are 4 integers between 0 and 5. Now the problem is simpler. The number of integers between 0 and c is equal to $c - 1$ (you can't include c as one of the integers). Therefore, the answer is **(C)**.

Picking Numbers is also a good strategy, since there are variables in the question and the answer choices. If $c = 3$, then $2c = 6$. There are two integers between 3 and 6, so plug $c = 3$ into the answer choices to see which one is equal to 2.

(A) $\frac{3}{2} \neq 2$

(B) $3 \neq 2$

(C) $3 - 1 = 2$
(D) $3 - 2 \neq 2$
(E) $3 + 1 \neq 2$

The only answer choice that equals 2 when $c = 3$ is **(C)**, so **(C)** is correct.

14. B, D

You're asked to find what $\frac{b}{a}$ could be; that may tell you there's more than one possible value for $\frac{b}{a}$. You're told the ratio of $2a$ to b is 8 times the ratio of b to a. That's awkward to keep track of in English—it's a little easier to write fractions. The ratio of $2a{:}b$ equals $8\left(\frac{b}{a}\right)$. So, $2\left(\frac{a}{b}\right) = 8\left(\frac{b}{a}\right)$, or $\frac{2a}{b} = \frac{8b}{a}$. By the Cross Product Property, you get $2a^2 = 8b^2$, or $a^2 = 4b^2$. Multiply each side of the equation by $\frac{1}{4a^2}$: $\frac{a^2}{4a^2} = \frac{4b^2}{4a^2}$. This is the same as $\frac{1}{4} = \frac{b^2}{a^2}$. Take the square root of both sides of the equation: $\pm\frac{1}{2} = \frac{b}{a}$. The ratio of b to a is $\frac{1}{2}$ or $-\frac{1}{2}$. So, **(B)** and **(D)** are the answers. This problem is also a great candidate for Backsolving, although since this question could have more than one correct answer, you would need to test all answer choices to see which ones work out.

15. 8

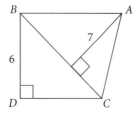

It is given that the area of triangle ABC is 35, and in the diagram, you're given a height for triangle ABC. If you use BC as the base of the triangle, the triangle's height is 7, so you can find the length of BC. When you find the length BC, the base of triangle ABC, what do you have? You have the hypotenuse of right triangle BDC.

Given the hypotenuse and the length of leg BD, which is given in the diagram as 6, you'll be able to find the third leg of the triangle, side DC, which is what you're looking for.

Okay, going back to triangle ABC, the area is 35 and the height is 7. The area of a triangle is $\frac{1}{2}$ base $\times$ height, so $\frac{1}{2}$ base $\times$ height is 35, $\frac{1}{2} \times 7 \times$ length BC is 35. That means $7 \times$ length BC is 70, so BC must have length 10. Now look at right triangle BDC. Here is a right triangle with one leg of length 6, the hypotenuse of length 10, and the third side unknown. That's one of the famous Pythagorean ratios—it's a 3:4:5 triangle. So DC must have length 2×4, or 8.

16. E

First, find the value of m. You are told that 3^m is 81. Well, 81 is 9×9 and 9 is 3^2. So you have $3^2 \times 3^2 = 81$ or $3 \times 3 \times 3 \times 3 = 81$. How many factors of 3 are there in 81? There are 4, so m has the value 4. Now 4^3 is $4 \times 4 \times 4$ is 64. So **(E)** is correct.

17. D, E

The problem states that x is between 0 and 1, so x must be a positive fraction (or decimal) less than 1. We can pick a number to get to the correct answer(s) here because both the question and the answer choices have variables. The decimal 0.5 is in the middle of the given range, so it's a good starting point.

(A) is false. Doubling any positive value always produces a greater value, not a lesser value.

(B) is false. $2 \times 0.5 = 1$; this choice is incorrect because 0.5 is a counter example.

(C) is false. $2 \times 0.5 = 1$; this choice is incorrect because 0.5 is a counter example for this statement also.

(D) is correct. $0.5^2 = 0.25$; the square of any number between 0 and 1 (exclusive) will be less than the original number. This is an example of that property.

(E) is correct. $0.25 < 1$; the square of any number between 0 and 1 (exclusive) will be less than 1. This is an example of that property. So, the correct answers are **(D)** and **(E)**.

18. C

To find how many categories had energy use greater than 150 million kilowatt-hours, you have to find out how many total kilowatt-hours were used in that year using the line graph. You see that 600 million kilowatt-hours were used in 1995. What is the relationship of 150 million kilowatt-hours to 600 million kilowatt-hours? It's 25 percent of 600 million kilowatt-hours, so you're looking for categories with more than 25 percent of the energy use for 1995. How many categories exceeded 25 percent? Just two, government and industrial. So your answer is **(C)**.

19. D

What you need to do for 1990 and 1995 is find the per capita personal use, then find the percent decrease from 1990 to 1995. To do that, let's plug in a value for the population of Country Y for 1990. Let's use 100 million for the '90s population. The per capita use in 1990 is the total personal use, which is 30 percent of 500 million or about 150 million. Set up 150 million kilowatt hours, the total personal use, as a proportion with 100 million people, the population. The per capita use is $\frac{3}{2}$ or 1.5. Going on to 1995, you are told the population increased by 20 percent, so in 1995 the population was 120 million—using our initial figure of 100 million. What was the total personal use of energy? It was a little bit less than 20 percent of your total 600 million, so call it 20 percent of 600 million, or 120 million. If total personal use is 120 million and there are 120 million people, that's 1 kilowatt hour per person. What's the percent decrease? It's

a decrease of $\frac{1}{3}$, or $33\frac{1}{3}$ percent. But remember, in 1995, they were using a little more energy for personal use than you figured. The correct answer must be a little greater than $33\frac{1}{3}$ percent, so 35 percent, **(D)**, is the correct answer.

20. A, D

The question requires that you choose all the correct answers, so you have no choice but to test all the statements. Before you start, note that the top graph shows kilowatt hours; the bottom graph shows usage by percent of the total.

Statement A says farm use of energy increased between 1990 and 2010. In 1990, 500 million kilowatt-hours were used. In 2010, 710 million kilowatt-hours were used. What was the percent of farm use in 1990? It was 30 percent of the total in 1990 and a little bit less than 30 percent, around 28 percent, in 2010. The percents are very close together, while the whole has become much larger from 1990 to 2010, so 30 percent of 500 million is less than 28 percent of 710 million. Farm use of energy did go up in that 20-year period, and statement **(A)** is a correct choice.

Statement B says that in 2010, industrial use of energy was greater than industrial use of energy in 1995. But what was it in 1995? Industrial use of energy in 1995 was 30 percent of 600 million. The percent comes from the bar graph; the total comes from the line chart. Okay, 30 percent of 600 million is 180 million. But what about 2010? In 2010 industrial use of energy was 20 percent of about 710 million kilowatt-hours. Well, 20 percent of 710 is 142 million. That's less than 180 million, isn't it? In fact, industrial use of energy went down from 1995 to 2010, so this can't be inferred from the graph.

Statement C says more people were employed by the government of Country Y in 2010 than in 1990. These graphs deal only with energy use, not with employment, so the statement cannot be inferred from the graphs.

Statement D compares the kilowatt hours used for farm purposes in the years 2000 and 2005. Estimate the kilowatt hours for each year: For 2000, multiply 10% $\times$ 650 million = 65 million. For 2005 multiply 20% $\times$ 675 million = 135 million. Although the numbers were rounded, it appears that the statement **(D)** is true: about twice as many kilowatt hours of energy were used for farm purposes in 2005 than in 2000.

To test Statement E, look at the distribution of the usage in the graph showing percents. The difference between the percents for government and personal use in 1990 shows that the types were not the most equally distributed in 1990.

Only **(A)** and **(D)** can be inferred from the graphs.

VERBAL REASONING SECTION 2 EXPLANATIONS:

1. B

"Instead" is a detour road sign that tells you that the second half of the sentence will say the opposite of the first half. That means diversification shouldn't "divert" the organization, so you're looking for a word that means the opposite of divert. The answer is **(B)**, *furthering*, which means "advancing or promoting." **(A)**, *undermining*, **(C)**, *retracting*, and **(E)**, *deterring*, are all the opposite of what you need—they say that diversification will negatively affect the historical purpose. Choice **(D)**, *classifying*, doesn't make sense in context.

2. B, D, G

The best way to approach the first blank is to consider the logic of this sentence and predict

an answer. A "keen" sense of smell is a positive attribute. What should a bee with a keen sense of smell be able to do with regard to kin and foe? To *promulgate* is to make known, in the sense of "to announce." *Discern* means "to perceive or recognize." And to *arbitrate* is to decide between disputants. A bee would want to "recognize" friend from foe, whether or not it did either of the other two things, and so **(B)**, *discern*, is the best choice.

The road sign "however" tells you that there is a "surprising deficiency" in another area, making bees unable to protect themselves from diseases. Which phrase most closely describes the desired response? Any of the three answer choices could work, but, as we said in the strategies section, the answer is in the question somewhere. Read the third sentence to see if it becomes clear. When you do, you'll note the key words "various diseases" matches one of the second blank's answer choices, *pathogens*. Let's hold onto **(D)** for now.

The third sentence is a bit convoluted, and some of the answer choices are uncommon words, so paraphrase it to put it into simpler terms and predict the answer: "Bees 'protect' their colony through grooming behavior." Only one of the answer choices, *minimizes incursions* **(G)** fits our prediction. If you substitute the other terms into the blank and re-read the sentence, you can confirm **(G)** as the correct choice; neither *implicating replication* or *simulates action* make sense in context.

Now that we have two of the blanks filled, we can return to blank (ii). When we read **(D)**, *pathogens*, into the sentence, the three sentences make sense together, and **(D)** is correct.

3. A, F, I

The key word in this sentence is "crisis." You need adjectives and verbs that play well off of it. If you don't know the meaning of *exigent*, you can use the process of elimination to identify the right answer. *Leviathan* means "gargantuan," and one wouldn't describe a need as physically great or imposing. You can eliminate *specious*—it means "false" and is the opposite of what you're looking for. That leaves **(A)** *exigent*, which means "immediate." It is the correct answer. Which of the actions would be required in a situation of "critical necessity"? Recall that there is a water crisis, so the resource involved is water. The word *ineffable* means "unable to be expressed," so it makes no sense in this context. However, if you didn't know that word, you could use the process of elimination to narrow your choices. If there were a water crisis, water would not be *abundant*, so you can eliminate **(E)**. That leaves **(F)**, *mobilize limited* resources. "Limited" makes sense in the context of the crisis, so it is the correct choice, and a solid guess if you weren't certain of the meaning of choice **(D)**. If you're galvanizing political efforts to stave off a crisis, it's unlikely you'd simply *request* **(G)** international attention—you'd demand, or *require*, **(I)**, it, You might want to *focus* it, but in context, **(I)** is the stronger choice.

4. E

The detour road sign "although" contrasts the honor Petain received for World War I with what he incurred during World War II. The sentence's structure implies that the word in the blank will have a negative charge, so you can rule out the positive answer choices **(A)**, *status* ("relative rank in a hierarchy"), and **(C)**, *kudos* ("congratulations"). Choice **(B)**, *reputation*, doesn't make sense—one earns a reputation, it is not incurred. Choice **(D)**, *recompense*, doesn't make sense either, since the French wouldn't compensate someone for something dishonorable. That leaves you with the correct answer, **(E)**, *obloquy*, "disgrace or public censure." One would heap *obloquy* on a person who's done something hateful, like collaborating with the enemy.

5. A, E, I

This is a long set of sentences, so you should paraphrase them to make the topic easier to get a handle on: "Although people don't think of cellophane as paper, this _____ material is made from the same stuff as paper bags. It was invented to coat fabric, but its usefulness became _____ and resulted in a _____ product."

For the first blank, you're looking for a term that describes cellophane. Even if you don't know what cellophane is, we can use the key words "clear plastic film" to complete the blank. The correct answer is **(A)**, *diaphanous*, which means "see-through." Choice **(B)**, *standardized*, although true, doesn't best complete the meaning of the sentence. Choice **(C)**, *opaque*, means the opposite of what we need here.

For the second blank, all the answer choices are two words, and a good technique in this situation is to try each choice in the blank to see which makes the most sense. Choice **(D)**, *unjustifiably marketable*, is incorrect—nothing in the text says that you can't justify this useful product's marketing. Choice **(E)**, *immediately apparent*, is correct. Choice **(F)**, *outrageously fashionable*, doesn't fit the context of the sentence.

Having filled in the first and second blanks, you have a strong sense of the meaning of the sentence: "Cellophane is useful and _____." Nothing in the sentences describe cellophane as **(G)**, *amorphous*, "shapeless," so eliminate it. Choice **(H)** is a trap—don't confuse *ingenuous*, "innocent," with "ingenious," or "brilliant." You would expect a product with "overwhelming usefulness" to be **(I)**, *ubiquitous*, "constantly present," and that's the correct answer.

6. D

From the detour road sign "unlike," you can tell that Hume isn't trying to determine whether an objective reality exists. Why wouldn't he do so? Following this logic reveals the right word for the sentence. Hume disregarded objective reality not because he thought the issue was *pragmatic* (A), "practical," or *challenging* (B). That would have made him want to investigate it. He probably didn't try because he felt that the issue was either unverifiable or uninteresting. Choice (D), *insoluble*, "not capable of being solved," fits the blank best. It's unclear that Hume would be "unlike most philosophers" if he thought the issue was (C) *theoretical* or (E) *esoteric* ("understood only by a select few"), so both are wrong.

7. A, F

This is a long sentence and the blank occurs in the middle, so paraphrase it. As you do so, note that the word *although* is a detour road sign that indicates a contrast. A good paraphrase is, "People smoke, even though nicotine has a _____ effect on their health." You are looking for a pair of synonyms that have a negative tone and mean something like "bad" or "harmful." Choice (A), *deleterious*, means "harmful," so it is correct. Choice (B), *addictive*, is not a synonym for harmful, but it's often used to describe smoking, so don't eliminate it yet.

Inimical and *antagonistic*, choices (C) and (D), both mean "hostile." If *inimical* was unfamiliar to you, you could use the roots strategy and think of a word or words that sound similar to it. *Intimidate* comes to mind; it has a negative tone and its meaning is similar to *antagonistic*. This is another example of a trap: this pair is synonymous and negatively charged, but the words don't accurately complete the meaning of the sentence.

Choices (E) *benign*, means "harmless," the opposite of what you want, so eliminate them.

Pernicious (F) means "destructive," and it, too, fits well in the sentence. That leaves three potential answers—(A), (B), and (F). Only two are synonyms, however: (A) and (F) create sentences with similar meanings, so they're right.

8. A, F

The phrase "to the public's great shock" is a key phrase—it tells you there's a contrast between what was expected ("peaceable reform") and what really happened. The correct answers must mean something like "violent rebellion." *Contumacious* is a difficult vocabulary word, so we'll use the process of elimination to go through all the answer choices. Choice (B), *endemic*, means "inherent," which doesn't fit the context of the sentence. Choices (C) and (E), *erratic* and *irresolute*, both mean "unpredictable" or "uncertain." If you weren't sure of *irresolute*, consider its root, *resolute*, and think of a similar word, *resolution* in this case. A resolution is something you commit to doing, and irresolute is its opposite, "unsure" or "unable to make a decision."

These two words are plausible choices because they imply that the group didn't fulfill its promises, but they don't work in context. You need a contrast with "peaceable reform" something that would result in people's shock—unpredictability and uncertainty aren't shocking.

Choice (D), *estimable*, "worthy," means the opposite of what you want. If you didn't know the meaning of this word, you could consider its root, *esti*: Think of words with a similar root that you *can* define, such as *esteem*. Knowing that esteem has a positive tone, you could deduce that *estimable* does as well, making it incorrect. That leaves you with choices (A) and **(F)**—*contumacious* and *seditious*—both of which mean "rebellious," and are the correct choices.

9. B, D

Some of the answer choices are fairly difficult words, but you can tell from the key word "concealed" that you want a word negative in tone. Based on that, two words pop out from the answer choices, *artifice* and *chicanery*, both of which are negative and both of which mean "deception." But you should go through the answer choices one at a time to confirm your selections.

Choice **(A)**, *cabal*, means "a secret group," and it doesn't work in context.

Choice **(B)**, *artifice*, sounds a lot like a word you're probably familiar with—"artificial," which means looking like one thing while actually being another. *Artifice* means "trickery." "Photo retouching and inflated claims" are forms of trickery, so this is one of the correct answers.

If you don't know the meaning of the word *hegemony* **(C)**, put it aside until you go through the other answer choices. Choice **(E)**, *dominance*, means "supremacy" or "domination," and doesn't make sense in context. Eliminate it. Choice **(D)**, *chicanery*, also means "deception and trickery," so it's also right. To determine the meaning of *imprecation*, choice **(F)**, think of a word with a similar root. One is precarious, which means "dangerous." Are advertising ploys dangerous? No. This word is too extreme to work in context. That leaves you with only *hegemony* outstanding. Even if its meaning is unclear, you have, through the process of elimination, two synonymous answer choices that fit well in context, and you should go with them. *Hegemony* means "influence" or "dominance." If you knew this definition,

you'd know that *hegemony* is a synonym for another answer choice, *dominance*, and this is another example of a question with two sets of synonyms in the answer choices.

10. B, C

While this sentence includes a classic detour road sign, "however," its structure is such that you can't identify what "however" is contradicting. As you've learned from Kaplan's strategies, key words can help you figure out the missing word in a sentence. The key words in this sentence are "conservative" and "unreceptive." You need to predict the kind of joke a conservative audience at a charity event would receive poorly. Choice **(A)**, *plucky*, means "brave," so eliminate it. Choices **(B)** and **(C)**—*ribald* and *coarse*—both mean "vulgar." These are likely correct, but continue to test the other choices before answering definitively. Choices **(D)**, **(F)**—*traitorous* and *treacherous*—are synonyms that mean "disloyal." Although the performers betrayed the spirit of the event, this is not the meaning of the words needed to describe the jokes. Choice **(E)**, *politic*, means "diplomatic." This has the opposite meaning of the word you're looking for, so eliminate it. The correct answers are *ribald* and *coarse*.

11. E

The first sentence expresses the passage's main idea (sharks are different from fish), and the second sentence explains one of the ways in which this is true (they have livers, not swim bladders). That's choice **(E)**. Since no opposing perspective is included, you can rule out **(A)**. Choice **(B)** reverses the roles of the two sentences; the second sentence supports the first, not vice versa. No opposing argument is addressed, and the author forms no intermediate conclusion, so **(C)** and **(D)** are incorrect.

12. C

This Inference question asks you to consider the information in the passage and speculate about the events that may have preceded those described. The phrase "for themselves" implies the patrons' ability to locate their own books, so it follows that they would previously have needed assistance from librarians, choice **(C)**. The passage says that Dewey was the first standardized method, but you have no basis to assume that no classification method existed before, **(A)**. Similarly, nothing suggests that libraries kept their methods confidential **(B)**. Although Dewey helped patrons find materials themselves, no information in the passage implies that this change affected librarians' jobs directly, so you can eliminate **(D)**. As for choice **(E)**, the passage implies that patrons may have had difficulty locating items, but to say that they were never able to understand the system is too extreme.

13. A, B

A lower risk of fatal disease meant that vaccination was safer than inoculation, **(A)**. Since the passage mentions "enormous variations" between batches of inoculum, the "standard dose" used in vaccines would be more likely to be consistent, so **(B)** is also correct. Choice **(C)** is incorrect because it deals with TB vaccines and inoculations, which goes beyond the scope of the passage.

14. C

The second half of the sentence this question refers to explains that health care providers couldn't predict the severity of disease due to the "disparities" in the doses given. The next sentence contrasts this practice with the "standard dose" of a vaccination, so inoculation must have used doses that had variations, or *inconsistencies*, **(C)**. *Incapacities*, **(A)**, and *ineffectiveness*, **(E)**, would suggest that the

inoculations were unsuccessful, which contradicts the first sentence of the passage. While the practice of inoculation could be said to have *weaknesses*, **(B)**, this choice doesn't make sense in relation to the second half of the sentence. Choice **(D)** is the antonym of the word given; if the inoculations had *resemblances*, they would all be relatively similar.

15. E

The passage as a whole is concerned with how to come up with a good definition of tragedy. In lines 9–14, the author leads into Scylla and Charybdis by mentioning "overly broad definitions" and "overly narrow ones," respectively. Just afterward, he calls this situation a "definitional dilemma." From these clues, you're thus led to infer that Scylla and Charybdis are names for the dangers that may befall anyone who tries to come up with a good definition of tragedy. **(E)** is in line with this inference. **(A)** cannot be correct because Terry Eagleton begs off providing a good definition in the first place. He seems to think that the task is simply impossible. So broad and narrow definitions, represented by Scylla and Charybdis, respectively, are not signs of Eagleton's principal faults. **(B)** is outside of scope. The author is making no larger claim about the significance of myth. Similarly, **(C)** is outside of scope. This we know from the talk of "origin of myth"; the latter has no place in the author's account and so is irrelevant. Like **(B)** and **(C)**, **(D)** is also outside of scope. Because the author makes no reference to other intellectual inquiries, you have no reason for believing that those are in any way applicable to the case at hand.

16. D

What is the main point of the passage? It is to criticize two authors' views of tragedy (paragraphs 1–2) and to generate a new necessary condition for tragedy (paragraph 3). The answer that most closely matches this understanding is **(D)**. Consider that **(A)** is too narrow: Mandel isn't even mentioned despite the fact that he is the "main character" in the passage. The problem with **(B)** is that it includes Eagleton in the author's criticism of Mandel. In other words, the author *does* criticize Mandel for not providing all the necessary conditions for tragedy. But he *does not* have anything explicit to say about whether Eagleton falls prey to the same problem. Consequently, **(B)** is a distortion. For its part, **(C)** is opposite. The author implies throughout the passage that tragedy can be definable. Though she pokes holes in both theorists' accounts, the author seems, if anything, more sympathetic to Mandel, who thinks that tragedy is definable, than she is to Eagleton, who does not. **(E)**, finally, is too strong because of the bit that follows the "in order to." In the final paragraph, the author doesn't provide you with a new definition of tragedy; she simply tells you that there's at least one necessary ingredient in tragedy that Mandel fails to pick up on. Think about the point about necessary and sufficient conditions this way: To make a quiche, it's necessary to use eggs. But eggs aren't enough for something to be a quiche. After all, eggs can be used in a lot of other things—cake and omelets, just to name a few. The author is making the same point about powerlessness in the realm of tragedy: it's necessary (or "absolutely essential") but not sufficient for something to be tragic.

17. A

This question tests your ability to identify GRE vocabulary words within the Reading Comprehension portion of the exam. At the very least, you should be thinking that the author *liked*, *esteemed*, and *pitied* these characters. He says as much when she describes them as being "well-educated, tireless, but spiritually drained" (lines 44–45). The only answer that comes

close is *laudatory*, meaning worthy of praise. *Conciliatory* means intending to placate, so this does not work. *Despondent* means very sad. You could infer that the characters themselves are despondent, but "the author's attitude" is surely not despondent. **(C)**, then, is opposite. *Myopic* means shortsighted, and that has nothing to do with the passage before you, let alone the author's attitude toward the protagonists in this work. So get rid of **(D)**. And *diffident* means being modest or timid, and that's not on target. In sum, none but **(A)** rings true.

18. B

This Inference question is essentially asking you to consider not only what Eagleton and Mandel have in common, but also what they do not. What do they have in common? According to the author, they don't give us an adequate conception of tragedy. And now what are the main differences between them? They take different approaches to the task, Eagleton throwing his hands up and saying, in effect, that tragedy can't be defined and Mandel digging his heels in and saying that it can. **(B)** captures what they share (that is, failure) and what they differ on (that is, the reasons for their respective failures). Regarding **(A)**, the author does not think that their ideas should be dismissed. Why would she have bothered methodically working through their ideas in the first place if this was her attitude toward their ideas? No, clearly she thinks that much can be learned from them. Thus, **(A)** is opposite. And **(C)**? Read the *very sad* bit as a shorthand description of Eagleton's view and the *inevitability requirement* bit as an aspect of Mandel's view. The author's ultimate assessment is that neither will do. What's more, she never says whether the first thing about sadness should be weighed *as heavily* as the second thing about inevitability. For both of these reasons, **(C)** can't be inferred. **(D)** can't be correct for two reasons. First, you can't validly infer from the fact that a work is very sad that the heroes have necessarily suffered greatly. The fact of great suffering is, at best, probable and not certain. Second, great suffering is not at the center of Mandel's view—as you know, the inevitability requirement is. The key word in **(E)** is *combine*. The author does examine different thinkers' ideas, but her strategy is not to combine those ideas; her strategy is to criticize these ideas. Consequently, **(E)** can't be inferred.

19. C

In this question, you should *only* look at paragraph 3. Make sure that "present conception of tragedy" refers to Mandel's view. Think about what the opening sentence is doing: it's making clear to you the author's chief complaint with Mandel. And then consider that the rest of the paragraph is trying to provide evidence for the complaint already mentioned.

Thus, **(C)** is correct. No such luck with **(A)**. Don't be fooled: all talk of genre and influence goes beyond the bounds of the passage. You run into a similar problem in **(B)**. Aesthetic value, supreme or otherwise, takes your eyes off the main focus of paragraph 3. The author, in short, has nothing to say about **(B)**. In sum, **(A)** and **(B)** are outside of scope. On the face of it, **(D)** looks pretty good. True, the author is worrying about something in Mandel's definition. However, he is not worrying about criteria—only about one criterion (the inevitability requirement, in fact). Consequently, **(D)** is opposite. Turning to **(E)**, we don't see much to recommend it. For one thing, the author is not defending conclusions (she is, as the question tells you, simply voicing dissatisfaction). For another, she is not pointing out a trap that Mandel is falling into.

20. E

To begin with, get the scope of the question squarely before you. The question has to do with the whole passage, not with one of its parts. Now think about the first two requirements. The first is that the protagonist is worthy of esteem; the second that he or she suffers greatly. Ask yourself: What do you think the author's opinion about these two requirements is? Does he like them? Dislike them? It's the first: he most likely thinks that they are good things. Evidence for the first part of this conclusion can be found in paragraph 3 where the author seems to look favorably on the characters in the modern tragedy *Three Sisters*. **(E)** puts this point even more delicately by making us see that both requirements are OK so long as they don't contradict the condition of powerlessness. And that is right. **(A)** is the opposite of the correct answer. From what you have read so far, the author provides no reason to believe that these requirements would not fit with the condition of powerlessness. With respect to **(B)**, the first condition isn't at all at odds with the condition of powerlessness. The author implies as much in paragraph 3 when she shows that good characters in works of tragedy necessarily feel powerless. **(C)** is also opposite. From all that you read in paragraph 3, you can reasonably conclude that the sisters do suffer a good deal. That leaves you with **(D)** to consider. **(D)** is without question quite tempting. Yet that both requirements should not figure prominently is outside of scope. You do have reason to believe that they should figure *in some way*, but we *can't know* for sure *how prominently* they should figure. Because of this, **(D)** is outside of scope. The answer is **(E)**.

QUANTITATIVE REASONING SECTION 2 EXPLANATIONS:

1. D

The perimeter of *ABC* is 40 and the length of *BC* is 12, and you want to compare the length of *AB* with 14. In an isosceles triangle, there are two sides with equal length, but you don't know whether side *BC* is one of those sides or not. If side *BC* is the unequal side, there are two unknown sides plus 12, and they have a sum of 40, the perimeter. The two remaining sides have a sum of 28, so each is 14. That would mean that *AB* and *AC* would have length 14. Then the answer would be **(C)**. If *BC* is one of the equal sides, however, there are two sides with length 12 and a third unknown side, and the sum is 40. Because 12 + 12 is 24, the third side has length 16. *AB* could be one of the sides of length 12 or the side of length 16. There are three possible lengths for side *AB*—16, 14, and 12—so the answer is **(D)**.

2. A

Plug 1 in for *x* and solve the equation for *y*. Perform the addition inside the parentheses first. You have 1 + 3 = 4 inside the parentheses. *y* = 4², 4² is 16, and 16 is greater than 9, so the answer is **(A)**.

3. B

In both quantities, use the basic formula: rate × time = distance. In Quantity A, 40 mph × 4 hours traveled gives you 160 miles. In Quantity B, 70 mph × $2\frac{1}{2}$ hours = 175 miles. As 175 is greater than 160, the answer is **(B)**.

4. D

This is intended to conjure up a picture of heavy cookies in one bag and light grapes in the other, but you can't assume that because cookies are usually bigger than grapes, these cookies weigh more than these grapes. Since you don't know how much each cookie and each grape weighs, you can't find the number of cookies or grapes, so the answer is **(D)**.

5. C

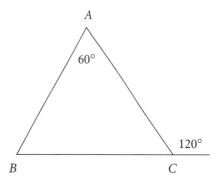

Here you have triangle *ABC*—base *BC* has been extended on one side and there is an exterior angle drawn in and labeled 120°. You want to compare side lengths *AB* and *BC*. In any triangle, the largest side will be opposite the largest angle, so you want to see which of these sides is opposite a larger angle. Angle *A* is labeled 60°, but is angle *C* less than, equal to, or greater than 60? Notice that the adjacent angle is 120°—the two together form a straight line, so their sum is 180°. And 180 − 120 = 60, so angle *C* is a 60° angle. Since the angles are equal, the sides are equal, and the answer is **(C)**.

6. A

Notice the way the diagram is set up—*a* + *b* is the same as *PQ*. The equation is 8*a* + 8*b* = 24. Divide both sides by 8. You end up with *a* + *b* = 3. *PQ* is 3 and because 3 is greater than 2, the answer is **(A)**. Note that you did not have to solve for *a* or *b* individually.

7. A

All you know is that *x* is less than *y*, but even though you don't know their values, you know enough to determine a relationship. In Quantity A, you have *y* − *x*, the larger number minus the smaller number, so you must get a positive difference, even if both numbers are negative. In Quantity B, you have the smaller number minus the larger number—this time the difference is negative. So you can determine a relationship—you know the answer is **(A)**, Quantity A is always greater than Quantity B.

8. D

Remember, area equals $\frac{1}{2} \times$ base $\times$ height. Both triangles have the same height, because they have the same apex point *A*. So the one with the larger base has the larger area. Which is bigger, *CB* or *DE*? You have no way to figure it out. You are not given any relationships or lengths for any of those segments, so the answer is **(D)**.

9. D

If the radius of each circle is 3, then the diameter of each circle is 6. Then *PS* and *QR* = 6, and *PQ* and *SR* = 12. The perimeter of rectangle *PQRS* = 6 + 12 + 6 + 12 = 36. The answer is **(D)**.

10. D

In this question, you have a fraction as a base and must consider various values for *x*, the exponent. Consider what happens when $x = 0$. Any base to the zero power equals 1; then $1 - \left(\frac{1}{4}\right)^x = 1 - 1 = 0$. You want the value of *x* that makes the expression greater than 0, so try $x = 1$.

$1 - \left(\frac{1}{4}\right)^x = 1 - \left(\frac{1}{4}\right) = \frac{3}{4}$ and the answer is **(D)**.

11. B

Begin with Cross Multiplication and use algebra to isolate $\frac{q}{p}$:

$\dfrac{p - q}{p} = \dfrac{2}{7}$

$7(p - q) = 2p$ Cross Multiplication

$7p - 7q = 2p$ Remove parentheses.

$5p = 7q$ Add $7q$; subtract $2p$ on both sides.

$\dfrac{5}{7} = \dfrac{q}{p}$ Divide both sides by $7p$.

Choice **(B)** is correct.

12. 0.9

The shaded region is a right triangle. So, use the numbers on the grid to calculate the base and height of the triangle. The length horizontally is $(-2.0) - (-0.5) = -2.0 + 0.5 = -1.5$. Simply use 1.5 as the base of the triangle. The height of the triangle is $1.6 - 0.4 = 1.2$. Use the equation for the area of a triangle: $A = \frac{1}{2} bh = \frac{1}{2} \times 1.5 \times 1.2 = 0.9$

The area is **0.9**.

13. D

The question asks for the number that is 850 percent greater than 8×10^3. First, determine the value of 8×10^3. That number is 8,000. To 8,000, you need to add 850% of 8,000. Here's what the math looks like:

$8{,}000 + 850\% \times 8{,}000 = 8{,}000 + 8.5 \times 8{,}000 = 8{,}000 + 68{,}000 = 76{,}000.$

In scientific notation, this is 7.6×10^4, choice **(D)**.

14. B, C, E

List the factors each number to check for all correct choices.

Number	Factors	Number of Factors
4	1, 2, 4	3
6	1, 2, 3, 6	4
8	1, 2, 4, 8	4
12	1, 2, 3, 4, 6, 12	6
14	1, 2, 7, 14	4

So the correct choices are **(B)**, **(C)**, and **(E)**.

15. 60

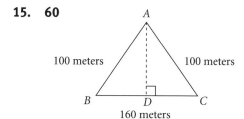

You're trying to find the shortest distance in meters a person would walk to go from point *A* to a point on side *BC* of the triangular field represented in the diagram. To get the shortest distance from point *A* to side *BC*, draw a perpendicular line from point *A* to side *BC*. Call the new vertex point *D*. Now two smaller right triangles, *ADC* and *ADB* have been created.

From the diagram, length *BC* is 160 meters, *AB* is 100 meters and *AC* is 100 meters. Each of the two right triangles formed has 100 meters as the length of its hypotenuse. What does that tell you about triangle *ABC*? *AB* and *AC* have the same length, so this is an isosceles triangle. That means that when you drew in the perpendicular distance from *A* down to *D*, you split the isosceles triangle *ABC* into two identical right triangles. Length *BD* is the same as length *CD*. So each of them is half of 160 meters, or 80 meters. Each right triangle has an hypotenuse of 100 meters and one leg of 80 meters. This is a 3:4:5 right triangle, with each member of the ratio multiplied by 20. So *AD* must have length **60**, and the minimum distance is 60 meters.

16. E

The average is $\dfrac{\text{The sum of terms}}{\text{The number of terms}}$. Here you have $y - z$ and the other number, which you can call x. The average of x and $y - z$ is $3y$, so $3y = \dfrac{x + y - z}{2}$. Multiplying both sides by 2 gives $6y = x + y - z$. Subtracting $y - z$ from both sides gives $5y + z = x$. So the other number, x, is $5y + z$, answer choice **(E)**.

17. B, D

Test each point. Substitute a value for x and compare the result to the given value for y in the ordered pair.

Let $x = -3$. $y = \dfrac{x^2}{x + 1} = \dfrac{(-3)^2}{-3 + 1} = \dfrac{9}{-2} \neq -5$

Let $x = -2$. $y = \dfrac{x^2}{x + 1} = \dfrac{(-2)^2}{-2 + 1} = \dfrac{4}{-1} = -4$

Let $x = -1$. $y = \dfrac{x^2}{x + 1} = \dfrac{(-1)^2}{-1 + 1} = \dfrac{1}{0} \neq -3$

Let $x = 1$. $y = \dfrac{x^2}{x + 1} = \dfrac{1^2}{1 + 1} = \dfrac{1}{2}$

Let $x = 3$. $y = \dfrac{x^2}{x + 1} = \dfrac{3^2}{3 + 1} = \dfrac{9}{4} \neq 2\dfrac{1}{2}$

So, the correct answers are **(B)** and **(D)**.

18. D

You're looking for the lowest ratio of males to females. In the double bar graph, the males outnumber females in each double bar, so you want the specialty in which the numbers of males and females are closest. Skimming the bar graphs, you can see that in pediatrics, the female graph and the male graph are closer than any of the others. Pediatrics **(D)** is the correct answer.

19. B

How many male general surgeon physicians were under 35 years old? The pie chart breaks down general surgery physicians by age, so work with that. And because you're looking for a number of general surgery physicians, you know that you're going to have to find the total number of general surgery physicians, and then break it down according to the percentages on the pie chart.

The number of female general surgery physicians in the under-35 category represented

3.5 percent of all the general surgery physicians. What this does is break that slice of the pie for under-35 into two smaller slices, one for men under 35 and one for women under 35. Now the whole slice for under-35-year-olds is 30 percent of the total, and the question states that the number of females under 35 is 3.5 percent of the total. So the difference between 30 percent and 3.5 percent (26.5 percent) must be the men in the under-35 category.

From the top graph, estimate the total number of general surgery physicians as 37,000 (35,000 male plus 2,000 female). Multiply 37,000 by 26.5%: $0.265 \times 37,000 = 9,805$, which is very close to **(B)**, the correct answer.

20. E

The bar graph doesn't give the total number of general practice physicians, but if you add the number of males to the number of females, you get the total number of GP physicians. To find the percent who are male, take the number of males and put it over the total number. There are about 2,000 women and about 23,000 men, making the total about 25,000. Well, if there are around 25,000 GP physicians altogether and 2,000 to 3,000 of them are female, that's around 10 percent. About 22,500 are male, which is 90 percent, **(E)**.

ANALYTICAL WRITING SCORING RUBRIC

6: "Outstanding" Essay

- Insightfully presents and convincingly supports an opinion on the issue or a critique of the argument
- Communicates ideas clearly and is generally well organized; connections are logical
- Demonstrates superior control of language: grammar, stylistic variety, and accepted conventions of writing; minor flaws may occur

5: "Strong" Essay

- Presents well-chosen examples and strongly supports an opinion on the issue or a critique of the argument
- Communicates ideas clearly and is generally well organized; connections are logical
- Demonstrates solid control of language: grammar, stylistic variety, and accepted conventions of writing; minor flaws may occur

4: "Adequate" Essay

- Presents and adequately supports an opinion on the issue or a critique of the argument
- Communicates ideas fairly clearly and is adequately organized; logical connections are satisfactory
- Demonstrates satisfactory control of language: grammar, stylistic variety, and accepted conventions of writing; some flaws may occur

3: "Limited" Essay

- Succeeds only partially in presenting and supporting an opinion on the issue or a critique of the argument
- Communicates ideas unclearly and is poorly organized
- Demonstrates less than satisfactory control of language: contains significant mistakes in grammar, usage, and sentence structure

2: "Weak" Essay

- Shows little success in presenting and supporting an opinion on the issue or a critique of the argument
- Struggles to communicate ideas; essay shows a lack of clarity and organization
- Meaning is impeded by many serious mistakes in grammar, usage, and sentence structure

1: "Fundamentally Deficient" Essay

- Fails to present a coherent opinion and/or evidence on the issue or a critique of the argument
- Fails to communicate ideas; essay is seriously unclear and disorganized
- Lacks meaning due to widespread and severe mistakes in grammar, usage, and sentence structure

0: "Unscorable" Essay

- Completely ignores topic
- Attempts to copy the assignments
- Written in a foreign language or contains undecipherable text

SAMPLE ESSAY RESPONSES
ISSUE ESSAY SAMPLE RESPONSE

At face value, the belief that "one should look upon any information described as 'factual' with skepticism since it may well be proven false in the future," seems ludicrous almost to the point of threatening anarchy. Yet not only does this belief prove well justified, it is also the linchpin around which our complex, highly technical society creates and consolidates its advances.

Science itself provides the best evidence and examples in support of this statement. One need look no further than contemporary medicine to see how far we have come from the days when illness was perceived as a sign of moral weakness or as a punishment from on high. In fact, the most outstanding characteristic of what we call "the scientific method" amounts to endless questioning of received theory in search of a more comprehensive explanation of what we perceive to be true. This iterative style of inquiry (and re-inquiry) perpetuates an ongoing scientific dialogue that catalyzes further breakthroughs in the developed world.

Furthermore, advances made through constant questioning are not limited to the scientific arena: The skeptical attitudes of ancient Greek philosophers, as well as those of Renaissance mariners, 19th century suffragists, and 20th century civil rights activists, have left the world a richer and more hopeful place. By refusing to accept the world as explained by contemporary "fact," these doubters helped give birth to societies and cultures in which human potential and accomplishment have been enabled to an unprecedented degree.

In contrast, those societies that cultivate adherence to received belief and a traditional non-skeptical approach have advanced very little over the centuries. In Tibet, for instance, the prayer wheels spin endlessly around a belief system as secure and unquestioning as the Himalayas themselves. While there may very well be things worth learning from such a society, Tibet has proven to lack adaptability and expansiveness and prefers to turn inward, away from the modern world. Such introspection has given Tibet neither immunity nor an array of defenses in the face of contemporary medical, social, and political problems. Thus, cultural inflexibility regarding received wisdom and convention comes with a price.

To conclude, it seems clear from the above discussion that a healthy skepticism remains the hallmark of Western epistemology as we face the future. A close look at the statement reveals that it is not advocating the wholesale rejection of orthodox thinking, but rather that we be open to redefining our assumptions. As the basis of our resiliency and creativity, this attitude offers the most positive prognosis for a society that revels in the solution of conundrums that its own constant questioning brings continually into view.

ARGUMENT ESSAY SAMPLE RESPONSE

In this memo, the owner of the Juniper Café concludes that cutting hours is the "best strategy for us to save money and remain in business without having to eliminate jobs." While the café's employees are undoubtedly grateful for the intent of the memo, they may see that its logic is flawed. First, the memo does not provide enough supporting evidence to prove that the money saved by cutting hours would exceed the money lost by losing early-morning and weekend clients. Second, the owner does not seem to evaluate other options that would either cut back on overhead or change the café's operation to bring in more revenue.

First, the owner relies on an unproven assumption about the cause of the overhead. He concludes, without justifying, that being open too many hours is causing too much overhead expense. There may be other causes, however, such as waste in other areas of management. While it is true that reducing café hours would save money spent on utilities, employee wages, and other operating costs, there is no evidence that those savings would outweigh the café's loss of business. The owner's message fails to give details of operating costs, wages, and utilities saved if the café is closed for the hours suggested by the memo. Perhaps the highest utility expenses are actually incurred between noon and 3 p.m., when the sun is the hottest and the café's air conditioning and refrigeration are most in use. The owner needs to do more research, including the habits and demography of the town. For example, since the café is located in the downtown area, perhaps *increasing* the number of hours the café is open would be a better solution.

Yes, it would cost more in overhead, but doing so might, in fact, make much more money for the café. Say, for instance, the Juniper becomes the only restaurant open on Friday and Saturday date nights, after the football games and movies let out. Second, the owner of the Juniper Café is not considering that the café serves a small American city. Cutting early-morning hours at a café, in a downtown area, where businesspeople and city workers most likely stop for coffee or breakfast on their way to work, seems very short-sighted and ill-informed. Are there one or more other cafés that will gladly steal business from 6 a.m. to 8 a.m. weekdays and that will perhaps win the permanent loyalty of those customers for lunch and dinner?

Furthermore, the owner does not seem to have evaluated other options to save the café. There are other places where overhead costs could potentially be cut. Certainly the owner would benefit from a brainstorming session with all employees, to get other ideas on the table. Maybe a new, lower-rent freezer storage facility is nearby. Maybe employees can suggest cutting waste in the purchasing department or dropping services the café doesn't need. It stands to reason that there is a plurality of ways to decrease overhead, aside from simply cutting hours.

In conclusion, the memo as it stands now does not logically prove that reduction in those particular hours will result in financial and future success for the café. There are several unstated assumptions upon which the argument turns, principally the assertion that simply being open for a certain number of hours is causing crippling overhead expenses. The owner's argument would profit enormously from further research, which may affect the hours he chooses to cut. Customer polling could show that few people eat or want coffee in that part of town between 2 p.m. and 5 p.m., and the café could be closed between lunch and dinner, adding flex hours or overlapping shifts for the staff. The memo lacks outlining what other restaurant services are available in the area and how or if they affect the 6 a.m. to 8 a.m. block and weekend hours. Once the marketing research and brainstorming is complete, the owner of the Juniper Café will make a better informed choice for his café's operating hours.

PART SIX

Test Day and Beyond

CHAPTER 22

Take Control of the Test

Now that you're familiar with the content that makes up each section of the GRE, and are armed with the strategies and techniques you'll need to tackle all of the question types, you're ready to turn your attention to building the right mentality and attitude that will help you succeed on test day. Let's first go over the basic principles of good test mentality.

KAPLAN'S 4 BASIC PRINCIPLES OF GOOD TEST MENTALITY

You are already armed with the weapons that you need to do well on the GRE. But you must wield those weapons with the right frame of mind and in the right spirit. This involves taking a certain stance toward the entire test and bolstering your stamina, confidence, and attitude.

TEST AWARENESS

To do your best on the GRE, keep in mind that the test is different from other tests you've taken before, both in terms of its content and in terms of its scoring system. If you took a test in high school or college and got a quarter of the questions wrong, you probably received a mediocre grade. Not so with the GRE. The test is geared so that even the very best test takers don't necessarily get every question right.

What does this mean for you? Well, just as you shouldn't let one tough Reading Comprehension passage ruin an entire section, you shouldn't let what you consider to be a subpar performance on one section ruin your performance on the entire test. If you allow that subpar section to rattle you, it sets in motion a downward spiral that could do serious damage to your score. Losing a few extra points won't do you in, but losing your head will. Keeping your composure is an important test-taking skill.

Also, you should remember that if you feel you've done poorly on a section, it could very well be the experimental section. You'll have the opportunity immediately after you've taken the test to think about whether you want to cancel your score. You might underestimate your performance, since you're more likely to remember the questions you thought were more difficult. The major takeaway is to stay confident throughout the test.

STAMINA

Overall, the GRE is a grueling experience. Remember, you'll be completing up to seven full-length sections on test day (Analytical Writing, two Verbal Reasoning, two Quantitative Reasoning, Experimental, and one Research). It is a true test of endurance, and some test takers run out of gas on the final few sections.

To avoid this, you must build up your test-taking stamina by taking as many full-length Practice Tests as possible several weeks before the test. If you do this, by test day, completing this test won't seem like such a daunting task.

When you register for the GRE, ETS will send you a free copy of its POWERPREP II® software, including two multi-stage Practice Tests. Or if you prefer, you may download the POWERPREP II® software yourself anytime at **gre.org**.

Another option, if you haven't already done so, would be to take a Kaplan course, either classroom-based or online. You could also set up special one-on-one tutoring sessions with Kaplan faculty. If you decide to go this route, visit **kaptest.com** or call 1-800-KAP-TEST for information on a Kaplan classroom or tutoring program.

CONFIDENCE

Confidence is self-sustaining, and unfortunately, so is its opposite—self-doubt. Confidence in your ability leads to quick, sure answers and an ease of concentration that translates into more points. If you lack confidence, you might lose concentration and end up reading sentences and answer choices two, three, or four times. This leads to timing difficulties, which only continue the downward spiral, causing anxiety and a tendency to rush. If you subscribe to the test-prep mindset that we've described, however, you'll be ready and able to take control of the test. Learn our techniques and then practice them over and over again. That's the way to score your best on the test.

ATTITUDE

Those who fear the test or consider it an extra hurdle in the long race toward graduate school usually don't fare as well as those who see the GRE as an opportunity to show off the reading and reasoning skills that graduate schools are looking for. In fact, consider this: the test is designed to reward you. Those who look forward to the GRE as a challenge—or, at least, who enjoy the opportunity to distinguish themselves from the rest of the applicant pack—tend to score better than do those who resent it.

It may sound a little dubious, but take our word for it: altering your approach is proven to raise scores. Here are a few steps you can take to make sure you develop the right GRE attitude:

- Look at the GRE as a challenge but try not to obsess over it; you certainly don't want to psych yourself out of the game.
- Remember that, yes, the GRE is obviously important, but contrary to what some people think, this one test will not singlehandedly determine the outcome of your life. In many cases, it's not even the most important piece of your graduate application.
- Since the test is predictable, think of the GRE as a reward for understanding the same core skills that show up all the time.
- Remember that you're more prepared than most people. You've trained with Kaplan. You have the tools you need, plus the know-how to use those tools.

Kaplan's basic principles of good test mentality are as follows:

- Be aware of the test and keep your composure even when you are struggling with a difficult question; missing one question won't ruin your score for a section.
- Build your stamina by taking as many Practice Tests as you can.
- Be confident; you are already well on your way to a great score!
- Stay positive; consider the GRE an opportunity rather than an obstacle.

THE KAPLAN ADVANTAGE™ STRESS-MANAGEMENT SYSTEM

Is it starting to feel as if your whole life is a buildup to the GRE? You've known about it for years, worried about it for months, and now spent at least a few weeks in solid preparation for it. As the test gets closer, you may find that your anxiety is on the rise. You shouldn't worry. Armed with the preparation strategies that you've learned from this book, you're in good shape for test day. To calm any pre-test jitters that you may have, however, let's go over a few strategies for the couple of days before the test.

TIPS FOR THE DAYS JUST BEFORE THE EXAM

- The best test takers do less and less as the test approaches. Taper off your study schedule and take it easy on yourself. Give yourself time off, especially the evening before the exam. By that time, if you've studied well, everything you need to know is firmly stored in your memory bank. In fact, it's in your best interest to marshal your physical and psychological resources for the last 24 hours or so before the test. Keep the test out of your consciousness; go to a movie, take a pleasant walk, or just relax. Eat healthy meals and steer clear of sugar and caffeine. And, of course, get plenty of rest that night, and also two nights before. It's hard to fall asleep earlier than you're used to, and you don't want to lie there worrying about the test.

- Most importantly, make sure you know where the test will be held and the easiest, quickest way to get there. You'll have great peace of mind by knowing that all the little details are set before test day.

- Visit the test site a few days in advance, particularly if you are especially anxious.

HANDLING STRESS DURING THE TEST

The biggest source of stress will be the test itself. Fear not! The following are methods to relieve your stress during the test:

- Keep moving forward instead of getting bogged down in a difficult question. You don't have to get everything right to achieve a solid score. So don't linger out of desperation on a question that is going nowhere even after you've spent considerable time on it.

- Breathe! Weak test takers tend to share one major trait: they don't breathe properly as the test proceeds. They might hold their breath without realizing it or breathe irregularly. Improper breathing hurts confidence and accuracy. Just as importantly, it interferes with clear thinking.

TEST DAY

The night before test day, gather the following things together:

- ID
- Admission ticket
- A watch
- Bottle of water
- Aspirin or other painkiller, in case you get a headache

- A snack, such as fruit or an energy bar, to keep your energy up for the later sections of the test
- Names of schools you'd like to receive your scores

Test day should start with a moderate, high-energy breakfast. Cereal, fruit, bagels, or eggs are good. Avoid doughnuts, pastries, or anything else with a lot of sugar. Also, unless you are utterly catatonic without it, it's a good idea to stay away from coffee.

Yes, perhaps you drink two cups every morning and don't even notice it. But it's different during the test. Coffee won't make you alert (your adrenaline will do that much more effectively); it will just give you the jitters. Kaplan has done experiments in which test takers go into one exam having drunk various amounts of coffee and another exam without having drunk coffee. The results indicate that even the most caffeine-addicted test takers will lose their focus midway through the second section if they've had coffee, but they report no alertness problems without it.

When you get to the test center, you will be seated at a computer station. Some administrative questions will be asked before the test begins, and once you're done with those, you're set to go. While you're taking the test, a small clock will count down the time you have left in each section. The computer will tell you when you're done with each section and when you've completed the test.

Here are some last-minute reminders to help guide your work on the test:

- Take a few minutes now to look back over your preparation and give yourself credit for all the work you put into it. Confidence is far more useful than distress.
- Give all answer choices a fair shot in Verbal Reasoning (especially Reading Comprehension), time permitting. For the Quantitative Reasoning section, go with the clearly correct answer as soon as you find it and forget the rest of the answer choices.
- Don't bother trying to figure out which section is the experimental section. It can't help you, and you might make a tragic mistake if you guess wrong. Instead, just do your best on every section.
- Dress in layers for maximum comfort. This way, you can adjust to the room's temperature accordingly.
- During the exam, try not to fixate on what your score is or how you're doing so far. It's counterproductive to continue to think about questions you've already answered or ones you haven't gotten to yet. If you worry about the next section, or the one you've just completed, you'll just feel overwhelmed. Instead, focus on

the question-by-question task of picking the correct answer choice. Try to take things one step at a time. Concentrate on each question, each passage, and each essay prompt—on the mechanics, in other words—and you'll avoid cognitive confusion.

After all the hard work that you've put in preparing for and taking the GRE, make sure you take time to celebrate afterwards. Plan to get together with friends the evening after the test. You prepared for the test ahead of time. You did your best. You're going to get a great score.

CHAPTER 23

Where and When to Apply

You probably know what you want to study as a graduate student, but where should you apply? The answer to this question is dependent on two main factors: which programs would be best for you, and which of these programs you can actually get into. This chapter will help you answer these questions—and many more you may have about the process of choosing a school for postgraduate study.

WHAT PROGRAMS YOU SHOULD CONSIDER

Once you've made the decision to pursue graduate studies, you should take the decision about where to go to school seriously—it will have a major influence on your daily life for the next several years and will influence your academic and career paths for years to come. Many students allow themselves to be influenced by a professor or mentor or school rankings, and then find they're unhappy in a certain program because of its location, workload, cost, or some unforeseen factor. If you complete your own research, even if it takes time and hard work, you will be happier with your own choice. Let's take a look at some of the factors you'll need to consider when choosing a school.

YOUR GOALS

Keep your goals in mind when evaluating graduate programs. Before you take the leap, it's important that you have a pretty clear idea where your interests really lie, what grad school life is like, and whether you're compatible with a particular program and its professors. Armed with this information, you should be able to successfully apply to the right programs, get accepted, and use your time in graduate school to help you get a head start on the post-graduation job search.

Students decide to enter master's and doctoral degree programs for a variety of reasons. Some want to pursue a career in academia. To teach at two-year colleges, you'll need at least a master's degree; to teach and do research at four-year colleges, universities, and graduate programs, you'll need a doctorate. Other people need graduate education to meet national and state licensing requirements in fields such as social work, engineering, and architecture. Some students want to change careers, while others expect an advanced degree to open up new opportunities in their current field.

Most master's programs are two years long, and master's students are generally one of two types: those on an academic track, where the degree programs focus on classical research and scholarship, and those on a practical track, where the degree program is actually a professional training course that qualifies people to enter or advance in a field such as social work or education.

Other options to consider if you're pursuing a master's degree are cooperative, joint, and interdisciplinary programs. In cooperative programs, you apply to, answer to, and graduate from one school, but you have access to classes, professors, and facilities at a cooperating school or schools as part of the program. In joint- or dual-degree programs, you work toward two degrees simultaneously, either within the same school or at two neighboring schools. Interdisciplinary programs are generally run by a committee consisting of faculty from a number of different departments. You apply to, register with, and are graduated by only one of the departments; you and your faculty committee design your curriculum.

Doctoral programs are designed to create scholars capable of independent research that will add new and significant knowledge to their fields. At first, you'll be regarded as an apprentice in your field. Your first year or two in the program will be spent on coursework, followed by "field" or "qualifying" exams. Once you've passed those exams, demonstrating that you have the basic factual and theoretical knowledge of your field down cold, you'll be permitted to move on to independent research in the form of your doctoral dissertation. During most of this time you can get financial aid in the form of teaching or research assistantships; in exchange for assisting professors in the classroom or the lab, you get a small stipend and/or tuition remission.

If you want to get a doctoral degree, you can get a master's and reapply to Ph.D. programs, or enter directly into the doctoral program. The first method gives you flexibility but generally takes longer, costs more in the long run, and means reliving the application process. However, some doctoral programs do require a full master's degree for acceptance.

PROGRAM REPUTATION

Although you shouldn't place too much stock in school and program rankings, you should consider a program's overall reputation. When you assess a program's reputation, don't just consider its national ranking, but think about whether it fits your goals and interests. You can get information from a variety of sources, formal and informal.

Each year, various groups publish rankings of graduate programs: *U.S. News and World Report* on American graduate programs, *Maclean's* on Canadian programs, and many others. These rankings can give you a general sense of the programs in your field and may include profiles of distinguished professors, but they tell you nothing about departmental politics, job placement records, or financial aid possibilities.

You should find out which programs are highly regarded in the areas that interest you. You can learn these details through professional associations (such as the American Psychological Association), comprehensive commercial directories of graduate programs (available through school or local libraries), and the Internet.

Don't forget to contact schools and departments directly. Most departments have a chairperson who is also the admissions contact; he or she can put you in touch with current students and alumni who are willing to discuss the program with you. The chair is usually willing to answer questions as well.

Try to speak to at least one current student and one alumnus from each program you're seriously considering. You'll find that many graduate students are quite outspoken about the strengths and weaknesses of professors, programs, and the state of the job market in their field.

If you're an undergraduate, or still have contacts from your undergraduate experience, ask your professors for their take on the various graduate programs. You'll often find that they have a great deal of inside information on academic and research trends, impending retirements, intellectual rivalries, and rising stars.

Remember, a program's reputation isn't everything, but the higher your school is regarded in the marketplace, the better your job prospects are likely to be upon graduation.

LOCATION

Two key questions you should consider regarding a school's location are: How will it affect the overall quality of your graduate school experience, and how will it affect your employability? Some students prefer an urban setting. Others prefer a more rustic environment. Cost of living can also be a factor.

Geography may be an important criterion for you. Perhaps your geographical choices are limited by a spouse's job or other family obligations. Perhaps you already know where you want to live after graduation. If you're planning on a career in academia, you'll probably want to choose a nationally known program, regardless of where it's located. If, on the other hand, your program involves a practical dimension (psychology, social work, education, or some interdisciplinary programs), you may want to concentrate your school search on the area in which you hope to live and work, at least initially.

CURRICULUM

To maximize the value of your graduate school experience, be sure that a department's areas of concentration match up with your own interests. Knowing a program's particular theoretical bent and practical selling points can help ensure that you choose a school that reflects your own needs and academic leanings. Does one school of thought, one style of research, predominate? If so, is there anyone else working in the department with a different theoretical framework? Will you have opportunities to work within a variety of theories and orientations? What special opportunities are available? How well are research programs funded? Do the professors have good records at rounding up grants? In field or clinical work, what are the options? Are programs available in your area of interest?

Find the environment that works best for you. Don't put yourself in a situation in which you don't have access to the courses or training you're seeking. It's your education. Your time. Your energy. Your investment in your future. By being proactive, you can help guarantee that you maximize your graduate school experience.

FACULTY

One of the most important decisions you make in your graduate school career will be your choice of advisor. This one person will help you with course selection as well as clinical, research, or field education opportunities; he or she can make or break the thesis/dissertation process. So when you investigate a department, look for a faculty member whose interests and personality are compatible with yours. Since this single person (your "dream advisor") may not be available, be sure to look for a couple of other professors with whom you might be able to work.

If one of your prime motivations in attending a certain program is to take classes from specific professors, make sure you'll have that opportunity. At the master's level, access to prominent professors is often limited to large, foundation-level lecture courses, where papers and exams are graded by the professor's graduate assistants or tutors. At the doctoral level, professors are generally much more accessible.

Is the department stable or changing? Find out whether the faculty is nearing retirement age. Impending retirements may not affect you in a two-year master's program, but this is a serious consideration in doctoral programs, which can (and often do) stretch on for over five years. If you have hopes of working with a distinguished professor, will he or she even be available for that time—or longer, if you get delayed? Will the department be large and stable enough to allow you to put together a good thesis or dissertation committee? Also try to find out whether younger members of the department are established. Do they get sufficient funding? Have they settled in to the institution enough that there are not likely to be political controversies?

PLACEMENT

Although some people attend graduate school for the love of knowledge, most want to enhance their career prospects in some way. When you graduate with your hard-won degree, what are your chances of getting your desired job?

You'll want to ask what kind of track record a given program has in placing its alumni. With today's highly competitive job market, it's especially important to find out when and where graduates have found work. If you're considering work in business, industry, local agencies, schools, health care facilities, or the government, find out whether these employers visit the campus to recruit. Major industries may visit science programs to interview prospective graduates. Some will even employ graduate students over the summer or part-time. If you're going into academia, find out whether recent grads have been able to find academic posts, how long the search took, and where they're working. Are they getting tenure-track positions at reasonably prestigious departments, or are they shifting from temporary appointment to temporary appointment with little hope of finding a stable position? Don't just look at the first jobs that a school's graduates take. Where are they in 5, 10, or even 25 years?

Your career is more like a marathon than a sprint. So take the long view. A strong indicator of a program's strength is the accomplishments of its alumni.

STUDENT BODY

Some graduate catalogs contain profiles of or statements by current master's and Ph.D. students. Sometimes this is an informal blurb on a few students—it's really marketing material—and sometimes it's a full listing of graduate students. Use this as a resource both to find out what everyone else in the program is up to, and to find current students you can interview about the school and the program.

Because much of your learning will come from your classmates, consider the makeup of your class. A school with a geographically, professionally, and ethnically diverse student body will expose you to far more viewpoints than will a school with a more homogeneous group. If you're an older applicant, ask yourself how you'll fit in with a predominantly younger group of students. For many, the fit is terrific, but for others, the transition can be tougher. The answer depends on you, but it's something to consider.

The student body, as well as the faculty, will have varied philosophical and political orientations. The theories and perspectives considered liberal in one program can be deemed conservative in another, and where you fit among your peers can have a lot of influence on your image and your opportunities. If you plan on an academic career, remember that your student colleagues will someday likely be your professional colleagues.

NETWORKING

Forging relationships—with your classmates, your professors and, in a larger sense, all the alumni—is a big part of the graduate-school experience. One of the things you'll take with you when you graduate, aside from an education, a diploma, and debt, is that network. And whether you thrive on networking or tend to shy away from it, it's a necessity. At some point it may help you advance your career, in academia or outside.

QUALITY OF LIFE

Your graduate school experience will extend far beyond your classroom learning, particularly for full-time students. That's why it's so important to find out as much as you can about the schools that interest you. For example, what activities would you like to participate in? Perhaps convenient recreational facilities or an intramural sports program is appealing. If you'd like to be involved in community activities, perhaps there's a school volunteer organization. Regardless of your interests, your ability to maintain balance in your life in the face of a rigorous academic challenge will help you keep a healthy outlook.

Housing is another quality-of-life issue to consider. Is campus housing available? Is off-campus housing convenient? Is it affordable? Where do most of the students live?

Quality of life is also an important consideration for spouses and significant others, especially if your school choice requires a move to a new city. When graduate school takes over your life, your spouse may feel left out. Find out what kind of groups and activities there are for families and partners. For example, are there any services to help your spouse find employment? Is child care available? Is there a good school system in the area?

FULL TIME VERSUS PART TIME

In a full-time program, you can focus your energy on your studies to maximize your learning. You're also likely to meet more people and forge closer relationships with your classmates. Many programs are oriented toward the full-time student and many top-tier programs don't offer part-time options. A part-time schedule may also make it difficult for you to take classes with the best professors.

There are, however, many compelling reasons for attending part-time. It may not be economically feasible for you to attend full-time. Or you may wish to continue gaining professional experience while earning the degree that will allow you to move on to the next level. If there's a possibility that you'll have to work while you're in school, particularly while you're in the coursework stage, check out the flexibility of any program that interests you. Are there night or weekend classes? When is the library open? What about the lab? Talk to students currently in the program, especially those who work. Part-time programs are often slow, which can be discouraging, especially when licensure or salary increases are at stake.

Although many students in full-time graduate programs support themselves with part-time work, their primary allegiance is to the graduate degree. Since graduate studies tend to become the focus of your life, if you can manage full-time or nearly full-time studies at the higher levels, do it. You can graduate earlier and start picking up the financial pieces that much sooner—often with a more secure base for your job search in the form of good support from your advisor.

Most master's programs are flexible about part-time studies, but doctoral programs are less so. Many doctoral programs expect a minimum amount of time "in residence"—that is, enrolled as a full-time student for a certain number of consecutive semesters. This requirement is usually listed in the catalog.

PROGRAM COSTS

Some graduate programs charge per credit or per hour, meaning that your tuition bill is calculated by the number of credits you take each semester. Other programs charge per semester or per year with a minimum and maximum number of credits you can take per semester for that flat fee. In general, per credit makes sense for part-time students, while per semester makes sense for full-time students. Generally speaking, the most expensive kind of graduate program (per semester) will be a master's degree at a private school. Loans are available to master's-level students, but grants, scholarships, and other forms of "free" financial assistance are harder to find. Furthermore, most private schools apply the same tuition rate to in-state and out-of-state residents. State colleges and universities usually give in-state residents a tuition break. Other forms of savings can come from finding the cheapest living and housing expenses and from working your way through the program as quickly as possible.

At the doctoral level, tuition remission (you don't pay any of it) and grants or stipends (they pay you) are common. Percentages of doctoral students in a program receiving full tuition remission plus stipend/grant money can range anywhere from 0 percent to 100 percent—every student in the program pays no tuition and receives some grant or stipend. In these programs, the major financial burden is the living expenses over the years of coursework, language requirements, qualifying and field exams, research, and the dissertation.

WHERE YOU CAN GET IN

Once you've developed a list of schools that meet your needs, take an objective look at your chances of getting into them.

A good way to get a sense of how graduate schools will perceive you is to make up a fact sheet with your GRE scores (or projected scores), your overall grade point average (GPA), as well as your GPA in your major, and your work experience. Outside activities and your personal statement will contribute to the overall "score" that admissions officers will use to evaluate you, but let's stick with the raw data for now.

The next step is to find a current source of information about graduate school programs. There are several guides published every year that provide data about acceptance rates for given years, as well as median GPA and GRE scores. You can also request this information directly from a given department. The school of your dreams may not care very much about your GPA, but it might be very interested in your GRE scores. Make sure you find out what your target school prioritizes in its search for worthy applicants.

One of the best ways to gauge whether you're in contention for a certain program is to compare your numbers to theirs. And remember that you needn't hit the nail on the head. Median is similar to average, so some applicants do better or worse than the GRE scores or GPA cited. And remember all the other factors that add up to make you a desirable applicant. Comparing numbers is merely a good way to get a preliminary estimate of your compatibility with the schools of your choice.

"SAFETY" SCHOOLS

Once you have some idea of where you fall in the applicant pool, you can begin to make decisions about your application strategy. No matter what your circumstances, it's wise to choose at least one school that is likely to accept you, a "safety" school. Make sure it's one that fits your academic goals and your economic circumstances. If your GRE scores and GPA are well above a school's median scores and you don't anticipate any problems with other parts of your record or application, you've probably found your safety school.

"WISHFUL THINKING" SCHOOLS

If your ideal program is one that you don't seem qualified for, apply to your "dream school" anyway. You may be surprised! GPA and GRE scores aren't the only criteria by which applicants are judged, and you may discover that you're admitted in spite of your academic background, on the merits of your personal statement, work samples, or other criteria. It's always worth a try. Some people underestimate their potential and apply only to safety schools. This can often lead to disappointment when they end up at one of these schools and discover that it doesn't provide the rigorous training they want.

WHEN TO APPLY

With the number of graduate school applications received by institutions of higher learning on the rise, the issue of when to apply for admission has become very important. There are perfect times to begin and end the application process. You should begin at least a year before you plan to enter school (sooner if you're a nontraditional candidate or are changing fields). Find out the following essential dates as early as possible and incorporate them into your own personal application schedule:

- Standardized test registration deadlines
- Transcript deadlines (some schools send out transcripts only on particular dates)
- Letters-of-recommendation due dates
- Application deadlines (submit your application as early as possible to ensure that you get a fair and comprehensive review)
- Financial aid forms deadlines (federal/state programs, universities, and independent sources of aid all have definite deadlines)

SETTING UP AN APPLICATION SCHEDULE

We've organized the following "seasonal" schedule to help you understand how to proceed through the admissions process.

Winter (18–20 months prior to start date)
- If you're a nontraditional applicant or plan to switch fields, begin investigating program requirements. Take courses to make up any missing portion of your background.

Spring (16–18 months prior to start date)
- Browse through program catalogs and collect information on different grants and loans. Create your own graduate school library.

Summer
- Request applications from schools. If they're not available yet, ask for last year's so you can get a feel for the questions you'll have to answer.
- Write a draft of your personal statement and show it to trusted friends and/or colleagues for feedback.

- Consider registering for the GRE in the fall. This will give you plenty of time to submit your scores with your application.
- Research your options for test preparation. Take the test included in this book to give you a good idea of where you stand with regard to the GRE.

Early Fall

- Ask for recommendations. Make sure that your recommenders know enough about you to write a meaningful letter. Ask them first if they would be willing to write you a recommendation and ask how much lead time they would need. Once your recommenders have agreed to write a recommendation, make sure to give them clear deadlines, so you can avoid any timing conflicts.

Late Fall

- Take the GRE.
- Request applications from schools, if you haven't already done so.
- Request institutional, state, and federal financial aid materials from school aid offices.
- Request information on independent grants and loans.
- Order transcripts from your undergraduate (and any graduate) institution(s).
- Follow up with your recommenders, and send a thank you note to those who sent their recommendations in already.

Winter

- Fill out applications. Mail them as early as possible.
- Fill out financial aid applications. Mail these early as well.
- Make sure your recommendation writers have the appropriate forms and directions for mailing. Remind them of deadline dates.

Spring

- Sit back and relax (if you can). Most schools indicate how long it will take to inform you of their decision. This is also a crucial time to solidify your financial plans as you begin to receive offers of aid (with any luck).

The timing described here is approximate, and you needn't follow it exactly. The most important thing for you to do is make yourself aware of strict deadlines well in advance so that you'll be able to devote plenty of quality time to your application. In the next chapter, we'll go over the application process in detail.

CHAPTER 24

How to Apply to Graduate School

You've taken the GRE and you've researched schools that offer the program you want. Now your first step in the application process is to order the application forms from the various schools that you've selected. Once the applications begin arriving, you'll notice one thing quickly: no two applications are exactly alike. Some ask you to write one essay or personal statement, and others may ask for three or more essays on various subjects. Some have very detailed forms requiring extensive background information; others are satisfied with your name and address and little else.

Despite these differences, most applications follow a general pattern with variations on the same kinds of questions. So read this section with the understanding that, although not all of it is relevant to every application, these guidelines will be valuable for just about any graduate school application you'll encounter.

HOW SCHOOLS EVALUATE APPLICANTS

Each graduate school has its own admissions policies and practices, but all programs evaluate your application based on a range of objective and subjective criteria. Regardless of which schools you are pursuing, understanding how admissions officers judge your candidacy can give you a leg up on the competition.

Generally, all admissions officers use the application process to measure your intellectual abilities, aptitude in your field of study, and personal characteristics. When you submit your application, admissions officers will evaluate the total package. Most admissions officers look for reasons to admit candidates, not reject them. Your challenge, therefore, is to distinguish yourself positively from the other candidates.

INTELLECTUAL ABILITY

To assess your intellectual ability, admissions officers look at two key factors: your academic record and your GRE score.

Academic Record

Your grade point average (GPA) is important, but it's just part of your academic profile. Admissions officers will consider the reputation of your undergraduate institution and the difficulty of your courses. Admissions officers are well aware that comparing GPAs from different schools and even different majors from the same school is like comparing apples and oranges. So they'll look closely at your transcript. Do your grades show an upward trend? How did you perform in your major? How did you fare in courses related to the program you're applying to?

Admissions officers focus primarily on your undergraduate performance, but they will consider all graduate studies and non-degree coursework that you have completed. Be sure to submit those transcripts. Generally, the GPA of applicants who are about to complete or have recently completed an undergraduate degree is given much more weight than that of applicants returning to school after several years.

If you have a poor academic record, it will be tougher to get into a top school, but it is by no means impossible. Your challenge is to find other ways to demonstrate your intellectual horsepower. High GRE scores, an intelligently written personal statement, and strong recommendations will help.

The GRE

You are already familiar with the GRE and are armed with strategies to score higher on the test. An integral part of the admissions process at virtually all schools, the GRE measures general verbal, quantitative, and analytical writing skills. Some programs, particularly in psychology and the sciences, require you to take one or more GRE Subject Tests as well. In addition to or instead of the GRE, some programs require the Miller Analogies Test (MAT). Be sure to check with the programs you're considering to see which tests they require.

When admissions officers review your GRE scores, they'll look at your Verbal Reasoning, Quantitative Reasoning, and Analytical Writing scores separately, particularly if they have any questions about your abilities in a certain area. Different programs give varying weight to each score. If you've taken the GRE more than once, schools will generally credit you with your highest score for each section, though some may average the scores or take the most recent.

Used by itself, the GRE may not be a perfect predictor of academic performance, but it is the single best one available. The GRE does not measure your intelligence, nor does it measure the likelihood of your success in your field. The revised GRE has been designed to predict with more certainty your success in graduate school. As with any standardized test, by preparing properly for the GRE, you can boost your score significantly. The strategies you practice and learn will help you decipher difficult academic text you may encounter in your future studies.

The GRE's Analytical Writing section includes two essays: one requiring you to express and support a position on a given issue, and one requiring you to critique the logic of a given argument. The essays you type into the computer are graded on a 0 to 6 scale, and those scores are sent to the schools you designate along with your 130–170 scores for the Verbal Reasoning and Quantitative Reasoning sections. The Analytical Writing section is designed to provide schools with information about your communications skills that is not otherwise detectable on the GRE. Essentially, it is another tool that schools can use to evaluate you. Graduate schools have recognized that the Analytical Writing section provides you with an opportunity to demonstrate your ability to think critically and communicate complex ideas in a very limited time period.

Even though the Analytical Writing section is scored separately from the multiple-choice sections, you should prepare for it with the same intensity that you put into preparing for the rest of the GRE.

Fellowships and Assistantships

Some graduate programs award fellowships and assistantships partly on the basis of GRE scores. Because most programs have limited funds and therefore limited positions to offer, the awards process can be quite competitive. Not only should you take your scores seriously, you should also confirm the submission deadline with your department. The financial aid deadline is usually earlier than the application deadline.

RELEVANT EXPERIENCE AND SKILLS

When evaluating your application, admissions officers look at work experience and other activities related to the program in question. In fields like psychology, social work, and health, your research and practical experience will play a role in the admissions decision. If you're applying to film, writing, or other arts programs, you'll be asked to submit samples of your work. And if you're planning on an academic career, your research and publications will be of particular interest to the admissions committee. The way you present yourself and your achievements should be tailored to the programs you're applying to.

You can communicate some of your abilities through the straightforward "data" part of your application. Be sure to describe your job and internship responsibilities. Be aware that your job title alone will not necessarily communicate enough about what you do or the level of your responsibilities. If you are asked to submit a resume or CV, make sure you illustrate your experience and on-the-job training in a way that highlights skills you already have and those you think will serve you well in your future field of study.

If you are working and applying to a graduate program in the same field, admissions officers will look at your overall career record. How have you progressed? Have you been an outstanding performer? What do your recommendation writers say about your performance? Have you progressed to increasingly higher levels of responsibility? If you have limited work experience, you will not be expected to match the accomplishments of an applicant with 10 years' experience, but you will be expected to demonstrate your abilities.

Extracurricular activities and community involvement also present opportunities for you to highlight your skills. For younger applicants, college activities play a more significant role than for more seasoned applicants. Your activities say a lot about who you are and what's important to you. Were you a campus leader? Did your activities require discipline and commitment? Did you work with a team? What did you learn from your involvement?

Active community involvement provides a way for you to demonstrate your skills and to impress admissions officers with your personal character. In fact, many applications ask directly about community activities. Getting involved in your community is a chance to do something worthwhile and enhance your application in the process.

PERSONAL CHARACTERISTICS

The third, and most subjective, criterion on which schools evaluate you is your personal character. Admissions officers judge you in this area primarily through your personal statement (and essays, if applicable), recommendations, and personal interview (if applicable). Although different schools emphasize different qualities, most seek candidates who demonstrate maturity, integrity, responsibility, and a clear sense of how they fit into their chosen field. The more competitive programs place special emphasis on these criteria because they have many qualified applicants for each available spot in the class.

WHO EVALUATES APPLICANTS

At most schools, the board includes professional admissions officers and/or faculty from the department you're applying to. At some schools, the authority to make admissions decisions lies with the graduate school itself, that is, with the central administration. At others, it lies with individual departments.

WHAT DECISIONS DO THEY MAKE?

Upon reviewing your application, the admissions board may make any number of decisions, including the following:

- *Admit:* Congratulations, you're in! But read the letter carefully. The board may recommend or, in some cases, require you to do some preparatory coursework to ensure that your quantitative or language skills are up to speed.

- *Reject:* At the top schools, there are far more qualified applicants than spaces in the class. Even though you were rejected, you can reapply at a later date. However, if you are considering reapplying, you need to understand why you were rejected and whether you have a reasonable chance of being admitted the next time around. Some schools will speak with you about your application, but they often wait until the end of the admissions season, by which time you may have accepted another offer.

- *Waiting list:* Schools use the waiting list to manage class size, leaving the applicant with a mixed message. The good news is that you are a strong enough candidate to have made the list. The bad news is there is no way to know with certainty whether you'll be accepted. Take heart, though, that schools do tend to look kindly upon wait-listed candidates who reapply in a subsequent year.

- *Request for an interview:* Schools at which an interview is not required may request that you interview prior to making their final decision. Your application may have raised some specific issues that you can address in an interview, or perhaps the board feels your personal statement did not give them a complete enough picture to render a decision. Look at this as a positive opportunity to strengthen your case.

PREPARING YOUR APPLICATION

A key part of getting into the graduate school of your choice is to develop a basic application strategy so you can present yourself in the best light.

Your Application as a Marketing Tool

When it comes to applying to graduate school, you are the product. Your application is your marketing document. Of course, marketing yourself doesn't mean that you should lie or even embellish; it just means that you need to make a tight presentation of the facts. Everything in your application should add up to a coherent whole and underscore the fact that you are not only qualified to be in the program but that you should be in it.

Many application forms have a comforting and accepting tone. *Why would you like to come to our program?* they ask. They do want an answer to that question, but what's even more important—the subtext for the whole application process—is the question: *Why should we accept you?* This is the question that your application will answer. And with some effective marketing strategies, your answer will be clear, concise, coherent, and strong.

MAXIMIZING THE VARIOUS PARTS OF YOUR APPLICATION

Let's take a close look at how you should approach the specific parts of your application.

Personal Statement

Your personal statement is a critical part of your application. The personal statement is where you can explain why you're applying to graduate school, what interests you about this program, and what your future goals are. The situations you choose to write about and the manner in which you present them can have a major bearing on the strength of your candidacy.

Writing an effective personal statement requires serious self-examination and sound strategic planning. What major personal and professional events have shaped you? What accomplishments best demonstrate your abilities? Remember, admissions officers are interested in getting to know you as a complete person. What you choose to write about sends clear signals about what's important to you and what your values are. You want the readers to put your essay down and think, "Wow! That was really interesting and memorable," and, "Wow! This person really knows why she's going into this program and has real contributions to make to the field."

Creating Your Statement

Your statement should demonstrate the patterns in your life that have led you to apply for the program. Part of demonstrating why you are right for the program involves demonstrating that you understand what the program is and where it will lead you. A personal statement requires honesty and distinctiveness. If you are heading to graduate school straight from undergraduate school, what has made you so certain that you know what you want to do with your life? If you are returning to school, particularly if you are changing fields, what has led you to this decision? You can use vignettes from your personal history, academic life, work life, and extracurricular activities to explain. If you are applying to a doctoral program, indicate which ideas, fields of research, or problems intrigue you. It's always a good idea to demonstrate familiarity with the field you want to enter.

You should start compiling information for your statement three or four months before you fill out your application. Write a draft once you've narrowed your list of potential topics. Have it edited by someone who knows you well. After rewriting, have someone whose opinion and writing skills you trust read your final draft, make suggestions, and above all, help you proofread.

General Personal Statement Tips

Once you've determined what you plan to write for your statement, keep the following tips in mind:

- *Length*: Schools are pretty specific about how long they want your statement to be. Adhere to their guidelines.

- *Spelling/typos/grammar*: Remember, your application is your marketing document. What would you think of a product that's promoted with sloppy materials containing typos, spelling errors, and grammatical mistakes?

- *Write in the active voice*: Candidates who write well have an advantage in the application process because they can state their case in a concise, compelling manner. Less effective writers commonly write "passively." For example:

    Passive voice: *The essays were written by me.*

    Active voice: *I wrote the essays.*

    Strong writing will not compensate for a lack of substance, but poor writing can torpedo an otherwise impressive candidate.

- *Tone*: On the one hand, you want to tout your achievements and present yourself as a poised, self-confident applicant. On the other hand, arrogance and self-importance do not go over well with admissions officers. Before you submit your application, be sure that you're comfortable with the tone as well as the content.

- *Creative approaches*: If you choose to submit a humorous or creative application, you are employing a high-risk, high-reward strategy. If you're confident you can pull it off, go for it. Be aware, though, that what may work for one admissions officer may fall flat with another. Admissions officers who review thousands of essays every year may consider your approach gimmicky or simply find it distracting. Remember, your challenge is to stand out in the applicant pool in a positive way. Don't let your creativity obscure the substance of your application.

Making Your Statement Distinctive

Depending on the amount of time you have and the amount of effort you're willing to put in, you can write a personal statement that will stand out from the crowd. One of the first mistakes that some applicants make is in thinking that "thorough" and "comprehensive" are sufficient qualities for their personal statement. They try to include as much information as possible, without regard for length limitations or strategic intent. Application readers dread reading these bloated personal statements. So how do you decide what to include? There are usually clear length guidelines, and admissions officers prefer that you adhere to them. So get rid of the idea of "comprehensive" and focus more on "distinctive."

Unless they ask for it, don't dwell on your weak points. A strong personal statement, for example, about how much you learned in your current position and how the experience and knowledge you've gained inspired you to apply to graduate school will give readers what they want—a quick image of who you are, how you got that way, and why you want to go to their school. One of the best ways to be distinctive is to sell your image briefly and accurately, including real-life examples to back up your points.

The admissions team wants to know about you, but there is the potential for including too much personal information. Beware of sharing reasons for applying that include furthering personal relationships, improving finances, or proving someone wrong.

"Distinctive" means that your statement should answer the questions that admissions officers think about while reading personal statements: What's different about this applicant? Why should we pick this applicant over others? Authentic enthusiasm can be a plus, and writing about parts of your life or career that are interesting and relevant helps grab a reader's attention.

THE INTERVIEW

In some programs, an interview with the department is conducted at the applicant's discretion: if you want one, you're welcome to ask. In other programs, only the most promising applicants are invited to interviews. Whether or not a department can pay your travel expenses depends on its financial circumstances. If you have the opportunity, definitely go to interview at your first-choice departments. There's no substitute for face-to-face contact with your potential colleagues, and by visiting the school you can check out the city or town where it is located. You should investigate cost-of-living and transportation options during your visit.

As you prepare for an interview, here are some tips.

- *Review your application.* If you've submitted your application prior to the interview, your interviewer is likely to use it as a guide and may ask specific questions about it. Be sure you remember what you wrote.

- *Be ready to provide examples and specifics*. Professionally trained interviewers are more likely to ask you about specific situations than to ask broad, open-ended questions. They can learn more by asking what you've done in situations than by asking what you think you'd do. Here are a few situations an interviewer may ask you to discuss: "Tell me about a recent accomplishment." "Discuss a recent situation in which you demonstrated leadership." "Give me an example of a situation where you overcame difficult circumstances." As you think about these situations, be prepared to discuss specifics—what you did and why you did it that way. You do not need to "script" or over-rehearse your responses, but you should go into the interview confident that you can field any question.

- *Be open and honest*. Don't struggle to think of "right" answers. The only right answers are those that are right for you. By responding openly and honestly, you'll find the interview less stressful, and you'll come across as a more genuine, attractive candidate.

- *Ask questions*. The interview is as much an opportunity for you to learn about the school as for the school to learn about you. Good questions demonstrate your knowledge about a particular program and your thoughtfulness about the entire process.

- *Follow proper professional decorum*. Be on time, dress appropriately, and follow up with thank-you letters. Treat the process as you would a job interview, which in many respects it is.

- *Watch your nonverbal cues*. Nonverbal communication is much more important than people realize. Maintain eye contact, keep good posture, sustain positive energy, and avoid nervous fidgeting. It will help you come across as confident, poised, and mature.

- *Be courteous to the administrative staff*. These people are colleagues of the board members, and how you treat them can have an impact, either positive or negative.

- *Relax and have fun*. Interviews are inherently stressful. But by being well prepared, you can enhance your prospects for admission, learn about the school, and enjoy yourself in the process.

RECOMMENDATIONS

Graduate schools will require at least three recommendations. Choose recommenders who can write meaningfully about your strengths. One of the more common mistakes is to sacrifice an insightful recommendation from someone who knows you well for a generic recommendation from a celebrity or a prominent professor. Admissions officers are not impressed by famous names. So unless that individual knows you and can write convincingly on your behalf, it's not a strategy worth pursuing. Good choices for recommenders include current and past supervisors, professors, academic and nonacademic advisers, and people you work with in community activities.

Many schools will specifically request an academic recommendation. Professors in your major are ideal recommenders, as they can vouch for your ability to study at the graduate level. If you don't have a professor who can recommend you, use a TA who knows your work well. Similarly, if requesting a recommendation from your employer would create an awkward situation, look for someone else who can comment on your skills. Your recommendations will confirm your strengths and, in some cases, help you overcome perceived weaknesses in your application.

If you wish to submit an extra recommendation, it's generally not a problem. Most schools will include the letter in your file, and those that don't will not penalize you for it. You should, however, send a note explaining why you have requested an additional recommendation so it does not appear that you disregarded the instructions. It's also a good idea to check with the admissions department before submitting an extra recommendation.

Asking for Recommendations

There are two fundamental rules of requesting recommendations: ask early and ask nicely. As soon as you decide to go to graduate school, you should start sizing up potential recommendation writers and let them know that you may ask them for a recommendation. This will give them plenty of time to think about what to say. Once they've agreed, let them know about deadlines well in advance to avoid potential scheduling conflicts. The more time they have, the better the job they'll do recommending you. As for asking nicely, you should let these people know you think highly of their opinion and you'd be happy and honored if they would consider writing you a letter of recommendation. You can help your recommenders by scheduling brief appointments with them to discuss your background; providing any forms required by the program; supplying stamped, addressed envelopes; and following up with them.

BEFORE YOU SUBMIT YOUR APPLICATION

When you've completed your personal statement and you're ready to submit your application, take two more steps to ensure that your application is as strong as it can be.

1. Be sure to read your personal statement in the context of your entire application.
   a. Does the total package make sense? Does it represent you favorably? Is everything consistent?
   b. Have you demonstrated your intellectual ability, relevant experience and skills, and personal characteristics?

    c. Most importantly, do you feel good about the application? After all, you don't want to be rejected on the basis of an application that you don't believe represents the real you.

2. Have someone you trust and respect review your application. Someone who has not been involved in writing the application may pick up spelling or grammatical errors that you've overlooked. In addition, because your application is an intensely personal document that requires significant self-examination, you may not be able to remain objective. Someone who knows you and can be frank will tell you whether your application has "captured" you most favorably. Note, however, that some schools prohibit you from using any outside help on your application. A last-minute once-over from a friend or family member is probably within reason, but you may want to directly ask the school what is permissible.

PUTTING IT ALL TOGETHER

There are no magic formulas that automatically admit you to, or reject you from, the school of your choice. Rather, your application is like a jigsaw puzzle. Each component— GPA, GRE scores, professional experience, school activities, recommendations—is a different piece of the puzzle.

Outstanding professional experience and personal characteristics may enable you to overcome a mediocre academic record. Conversely, outstanding academic credentials will not ensure your admission to a top-tier program if you do not demonstrate strong relevant skills and experience, as well as solid personal character. Your challenge in preparing your application is to convince the admissions board that all of the pieces in your background fit together to form a substantial and unique puzzle.

CONGRATULATIONS!

You have all of the tools you need to put together a stand-out application package, including a top GRE score. Best of luck, and remember, your Kaplan training will be with you each step of the way.

A SPECIAL NOTE FOR INTERNATIONAL STUDENTS

About a quarter of a million international students pursue advanced academic degrees at the master's or Ph.D. level at U.S. universities each year. This trend of pursuing higher education in the United States, particularly at the graduate level, is expected to continue. Business, management, engineering, and the physical and life sciences are popular areas of study for students coming to the United States from other countries.

Along with these academic options, international students are also taking advantage of opportunities for research grants, teaching assistantships, and practical training or work experience in U.S. graduate departments.

If you are not from the United States but are considering attending a graduate program at a university in the United States, here is what you'll need to get started.

- If English is not your first language, start there. You will probably need to take the Test of English as a Foreign Language (TOEFL) or show some other evidence that you're proficient in English prior to gaining admission to a graduate program. Graduate programs will vary on what is an acceptable TOEFL score. For degrees in business, journalism, management, or the humanities, a minimum TOEFL score of 600 (250 on the computer-based TOEFL) or better is expected. For the hard sciences and computer technology, a TOEFL score of 550 (213 on the computer-based TOEFL) is a common minimum requirement.

- You may also need to take the GRE. The strategies in this book are designed to help you maximize your score on the computer-based GRE exam. However, most sites outside the United States and Canada offer only the paper-and-pencil version of the GRE exam. Fortunately, most strategies can be applied to the pencil-and-paper version as well. For additional paper-and-pencil strategies, see Chapter 2.

- Because admission to many graduate programs is quite competitive, you may want to select three or four programs you would like to attend and complete applications for each program.

- Selecting the correct graduate school is very different from selecting a suitable undergraduate institution. You should research the qualifications and interests of faculty members teaching and doing research in your chosen field. Look for professors who share your specialty.

- You need to begin the application process at least a year in advance. Be aware that many programs offer only August or September start dates. Find out application deadlines and plan accordingly.

- Finally, you will need to obtain an I–20 Certificate of Eligibility in order to obtain an F-1 Student Visa to study in the United States.

KAPLAN ENGLISH PROGRAMS*

If you need more help with the complex process of graduate school admissions, assistance preparing for the TOEFL or GRE, or help building your English language skills in general, you may be interested in Kaplan's programs for international students.

---

* Kaplan is authorized under federal law to enroll nonimmigrant alien students. Kaplan is accredited by ACCET (Accrediting Council for Continuing Education and Training).

Kaplan English Programs were designed to help students and professionals from outside the United States meet their educational and career goals. At locations throughout the United States, international students take advantage of Kaplan's programs to help them improve their academic and conversational English skills; to raise their scores on the TOEFL, GRE, and other standardized exams; and to gain admission to the schools of their choice. Our staff and instructors give international students the individualized instruction they need to succeed. Here is a brief description of some of Kaplan's programs for international students.

General Intensive English

Kaplan's General Intensive English course is the fastest and most effective way for students to improve their English. This full-time program integrates the four key elements of language learning—listening, speaking, reading, and writing. The challenging curriculum and intensive schedule are designed for both the general language learner and the academically bound student.

TOEFL and Academic English

Our world-famous TOEFL course prepares you for the TOEFL and teaches you the academic language and skills needed to succeed in a university. Designed for high-intermediate to advanced-level English speakers, our course includes TOEFL-focused reading, writing, listening, speaking, vocabulary, and grammar instruction.

General English

Our General English course is a semi-intensive program designed for students who want to improve their listening and speaking skills without the time commitment of an intensive program. With morning class time and flexible computer lab hours throughout the week, our General English course is perfect for every schedule.

GRE FOR INTERNATIONAL STUDENTS

The GRE is required for admission to many graduate programs in the United States. Nearly a half million people take the GRE each year. A high score can help you stand out from other test takers. This course, designed especially for nonnative English speakers, includes the skills you need to succeed on each section of the GRE, as well as access to Kaplan's exclusive computer-based practice materials and extra Verbal practice.

OTHER KAPLAN PROGRAMS

Since 1938, more than 3 million students have come to Kaplan to advance their studies, prepare for entry to American universities, and further their careers. In addition to the above programs, Kaplan offers courses to prepare for the SAT, GMAT, LSAT, MCAT, DAT, USMLE, NCLEX, and other standardized exams at locations throughout the United States.

APPLYING TO KAPLAN ENGLISH PROGRAMS

To get more information, or to apply for admission to any of Kaplan's programs for international students and professionals, contact us at

Kaplan English Programs

700 South Flower, Suite 2900

Los Angeles, CA 90017, USA

Phone (if calling from within the United States): (800) 818-9128

Phone (if calling from outside the United States): (213) 452-5800

Fax: (213) 892-1360

Website: kaptest.com/kep_domestic

GRE Resources

Kaplan's Word Groups

The following lists contain a lot of common GRE words grouped together by meaning. Make flashcards from these lists and look over your cards a few times a week from now until the day of the test. Look over the word group lists once or twice a week for 30 seconds every week until the test. If you don't have much time until the exam date, look over your lists more frequently. Then, by the day of the test, you should have a rough idea of what most of the words on your lists mean.

Note: The categories in which these words are listed are *general* and should *not* be interpreted as the exact definitions of the words.

Abbreviated Communication

abridge
compendium
cursory
curtail
syllabus
synopsis
terse

Act Quickly

abrupt
apace
headlong
impetuous
precipitate

Assist

abet
advocate
ancillary
bolster
corroborate
countenance
espouse
mainstay
munificent
proponent
stalwart
sustenance

Bad Mood

bilious
dudgeon
irascible
pettish
petulant
pique
querulous
umbrage
waspish

Beginner/Amateur

dilettante
fledgling
neophyte
novitiate
proselyte
tyro

Beginning/Young

burgeoning
callow
engender
inchoate
incipient
nascent

Biting (as in wit or temperament)

acerbic
acidulous
acrimonious
asperity
caustic
mordacious
mordant
trenchant

Bold

audacious
courageous
dauntless

Boring

banal
fatuous
hackneyed
insipid
mundane
pedestrian
platitude
prosaic
quotidian
trite

Carousal

bacchanalian
debauchery
depraved
dissipated
iniquity
libertine
libidinous
licentious
reprobate
ribald
salacious

sordid
turpitude

Changing Quickly

capricious
mercurial
volatile

Copy

counterpart
emulate
facsimile
factitious
paradigm
precursor
quintessence
simulated
vicarious

Criticize/Criticism

aspersion
belittle
berate
calumny
castigate
decry
defamation
denounce
deride/derisive
diatribe
disparage
excoriate
gainsay
harangue
impugn
inveigh
lambaste
objurgate
obloquy
opprobrium
pillory
rebuke
remonstrate
reprehend
reprove
revile
tirade
vituperate

Death/Mourning

bereave
cadaver
defunct
demise
dolorous
elegy
knell
lament
macabre
moribund
obsequies
sepulchral
wraith

Denying of Self

abnegate
abstain
ascetic
spartan
stoic
temperate

Dictatorial

authoritarian
despotic
dogmatic
hegemonic (hegemony)
imperious
peremptory
tyrannical

Difficult to Understand

abstruse
ambiguous
arcane
bemusing
cryptic
enigmatic
esoteric
inscrutable
obscure
opaque
paradoxical
perplexing
recondite
turbid

Disgusting/Offensive

defile
fetid
invidious
noisome
odious
putrid
rebarbative

Easy to Understand

articulate
cogent
eloquent
evident
limpid
lucid
pellucid

Eccentric/Dissimilar

aberrant
anachronism
anomalous
discrete
eclectic
esoteric
iconoclast

Embarrass

abash
chagrin
compunction
contrition
diffidence
expiate
foible
gaucherie
rue

Equal

equitable
equity
tantamount

Falsehood

apocryphal
canard
chicanery
dissemble

duplicity
equivocate
erroneous
ersatz
fallacious
feigned
guile
mendacious/mendacity
perfidy
prevaricate
specious
spurious

Family

conjugal
consanguine
distaff
endogamous
filial
fratricide
progenitor
scion

Favoring/not Impartial

ardor/ardent
doctrinaire
fervid
partisan
tendentious
zealot

Forgive

absolve
acquit
exculpate
exonerate
expiate
palliate
redress
vindicate

Funny

chortle
droll
facetious
flippant
gibe
jocular

levity
ludicrous
raillery
riposte
simper

Gaps/Openings

abatement
aperture
fissure
hiatus
interregnum
interstice
lull
orifice
rent
respite
rift

Generous/Kind

altruistic
beneficent
clement
largess
magnanimous
munificent
philanthropic
unstinting

Greedy

avaricious
covetous
mercenary
miserly
penurious
rapacious
venal

Hardhearted

asperity
baleful
dour
fell
malevolent
mordant
sardonic

scathing
truculent
vitriolic
vituperation

Harmful

baleful
baneful
deleterious
inimical
injurious
insidious
minatory
perfidious
pernicious

harsh-sounding

cacophony
din
dissonant
raucous
strident

Hatred

abhorrence
anathema
antagonism
antipathy
detestation
enmity
loathing
malice
odium
rancor

Healthy

beneficial
salubrious
salutary

Hesitate

dither
oscillate
teeter
vacillate
waver

Hostile

antithetic
churlish
curmudgeon
irascible
malevolent
misanthropic
truculent
vindictive

Innocent/Inexperienced

credulous
gullible
ingenuous
naive
novitiate
tyro

Insincere

disingenuous
dissemble
fulsome
ostensible
unctuous

Investigate

appraise
ascertain
assay
descry
peruse

Lazy/Sluggish

indolent
inert
lackadaisical
languid
lassitude
lethargic
phlegmatic
quiescent
slothful
torpid

luck

adventitious
amulet
auspicious
fortuitous
kismet
optimum
portentous
propitiate
propitious
providential
talisman

Nag

admonish
cavil
belabor
enjoin
exhort
harangue
hector
martinet
remonstrate
reproof

Nasty

fetid
noisome
noxious

Not a Straight Line

askance
awry
careen
carom
circuitous
circumvent
gyrate
labyrinth
meander
oblique
serrated
sidle
sinuous
undulating
vortex

Overblown/Wordy

bombastic
circumlocution
garrulous
grandiloquent
loquacious
periphrastic
prolix
rhetoric
turgid
verbose

Pacify/Satisfy

ameliorate
appease
assuage
defer
mitigate
mollify
placate
propitiate
satiate
slake
sooth

Pleasant-Sounding

euphonious
harmonious
melodious
sonorous

Poor

destitute
esurient
impecunious
indigent

Praise

acclaim
accolade
aggrandize
encomium
eulogize
extol
fawn
laud/laudatory
venerate/veneration

Predict

augur
auspice
fey
harbinger
portentous
presage
prescient
prognosticate

Prevent/Obstruct

discomfort
encumber
fetter
forfend
hinder
impede
inhibit
occlude

Smart/Learned

astute
canny
erudite
perspicacious

Sorrow

disconsolate
doleful
dolor
elegiac
forlorn
lament
lugubrious
melancholy
morose
plaintive
threnody

Stubborn

implacable
inexorable
intractable
intransigent
obdurate
obstinate
recalcitrant

refractory
renitent
untoward
vexing

Terse

compendious
curt
laconic
pithy
succinct
taciturn

Time/Order/Duration

anachronism
antecede
antedate
anterior
archaic
diurnal
eon
ephemeral
epoch
fortnight
millennium
penultimate
synchronous
temporal

Timid/Timidity

craven
diffident
pusillanimous
recreant
timorous
trepidation

Truth

candor/candid
fealty
frankness
indisputable
indubitable
legitimate
probity
sincere
veracious
verity

Unusual

aberration
anomaly
iconoclast
idiosyncrasy

Walking About

ambulatory
itinerant
peripatetic

Wandering

discursive
expatiate
forage
itinerant
peregrination
peripatetic
sojourn

Weaken

adulterate
enervate

exacerbate
inhibit
obviate
stultify
undermine
vitiate

Wisdom

adage
aphorism
apothegm
axiom
bromide
dictum
epigram
platitude
sententious
truism

Withdrawal/Retreat

abeyance
abjure
abnegation
abortive
abrogate
decamp
demur
recant
recidivism
remission
renege
rescind
retrograde

Kaplan's Root List

Kaplan's Root List can boost your knowledge of GRE-level words, and that can help you get more questions right. No one can predict exactly which words will show up on your test, but there are certain words that the test makers favor. The Root List gives you the component parts of many typical GRE words. Knowing these words can help you because you may run across them on your GRE. Also, becoming comfortable with the types of words that pop up will reduce your anxiety about the test.

Knowing roots can help you in two more ways. First, instead of learning one word at a time, you can learn a whole group of words that contain a certain root. They'll be related in meaning, so if you remember one, it will be easier for you to remember others. Second, roots can often help you decode an unknown GRE word. If you recognize a familiar root, you could get a good enough grasp of the word to answer the question.

A: without

amoral: neither moral nor immoral
atheist: one who does not believe in God
atypical: not typical
anonymous: of unknown authorship or origin
apathy: lack of interest or emotion
atrophy: the wasting away of body tissue
anomaly: an irregularity
agnostic: one who questions the existence of God

AB/ABS: off, away from, apart, down

abduct: to take by force
abhor: to hate, detest
abolish: to do away with, make void
abstract: conceived apart from concrete realities, specific objects, or actual instances
abnormal: deviating from a standard
abdicate: to renounce or relinquish a throne
abstinence: forbearance from any indulgence of appetite
abstruse: hard to understand; secret, hidden

AC/ACR: sharp, bitter

acid: something that is sharp, sour, or ill-natured
acute: sharp at the end; ending in a point
acerbic: sour or astringent in taste; harsh in temper
acrid: sharp or biting to the taste or smell
acrimonious: caustic, stinging, or bitter in nature
exacerbate: to increase bitterness or violence; aggravate

ACT/AG: to do; to drive; to force; to lead

agile: quick and well-coordinated in movement; active, lively
agitate: to move or force into violent, irregular action
litigate: to make the subject of a lawsuit
prodigal: wastefully or recklessly extravagant
pedagogue: a teacher
synagogue: a gathering or congregation of Jews for the purpose of religious worship

AD/AL: to, toward, near

adapt: adjust or modify fittingly
adjacent: near, close, or contiguous; adjoining
addict: to give oneself over, as to a habit or pursuit
admire: to regard with wonder, pleasure, and approval
address: to direct a speech or written statement to
adhere: to stick fast; cleave; cling
adjoin: to be close or in contact with
advocate: to plead in favor of

AL/ALI/ALTER: other, another

alternative: a possible choice
alias: an assumed name; another name
alibi: the defense by an accused person that he or she was verifiably elsewhere at the time of the crime with which he or she is charged
alien: one born in another country; a foreigner
alter ego: the second self; a substitute or deputy
altruist: a person unselfishly concerned for the welfare of others
allegory: figurative treatment of one subject under the guise of another

AM: love

amateur: a person who engages in an activity for pleasure rather than financial or professional gain
amatory: of or pertaining to lovers or lovemaking
amenity: agreeable ways or manners
amorous: inclined to love, esp. sexual love
enamored: inflamed with love; charmed; captivated
amity: friendship; peaceful harmony
inamorata: a female lover
amiable: having or showing agreeable personal qualities
amicable: characterized by exhibiting good will

AMB: to go; to walk

ambient: moving freely; circulating
ambitious: desirous of achieving or obtaining power
preamble: an introductory statement
ambassador: an authorized messenger or representative
ambulance: a wheeled vehicle equipped for carrying sick people, usually to a hospital

ambulatory: of, pertaining to, or capable of walking

ambush: the act of lying concealed so as to attack by surprise

perambulator: one who makes a tour of inspection on foot

AMBI/AMPH: both, more than one, around

ambiguous: open to various interpretations

amphibian: any cold-blooded vertebrate, the larva of which is aquatic and the adult of which is terrestrial; a person or thing having a twofold nature

ambidextrous: able to use both hands equally well

ANIM: of the life, mind, soul, spirit

unanimous: in complete accord

animosity: a feeling of ill will or enmity

animus: hostile feeling or attitude

equanimity: mental or emotional stability, especially under tension

magnanimous: generous in forgiving an insult or injury

ANNUI/ENNI: year

annual: of, for, or pertaining to a year; yearly

anniversary: the yearly recurrence of the date of a past event

annuity: a specified income payable at stated intervals

perennial: lasting for an indefinite amount of time

annals: a record of events, esp. a yearly record

ANTE: before

anterior: placed before

antecedent: existing, being, or going before

antedate: precede in time

antebellum: before the war (especially the American Civil War)

antediluvian: belonging to the period before the biblical flood; very old or old-fashioned

ANTHRO/ANDR: man, human

anthropology: the science that deals with the origins of humankind

android: robot; mechanical man

misanthrope: one who hates humans or humanity

philanderer: one who carries on flirtations

androgynous: being both male and female

androgen: any substance that promotes masculine characteristics

anthropocentric: regarding humanity as the central fact of the universe

ANTI: against

antibody: a protein naturally existing in blood serum that reacts to overcome the toxic effects of an antigen

antidote: a remedy for counteracting the effects of poison, disease, etc.

antiseptic: free from germs; particularly clean or neat

antipathy: aversion

antipodal: on the opposite side of the globe

APO: away

apology: an expression of one's regret or sorrow for having wronged another

apostle: one of the 12 disciples sent forth by Jesus to preach the gospel

apocalypse: revelation; discovery; disclosure

apogee: the highest or most distant point

apocryphal: of doubtful authorship or authenticity

apostasy: a total desertion of one's religion, principles, party, cause, etc.

ARCH/ARCHI/ARCHY: chief, principal, ruler

architect: the devisor, maker, or planner of anything

archenemy: chief enemy

monarchy: a government in which the supreme power is lodged in a sovereign

anarchy: a state or society without government or law

oligarchy: a state or society ruled by a select group

AUTO: self

automatic: self-moving or self-acting
autocrat: an absolute ruler
autonomy: independence or freedom

BE: to be; to have a particular quality; to exist

belittle: to regard something as less impressive than it apparently is
bemoan: to express pity for
bewilder: to confuse or puzzle completely
belie: to misrepresent; to contradict

BEL/BEL: war

antebellum: before the war
rebel: a person who resists authority, control, or tradition
belligerent: warlike, given to waging war

BEN/BON: good

benefit: anything advantageous to a person or thing
benign: having a kindly disposition
benediction: act of uttering a blessing
benevolent: desiring to do good to others
bonus: something given over and above what is due
bona fide: in good faith; without fraud

BI: twice, double

binoculars: involving two eyes
biennial: happening every two years
bilateral: pertaining to or affecting two or both sides
bilingual: able to speak one's native language and another with equal facility
bipartisan: representing two parties

CAD/CID: to fall; to happen by chance

accident: happening by chance; unexpected
coincidence: a striking occurrence of two or more events at one time, apparently by chance
decadent: decaying; deteriorating
cascade: a waterfall descending over a steep surface
recidivist: one who repeatedly relapses, as into crime

CANT/CENT/CHANT: to sing

accent: prominence of a syllable in terms of pronunciation
chant: a song; singing
enchant: to subject to magical influence; bewitch
recant: to withdraw or disavow a statement
incantation: the chanting of words purporting to have magical power
incentive: that which incites action

CAP/CIP/CEPT: to take; to get

capture: to take by force or stratagem
anticipate: to realize beforehand; foretaste or foresee
susceptible: capable of receiving, admitting, undergoing, or being affected by something
emancipate: to free from restraint
percipient: having perception; discerning; discriminating
precept: a commandment or direction given as a rule of conduct

CAP/CAPIT/CIPIT: head, headlong

capital: the city or town that is the official seat of government
disciple: one who is a pupil of the doctrines of another
precipitate: to hasten the occurrence of; to bring about prematurely
precipice: a cliff with a vertical face
capitulate: to surrender unconditionally or on stipulated terms
caption: a heading or title

CARD/CORD/COUR: heart

cardiac: pertaining to the heart
encourage: to inspire with spirit or confidence
concord: agreement; peace, amity
discord: lack of harmony between persons or things
concordance: agreement, concord, harmony

CARN: flesh

carnivorous: eating flesh
carnage: the slaughter of a great number of people

carnival: a traveling amusement show

reincarnation: rebirth of a soul in a new body

incarnation: a being invested with a bodily form

CAST/CHAST: cut

cast: to throw or hurl; fling

caste: a hereditary social group, limited to people of the same rank

castigate: to punish in order to correct

chastise: to discipline, esp. by corporal punishment

chaste: free from obscenity; decent

CED/CEED/CESS: to go; to yield; to stop

antecedent: existing, being, or going before

concede: to acknowledge as true, just, or proper; admit

predecessor: one who comes before another in an office, position, etc.

cessation: a temporary or complete discontinuance

incessant: without stop

CENTR: center

concentrate: to bring to a common center; to converge, to direct toward one point

eccentric: off-center

concentric: having a common center, as in circles or spheres

centrifuge: an apparatus that rotates at high speed that separates substances of different densities using centrifugal force

centrist: of or pertaining to moderate political or social ideas

CERN/CERT/CRET/CRIM/CRIT: to separate; to judge; to distinguish; to decide

discrete: detached from others, separate

ascertain: to make sure of; to determine

certitude: freedom from doubt

discreet: judicious in one's conduct of speech, esp. with regard to maintaining silence about something of a delicate nature

hypocrite: a person who pretends to have beliefs that she does not

criterion: a standard of judgment or criticism

CHRON: time

synchronize: to occur at the same time or agree in time

chronology: the sequential order in which past events occurred

anachronism: an obsolete or archaic form

chronic: constant, habitual

chronometer: a time piece with a mechanism to adjust for accuracy

CIRCU: around, on all sides

circumference: the outer boundary of a circular area

circumstances: the existing conditions or state of affairs surrounding and affecting an agent

circuit: the act of going or moving around

circumambulate: to walk about or around

circuitous: roundabout, indirect

CIS: to cut

scissors: cutting instrument for paper

precise: definitely stated or defined

exorcise: to seek to expel an evil spirit by ceremony

incision: a cut, gash, or notch

incisive: penetrating, cutting

CLA/CLO/CLU: shut, close

conclude: to bring to an end; finish; to terminate

claustrophobia: an abnormal fear of enclosed places

disclose: to make known, reveal, or uncover

exclusive: not admitting of something else; shutting out others

cloister: a courtyard bordered with covered walks, esp. in a religious institution

preclude: to prevent the presence, existence, or occurrence of

CLAIM/CLAM: to shout; to cry out

exclaim: to cry out or speak suddenly and vehemently

proclaim: to announce or declare in an official way

clamor: a loud uproar

disclaim: to deny interest in or connection with

reclaim: to claim or demand the return of a right or possession

CLI: to lean toward

decline: to cause to slope or incline downward

recline: to lean back

climax: the most intense point in the development of something

proclivity: inclination, bias

disinclination: aversion, distaste

CO/COL/COM/CON: with, together

connect: to bind or fasten together

coerce: to compel by force, intimidation, or authority

compatible: capable of existing together in harmony

collide: to strike one another with a forceful impact

collaborate: to work with another, cooperate

conciliate: to placate, win over

commensurate: suitable in measure, proportionate

COUR/CUR: running; a course

recur: to happen again

curriculum: the regular course of study

courier: a messenger traveling in haste who bears news

excursion: a short journey or trip

cursive: handwriting in flowing strokes with the letters joined together

concur: to accord in opinion; agree

incursion: a hostile entrance into a place, esp. suddenly

cursory: going rapidly over something; hasty; superficial

CRE/CRESC/CRET: to grow

accrue: to be added as a matter of periodic gain

creation: the act of producing or causing to exist

increase: to make greater in any respect

increment: something added or gained; an addition or increase

accretion: an increase by natural growth

CRED: to believe; to trust

incredible: unbelievable

credentials: anything that provides the basis for belief

credo: any formula of belief

credulity: willingness to believe or trust too readily

credit: trustworthiness

CRYP: hidden

crypt: a subterranean chamber or vault

apocryphal: of doubtful authorship or authenticity

cryptology: the science of interpreting secret writings, codes, ciphers, and the like

cryptography: procedures of making and using secret writing

CUB/CUMB: to lie down

cubicle: any small space or compartment that is partitioned off

succumb: to give away to superior force; yield

incubate: to sit upon for the purpose of hatching

incumbent: holding an indicated position

recumbent: lying down; reclining; leaning

CULP: blame

culprit: a person guilty for an offense

culpable: deserving blame or censure

inculpate: to charge with fault

mea culpa: through my fault; my fault

DAC/DOC: to teach

doctor: someone licensed to practice medicine; a learned person

doctrine: a particular principle advocated, as of a government or religion

indoctrinate: to imbue a person with learning

docile: easily managed or handled; tractable

didactic: intended for instruction

DE: away, off, down, completely, reversal

descend: to move from a higher to a lower place

decipher: to make out the meaning; to interpret

defile: to make foul, dirty, or unclean

defame: to attack the good name or reputation of

deferential: respectful; to yield to judgment

delineate: to trace the outline of; sketch or trace in outline

DEM: people

democracy: government by the people

epidemic: affecting at the same time a large number of people, and spreading from person to person

endemic: peculiar to a particular people or locality

pandemic: general, universal

demographics: vital and social statistics of populations

DI/DIA: apart, through

dialogue: conversation between two or more persons

diagnose: to determine the identity of something from the symptoms

dilate: to make wider or larger; to cause to expand

dilatory: inclined to delay or procrastinate

dichotomy: division into two parts, kinds, etcetera

DIC/DICT/DIT: to say; to tell; to use words

dictionary: a book containing a selection of the words of a language

predict: to tell in advance

verdict: judgment, decree

interdict: to forbid; prohibit

DIGN: worth

dignity: nobility or elevation of character; worthiness

dignitary: a person who holds a high rank or office

deign: to think fit or in accordance with one's dignity

condign: well deserved; fitting; adequate

disdain: to look upon or treat with contempt

DIS/DIF: away from, apart, reversal, not

disperse: to drive or send off in various directions

disseminate: to scatter or spread widely; promulgate

dissipate: to scatter wastefully

dissuade: to deter by advice or persuasion

diffuse: to pour out and spread, as in a fluid

DOG/DOX: opinion

orthodox: sound or correct in opinion or doctrine

paradox: an opinion or statement contrary to accepted opinion

dogma: a system of tenets, as of a church

DOL: suffer, pain

condolence: expression of sympathy with one who is suffering

indolence: a state of being lazy or slothful

doleful: sorrowful, mournful

dolorous: full of pain or sorrow, grievous

DON/DOT/DOW: to give

donate: to present as a gift or contribution

pardon: kind indulgence, forgiveness

antidote: something that prevents or counteracts ill effects

anecdote: a short narrative about an interesting event

endow: to provide with a permanent fund

DUB: doubt

dubious: doubtful

dubiety: doubtfulness

indubitable: unquestionable

DUC/DUCT: to lead

abduct: to carry off or lead away

conduct: personal behavior, way of acting

conducive: contributive, helpful

induce: to lead or move by influence

induct: to install in a position with formal ceremonies

produce: to bring into existence; give cause to

DUR: hard

endure: to hold out against; to sustain without yielding

durable: able to resist decay

duress: compulsion by threat, coercion

dour: sullen, gloomy

duration: the length of time something exists

DYS: faulty, abnormal

dystrophy: faulty or inadequate nutrition or development

dyspepsia: impaired digestion

dyslexia: an impairment of the ability to read due to a brain defect

dysfunctional: poorly functioning

E/EF/EX: out, out of, from, former, completely

evade: to escape from, avoid

exclude: to shut out; to leave out

extricate: to disentangle, release

exonerate: to free or declare free from blame

expire: to come to an end, cease to be valid

efface: to rub or wipe out; surpass, eclipse

EPI: upon

epidemic: affecting a large number of people at the same time and spreading from person to person

epilogue: a concluding part added to a literary work

epidermis: the outer layer of the skin

epigram: a witty or pointed saying tersely expressed

epithet: a word or phrase, used invectively as a term of abuse

EQU: equal, even

equation: the act of making equal

adequate: equal to the requirement or occasion

equidistant: equally distant

iniquity: gross injustice; wickedness

ERR: to wander

err: to go astray in thought or belief, to be mistaken

error: a deviation from accuracy or correctness

erratic: deviating from the proper or usual course in conduct

arrant: downright, thorough, notorious

ESCE: becoming

adolescent: between childhood and adulthood

obsolescent: becoming obsolete

incandescent: glowing with heat, shining

convalescent: recovering from illness

reminiscent: reminding or suggestive of

EU: good, well

euphemism: pleasant-sounding term for something unpleasant

eulogy: speech or writing in praise or commendation

eugenics: improvement of qualities of race by control of inherited characteristics

euthanasia: killing a person painlessly, usually one who has an incurable, painful disease

euphony: pleasantness of sound

EXTRA: outside, beyond

extraordinary: beyond the ordinary

extract: to take out, obtain against a person's will

extradite: to hand over (person accused of crime) to state where crime was committed

extrasensory: derived by means other than known senses

extrapolate: to estimate (unknown facts or values) from known data

FAB/FAM: speak

fable: fictional tale, esp. legendary

affable: friendly, courteous

ineffable: too great for description in words; that which must not be uttered

famous: well known, celebrated

defame: attack good name of

FAC/FIC/FIG/FAIT/FEIT/FY: to do; to make

factory: building for manufacture of goods

faction: small dissenting group within larger one, esp. in politics

deficient: incomplete or insufficient

prolific: producing many offspring or much output

configuration: manner of arrangement, shape

ratify: to confirm or accept by formal consent

effigy: sculpture or model of person

counterfeit: imitation, forgery

FER: to bring; to carry; to bear

offer: to present for acceptance, refusal, or consideration

confer: to grant, bestow

referendum: to vote on political question open to the entire electorate proffer: to offer

proliferate: to reproduce; produce rapidly

FERV: to boil; to bubble

fervor: passion, zeal

fervid: ardent, intense

effervescent: with the quality of giving off bubbles of gas

FID: faith, trust

confide: to entrust with a secret

affidavit: written statement on oath

fidelity: faithfulness, loyalty

fiduciary: of a trust; held or given in trust

infidel: disbeliever in the supposed true religion

FIN: end

final: at the end; coming last

confine: to keep or restrict within certain limits; imprison

definitive: decisive, unconditional, final

infinite: boundless; endless

infinitesimal: infinitely or very small

FLAG/FLAM: to burn

flammable: easily set on fire

flambeau: a lighted torch

flagrant: blatant, scandalous

conflagration: a large destructive fire

FLECT/FLEX: to bend

deflect: to bend or turn aside from a purpose

flexible: able to bend without breaking

inflect: to change or vary pitch of

reflect: to throw back

genuflect: to bend knee, esp. in worship

FLU/FLUX: to flow

fluid: substance, esp. gas or liquid, capable of flowing freely

fluctuation: something that varies, rising and falling

effluence: flowing out of (light, electricity, etc.)

confluence: merging into one

mellifluous: pleasing, musical

FORE: before

foresight: care or provision for future

foreshadow: be warning or indication of (future event)

forestall: to prevent by advance action

forthright: straightforward, outspoken, decisive

FORT: chance

fortune: chance or luck in human affairs

fortunate: lucky, auspicious

fortuitous: happening by luck

FORT: strength

fortify: to provide with fortifications; strengthen

fortissimo: very loud

forte: strong point; something a person does well

FRA/FRAC/FRAG/FRING: to break

fracture: breakage, esp. of a bone

fragment: a part broken off

fractious: irritable, peevish

refractory: stubborn, unmanageable, rebellious

infringe: to break or violate (a law, etc.)

FUS: to pour

profuse: lavish, extravagant, copious

fusillade: continuous discharge of firearms or outburst of criticism

suffuse: to spread throughout or over from within

diffuse: to spread widely or thinly

infusion: infusing; liquid extract so obtained

GEN: birth, creation, race, kind

generous: giving or given freely

genetics: study of heredity and variation among animals and plants

gender: classification roughly corresponding to the two sexes and sexlessness

carcinogenic: producing cancer

congenital: existing or as such from birth

progeny: offspring, descendants

miscegenation: interbreeding of races

GN/GNO: know

agnostic: person who believes that the existence of God is not provable ignore: to refuse to take notice of

ignoramus: a person lacking knowledge, uninformed

recognize: to identify as already known

incognito: with one's name or identity concealed

prognosis: to forecast, especially of disease

diagnose: to make an identification of disease or fault from symptoms

GRAD/GRESS: to step

progress: forward movement

aggressive: given to hostile act or feeling

degrade: to humiliate, dishonor, reduce to lower rank

digress: to depart from main subject

egress: going out; way out

regress: to move backward, revert to an earlier state

GRAT: pleasing

grateful: thankful

ingratiate: to bring oneself into favor

gratuity: money given for good service

gracious: kindly, esp. to inferiors; merciful

HER/HES: to stick

coherent: logically consistent; having waves in phase and of one wavelength

adhesive: tending to remain in memory; sticky; an adhesive substance

inherent: involved in the constitution or essential character of something

adherent: able to adhere; believer or advocate of a particular thing

heredity: the qualities genetically derived from one's ancestors and the transmission of those qualities

(H)ETERO: different

heterosexual: of or pertaining to sexual orientation toward members of the opposite sex; relating to different sexes

heterogeneous: of other origin: not originating in the body

heterodox: different from acknowledged standard; holding unorthodox opinions or doctrines

(H)OM: same

homogeneous: of the same or a similar kind of nature; of uniform structure of composition throughout

homonym: one of two or more words spelled and pronounced alike but different in meaning

homosexual: of, relating to, or exhibiting sexual desire toward a member of one's own sex

anomaly: deviation from the common rule

homeostasis: a relatively stable state of equilibrium

HYPER: over, excessive

hyperactive: excessively active

hyperbole: purposeful exaggeration for effect

hyperglycemia: an abnormally high concentration of sugar in the blood

HYPO: under, beneath, less than

hypodermic: relating to the parts beneath the skin

hypochondriac: one affected by extreme depression of mind or spirits often centered on imaginary physical ailments

hypocritical: affecting virtues or qualities one does not have

hypothesis: assumption subject to proof

IDIO: one's own

idiot: an utterly stupid person

idiom: a language, dialect, or style of speaking particular to a people

idiosyncrasy: peculiarity of temperament; eccentricity

IM/IN/EM/EN: in, into

embrace: to clasp in the arms; to include or contain

enclose: to close in on all sides

intrinsic: belonging to a thing by its very nature

influx: the act of flowing in; inflow

implicit: not expressly stated; implied

incarnate: given a bodily, esp. a human, form

indigenous: native; innate, natural

IM/IN: not, without

inactive: not active

innocuous: not harmful or injurious

indolence: showing a disposition to avoid exertion; slothful

impartial: not partial or biased; just

indigent: deficient in what is requisite

INTER: between, among

interstate: connecting or jointly involving states

interim: a temporary or provisional arrangement; meantime

interloper: one who intrudes in the domain of others

intermittent: stopping or ceasing for a time

intersperse: to scatter here and there

JECT: to throw; to throw down

inject: to place (quality, etc.) where needed in something

dejected: sad, depressed

eject: to throw out, expel

conjecture: formation of opinion on incomplete information

abject: utterly hopeless, humiliating, or wretched

JOIN/JUNCT: to meet; to join

junction: the act of joining; combining

adjoin: to be next to and joined with

subjugate: to conquer

rejoinder: to reply, retort

junta: (usually military) clique taking power after a coup d'état

JUR: to swear

perjury: willful lying while on oath

abjure: to renounce on oath

adjure: to beg or command

LAV/LUT/LUV: to wash

lavatory: a room with equipment for washing hands and face

dilute: to make thinner or weaker by the addition of water

pollute: to make foul or unclean

deluge: a great flood of water

antediluvian: before the biblical flood; extremely old

ablution: act of cleansing

LECT/LEG: to select, to choose

collect: to gather together or assemble

elect: to choose; to decide

select: to choose with care

eclectic: selecting ideas, etc. from various sources

predilection: preference, liking

LEV: lift, light, rise

relieve: to mitigate; to free from a burden

alleviate: to make easier to endure, lessen

relevant: bearing on or pertinent to information at hand

levee: embankment against river flooding

levitate: to rise in the air or cause to rise

levity: humor, frivolity, gaiety

LOC/LOG/LOQU: word, speech

dialogue: conversation, esp. in a literary work

elocution: art of clear and expressive speaking

prologue: introduction to poem, play, etc.

eulogy: speech or writing in praise of someone

colloquial: of ordinary or familiar conversation

grandiloquent: pompous or inflated in language

loquacious: talkative

LUC/LUM/LUS: light

illustrate: to make intelligible with examples or analogies

illuminate: to supply or brighten with light

illustrious: highly distinguished

translucent: permitting light to pass through

lackluster: lacking brilliance or radiance

lucid: easily understood, intelligible

luminous: bright, brilliant, glowing

LUD/LUS: to play

allude: to refer casually or indirectly

illusion: something that deceives by producing a false impression of reality

ludicrous: ridiculous, laughable

delude: to mislead the mind or judgment of, deceive

elude: to avoid capture or escape defection by

prelude: a preliminary to an action, event, etc.

MAG/MAJ/MAX: big

magnify: to increase the apparent size of

magnitude: greatness of size, extent, or dimensions

maximum: the highest amount, value, or degree attained

magnate: a powerful or influential person

magnanimous: generous in forgiving an insult or injury

maxim: an expression of general truth or principle

MAL/MALE: bad, ill, evil, wrong

malfunction: failure to function properly

malicious: full of or showing malice

malign: to speak harmful untruths about, to slander

malady: a disorder or disease of the body

maladroit: clumsy, tactless

malapropism: humorous misuse of a word

malfeasance: misconduct or wrongdoing often committed by a public official

malediction: a curse

MAN: hand

manual: operated by hand

manufacture: to make by hand or machinery

emancipate: to free from bondage

manifest: readily perceived by the eye or the understanding

mandate: an authoritative order or command

MIN: small

minute: a unit of time equal to one-sixtieth of an hour, or sixty seconds

minutiae: small or trivial details

miniature: a copy or model that represents something in greatly reduced size

diminish: to lessen

diminution: the act or process of diminishing

MIN: to project, to hang over

eminent: towering above others; projecting

imminent: about to occur; impending

prominent: projecting outward

preeminent: superior to or notable above all others

minatory: menacing, threatening

MIS/MIT: to send

transmit: to send from one person, thing, or place to another

emissary: a messenger or agent sent to represent the interests of another

intermittent: stopping and starting at intervals

remit: to send money

remission: a lessening of intensity or degree

MISC: mixed

miscellaneous: made up of a variety of parts or ingredients

miscegenation: the interbreeding of races, esp. marriage between white and nonwhite persons

promiscuous: consisting of diverse and unrelated parts or individuals

MON/MONIT: to remind; to warn

monument: a structure, such as a building, tower, or sculpture, erected as a memorial

monitor: one that admonishes, cautions, or reminds

summon: to call together; convene

admonish: to counsel against something; caution

remonstrate: to say or plead in protect, objection, or reproof

premonition: forewarning, presentiment

MORPH: shape

amorphous: without definite form; lacking a specific shape

metamorphosis: a transformation, as by magic or sorcery

anthropomorphism: attribution of human characteristics to inanimate objects, animals, or natural phenomena

MORT: death

immortal: not subject to death

morbid: susceptible to preoccupation with unwholesome matters

moribund: dying, decaying

MUT: change

commute: to substitute; exchange; interchange
mutation: the process of being changed
transmutation: the act of changing from one form into another
permutation: a complete change; transformation
immutable: unchangeable, invariable

NAT/NAS/NAI: to be born

natural: present due to nature, not to artificial or man-made means
native: belonging to one by nature; inborn; innate
naive: lacking worldliness and sophistication; artless
cognate: related by blood; having a common ancestor
renaissance: rebirth, esp. referring to culture
nascent: starting to develop

NIC/NOC/NOX: harm

innocent: uncorrupted by evil, malice, or wrong-doing
noxious: injurious or harmful to health or morals
obnoxious: highly disagreeable or offensive
innocuous: having no adverse effect; harmless

NOM: rule, order

astronomy: the scientific study of the universe beyond the earth
economy: the careful or thrifty use of resources, as of income, materials, or labor
gastronomy: the art or science of good eating
taxonomy: the science, laws, or principles of classification
autonomy: independence, self-governance

NOM/NYM/NOUN/NOWN: name

synonym: a word having a meaning similar to that of another word of the same language
anonymous: having an unknown or unacknowledged name
nominal: existing in name only; negligible
nominate: to propose by name as a candidate
nomenclature: a system of names; systematic naming
acronym: a word formed from the initial letters of a name

NOUNC/NUNC: to announce

announce: to proclaim
pronounce: to articulate
renounce: to give up, especially by formal announcement

NOV/NEO/NOU: new

novice: a person new to any field or activity
renovate: to restore to an earlier condition
innovate: to begin or introduce something new
neologism: a newly coined word, phrase, or expression
neophyte: a recent convert
nouveau riche: one who has lately become rich

OB/OC/OF/OP: toward, to, against, over

obese: extremely fat, corpulent
obstinate: stubbornly adhering to an idea, inflexible
obstruct: to block or fill with obstacles
oblique: having a slanting or sloping direction
obstreperous: noisily defiant, unruly
obtuse: not sharp, pointed, or acute in any form
obfuscate: to render indistinct or dim; darken
obsequious: overly submissive

OMNI: all

omnibus: an anthology of the works of one author or of writings on related subjects
omnipresent: everywhere at one time
omnipotent: all powerful
omniscient: having infinite knowledge

PAC/PEAC: peace

appease: to bring peace to
pacify: to ease the anger or agitation of
pacifier: something or someone that eases the anger or agitation of
pact: a formal agreement, as between nations

PAN: all, everyone

panorama: an unobstructed and wide view of an extensive area
panegyric: formal or elaborate praise at an assembly
panoply: a wide-ranging and impressive array or display

pantheon: a public building containing tombs or memorials of the illustrious dead of a nation

pandemic: widespread, general, universal

PAR: equal

par: an equality in value or standing

parity: equally, as in amount, status, or character

apartheid: any system or caste that separates people according to race, etc.

disparage: to belittle, speak disrespectfully about

disparate: essentially different

PARA: next to, beside

parallel: extending in the same direction

parasite: an organism that lives on or within a plant or animal of another species, from which it obtains nutrients

parody: to imitate for purposes of satire

parable: a short, allegorical story designed to illustrate a moral lesson or religious principle

paragon: a model of excellence

paranoid: suffering from a baseless distrust of others

PAS/PAT/ PATH: feeling, suffering, disease

sympathy: harmony or agreement in feeling

empathy: the identification with the feelings or thoughts of others

compassion: a feeling of deep sympathy for someone struck by misfortune, accompanied by a desire to alleviate suffering

dispassionate: devoid of personal feeling or bias

impassive: showing or feeling no emotion

sociopath: a person whose behavior is antisocial and who lacks a sense of moral responsibility

pathogenic: causing disease

PAU/PO/POV/PU: few, little, poor

poverty: the condition of being poor

paucity: smallness of quantity; scarcity; scantiness

pauper: a person without any personal means of support

impoverish: to deplete

pusillanimous: lacking courage or resolution

puerile: childish, immature

PED: child, education

pedagogue: a teacher

pediatrician: a doctor who primarily has children as patients

pedant: one who displays learning ostentatiously

encyclopedia: book or set of books containing articles on various topics, covering all branches of knowledge or of one particular subject

PED/POD: foot

pedal: a foot-operated lever or part used to control

pedestrian: a person who travels on foot

expedite: to speed up the progress of

impede: to retard progress by means of obstacles or hindrances

podium: a small platform for an orchestra conductor, speaker, etc.

antipodes: places diametrically opposite each other on the globe

PEN/PUN: to pay; to compensate

penal: of or pertaining to punishment, as for crimes

penalty: a punishment imposed for a violation of law or rule

punitive: serving for, concerned with, or inflicting punishment

penance: a punishment undergone to express regret for a sin

penitent: contrite

PEND/PENS: to hang; to weight; to pay

depend: to rely; to place trust in

stipend: a periodic payment; fixed or regular pay

compensate: to counterbalance, offset

indispensable: absolutely necessary, essential, or requisite

appendix: supplementary material at the end of a text

appendage: a limb or other subsidiary part that diverges from the central structure

PER: completely

persistent: lasting or enduring tenaciously

perforate: to make a way through or into something

perplex: to cause to be puzzled or bewildered over what is not understood

peruse: to read with thoroughness or care

perfunctory: performed merely as routine duty

pertinacious: resolute

perspicacious: shrewd, astute

PERI: around

perimeter: the border or outer boundary of a two-dimensional figure

periscope: an optical instrument for seeing objects in an obstructed field of vision

peripatetic: walking or traveling about; itinerant

PET/PIT: to go; to seek; to strive

appetite: a desire for food or drink

compete: to strive to outdo another for acknowledgment

petition: a formally drawn request soliciting some benefit

centripetal: moving toward the center

impetuous: characterized by sudden or rash action or emotion

petulant: showing sudden irritation, esp. over some annoyance

PHIL: love

philosophy: the rational investigation of the truths and principles of being, knowledge, or conduct

philatelist: one who loves or collects postage stamps

philology: the study of literary texts to establish their authenticity and determine their meaning

bibliophile: one who loves or collects books

PLAC: to please

placid: pleasantly calm or peaceful

placebo: a substance with no pharmacological effect which acts to placate a patient who believes it to be a medicine

implacable: unable to be pleased

complacent: self-satisfied, unconcerned

complaisant: inclined or disposed to please

PLE: to fill

complete: having all parts or elements

deplete: to decrease seriously or exhaust the supply of

supplement: something added to supply a deficiency

implement: an instrument, tool, or utensil for accomplishing work

replete: abundantly supplied

plethora: excess, overabundance

PLEX/PLIC/PLY: to fold, twist, tangle, or bend

complex: composed of many interconnected parts

replica: any close copy or reproduction

implicit: not expressly stated, implied

implicate: to show to be involved, usually in an incriminating manner

duplicity: deceitfulness in speech or conduct, double-dealing

supplicate: to make humble and earnest entreaty

PON/POS/POUND: to put; to place

component: a constituent part, elemental ingredient

expose: to lay open to danger, attack, or harm

expound: to set forth in detail

juxtapose: to place close together or side by side, esp. for contract

repository: a receptacle or place where things are deposited

PORT: to carry

import: to bring in from a foreign country

export: to transmit abroad

portable: easily carried

deportment: conduct, behavior

disport: to divert or amuse oneself

importune: to urge or press with excessive persistence

POST: after

posthumous: after death

posterior: situated at the rear

posterity: succeeding in future generations collectively

post facto: after the fact

PRE: before

precarious: dependent on circumstances beyond one's control

precocious: unusually advanced or mature in mental development or talent

premonition: a feeling of anticipation over a future event

presentiment: foreboding

precedent: an act that serves as an example for subsequent situations

precept: a commandment given as a rule of action or conduct

PREHEND/PRISE: to take; to get; to seize

surprise: to strike with an unexpected feeling of wonder or astonishment

enterprise: a project undertaken

reprehensible: deserving rebuke or censure

comprise: to include or contain

reprisals: retaliation against an enemy

apprehend: to take into custody

PRO: much, for, a lot

prolific: highly fruitful

profuse: spending or giving freely

prodigal: wastefully or recklessly extravagant

prodigious: extraordinary in size, amount, or extent

proselytize: to convert or attempt to recruit

propound: to set forth for consideration

provident: having or showing foresight

PROB: to prove; to test

probe: to search or examine thoroughly

approbation: praise, consideration

opprobrium: the disgrace incurred by shameful conduct

reprobate: a depraved or wicked person

problematic: questionable

probity: honesty, high-mindedness

PUG: to fight

pugnacious: to quarrel or fight readily

impugn: to challenge as false

repugnant: objectionable or offensive

pugilist: a fighter or boxer

PUNC/PUNG/POIGN: to point; to prick

point: a sharp or tapering end

puncture: the act of piercing

pungent: caustic or sharply expressive

compunction: a feeling of uneasiness for doing wrong

punctilious: strict or exact in the observance of formalities

expunge: to erase, eliminate completely

QUE/QUIS: to seek

acquire: to come into possession of

exquisite: of special beauty or charm

conquest: vanquishment

inquisitive: given to research, eager for knowledge

query: a question, inquiry

querulous: full of complaints

perquisite: a gratuity, tip

QUI: quiet

quiet: making little or no sound

disquiet: lack of calm or peace

tranquil: free from commotion or tumult

acquiesce: to comply, give in

quiescence: the condition of being at rest, still, inactive

RID/RIS: to laugh

riddle: a conundrum

derision: the act of mockery

risible: causing laughter

ROG: to ask

interrogate: to ask questions of, esp. formally

arrogant: making claims to superior importance or rights

abrogate: to abolish by formal means

surrogate: a person appointed to act for another

derogatory: belittling, disparaging

arrogate: to claim unwarrantably or presumptuously

SACR/SANCT/SECR: sacred

sacred: devoted or dedicated to a deity or religious purpose

sacrifice: the offering of some living or inanimate thing to a deity in homage

sanctify: to make holy

sanction: authoritative permission or approval

execrable: abominable

sacrament: something regarded as possessing sacred character

sacrilege: the violation of anything sacred

SAL/SIL/SAULT/SULT: to leap, to jump

insult: to treat with contemptuous rudeness

assault: a sudden or violent attack

somersault: to roll the body end over end, making a complete revolution

salient: prominent or conspicuous

resilient: able to spring back to an original form after compression

insolent: boldly rude or disrespectful

exult: to show or feel triumphant joy

desultory: at random, unmethodical

SCI: to know

conscious: aware of one's own existence

conscience: the inner sense of what is right or wrong, impelling one toward right action

unconscionable: unscrupulous

omniscient: knowing everything

prescient: having knowledge of things before they happen

SCRIBE/SCRIP: to write

scribble: to write hastily or carelessly

describe: to tell or depict in words

script: handwriting

postscript: any addition or supplement

proscribe: to condemn as harmful or odious

ascribe: to credit or assign, as to a cause or course

conscription: draft

transcript: a written or typed copy

circumscribe: to draw a line around

SE: apart

select: to choose in preference to another

separate: to keep apart, divide

seduce: to lead astray

segregate: to separate or set apart from others

secede: to withdraw formally from an association

sequester: to remove or withdraw into solitude or retirement

sedition: incitement of discontent or rebellion against a government

SEC/SEQU: to follow

second: next after the first

prosecute: to seek to enforce by legal process

sequence: the following of one thing after another

obsequious: fawning

non sequitur: an inference or a conclusion that does not follow from the premises

SED/SESS/SID: to sit; to be still; to plan; to plot

preside: to exercise management or control

resident: a person who lives in a place

sediment: the matter that settles to the bottom of a liquid

dissident: disagreeing, as in opinion or attitude

residual: remaining, leftover

subsidiary: serving to assist or supplement

insidious: intended to entrap or beguile

assiduous: diligent, persistent, hardworking

SENS/SENT: to feel; to be aware

sense: any of the faculties by which humans and animals perceive stimuli originating outside the body

sensory: of or pertaining to the senses or sensation

sentiment: an attitude or feeling toward something

presentiment: a feeling that something is about to happen

dissent: to differ in opinion, esp. from the majority

resent: to feel or show displeasure

sentinel: a person or thing that stands watch

insensate: without feeling or sensitivity

SOL: to loosen; to free

dissolve: to make a solution of, as by mixing in a liquid

soluble: capable of being dissolved or liquefied

resolution: a formal expression of opinion or intention made

dissolution: the act or process of dissolving into parts or elements

dissolute: indifferent to moral restraints

absolution: forgiveness for wrongdoing

SPEC/SPIC/SPIT: to look; to see

perspective: one's mental view of facts, ideas, and their interrelationships

speculation: the contemplation or consideration of some subject

suspicious: inclined to suspect

spectrum: a broad range of related things that form a continuous series

retrospective: contemplative of past situations

circumspect: watchful and discreet, cautious

perspicacious: having keen mental perception and understanding

conspicuous: easily seen or noticed; readily observable

specious: deceptively attractive

STA/STI: to stand; to be in place

static: of bodies or forces at rest or in equilibrium

destitute: without means of subsistence

obstinate: stubbornly adhering to a purpose, opinion, or course of action

constitute: to make up

stasis: the state of equilibrium or inactivity caused by opposing equal forces

apostasy: renunciation of an object of one's previous loyalty

SUA: smooth

suave: smoothly agreeable or polite

persuade: to encourage; to convince

dissuade: to deter

assuage: to make less severe, ease, relieve

SUB/SUP: below

submissive: inclined or ready to submit

subsidiary: serving to assist or supplement

subliminal: existing or operating below the threshold of confidence

subtle: thin, tenuous, or rarefied

subterfuge: an artifice or expedient used to evade a rule

supposition: the act of assuming

SUPER/SUR: above

surpass: to go beyond in amount, extent, or degree

superlative: the highest kind or order

supersede: to replace in power, as by another person or thing

supercilious: arrogant, haughty, condescending

superfluous: extra, more than necessary

surmount: to get over or across, to prevail

surveillance: a watch kept over someone or something

TAC/TIC: to be silent

reticent: disposed to be silent or not to speak freely

tacit: unspoken understanding

taciturn: uncommunicative

TAIN/TEN/TENT/TIN: to hold

detain: to keep from proceeding

pertain: to have reference or relation

tenacious: holding fast

abstention: the act of refraining voluntarily

tenure: the holding or possessing of anything

tenable: capable of being held, maintained, or defended

sustenance: nourishment, means of livelihood

pertinacious: persistent, stubborn

TEND/TENS/TENT/TENU: to stretch; to thin

tension: the act of stretching or straining

tentative: of the nature of, or done as a trial, attempt

tendentious: having a predisposition towards a point of view

distend: to expand by stretching

attenuate: to weaken or reduce in force

extenuating: making less serious by offering excuses

contentious: quarrelsome, disagreeable, belligerent

THEO: god

atheist: one who does not believe in a deity or divine system

theocracy: a form of government in which a deity is recognized as the supreme ruler

theology: the study of divine things and the divine faith

apotheosis: glorification, glorified ideal

TRACT: to drag; to pull; to draw

tractor: a powerful vehicle used to pull farm machinery

attract: to draw either by physical force or by an appeal to emotions or senses

contract: a legally binding document

detract: to take away from, esp. a positive thing

abstract: to draw or pull away, remove

tractable: easily managed or controlled

protract: to prolong, draw out, extend

TRANS: across

transaction: the act of carrying on or conduct to a conclusion or settlement

transparent: easily seen through, recognized, or detected

transition: a change from one way of being to another

transgress: to violate a law, command, or moral code

transcendent: going beyond ordinary limits

intransigent: refusing to agree or compromise

US/UT: to use

abuse: to use wrongly or improperly

usage: a customary way of doing something

usurp: to seize and hold

utilitarian: efficient, functional, useful

VEN/VENT: to come or to move toward

convene: to assemble for some public purpose

venturesome: showing a disposition to undertake risks

intervene: to come between disputing factions, mediate

contravene: to come into conflict with

adventitious: accidental

VER: truth

verdict: any judgment or decision

veracious: habitually truthful

verity: truthfulness

verisimilitude: the appearance or semblance of truth

aver: to affirm, to declare to be true

VERD: green

verdant: green with vegetation; inexperienced

verdure: fresh, rich vegetation

VERS/VERT: to turn

controversy: a public dispute involving a matter of opinion

revert: to return to a former habit

diverse: of a different kind, form, character

aversion: dislike

introvert: a person concerned primarily with inner thoughts and feelings

extrovert: an outgoing person

inadvertent: unintentional

covert: hidden, clandestine

avert: to turn away from

VI: life

vivid: strikingly bright or intense

vicarious: performed, exercised, received, or suffered in place of another

viable: capable of living

vivacity: the quality of being lively, animated, spirited

joie de vivre: joy of life (French expression)

convivial: sociable

VID/VIS: to see

evident: plain or clear to the sight or understanding

video: the elements of television pertaining to the transmission or reception of the image

adviser: one who gives counsel

survey: to view in a general or comprehensive way

vista: a view or prospect

VIL: base, mean

vilify: to slander, to defame

revile: to criticize with harsh language

vile: loathsome, unpleasant

VOC/VOK: to call

vocabulary: the stock of words used by or known to a particular person or group

advocate: to support or urge by argument

equivocate: to use ambiguous or unclear expressions

vocation: a particular occupation

avocation: something one does in addition to a principle occupation

vociferous: crying out noisily

convoke: to call together

invoke: to call on a deity

VOL: to wish

voluntary: undertaken of one's own accord or by free choice

malevolent: characterized by or expressing bad will

benevolent: characterized by or expressing goodwill

volition: free choice, free will; act of choosing

VOR: to eat

voracious: having a great appetite

carnivorous: meat-eating

omnivorous: eating or absorbing everything

Top GRE Words in Context

The GRE tests the same kinds of words over and over again. Here you will find the most popular GRE words with their definitions in context to help you to remember them. If you see a word that's unfamiliar to you, take a moment to study the definition and, most importantly, reread the sentence with the word's definition in mind.

Remember: Learning vocabulary words in context is one of the best ways for your brain to retain the words' meanings. A broader vocabulary will serve you well on all four GRE Verbal question types and will also be extremely helpful in the Analytical Writing section.

ABATE: to reduce in amount, degree, or severity

As the hurricane's force ABATED, the winds dropped and the sea became calm.

ABSCOND: to leave secretly

The patron ABSCONDED from the restaurant without paying his bill by sneaking out the back door.

ABSTAIN: to choose not to do something:

She ABSTAINED from choosing a mouthwatering dessert from the tray.

ABYSS: an extremely deep hole

The submarine dove into the ABYSS to chart the previously unseen depths.

ADULTERATE: to make impure

The chef made his ketchup last longer by ADULTERATING it with water.

ADVOCATE: to speak in favor of

The vegetarian ADVOCATED a diet containing no meat.

AESTHETIC: concerning the appreciation of beauty

Followers of the AESTHETIC Movement regarded the pursuit of beauty as the only true purpose of art.

AGGRANDIZE: to increase in power, influence, and reputation

The supervisor sought to AGGRANDIZE herself by claiming that the achievements of her staff were actually her own.

ALLEVIATE: to make more bearable

Taking aspirin helps to ALLEVIATE a headache.

AMALGAMATE: to combine; to mix together

Giant Industries AMALGAMATED with Mega Products to form Giant-Mega Products Incorporated.

AMBIGUOUS: doubtful or uncertain; able to be interpreted several ways

The directions she gave were so AMBIGUOUS that we disagreed on which way to turn.

AMELIORATE: to make better; to improve

The doctor was able to AMELIORATE the patient's suffering using painkillers.

ANACHRONISM: something out of place in time

The aged hippie used ANACHRONISTIC phrases like *groovy* and *far out* that had not been popular for years.

ANALOGOUS: similar or alike in some way; equivalent to

In the Newtonian construct for explaining the existence of God, the universe is ANALOGOUS to a mechanical timepiece, the creation of a divinely intelligent "clockmaker."

ANOMALY: deviation from what is normal

Albino animals may display too great an ANOMALY in their coloring to attract normally colored mates.

ANTAGONIZE: to annoy or provoke to anger

The child discovered that he could ANTAGONIZE the cat by pulling its tail.

ANTIPATHY: extreme dislike

The ANTIPATHY between the French and the English regularly erupted into open warfare.

APATHY: lack of interest or emotion

The APATHY of voters is so great that less than half the people who are eligible to vote actually bother to do so.

ARBITRATE: to judge a dispute between two opposing parties

Since the couple could not come to agreement, a judge was forced to ARBITRATE their divorce proceedings.

ARCHAIC: ancient, old-fashioned

Her ARCHAIC Commodore computer could not run the latest software.

ARDOR: intense and passionate feeling

Bishop's ARDOR for the landscape was evident when he passionately described the beauty of the scenic Hudson Valley.

ARTICULATE: able to speak clearly and expressively

She is such an ARTICULATE defender of labor that unions are among her strongest supporters.

ASSUAGE: to make something unpleasant less severe

Serena used aspirin to ASSUAGE her pounding headache.

ATTENUATE: to reduce in force or degree; to weaken

The Bill of Rights ATTENUATED the traditional power of governments to change laws at will.

AUDACIOUS: fearless and daring

Her AUDACIOUS nature allowed her to fulfill her dream of skydiving.

AUSTERE: severe or stern in appearance; undecorated

The lack of decoration makes military barracks seem AUSTERE to the civilian eye.

BANAL: predictable, clichéd, boring

He used BANAL phrases like *Have a nice day*, or *Another day, another dollar.*

BOLSTER: to support; to prop up

The presence of giant footprints BOLSTERED the argument that Sasquatch was in the area.

BOMBASTIC: pompous in speech and manner

The ranting of the radio talk-show host was mostly BOMBASTIC; his boasting and outrageous claims had no basis in fact.

CACOPHONY: harsh, jarring noise

The junior high orchestra created an almost unbearable CACOPHONY as they tried to tune their instruments.

CANDID: impartial and honest in speech

The observations of a child can be charming since they are CANDID and unpretentious.

CAPRICIOUS: changing one's mind quickly and often

Queen Elizabeth I was quite CAPRICIOUS; her courtiers could never be sure which of their number would catch her fancy.

CASTIGATE: to punish or criticize harshly

Many Americans are amazed at how harshly the authorities in Singapore CASTIGATE perpetrators of what would be considered minor crimes in the United States.

CATALYST: something that brings about a change in something else

The imposition of harsh taxes was the CATALYST that finally brought on the revolution.

CAUSTIC: biting in wit

Dorothy Parker gained her reputation for CAUSTIC wit from her cutting, yet clever, insults.

CHAOS: great disorder or confusion

In many religious traditions, God created an ordered universe from CHAOS.

CHAUVINIST: someone prejudiced in favor of a group to which he or she belongs

The attitude that men are inherently superior to women and therefore must be obeyed is common among male CHAUVINISTS.

CHICANERY: deception by means of craft or guile

Dishonest used car sales people often use CHICANERY to sell their beat-up old cars.

COGENT: convincing and well reasoned

Swayed by the COGENT argument of the defense, the jury had no choice but to acquit the defendant.

CONDONE: to overlook, pardon, or disregard

Some theorists believe that failing to prosecute minor crimes is the same as CONDONING an air of lawlessness.

CONVOLUTED: intricate and complicated

Although many people bought *A Brief History of Time*, few could follow its CONVOLUTED ideas and theories.

CORROBORATE: to provide supporting evidence

Fingerprints CORROBORATED the witness's testimony that he saw the defendant in the victim's apartment.

CREDULOUS: too trusting; gullible

Although some four-year-olds believe in the Easter Bunny, only the most CREDULOUS nine-year-olds also believe in him.

CRESCENDO: steadily increasing volume or force

The CRESCENDO of tension became unbearable as Evel Knievel prepared to jump his motorcycle over the school buses.

DECORUM: appropriateness of behavior or conduct; propriety

The countess complained that the vulgar peasants lacked the DECORUM appropriate for a visit to the palace.

DEFERENCE: respect, courtesy

The respectful young law clerk treated the Supreme Court justice with the utmost DEFERENCE.

DERIDE: to speak of or treat with contempt; to mock

The awkward child was often DERIDED by his "cooler" peers.

DESICCATE: to dry out thoroughly

After a few weeks of lying on the desert's baking sands, the cow's carcass became completely DESICCATED.

DESULTORY: jumping from one thing to another; disconnected

Diane had a DESULTORY academic record; she had changed majors 12 times in three years.

DIATRIBE: an abusive, condemnatory speech

The trucker bellowed a DIATRIBE at the driver who had cut him off.

DIFFIDENT: lacking self-confidence

Steve's DIFFIDENT manner during the job interview stemmed from his nervous nature and lack of experience in the field.

DILATE: to make larger; to expand

When you enter a darkened room, the pupils of your eyes DILATE to let in more light.

DILATORY: intended to delay

The congressman used DILATORY measures to delay the passage of the bill.

DILETTANTE: someone with an amateurish and superficial interest in a topic

Jerry's friends were such DILETTANTES that they seemed to have new jobs and hobbies every week.

DIRGE: a funeral hymn or mournful speech

Melville wrote the poem "A DIRGE for James McPherson" for the funeral of a Union general who was killed in 1864.

DISABUSE: to set right; to free from error

Galileo's observations DISABUSED scholars of the notion that the sun revolved around the earth.

DISCERN: to perceive; to recognize

It is easy to DISCERN the difference between butter and butter-flavored topping.

DISPARATE: fundamentally different; entirely unlike

Although the twins appear to be identical physically, their personalities are DISPARATE.

DISSEMBLE: to present a false appearance; to disguise one's real intentions or character

The villain could DISSEMBLE to the police no longer—he admitted the deed and tore up the floor to reveal the body of the old man.

DISSONANCE: a harsh and disagreeable combination, of ten of sounds

Cognitive DISSONANCE is the inner conflict produced when long-standing beliefs are contradicted by new evidence.

DOGMA: a firmly held opinion, often a religious belief

Linus's central DOGMA was that children who believed in the Great Pumpkin would be rewarded.

DOGMATIC: dictatorial in one's opinions

The dictator was DOGMATIC—he, and only he, was right.

DUPE: to deceive; a person who is easily deceived

Bugs Bunny was able to DUPE Elmer Fudd by dressing up as a lady rabbit.

ECLECTIC: selecting from or made up from a variety of sources

Budapest's architecture is an ECLECTIC mix of Eastern and Western styles.

EFFICACY: effectiveness

The EFFICACY of penicillin was unsurpassed when it was first introduced; the drug completely eliminated almost all bacterial infections for which it was administered.

ELEGY: a sorrowful poem or speech

Although Thomas Gray's "ELEGY Written in a Country Churchyard" is about death and loss, it urges its readers to endure this life and to trust in spirituality.

ELOQUENT: persuasive and moving, especially in speech

The Gettysburg Address is moving not only because of its lofty sentiments but also because of its ELOQUENT words.

EMULATE: to copy; to try to equal or excel

The graduate student sought to EMULATE his professor in every way, copying not only how she taught but also how she conducted herself outside of class.

ENERVATE: to reduce in strength

The guerrillas hoped that a series of surprise attacks would ENERVATE the regular army.

ENGENDER: to produce, cause, or bring about

His fear and hatred of clowns was ENGENDERED when he witnessed the death of his father at the hands of a clown.

ENIGMA: a puzzle; a mystery

Speaking in riddles and dressed in old robes, the artist gained a reputation as something of an ENIGMA.

ENUMERATE: to count, list, or itemize

Moses returned from the mountain with tablets on which the commandments were ENUMERATED.

EPHEMERAL: lasting a short time

The lives of mayflies seem EPHEMERAL to us, since the flies' average life span is a matter of hours.

EQUIVOCATE: to use expressions of double meaning in order to mislead

When faced with criticism of her policies, the politician EQUIVOCATED and left all parties thinking she agreed with them.

ERRATIC: wandering and unpredictable

The plot seemed predictable until it suddenly took a series of ERRATIC turns that surprised the audience.

ERUDITE: learned, scholarly, bookish

The annual meeting of philosophy professors was a gathering of the most ERUDITE, well-published individuals in the field.

ESOTERIC: known or understood by only a few

Only a handful of experts are knowledgeable about the ESOTERIC world of particle physics.

ESTIMABLE: admirable

Most people consider it ESTIMABLE that Mother Teresa spent her life helping the poor of India.

EULOGY: speech in praise of someone

His best friend gave the EULOGY, outlining his many achievements and talents.

EUPHEMISM: use of an inoffensive word or phrase in place of a more distasteful one

The funeral director preferred to use the EUPHEMISM *sleeping* instead of the word *dead*.

EXACERBATE: to make worse

It is unwise to take aspirin to try to relieve heartburn; instead of providing relief, the drug will only EXACERBATE the problem.

EXCULPATE: to clear from blame; prove innocent

The adversarial legal system is intended to convict those who are guilty and to EXCULPATE those who are innocent.

EXIGENT: urgent; requiring immediate action

The patient was losing blood so rapidly that it was EXIGENT to stop the source of the bleeding.

EXONERATE: to clear of blame

The fugitive was EXONERATED when another criminal confessed to committing the crime.

EXPLICIT: clearly stated or shown; forthright in expression

The owners of the house left a list of EXPLICIT instructions detailing their house-sitter's duties, including a schedule for watering the house plants.

FANATICAL: acting excessively enthusiastic; filled with extreme, unquestioned devotion

The stormtroopers were FANATICAL in their devotion to the emperor, readily sacrificing their lives for him.

FAWN: to grovel

The understudy FAWNED over the director in hopes of being cast in the part on a permanent basis.

FERVID: intensely emotional; feverish

The fans of Maria Callas were unusually FERVID, doing anything to catch a glimpse of the great opera singer.

FLORID: excessively decorated or embellished

The palace had been decorated in a FLORID style; every surface had been carved and gilded.

FOMENT: to arouse or incite

The protesters tried to FOMENT feeling against the war through their speeches and demonstrations.

FRUGALITY: a tendency to be thrifty or cheap

Scrooge McDuck's FRUGALITY was so great that he accumulated enough wealth to fill a giant storehouse with money.

GARRULOUS: tending to talk a lot

The GARRULOUS parakeet distracted its owner with its continuous talking.

GREGARIOUS: outgoing, sociable

She was so GREGARIOUS that when she found herself alone, she felt quite sad.

GUILE: deceit or trickery

Since he was not fast enough to catch the roadrunner on foot, the coyote resorted to GUILE in an effort to trap his enemy.

GULLIBLE: easily deceived

The con man pretended to be a bank officer so as to fool GULLIBLE bank customers into giving him their account information.

HOMOGENOUS: of a similar kind

The class was fairly HOMOGENOUS, since almost all of the students were senior journalism majors.

ICONOCLAST: one who opposes established beliefs, customs, and institutions

His lack of regard for traditional beliefs soon established him as an ICONOCLAST.

IMPERTURBABLE: not capable of being disturbed

The counselor had so much experience dealing with distraught children that she seemed IMPERTURBABLE, even when faced with the wildest tantrums.

IMPERVIOUS: impossible to penetrate; incapable of being affected

A good raincoat will be IMPERVIOUS to moisture.

IMPETUOUS: quick to act without thinking

It is not good for an investment broker to be IMPETUOUS, since much thought should be given to all the possible options.

IMPLACABLE: unable to be calmed down or made peaceful

His rage at the betrayal was so great that he remained IMPLACABLE for weeks.

INCHOATE: not fully formed; disorganized

The ideas expressed in Nietzsche's mature work also appear in an INCHOATE form in his earliest writing.

INGENUOUS: showing innocence or childlike simplicity

She was so INGENUOUS that her friends feared that her innocence and trustfulness would be exploited when she visited the big city.

INIMICAL: hostile, unfriendly

Even though the children had grown up together, they were INIMICAL to each other at school.

INNOCUOUS: harmless

Some snakes are poisonous, but most species are INNOCUOUS and pose no danger to humans.

INSIPID: lacking interest or flavor

The critic claimed that the painting was INSIPID, containing no interesting qualities at all.

INTRANSIGENT: uncompromising; refusing to be reconciled

The professor was INTRANSIGENT on the deadline, insisting that everyone turn the assignment in at the same time.

INUNDATE: to overwhelm; to cover with water

The tidal wave INUNDATED Atlantis, which was lost beneath the water.

IRASCIBLE: easily made angry

Attila the Hun's IRASCIBLE and violent nature made all who dealt with him fear for their lives.

LACONIC: using few words

She was a LACONIC poet who built her reputation on using words as sparingly as possible.

LAMENT: to express sorrow; to grieve

The children continued to LAMENT the death of the goldfish weeks after its demise.

LAUD: to give praise; to glorify

Parades and fireworks were staged to LAUD the success of the rebels.

LAVISH: to give unsparingly (v.); extremely generous or extravagant (adj.)

She LAVISHED the puppy with so many treats that it soon became overweight and spoiled.

LETHARGIC: acting in an indifferent or slow, sluggish manner

The clerk was so LETHARGIC that, even when the store was slow, he always had a long line in front of him.

LOQUACIOUS: talkative

She was naturally LOQUACIOUS, which was a problem in situations in which listening was more important than talking.

LUCID: clear and easily understood

The explanations were written in a simple and LUCID manner so that students were immediately able to apply what they learned.

LUMINOUS: bright, brilliant, glowing

The park was bathed in LUMINOUS sunshine, which warmed the bodies and the souls of the visitors.

MALINGER: to evade responsibility by pretending to be ill

A common way to avoid the draft was by MALINGERING—pretending to be mentally or physically ill so as to avoid being taken by the Army.

MALLEABLE: capable of being shaped

Gold is the most MALLEABLE of precious metals; it can easily be formed into almost any shape.

METAPHOR: a figure of speech comparing two different things; a symbol

The METAPHOR "a sea of troubles" suggests a lot of troubles by comparing their number to the vastness of the sea.

METICULOUS: extremely careful about details

To find all the clues at the crime scene, the investigators METICULOUSLY examined every inch of the area.

MISANTHROPE: a person who dislikes others

The character Scrooge in *A Christmas Carol* is such a MISANTHROPE that even the sight of children singing makes him angry.

MITIGATE: to soften; to lessen

A judge may MITIGATE a sentence if she decides that a person committed a crime out of need.

MOLLIFY: to calm or make less severe

Their argument was so intense that is was difficult to believe any compromise would MOLLIFY them.

MONOTONY: lack of variation

The MONOTONY of the sound of the dripping faucet almost drove the research assistant crazy.

NAIVE: lacking sophistication or experience

Having never traveled before, the elementary school students were more NAIVE than their high school counterparts on the field trip.

OBDURATE: hardened in feeling; resistant to persuasion

The president was completely OBDURATE on the issue, and no amount of persuasion would change his mind.

OBSEQUIOUS: overly submissive and eager to please

The OBSEQUIOUS new associate made sure to compliment her supervisor's tie and agree with him on every issue.

OBSTINATE: stubborn, unyielding

The OBSTINATE child could not be made to eat any food that he disliked.

OBVIATE: to prevent; to make unnecessary

The river was shallow enough to wade across at many points, which OBVIATED the need for a bridge.

OCCLUDE: to stop up; to prevent the passage of

A shadow is thrown across the earth's surface during a solar eclipse, when the light from the sun is OCCLUDED by the moon.

ONEROUS: troublesome and oppressive; burdensome

The assignment was so extensive and difficult to manage that it proved ONEROUS to the team in charge of it.

OPAQUE: impossible to see through; preventing the passage of light

The heavy buildup of dirt and grime on the windows almost made them OPAQUE.

OPPROBRIUM: public disgrace

After the scheme to embezzle the elderly was made public, the treasurer resigned in utter OPPROBRIUM.

OSTENTATION: excessive showiness

The OSTENTATION of the Sun King's court is evident in the lavish decoration and luxuriousness of his palace at Versailles.

PARADOX: a contradiction or dilemma

It is a PARADOX that those most in need of medical attention are often those least able to obtain it.

PARAGON: model of excellence or perfection

She is the PARAGON of what a judge should be: honest, intelligent, hardworking, and just.

PEDANT: someone who shows off learning

The graduate instructor's tedious and excessive commentary on the subject soon gained her a reputation as a PEDANT.

PERFIDIOUS: willing to betray one's trust

The actress's PERFIDIOUS companion revealed all of her intimate secrets to the gossip columnist.

PERFUNCTORY: done in a routine way; indifferent

The machinelike bank teller processed the transaction and gave the waiting customer a PERFUNCTORY smile.

PERMEATE: to penetrate

This miraculous new cleaning fluid is able to PERMEATE stains and dissolve them in minutes!

PHILANTHROPY: charity; a desire or effort to promote goodness

New York's Metropolitan Museum of Art owes much of its collection to the PHILANTHROPY of private collectors who willed their estates to the museum.

PLACATE: to soothe or pacify

The burglar tried to PLACATE the snarling dog by saying "Nice doggy," and offering it a treat.

PLASTIC: able to be molded, altered, or bent

The new material was very PLASTIC and could be formed into products of vastly different shape.

PLETHORA: excess

Assuming that more was better, the defendant offered the judge a PLETHORA of excuses.

PRAGMATIC: practical as opposed to idealistic

While daydreaming gamblers think they can get rich by frequenting casinos, PRAGMATIC gamblers realize that the odds are heavily stacked against them.

PRECIPITATE: to throw violently or bring about abruptly; lacking deliberation

Upon learning that the couple married after knowing each other only two months, friends and family members expected such a PRECIPITATE marriage to end in divorce.

PREVARICATE: to lie or deviate from the truth

Rather than admit that he had overslept again, the employee PREVARICATED and claimed that heavy traffic had prevented him from arriving at work on time.

PRISTINE: fresh and clean; uncorrupted

Since concerted measures had been taken to prevent looting, the archeological site was still PRISTINE when researchers arrived.

PRODIGAL: lavish, wasteful

The PRODIGAL son quickly wasted all of his inheritance on a lavish lifestyle devoted to pleasure.

PROLIFERATE: to increase in number quickly

Although she only kept two guinea pigs initially, they PROLIFERATED to such an extent that she soon had dozens.

PROPITIATE: to conciliate; to appease

The management PROPITIATED the irate union by agreeing to raise wages for its members.

PROPRIETY: correct behavior; obedience to rules and customs

The aristocracy maintained a high level of PROPRIETY, adhering to even the most minor social rules.

PRUDENCE: wisdom, caution, or restraint

The college student exhibited PRUDENCE by obtaining practical experience along with her studies, which greatly strengthened her résumé.

PUNGENT: sharp and irritating to the senses

The smoke from the burning tires was extremely PUNGENT.

QUIESCENT: motionless

Many animals are QUIESCENT over the winter months, minimizing activity in order to conserve energy.

RAREFY: to make thinner or sparser

Since the atmosphere RAREFIES as altitudes increase, the air at the top of very tall mountains is too thin to breathe.

REPUDIATE: to reject the validity of

The old woman's claim that she was Russian royalty was REPUDIATED when DNA tests showed she was of no relation to them.

RETICENT: silent, reserved

Physically small and RETICENT in her speech, Joan Didion often went unnoticed by those upon whom she was reporting.

RHETORIC: effective writing or speaking

Lincoln's talent for RHETORIC was evident in his beautifully expressed Gettysburg Address.

SATIATE: to satisfy fully or overindulge

His desire for power was so great that nothing less than complete control of the country could SATIATE it.

SOPORIFIC: causing sleep or lethargy

The movie proved to be so SOPORIFIC that soon loud snores were heard throughout the theater.

SPECIOUS: deceptively attractive; seemingly plausible but fallacious

The student's SPECIOUS excuse for being late sounded legitimate but was proved otherwise when her teacher called her home.

STIGMA: a mark of shame or discredit

In *The Scarlet Letter*, Hester Prynne was required to wear the letter *A* on her clothes as a public STIGMA for her adultery.

STOLID: unemotional; lacking sensitivity

The prisoner appeared STOLID and unaffected by the judge's harsh sentence.

SUBLIME: lofty or grand

The music was so SUBLIME that it transformed the rude surroundings into a special place.

TACIT: done without using words

Although not a word had been said, everyone in the room knew that a TACIT agreement had been made about which course of action to take.

TACITURN: silent, not talkative

The clerk's TACITURN nature earned him the nickname "Silent Bob."

TIRADE: long, harsh speech or verbal attack

Observers were shocked at the manager's TIRADE over such a minor mistake.

TORPOR: extreme mental and physical sluggishness

After surgery, the patient experienced TORPOR until the anesthesia wore off.

TRANSITORY: temporary, lasting a brief time

The reporter lived a TRANSITORY life, staying in one place only long enough to cover the current story.

VACILLATE: to sway physically; to be indecisive

The customer held up the line as he VACILLATED between ordering chocolate chip or rocky road ice cream.

VENERATE: to respect deeply

In a traditional Confucian society, the young VENERATE their elders, deferring to the elders' wisdom and experience.

VERACITY: filled with truth and accuracy

She had a reputation for VERACITY, so everyone trusted her description of events.

VERBOSE: wordy

The professor's answer was so VERBOSE that his student forgot what the original question had been.

VEX: to annoy

The old man who loved his peace and quiet was VEXED by his neighbor's loud music.

VOLATILE: easily aroused or changeable; lively or explosive

His VOLATILE personality made it difficult to predict his reaction to anything.

WAVER: to fluctuate between choices

If you WAVER too long before making a decision about which testing site to register for, you may not get your first choice.

WHIMSICAL: acting in a fanciful or capricious manner; unpredictable

The ballet was WHIMSICAL, delighting the children with its imaginative characters and unpredictable sets.

ZEAL: passion, excitement

She brought her typical ZEAL to the project, sparking enthusiasm in the other team members.

COMMONLY CONFUSED WORDS

Already—by this or that time, previously
He already completed his work.

All ready—completely prepared
The students were all ready to take their exam.

Altogether—entirely, completely
I am altogether certain that I turned in my homework.

All together—in the same place
She kept the figurines all together on her mantle.

Capital—a city containing the seat of government, the wealth or funds owned by a business or individual, resources
Atlanta is the capital of Georgia.
The company's capital gains have diminished in recent years.

Capitol—the building in which a legislative body meets
Our trip included a visit to the Capitol building in Washington, D.C.

Coarse—rough, not smooth; lacking refinement
The truck's large wheels enabled it to navigate the coarse, rough terrain.
His coarse language prevented him from getting hired for the job.

Course—path, series of classes or studies
James's favorite course is biology.
The doctor suggested that Amy rest and let the disease run its course.

Here—in this location
George Washington used to live here.

Hear—to listen to or to perceive by the ear
Did you hear the question?

Its—a personal pronoun that shows possession
Please put the book back in its place.

It's—the contraction of it is or it has
It's snowing outside.
It's been too long.

Lead—to act as a leader, to go first, or to take a superior position
The guide will lead us through the forest.

Led—past tense of lead
The guide led us through the forest.

Lead—a metal
It is dangerous to inhale fumes from paint containing lead.

Loose—free, to set free, not tight
She always wears loose clothing when she does yoga.

Lose—to become without
Use a bookmark so you don't lose your place in your book.

Passed—the past tense of pass, an euphemism for someone dying
We passed by her house on Sunday.

Past—that which has gone by or elapsed in time,
In the past, Abby never used to study.
We drove past her house.

Principal—the head of a school, main or important
The quarterback's injury is the principal reason the team lost.
The principal of the school meets with parents regularly.

Principle—a fundamental law or truth
The laws of motion are among the most important principles in physics.

Stationary—fixed, not moving
Thomas rode a stationary bicycle at the gym.

Stationery—paper used for letter writing
The principal's stationery has the school's logo on the top.

Their—possessive of they
Paul and Ben studied for their test together.

There—a place, in that matter or respect
There are several question types on the GRE.
Please hang up your jacket over there.

They're—contraction of they are
Be careful of the bushes as they're filled with thorns.

Math Reference

The math on the GRE covers a lot of ground—from number properties and arithmetic to basic algebra and symbol problems to geometry and statistics. Don't let yourself be intimidated.

We've highlighted the 100 most important concepts that you need to know and divided them into three levels. The GRE Quantitative sections test your understanding of a relatively limited number of mathematical concepts, all of which you will be able to master.

Level 1 consists of foundational math topics. Though these topics may seem basic, review this list so that you are aware that these skills may play a part in the questions you will answer on the GRE. Look over the Level 1 list to make sure you're comfortable with the basics.

Level 2 is where most people start their review of math. Level 2 skills and formulas come into play quite frequently on the GRE. If the skills needed to handle Level 1 or 2 topics are keeping you from feeling up to the tasks expected on the GRE Quantitative section, you might consider taking the Kaplan GRE Math Refresher course.

Level 3 represents the most challenging math concepts you'll find on the GRE. Don't spend a lot of time on Level 3 if you still have gaps in Level 2, but once you've mastered Level 2, tackling Level 3 can put you over the top.

Level 1

1. How to add, subtract, multiply, and divide WHOLE NUMBERS

You can check addition with subtraction.

$$17 + 5 = 22 \qquad 22 - 5 = 17$$

You can check multiplication with division.

$$5 \times 28 = 140 \qquad 140 \div 5 = 28$$

2. How to add, subtract, multiply, and divide FRACTIONS

Find a common denominator before adding or subtracting fractions.

$$\frac{4}{5} + \frac{3}{10} = \frac{8}{10} + \frac{3}{10} = \frac{11}{10} \text{ or } 1\frac{1}{10}$$

$$2 - \frac{3}{8} = \frac{16}{8} - \frac{3}{8} = \frac{13}{8} \text{ or } 1\frac{5}{8}$$

To multiply fractions, multiply the numerators first and then multiply the denominators. Simplify if necessary.

$$\frac{3}{4} \times \frac{1}{6} = \frac{3}{24} = \frac{1}{8}$$

You can also reduce before multiplying numerators and denominators. This keeps the products small.

$$\frac{5}{8} \times \frac{2}{15} = \frac{\overset{1}{\cancel{5}}}{\underset{4}{\cancel{8}}} \times \frac{\overset{1}{\cancel{2}}}{\underset{3}{\cancel{15}}} = \frac{1}{12}$$

To divide by a fraction, multiply by its reciprocal. To write the reciprocal of a fraction, flip the numerator and the denominator.

$$5 \div \frac{1}{3} = \frac{5}{1} \times \frac{3}{1} = 15 \qquad \frac{1}{3} \div \frac{4}{5} = \frac{1}{3} \times \frac{5}{4} = \frac{5}{12}$$

3. How to add, subtract, multiply, and divide DECIMALS

To add or subtract, align the decimal points and then add or subtract normally. Place the decimal point in the answer directly below existing decimal points.

$$\begin{array}{r} 3.25 \\ + 4.4 \\ \hline 7.65 \end{array} \qquad \begin{array}{r} 7.65 \\ - 4.4 \\ \hline 3.25 \end{array}$$

To multiply with decimals, multiply the digits normally and count off decimal places (equal to the total number of places in the factors) from the right.

$$2.5 \times 2.5 = 6.25$$
$$0.06 \times 2{,}000 = 120.00 = 120$$

To divide by a decimal, move the decimal point in the divisor to the right to form a whole number; move the decimal point in the dividend the same number of places. Divide as though there were no decimals, then place the decimal point in the quotient.

$$6.25 \div 2.5$$
$$= 62.5 \div 25 = 2.5$$

4. How to convert FRACTIONS TO DECIMALS and DECIMALS TO FRACTIONS

To convert a fraction to a decimal, divide the numerator by the denominator.

$$\frac{4}{5} = 0.8 \qquad \frac{4}{50} = 0.08 \qquad \frac{4}{500} = 0.008$$

To convert a decimal to a fraction, write the digits in the numerator and use the decimal name in the denominator.

$$0.003 = \frac{3}{1{,}000} \qquad 0.03 = \frac{3}{100} \qquad 0.3 = \frac{3}{10}$$

5. How to add, subtract, multiply, and divide POSITIVE AND NEGATIVE NUMBERS

When addends (the numbers being added) have the same sign, add their absolute values; the sum has the same sign as the addends. But when addends have different signs, subtract the absolute values; the sum has the sign of the greater absolute value.

$$3 + 9 = 12, \text{ but } -3 + (-9) = -12$$
$$3 + (-9) = -6, \text{ but } -3 + 9 = 6$$

In multiplication and division, when the signs are the same, the product/quotient is positive. When the signs are different, the product/quotient is negative.

$$6 \times 7 = 42 \text{ and } -6 \times (-7) = 42$$
$$-6 \times 7 = -42 \text{ and } 6 \times (-7) = -42$$
$$96 \div 8 = 12 \text{ and } -96 \div (-8) = 12$$
$$-96 \div 8 = -12 \text{ and } 96 \div (-8) = -12$$

6. How to plot points on the NUMBER LINE

To plot the point 4.5 on the number line, start at 0, go right to 4.5, halfway between 4 and 5.

To plot the point −2.5 on the number line, start at 0, go left to −2.5, halfway between −2 and −3.

7. How to plug a number into an ALGEBRAIC EXPRESSION

To evaluate an algebraic expression, choose numbers for the variables or use the numbers assigned to the variables.

Evaluate $4np + 1$ when $n = -4$ and $p = 3$.

$4np + 1 = 4(-4)(3) + 1 = -48 + 1 = -47$

8. How to SOLVE a simple LINEAR EQUATION

Use algebra to isolate the variable. Do the same steps to both sides of the equation.

$$28 = -3x - 5$$
$$28 + 5 = -3x - 5 + 5 \quad \text{Add 5.}$$
$$33 = -3x$$
$$\frac{33}{-3} = \frac{-3x}{-3} \quad \text{Divide by } -3.$$
$$-11 = x$$

9. How to add and subtract LINE SEGMENTS

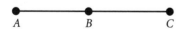

If $AB = 6$ and $BC = 8$, then $AC = 6 + 8 = 14$.
If $AC = 14$ and $BC = 8$, then $AB = 14 - 8 = 6$.

10. How to find the THIRD ANGLE of a TRIANGLE, given the other two angles

Use the fact that the sum of the measures of the interior angles of a triangle always sum to 180°.

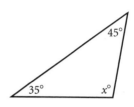

$$35 + 45 + x = 180$$
$$80 + x = 180$$
$$x = 100$$

Level 2

11. How to use PEMDAS

When you're given a complex arithmetic expression, it's important to know the order of operations. Just remember PEMDAS (as in "Please excuse my dear Aunt Sally"). What PEMDAS means is this: Clean up **Parentheses** first (Nested sets of parentheses are worked from the innermost set to the outermost set.); then deal with **Exponents** (or **Radicals**); then do the **Multiplication** and **Division** together, going from left to right; and finally do the **Addition** and **Subtraction** together, again going from left to right.

Example:

$$9 - 2 \times (5 - 3)^2 + 6 \div 3 =$$

Begin with the parentheses:

$$9 - 2 \times (2)^2 + 6 \div 3 =$$

Then do the exponent:

$$9 - 2 \times 4 + 6 \div 3 =$$

Now do multiplication and division from left to right:

$$9 - 8 + 2 =$$

Finally, do addition and subtraction from left to right:

$$1 + 2 = 3$$

12. How to use the PERCENT FORMULA

Identify the part, the percent, and the whole.

$$Part = Percent \times Whole$$

Find the part.

Example:

What is 12 percent of 25?

Setup:

$$Part = \frac{12}{100} \times 25 = \frac{300}{100} = 3$$

Find the percent.

Example:

45 is what percent of 9?

Setup:

$$45 = \frac{percent}{100} \times 9$$

$$\frac{45}{9} \times 100\% = 500\%$$

Find the whole.

Example:

15 is $\frac{3}{5}$ percent of what number?

Setup:

$$15 = \frac{3}{5}\left(\frac{1}{100}\right) \times Whole$$

$$15 = \frac{3}{500} \times Whole$$

$$Whole = 15\left(\frac{500}{3}\right) = \frac{7,500}{3} = 2,500$$

13. How to use the PERCENT INCREASE/ DECREASE FORMULAS

Identify the original whole and the amount of increase/decrease.

$$Percent\ increase = \frac{Amount\ of\ increase}{Original\ whole} \times 100\%$$

$$Percent\ decrease = \frac{Amount\ of\ decrease}{Original\ whole} \times 100\%$$

Example:

The price goes up from $80 to $100. What is the percent increase?

Setup:

$$Percent\ increase = \frac{20}{80} \times 100\%$$

$$= 0.25 \times 100\% = 25\%$$

14. How to predict whether a sum, difference, or product will be ODD or EVEN

Don't bother memorizing the rules. Just take simple numbers like 2 for even numbers and 3 for odd numbers and see what happens.

Example:

If m is even and n is odd, is the product mn odd or even?

Setup:

Say $m = 2$ and $n = 3$.
2×3 is even, so mn is even.

15. How to recognize MULTIPLES OF 2, 3, 4, 5, 6, 9, 10, and 12

  2: Last digit is even

  3: Sum of digits is a multiple of 3

  4: Last two digits are a multiple of 4

  5: Last digit is 5 or 0

  6: Sum of digits is a multiple of 3, and last digit is even

  9: Sum of digits is a multiple of 9

10: Last digit is 0

12: Sum of digits is a multiple of 3, and last two digits are a multiple of 4

16. How to find a COMMON FACTOR of two numbers

Break both numbers down to their prime factors to see which they have in common. Then multiply the shared prime factors to find all common factors.

Example:

What factors greater than 1 do 135 and 225 have in common?

Setup:

First find the prime factors of 135 and 225; $135 = 3 \times 3 \times 3 \times 5$, and $225 = 3 \times 3 \times 5 \times 5$. The numbers share $3 \times 3 \times 5$ in common. Thus, aside from 3 and 5, the remaining common factors can be found by multiplying 3, 3, and 5 in every possible combination: $3 \times 3 = 9$, $3 \times 5 = 15$, and $3 \times 3 \times 5 = 45$. To summarize, the common factors of 135 and 225 are: 3, 5, 9, 15, and 45.

17. How to find a COMMON MULTIPLE of two numbers

The product of two numbers is the easiest common multiple to find, but it is not always the least common multiple.

Example:

What is the least common multiple of 28 and 42?

Setup:

$$28 = 2 \times 2 \times 7$$
$$42 = 2 \times 3 \times 7$$

The LCM can be found by finding the prime factorization of each number, then seeing the greatest number of times each factor is used. Multiply each prime factor the greatest number of times it appears.

In 28, 2 is used twice. In 42, 2 is used once. In 28, 7 is used once. In 42, 7 is used once, and three is used once. So you multiply each factor the greatest number of times it appears in a prime factorization:

$$LCM = 2 \times 2 \times 3 \times 7 = 84$$

18. How to find the AVERAGE or ARITHMETIC MEAN

$$Average = \frac{Sum\ of\ terms}{Number\ of\ terms}$$

Example:

What is the average of 3, 4, and 8?

Setup:

$$Average = \frac{3 + 4 + 8}{3} = \frac{15}{3} = 5$$

19. How to use the AVERAGE to find the SUM

$$Sum = (Average) \times (Number\ of\ terms)$$

Example:

17.5 is the average (arithmetic mean) of 24 numbers.

What is the sum of the 24 numbers?

Setup:

$$Sum = 17.5 \times 24 = 420$$

20. How to find the AVERAGE of CONSECUTIVE NUMBERS

The average of evenly spaced numbers is simply the average of the smallest number and the largest number. The average of all the integers from 13 to 77, for example, is the same as the average of 13 and 77:

$$\frac{13 + 77}{2} = \frac{90}{2} = 45$$

21. How to COUNT CONSECUTIVE NUMBERS

The number of integers from A to B inclusive is $B - A + 1$.

Example:

How many integers are there from 73 through 419, inclusive?

Setup:

$$419 - 73 + 1 = 347$$

22. How to find the SUM OF CONSECUTIVE NUMBERS

$$Sum = (Average) \times (Number\ of\ terms)$$

Example:

What is the sum of the integers from 10 through 50, inclusive?

Setup:

Average $= (10 + 50) \div 2 = 30$
Number of terms $= 50 - 10 + 1 = 41$
Sum $= 30 \times 41 = 1,230$

23. How to find the MEDIAN

Put the numbers in numerical order and take the middle number.

Example:

What is the median of 88, 86, 57, 94, and 73?

Setup:

First, put the numbers in numerical order, then take the middle number:

$$57, 73, 86, 88, 94$$

The median is 86.

In a set with an even number of numbers, take the average of the two in the middle.

Example:

What is the median of 88, 86, 57, 73, 94, and 100?

Setup:

First, put the numbers in numerical order.

57, 73, 86, 88, 94, 100

Because 86 and 88 are the two numbers in the middle:

(86 + 88) ÷ 2 = 174 ÷ 2 = 87 is the median.

24. How to find the MODE

Take the number that appears most often. For example, if your test scores were 88, 57, 68, 85, 98, 93, 93, 84, and 81, the mode of the scores would be 93 because it appears more often than any other score. (If there's a tie for most often, then there's more than one mode. If there is only one of each number in a set, there is no mode.)

25. How to find the RANGE

Take the positive difference between the greatest and least values. Using the example under "How to find the MODE" above, if your test scores were 88, 57, 68, 85, 98, 93, 93, 84, and 81, the range of the scores would be 41, the greatest value minus the least value (98 − 57 = 41).

26. How to use actual numbers to determine a RATIO

To find a ratio, put the number associated with *of* on the top and the word associated with *to* on the bottom.

$$Ratio = \frac{of}{to}$$

The ratio of 20 oranges to 12 apples is $\frac{20}{12}$, or $\frac{5}{3}$. Ratios should always be reduced to lowest terms.

27. How to use a ratio to determine an ACTUAL NUMBER

Set up a proportion using the given ratio.

Example:

The ratio of boys to girls is 3 to 4. If there are 135 boys, how many girls are there?

Setup:

$$\frac{3}{4} = \frac{135}{g}$$
$$3 \times g = 4 \times 135$$
$$3g = 540$$
$$g = 180$$

28. How to use actual numbers to determine a RATE

Identify the quantities and the units to be compared. Keep the units straight.

Example:

Anders typed 9,450 words in $3\frac{1}{2}$ hours. What was his rate in words per minute?

Setup:

First convert $3\frac{1}{2}$ hours to 210 minutes. Then set up the rate with words on top and minutes on bottom (because "per" means "divided by"):

$$\frac{9,450 \text{ words}}{210 \text{ minutes}} = 45 \text{ words per minute}$$

29. How to deal with TABLES, GRAPHS, AND CHARTS

Read the question and all labels carefully. Ignore extraneous information and zero in on what the question asks for. Take advantage of the spread in the answer choices by approximating the answer whenever possible and choosing the answer choice closest to your approximation.

30. How to count the NUMBER OF POSSIBILITIES

You can use multiplication to find the number of possibilities when items can be arranged in various ways.

Example:

How many three-digit numbers can be formed with the digits 1, 3, and 5 each used only once?

Setup:

Look at each digit individually. The first digit (or, the hundreds digit) has three possible numbers to plug in: 1, 3, or 5. The second digit (or, the tens digit) has two possible numbers, since one has already been plugged in. The last digit (or, the ones digit) has only one remaining possible number. Multiply the possibilities together: $3 \times 2 \times 1 = 6$.

31. How to calculate a simple PROBABILITY

$$Probability = \frac{Number\ of\ favorable\ outcomes}{Total\ number\ of\ possible\ outcomes}$$

Example:

What is the probability of throwing a 5 on a fair six-sided die?

Setup:

There is one favorable outcome—throwing a 5. There are 6 possible outcomes—one for each side of the die.

$$Probability = \frac{1}{6}$$

32. How to work with new SYMBOLS

If you see a symbol you've never seen before, don't be alarmed. It's just a made-up symbol whose operation is defined by the problem. Everything you need to know is in the question stem. Just follow the instructions.

33. How to SIMPLIFY BINOMIALS

A binomial is a sum or difference of two terms. To simplify two binomials that are multiplied together use the FOIL method. Multiply the First terms, then the Outer terms, followed by the Inner terms and the Last terms. Lastly, combine like terms.

Example:

$$(3x + 5)(x - 1) =$$
$$3x^2 - 3x + 5x - 5 =$$
$$3x^2 + 2x - 5$$

34. How to FACTOR certain POLYNOMIALS

A polynomial is an expression consisting of the sum of two or more terms, where at least one of the terms is a variable.

Learn to spot these classic equations.

$$ab + ac = a(b + c)$$
$$a^2 + 2ab + b^2 = (a + b)^2$$
$$a^2 - 2ab + b^2 = (a - b)^2$$
$$a^2 - b^2 = (a - b)(a + b)$$

35. How to solve for one variable IN TERMS OF ANOTHER

To find x "in terms of" y, isolate x on one side, leaving y as the only variable on the other.

36. How to solve an INEQUALITY

Treat it much like an equation—adding, subtracting, multiplying, and dividing both sides by the same thing. Just remember to reverse the inequality sign if you multiply or divide by a negative quantity.

Example:

Rewrite $7 - 3x > 2$ in its simplest form.

Setup:

$$7 - 3x > 2$$

First, subtract 7 from both sides:

$$7 - 3x - 7 > 2 - 7$$

So $-3x > -5$.

Now divide both sides by -3, and remember to reverse the inequality sign:

$$x < \frac{5}{3}$$

37. How to handle ABSOLUTE VALUES

The *absolute value* of a number n, denoted by $|n|$, is defined as n if $n \geq 0$ and $-n$ if $n < 0$. The absolute value of a number is the distance from zero to the number on the number line. The absolute value of a number or expression is always positive.

$$|-5| = 5$$

If $|x| = 3$, then x could be 3 or -3.

Example:

If $|x - 3| < 2$, what is the range of possible values for x?

Setup:

Represent the possible range for $x - 3$ on a number line.

$|x - 3| < 2$, so $(x - 3) < 2$ and $(x - 3) > -2$
$x - 3 < 2$ and $x - 3 > -2$
$x < 2 + 3$ and $x > -2 + 3$
$x < 5$ and $x > 1$
So $1 < x < 5$.

38. How to TRANSLATE ENGLISH INTO ALGEBRA

Look for the key words and systematically turn phrases into algebraic expressions and sentences into equations.

Here's a table of keywords that you may have to translate into mathematical terms:

Operation	Keywords
Addition	sum, plus, and, added to, more than, increased by, combined with, exceeds, total, greater than
Subtraction	difference between, minus, subtracted from, decreased by, diminished by, less than, reduced by
Multiplication	of, product, times, multiplied by, twice, double, triple, half
Division	quotient, divided by, per, out of, ratio of ___ to ___
Equals	equals, is, was, will be, the result is, adds up to, costs, is the same as

39. How to find an ANGLE formed by INTERSECTING LINES

Vertical angles are equal. Angles along a line add up to 180°.

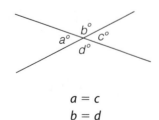

$a = c$
$b = d$
$a + b = 180°$
$a + b + c + d = 360°$

40. How to find an angle formed by a TRANSVERSAL across PARALLEL LINES

All the acute angles are equal. All the obtuse angles are equal. An acute plus an obtuse equals 180°.

Example:

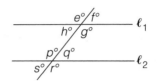

ℓ_1 is parallel to ℓ_2

$e = g = p = r$
$f = h = q = s$
$e + q = g + s = 180°$

41. How to find the AREA of a TRIANGLE

$$Area = \frac{1}{2}(base)(height)$$

Base and height must be perpendicular to each other. Height is measured by drawing a perpendicular line segment from the base—which can be any side of the triangle—to the angle opposite the base.

Example:

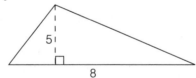

Setup:

$$Area = \frac{1}{2}(8)(5) = 20$$

42. How to work with ISOSCELES TRIANGLES

Isosceles triangles have two equal sides and two equal angles. If a GRE question tells you that a triangle is isoceles, you can bet that you'll need to use that information to find the length of a side or a measure of an angle.

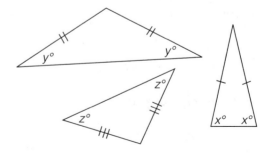

43. How to work with EQUILATERAL TRIANGLES

Equilateral triangles have three equal sides and three 60° angles. If a GRE question tells you that a triangle is equilateral, you can bet that you'll need to use that information to find the length of a side or a measure of an angle.

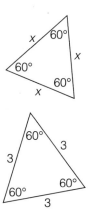

44. How to work with SIMILAR TRIANGLES

In similar triangles, corresponding angles are equal, and corresponding sides are proportional. If a GRE question tells you that triangles are similar, use the properties of similar triangles to find the length of a side or the measure of an angle.

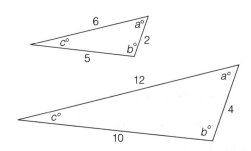

45. How to find the HYPOTENUSE or a LEG of a RIGHT TRIANGLE

For all right triangles, Pythagorean theorem: $a^2 + b^2 = c^2$ where a and b are the legs and c is the hypotenuse.

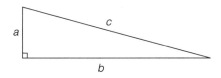

46. How to spot SPECIAL RIGHT TRIANGLES

3:4:5

5:12:13

30°-60°-90°

45°-45°-90°

These numbers (3, 4, 5 and 5, 12, 13) represent the ratio of the side lengths of these triangles.

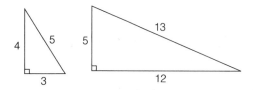

Likewise, the numbers 1, $\sqrt{3}$, 2 and 1, 1, $\sqrt{2}$ represent the ratios of the side lengths of these special triangles.

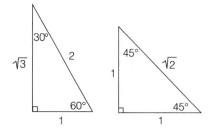

47. How to find the PERIMETER of a RECTANGLE

$$Perimeter = 2(length + width)$$

Example:

Setup:

$$Perimeter = 2(2 + 5) = 14$$

48. How to find the AREA of a RECTANGLE

Area = *(length)(width)*

Example:

Setup:

Area = 2 × 5 = 10

49. How to find the AREA of a SQUARE

Area = *(side)²*

Example:

Setup:

Area = 3^2 = 9

50. How to find the AREA of a PARALLELOGRAM

Area = *(base)(height)*

Example:

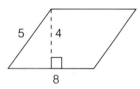

Setup:

Area = 8 × 4 = 32

51. How to find the AREA of a TRAPEZOID

A trapezoid is a quadrilateral having only two parallel sides. You can always drop a perpendicular line or two to break the figure into a rectangle and a triangle or two triangles. Use the area formulas for those familiar shapes. Alternatively, you could apply the general formula for the area of a trapezoid:

Area = *(Average of parallel sides)* × *(height)*

Example:

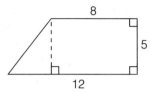

Setup:

Area of rectangle = 8 × 5 = 40

Area of triangle = $\frac{1}{2}$(4 × 5) = 10

Area of trapezoid = 40 + 10 = 50

or Area of trapezoid = $\left(\frac{8+12}{2}\right)$ × 5 = 50

52. How to find the CIRCUMFERENCE of a CIRCLE

Circumference = *2πr, where r is the radius*

Circumference = *πd, where d is the diameter*

Example:

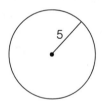

Setup:

Circumference = 2π(5) = 10π

53. How to find the AREA of a CIRCLE

Area = *πr² where r is the radius*

Example:

Setup:

Area = π × 5^2 = 25π

54. How to find the DISTANCE BETWEEN POINTS on the coordinate plane

If two points have the same *x* coordinates or the same *y* coordinates—that is, they make a line segment that is parallel to an axis—all you have to do is subtract the numbers that are different. Just remember that distance is always positive.

Example:

What is the distance from (2, 3) to (−7, 3)?

Setup:

The *y's* are the same, so just subtract the *x's*: $2 − (−7) = 9$.

If the points have different *x* coordinates and different *y* coordinates, make a right triangle and use the Pythagorean theorem or apply the special right triangle attributes if applicable.

Example:

What is the distance from (2, 3) to (−1, −1)?

Setup:

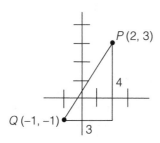

It's a 3:4:5 triangle!
$PQ = 5$

55. How to find the SLOPE of a LINE

$$Slope = \frac{rise}{run} = \frac{change\ in\ y}{change\ in\ x}$$

Example:

What is the slope of the line that contains the points (1, 2) and (4, −5)?

Setup:

$$Slope = \frac{−5 − 2}{4 − 1} = \frac{−7}{3}$$

Level 3

56. How to determine COMBINED PERCENT INCREASE/DECREASE

Start with 100 as a starting value.

Example:

A price rises by 10 percent one year and by 20 percent the next. What's the combined percent increase?

Setup:

Say the original price is $100.

Year one:
$100 + (10% of 100) = 100 + 10 = 110$

Year two:
$110 + (20% of 110) = 110 + 22 = 132$

From 100 to 132—That's a 32 percent increase.

57. How to find the ORIGINAL WHOLE before percent increase/decrease

Think of a 15 percent increase over *x* as 1.15*x* and set up an equation.

Example:

After decreasing by 5 percent, the population is now 57,000. What was the original population?

Setup:

$0.95 ×$ (Original population) $= 57,000$
Divide both sides by 0.95.
Original population $= 57,000 ÷ 0.95 = 60,000$

58. How to solve a SIMPLE INTEREST problem

With simple interest, the interest is computed on the principal only and is given by:

interest = (principal) × (interest rate*) × (time**)

* expressed as a decimal
** expressed in years or fraction of a year

Example:

If $12,000 is invested at 6 percent simple annual interest, how much interest is earned after 9 months?

Setup:

$$(12,000) × (0.06) × \left(\frac{9}{12}\right) = \$540$$

59. How to solve a COMPOUND INTEREST problem

If interest is compounded, the interest is computed on the principal as well as on any interest earned. To compute compound interest:

$$(\textit{Final balance}) = (\textit{Principal}) \times \left(1 + \frac{\textit{Interest rate}}{C}\right)^{(\textit{time})(C)}$$

where C = the number of times compounded annually

Example:

If \$10,000 is invested at 8 percent annual interest, compounded semiannually, what is the balance after 1 year?

Setup:

Final balance

$$= (10,000) \times \left(1 + \frac{0.08}{2}\right)^{(1)(2)}$$

$$= (10,000) \times (1.04)^2$$

$$= \$10,816$$

60. How to solve a REMAINDERS problem

Pick a number that fits the given conditions and see what happens.

Example:

When n is divided by 7, the remainder is 5. What is the remainder when $2n$ is divided by 7?

Setup:

Find a number that leaves a remainder of 5 when divided by 7. You can find such a number by taking any multiple of 7 and adding 5 to it. A good choice would be 12. If $n = 12$, then $2n = 24$, which when divided by 7 leaves a remainder of 3.

61. How to solve a DIGITS problem

Use a little logic—and some trial and error.

Example:

If A, B, C, and D represent distinct digits in the addition problem below, what is the value of D?

$$\begin{array}{r} AB \\ + BA \\ \hline CDC \end{array}$$

Setup:

Two 2-digit numbers will add up to at most something in the 100s, so $C = 1$. B plus A in the units column gives a 1, and since A and B in the tens column don't add up to C, it can't simply be that $B + A = 1$. It must be that $B + A = 11$, and a 1 gets carried. In fact, A and B can be any pair of digits that add up to 11 (3 and 8, 4 and 7, etc.), but it doesn't matter what they are: they always give you the same value for D which is 2:

$$\begin{array}{r} 47 \\ + 74 \\ \hline 121 \end{array} \qquad \begin{array}{r} 83 \\ + 38 \\ \hline 121 \end{array}$$

62. How to find a WEIGHTED AVERAGE

Give each term the appropriate "weight."

Example:

The girls' average score is 30. The boys' average score is 24. If there are twice as many boys as girls, what is the overall average?

Setup:

$$\text{Weighted avg.} = \frac{1 \times 30 + 2 \times 24}{3} = \frac{78}{3} = 26$$

HINT:

Don't just average the averages.

63. How to find the NEW AVERAGE when a number is added or deleted

Use the sum of the terms of the old average to help you find the new average.

Example:

Michael's average score after four tests is 80. If he scores 100 on the fifth test, what's his new average?

Setup:

Find the original sum from the original average:

$$\text{Original sum} = 4 \times 80 = 320$$

Add the fifth score to make the new sum:

$$\text{New sum} = 320 + 100 = 420$$

Find the new average from the new sum:

$$\text{New average} = \frac{420}{5} = 84$$

64. How to use the ORIGINAL AVERAGE and NEW AVERAGE to figure out WHAT WAS ADDED OR DELETED

Use the sums.

Number added = (New sum) − (Original sum)
Number deleted = (Original sum) − (New sum)

Example:

The average of five numbers is 2. After one number is deleted, the new average is −3. What number was deleted?

Setup:

Find the original sum from the original average:

Original sum = 5 × 2 = 10

Find the new sum from the new average:

New sum = 4 × (−3) = −12

The difference between the original sum and the new sum is the answer.

Number deleted = 10 − (−12) = 22

65. How to find an AVERAGE RATE

Convert to totals.

$$Average\ A\ per\ B = \frac{Total\ A}{Total\ B}$$

Example:

If the first 500 pages have an average of 150 words per page, and the remaining 100 pages have an average of 450 words per page, what is the average number of words per page for the entire 600 pages?

Setup:

Total pages = 500 + 100 = 600
Total words = (500 × 150) + (100 × 450)
= 120,000

$$Average\ words\ per\ page = \frac{120,000}{600} = 200$$

To find an average speed, you also convert to totals.

$$Average\ speed = \frac{Total\ distance}{Time}$$

Example:

Rosa drove 120 miles one way at an average speed of 40 miles per hour and returned by the same 120-mile route at an average speed of 60 miles per hour. What was Rosa's average speed for the entire 240-mile round trip?

Setup:

To drive 120 miles at 40 mph takes 3 hours. To return at 60 mph takes 2 hours. The total time, then, is 5 hours.

$$Average\ speed = \frac{240\ miles}{5\ hours} = 48\ mph$$

66. How to solve a COMBINED WORK PROBLEM

In a combined work problem, you are given the rate at which people or machines perform work individually and asked to compute the rate at which they work together (or vice versa). The work formula states: *The inverse of the time it would take everyone working together equals the sum of the inverses of the times it would take each working individually.* In other words:

$$\frac{1}{r} + \frac{1}{s} = \frac{1}{t}$$

where r and s are, for example, the number of hours it would take Rebecca and Sam, respectively, to complete a job working by themselves, and t is the number of hours it would take the two of them working together. Remember that all these variables must stand for units of TIME, and must all refer to the amount of time it takes to do the same task.

Example:

If it takes Joe 4 hours to paint a room and Pete twice as long to paint the same room, how long would it take the two of them, working together, to paint the same room, if each of them works at his respective individual rate?

Setup:

Joe takes 4 hours, so Pete takes 8 hours; thus:

$$\frac{1}{4} + \frac{1}{8} = \frac{1}{t}$$
$$\frac{2}{8} + \frac{1}{8} = \frac{1}{t}$$
$$\frac{3}{8} = \frac{1}{t}$$
$$t = \frac{1}{\left(\frac{3}{8}\right)} = \frac{8}{3}$$

So it would take them $\frac{8}{3}$ hours, or 2 hours 40 minutes, to paint the room together.

67. How to determine a COMBINED RATIO

Multiply one or both ratios by whatever you need to in order to get the terms they have in common to match.

Example:

The ratio of *a* to *b* is 7:3. The ratio of *b* to *c* is 2:5. What is the ratio of *a* to *c* ?

Setup:

Multiply each member of *a*:*b* by 2 and multiply each member of *b*:*c* by 3, and you get *a*:*b* = 14:6 and *b*:*c* = 6:15. Now that the *b*s match, you can write *a*:*b*:*c* = 14:6:15 and then say *a*:*c* = 14:15.

68. How to solve a DILUTION or MIXTURE problem

In dilution or mixture problems, you have to determine the characteristics of a resulting mixture when different substances are combined. Or, alternatively, you have to determine how to combine different substances to produce a desired mixture. There are two approaches to such problems—the straightforward setup and the balancing method.

Example:

If 5 pounds of raisins that cost $1 per pound are mixed with 2 pounds of almonds that cost $2.40 per pound, what is the cost per pound of the resulting mixture?

Setup:

The straightforward setup:

($1)(5) + ($2.40)(2) = $9.80 = total cost for 7 pounds of the mixture

The cost per pound is $\$\frac{9.80}{7}$ = $1.40.

Example:

How many liters of a solution that is 10 percent alcohol by volume must be added to 2 liters of a solution that is 50 percent alcohol by volume to create a solution that is 15 percent alcohol by volume?

Setup:

The balancing method: Make the weaker and stronger (or cheaper and more expensive, etc.) substances balance. That is, (percent difference between the weaker solution and the desired solution) × (amount of weaker solution) = (percent difference between the stronger solution and the desired solution) × (amount of stronger solution). Make *n* the amount, in liters, of the weaker solution.

$$n(15 - 10) = 2(50 - 15)$$
$$5n = 2(35)$$
$$n = \frac{70}{5} = 14$$

So 14 liters of the 10 percent solution must be added to the original, stronger solution.

69. How to solve a GROUP problem involving BOTH/NEITHER

Some GRE word problems involve two groups with overlapping members and possibly elements that belong to neither group. It's easy to identify this type of question because the words *both* and/or *neither* appear in the question. These problems are quite workable if you just memorize the following formula:

Group 1 + Group 2 + Neither − Both = Total

Example:

Of the 120 students at a certain language school, 65 are studying French, 51 are studying Spanish, and 53 are studying neither language. How many are studying both French and Spanish?

Setup:

$$65 + 51 + 53 - \text{Both} = 120$$
$$169 - \text{Both} = 120$$
$$\text{Both} = 49$$

70. How to solve a GROUP problem involving EITHER/OR CATEGORIES

Other GRE word problems involve groups with distinct "either/or" categories (male/female, blue-collar/white-collar, etc.). The key to solving this type of problem is to organize the information in a grid.

Example:

At a certain professional conference with 130 attendees, 94 of the attendees are doctors, and the rest are dentists. If 48 of the attendees are women and $\frac{1}{4}$ of the dentists in attendance are women, how many of the attendees are male doctors?

Setup:

To complete the grid, use the information in the problem, making each row and column add up to the corresponding total:

	Doctors	Dentists	Total
Male	55	27	82
Female		9	48
Total	94	36	130

After you've filled in the information from the question, use simple arithmetic to fill in the remaining boxes until you get the number you are looking for—in this case, that 55 of the attendees are male doctors.

71. How to work with FACTORIALS

You may see a problem involving factorial notation. If n is an integer greater than 1, then n factorial, denoted by $n!$, is defined as the product of all the integers from 1 to n. In other words:

$$2! = 2 \times 1 = 2$$
$$3! = 3 \times 2 \times 1 = 6$$
$$4! = 4 \times 3 \times 2 \times 1 = 24, \text{ etc.}$$

By definition, $0! = 1$.

Also note: $6! = 6 \times 5! = 6 \times 5 \times 4!$, etc. Most GRE factorial problems test your ability to factor and/or cancel.

Example:

$$\frac{8!}{6! \times 2!} = \frac{8 \times 7 \times 6!}{6! \times 2 \times 1} = 28$$

72. How to solve a PERMUTATION problem

Factorials are useful for solving questions about permutations (i.e., the number of ways to arrange elements sequentially). For instance, to figure out how many ways there are to arrange 7 items along a shelf, you would multiply the number of possibilities for the first position times the number of possibilities remaining for the second position, and so on—in other words: $7 \times 6 \times 5 \times 4 \times 3 \times 2 \times 1$, or $7!$.

If you're asked to find the number of ways to arrange a smaller group that's being drawn from a larger group, you can either apply logic, or you can use the permutation formula:

$$_nP_k = \frac{n!}{(n-k)!}$$

where $n = $ (# in the larger group) and
$k = $ (# you're arranging).

Example:

Five runners run in a race. The runners who come in first, second, and third place will win gold, silver, and bronze medals respectively. How many possible outcomes for gold, silver, and bronze medal winners are there?

Setup:

Any of the 5 runners could come in first place, leaving 4 runners who could come in second place, leaving 3 runners who could come in third place, for a total of $5 \times 4 \times 3 = 60$ possible outcomes for gold, silver, and bronze medal winners. Or, using the formula:

$$_5P_3 = \frac{5!}{(5-3)!} = \frac{5!}{2!} = \frac{5 \times 4 \times 3 \times \cancel{2} \times \cancel{1}}{\cancel{2} \times \cancel{1}}$$
$$= 5 \times 4 \times 3 = 60$$

73. How to solve a COMBINATION problem

If the order or arrangement of the smaller group that's being drawn from the larger group does NOT matter, you are looking for the numbers of combinations, and a different formula is called for:

$$_nC_k = \frac{n!}{k!(n-k)!}$$

where $n = $ (# in the larger group) and
$k = $ (# you're choosing).

Example:

How many different ways are there to choose 3 delegates from 8 possible candidates?

Setup:

$$_8C_3 = \frac{8!}{3!\,(8-3)!} = \frac{8!}{3! \times 5!}$$
$$= \frac{8 \times 7 \times \cancel{6} \, \cancel{5} \, \cancel{4} \, \cancel{3} \, \cancel{2} \, \cancel{1}}{\cancel{3} \times \cancel{2} \times 1 \times \cancel{5} \times \cancel{4} \times \cancel{3} \times \cancel{2} \times \cancel{1}}$$
$$= 8 \times 7 = 56$$

So there are 56 different possible combinations.

74. How to solve PROBABILITY problems where probabilities must be multiplied

Suppose that a random process is performed. Then there is a set of possible outcomes that can occur. An event is a set of possible outcomes. We are concerned with the probability of events.

When all the outcomes are all equally likely, the basic probability formula is:

$$Probability = \frac{Number\ of\ favorable\ outcomes}{Number\ of\ possible\ outcomes}$$

Many more difficult probability questions involve finding the probability that several events occur. Let's consider first the case of the probability that two events occur. Call these two events A and B. The probability that both events occur is the probability that event A occurs multiplied by the probability that event B occurs given that event A occurred. The probability that B occurs given that A occurs is called the conditional probability that B occurs given that A occurs. Except when events A and B do not depend on one another, the probability that B occurs given that A occurs is not the same as the probability that B occurs.

The probability that three events A, B, and C occur is the probability that A occurs multiplied by the conditional probability that B occurs given that A occurred multiplied by the conditional probability that C occurs given that both A and B have occurred.

This can be generalized to any number of events, where the number of events is an integer greater than 3.

Example:

If 2 students are chosen at random to run an errand from a class with 5 girls and 5 boys, what is the probability that both students chosen will be girls?

Setup:

The probability that the first student chosen will be a girl is $\frac{5}{10} = \frac{1}{2}$, and since there would be 4 girls and 5 boys left out of 9 students, the probability that the second student chosen will be a girl (given that the first student chosen is a girl) is $\frac{4}{9}$. Thus the probability that both students chosen

will be girls is $\frac{1}{2} \times \frac{4}{9} = \frac{2}{9}$. There was conditional probability here because the probability of choosing the second girl was affected by another girl being chosen first.

Now let's consider another example where a random process is repeated.

Example:

If a fair coin is tossed 4 times, what's the probability that at least 3 of the 4 tosses will be heads?

Setup:

There are 2 possible outcomes for each toss, so after 4 tosses, there are $2 \times 2 \times 2 \times 2 = 16$ possible outcomes.

We can list the different possible sequences where at least 3 of the 4 tosses are heads. These sequences are

HHHT

HHTH

HTHH

THHH

HHHH

Thus, the probability that at least 3 of the 4 tosses will come up heads is:

$$\frac{Number\ of\ favorable\ outcomes}{Number\ of\ possible\ outcomes} = \frac{5}{16}$$

We could have also solved this question using the combinations formula. The probability of a head is $\frac{1}{2}$, and the probability of a tail is $\frac{1}{2}$. The probability of any particular sequence of heads and tails resulting from 4 tosses is $\frac{1}{2} \times \frac{1}{2} \times \frac{1}{2} \times \frac{1}{2}$, which is $\frac{1}{16}$.

Suppose that the result each of the four tosses is recorded in each of the four spaces.

____ ____ ____ ____

Thus, we would record an H for head or a T for tails in each of the 4 spaces.

The number of ways of having exactly 3 heads among the 4 tosses is the number of ways of choosing 3 of the 4 spaces above to record an H for heads.

The number of ways of choosing 3 of the 4 spaces is

$$_4C_3 = \frac{4!}{3!(4-3)!} = \frac{4!}{3!(1)!} = \frac{4 \times 3 \times 2 \times 1}{3 \times 2 \times 1 \times 1} = 4$$

The number of ways of having exactly 4 heads among the 4 tosses is 1.

If we use the combinations formula, using the definition that $0! = 1$, then

$$_4C_4 = \frac{4!}{4!(4-4)!} = \frac{4!}{4!(0)!}$$
$$= \frac{4 \times 3 \times 2 \times 1}{4 \times 3 \times 2 \times 1 \times 1} = 1$$

Thus, $_4C_3 = 4$ and $_4C_4 = 1$. So the number of different sequences containing at least 3 heads is $4 + 1 = 5$.

The probability of having at least 3 heads is $\frac{5}{16}$.

75. How to deal with STANDARD DEVIATION

Like mean, mode, median, and range, standard deviation is a term used to describe sets of numbers. Standard deviation is a measure of how spread out a set of numbers is (how much the numbers deviate from the mean). The greater the spread, the higher the standard deviation. You'll never actually have to calculate the standard deviation on test day, but seeing how it's calculated can be helpful in understanding the concept:

- Find the average (arithmetic mean) of the set.
- Find the differences between the mean and each value in the set.
- Square each of the differences.
- Find the average of the squared differences.
- Take the positive square root of the average.

Although you won't have to calculate standard deviation on the GRE, you may be asked to compare standard deviations between sets of data or otherwise demonstrate that you understand what standard deviation means.

Example:

High temperatures, in degrees Fahrenheit, in two cities over five days:

September	1	2	3	4	5
City A	54	61	70	49	56
City B	62	56	60	67	65

For the five day period listed, which city had the greater standard deviation in high temperatures?

Setup:

Even without trying to calculate them out, one can see that City *A* has the greater spread in temperatures and, therefore, the greater standard deviation in high temperatures. If you were to go ahead and calculate the standard deviations following the steps described above, you would find that the standard deviation in high temperatures for City $A = \sqrt{\frac{254}{5}} \approx 7.1$, while the standard deviation for City $B = \sqrt{\frac{74}{5}} \approx 3.8$.

76. How to MULTIPLY/DIVIDE VALUES WITH EXPONENTS POWERS

Add/subtract the exponents.

Example:

$$x^a \times x^b = x^{a+b}$$
$$2^3 \times 2^4 = 2^7$$

Example:

$$\frac{x^c}{x^d} = x^{c-d}$$
$$\frac{5^6}{5^2} = 5^4$$

77. How to handle a value with an EXPONENT RAISED TO AN EXPONENT

Multiply the exponents.

Example:

$$(x^a)^b = x^{ab}$$
$$(3^4)^5 = 3^{20}$$

78. How to handle POWERS with a base of ZERO and POWERS with an EXPONENT of ZERO

Zero raised to any nonzero exponent equals zero.

Example:

$$0^4 = 0^{12} = 0^1 = 0$$

Any nonzero number raised to the exponent 0 equals 1.

Example:

$$3^0 = 15^0 = (0.34)^0 = (-345)^0 = \pi^0 = 1$$

The lone exception is 0 raised to the 0 power, which is *undefined*.

79. How to handle NEGATIVE POWERS

A number raised to the exponent −x is the reciprocal of that number raised to the exponent x.

Example:

$$n^{-1} = \frac{1}{n}, \, n^{-2} = \frac{1}{n^2}, \text{ and so on.}$$

$$5^{-3} = \frac{1}{5^3} = \frac{1}{5 \times 5 \times 5} = \frac{1}{125}$$

80. How to handle FRACTIONAL POWERS

Fractional exponents relate to roots. For instance, $x^{\frac{1}{2}} = \sqrt{x}$.

Likewise, $x^{\frac{1}{3}} = \sqrt[3]{x}, x^{\frac{2}{3}} = \sqrt[3]{x^2}$, and so on.

Example:

$$(x-2)^{\frac{1}{2}} = x^{(-2)\left(\frac{1}{2}\right)} = x^{-1} = \frac{1}{x}$$

$$4^{\frac{1}{2}} = \sqrt{4} = 2$$

81. How to handle CUBE ROOTS

The cube root of x is just the number that when used as a factor 3 times (i.e., cubed) gives you x. Both positive and negative numbers have one and only one cube root, denoted by the symbol $\sqrt[3]{}$, and the cube root of a number is always the same sign as the number itself.

Example:

$$(-5) \times (-5) \times (-5) = -125, \text{ so } \sqrt[3]{-125}$$
$$= -5$$

$$\frac{1}{2} \times \frac{1}{2} \times \frac{1}{2} = \frac{1}{8}, \text{ so } \sqrt[3]{\frac{1}{8}} = \frac{1}{2}$$

82. How to ADD, SUBTRACT, MULTIPLY, and DIVIDE ROOTS

You can add/subtract roots only when the parts inside the $\sqrt{}$ are identical.

Example:

$$\sqrt{2} + 3\sqrt{2} = 4\sqrt{2}$$
$$\sqrt{2} - 3\sqrt{2} = -2\sqrt{2}$$
$$\sqrt{2} + \sqrt{3} \quad \text{cannot be combined.}$$

To multiply/divide roots, deal with what's inside the $\sqrt{}$ and outside the $\sqrt{}$ separately.

Example:

$$(2\sqrt{3})(7\sqrt{5}) = (2 \times 7)(\sqrt{3 \times 5}) = 14\sqrt{15}$$

$$\frac{10\sqrt{21}}{5\sqrt{3}} = \frac{10}{5}\sqrt{\frac{21}{3}} = 2\sqrt{7}$$

83. How to SIMPLIFY A RADICAL

Look for factors of the number under the radical sign that are perfect squares; then find the square root of those perfect squares. Keep simplifying until the term with the square root sign is as simplified as possible: there are no other perfect square factors (4, 9, 16, 25, 36…) inside the $\sqrt{}$. Write the perfect squares as separate factors and "unsquare" them.

Example:

$$\sqrt{48} = \sqrt{16} \times \sqrt{3} = 4\sqrt{3}$$
$$\sqrt{180} = \sqrt{36} \times \sqrt{5} = 6\sqrt{5}$$

84. How to solve certain QUADRATIC EQUATIONS

Manipulate the equation (if necessary) into the "_____ = 0" form, factor the left side (reverse FOIL by finding two numbers whose product is the constant and whose sum is the coefficient of the term without the exponent), and break the quadratic into two simple expressions. Then find the value(s) for the variable that make either expression = 0.

Example:

$$x^2 + 6 = 5x$$
$$x^2 - 5x + 6 = 0$$
$$(x - 2)(x - 3) = 0$$
$$x - 2 = 0 \text{ or } x - 3 = 0$$
$$x = 2 \text{ or } 3$$

Example:

$$x^2 = 9$$
$$x = 3 \text{ or } -3$$

85. How to solve MULTIPLE EQUATIONS

When you see two equations with two variables on the GRE, they're probably easy to combine in such a way that you get something closer to what you're looking for.

Example:

If $5x - 2y = -9$ and $3y - 4x = 6$, what is the value of $x + y$?

Setup:

The question doesn't ask for x and y separately, so don't solve for them separately if you don't have to. Look what happens if you just rearrange a little and "add" the equations:

$$\begin{array}{r} 5x - 2y = -9 \\ +[-4x + 3y = 6] \\ \hline x + y = -3 \end{array}$$

86. How to solve a SEQUENCE problem

The notation used in sequence problems scares many test takers, but these problems aren't as bad as they look. In a sequence problem, the nth term in the sequence is generated by performing an operation, which will be defined for you, on either n or on the previous term in the sequence. For instance, if you are referring to the fourth term in a sequence, it is called n_4 in sequence notation. Familiarize yourself with sequence notation and you should have no problem.

Example:

What is the positive difference between the fifth and fourth terms in the sequence 0, 4, 18, ... whose nth term is $n^2(n - 1)$?

Setup:

Use the definition given to come up with the values for your terms:

$$n_5 = 5^2(5 - 1) = 25(4) = 100$$
$$n_4 = 4^2(4 - 1) = 16(3) = 48$$

So the positive difference between the fifth and fourth terms is $100 - 48 = 52$.

87. How to solve a FUNCTION problem

You may see function notation on the GRE. An algebraic expression of only one variable may be defined as a function, usually symbolized by f or g, of that variable.

Example:

What is the minimum value of x in the function $f(x) = x^2 - 1$?

Setup:

In the function $f(x) = x^2 - 1$, if x is 1, then $f(1) = 1^2 - 1 = 0$. In other words, by inputting 1 into the function, the output $f(x) = 0$. Every number inputted has one and only one output (although the reverse is not necessarily true). You're asked to find the minimum value, so how would you minimize the expression $f(x) = x^2 - 1$? Since x^2 cannot be negative, in this case $f(x)$ is minimized by making $x = 0$: $f(0) = 0^2 - 1 = -1$, so the minimum value of the function is -1.

88. How to handle GRAPHS of FUNCTIONS

You may see a problem that involves a function graphed onto the xy-coordinate plane, often called a "rectangular coordinate system" on the GRE. When graphing a function, the output, $f(x)$, becomes the y-coordinate. For example, in the previous example, $f(x) = x^2 - 1$, you've already determined 2 points, $(1, 0)$ and $(0, -1)$. If you were to keep plugging in numbers to determine more points and then plotted those points on the xy-coordinate plane, you would come up with something like this:

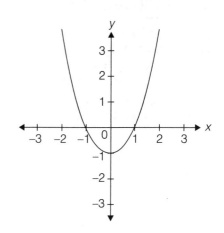

This curved line is called a *parabola*. In the event that you should see a parabola on the GRE (it could be upside down or more narrow or wider than the one shown), you will most likely be asked to choose which equation the parabola is describing. These questions can be surprisingly easy to answer. Pick out obvious points on the graph, such as (1, 0) and (0, −1) above, plug these values into the answer choices, and eliminate answer choices that don't jibe with those values until only one answer choice is left.

89. How to handle LINEAR EQUATIONS

You may also encounter linear equations on the GRE. A linear equation is often expressed in the form

$$y = mx + b, \text{ where}$$

$$m = \text{the slope of the line} = \frac{rise}{run}$$

$$b = \text{the } y\text{-intercept (the point where the line crosses the } y\text{-axis)}$$

For instance, a slope of 3 means that the line rises 3 steps for every 1 step it makes to the right. A line with positive slope slopes up from left to right. A line with negative slope slopes down from left to right. A slope of zero (e.g., $y = 5$) is a flat (horizontal) line.

Example:

The graph of the linear equation

$$y = -\frac{3}{4}x + 3 \text{ is this:}$$

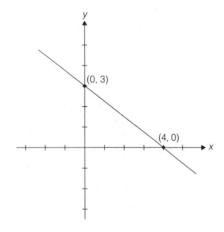

Note:

The equation could also be written in the form $3x + 4y = 12$, but this form does not readily describe the slope and y-intercept of the line.

To get a better handle on an equation written in this form, you can solve for y to write it in its more familiar form. Or, if you're asked to choose which equation the line is describing, you can pick obvious points, such as (0, 3) and (4, 0) in this example and use these values to eliminate answer choices until only one answer is left.

90. How to find the x- and y-INTERCEPTS of a line

The x-intercept of a line is the value of x where the line crosses the x-axis. In other words, it's the value of x when $y = 0$. Likewise, the y-intercept is the value of y where the line crosses the y-axis (i.e., the value of y when $x = 0$). The y-intercept is also the value b when the equation is in the form: $y = mx + b$. For instance, in the line shown in the previous example, the x-intercept is 4 and the y-intercept is 3.

91. How to find the MAXIMUM and MINIMUM lengths for a SIDE of a TRIANGLE

If you know $n = $ the lengths of two sides of a triangle, you know that the third side is somewhere between the positive difference and the sum.

Example:

The length of one side of a triangle is 7. The length of another side is 3. What is the range of possible lengths for the third side?

Setup:

The third side is greater than the difference (7 − 3 = 4) and less than the sum (7 + 3 = 10).

92. How to find one angle or the sum of all the ANGLES of a REGULAR POLYGON

The term "regular" means all angles in the polygon are of equal measure.

Sum of the interior angles in a polygon with n sides =

$$(n - 2) \times 180$$

Degree measure of one angle in a regular polygon with n sides =

$$\frac{(n-2) \times 180}{n}$$

Example:

What is the measure of one angle of a regular pentagon?

Setup:

Since a pentagon is a five-sided figure, plug $n = 5$ into the formula:

Degree measure of one angle

$$= \frac{(5-2) \times 180}{5} = \frac{540}{5} = 108$$

93. How to find the LENGTH of an ARC

Think of an arc as a fraction of the circle's circumference. Use the measure of an interior angle of a circle, which has 360 degrees around the central point, to determine the length of an arc.

$$\text{Length of } arc = \frac{n}{360} \times 2\pi r$$

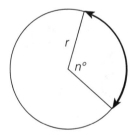

94. How to find the AREA of a SECTOR

Think of a sector as a fraction of the circle's area. Again, set up the interior angle measure as a fraction of 360, which is the degree measure of a circle a round the central point.

$$\text{Area of sector} = \frac{n}{360} \times \pi r^2$$

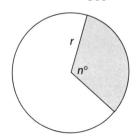

95. How to find the dimensions or area of an INSCRIBED or CIRCUMSCRIBED FIGURE

Look for the connection. Is the diameter the same as a side or a diagonal?

Example:

If the area of the square is 36, what is the circumference of the circle?

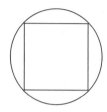

Setup:

To get the circumference, you need the diameter or radius. The circle's diameter is also the square's diagonal. The diagonal of the square is $6\sqrt{2}$. This is because the diagonal of the square transforms it into two separate 45°-45°-90° triangles (see #46). So, the diameter of the circle is $6\sqrt{2}$.

$$\text{Circumference} = \pi(\text{diameter}) = 6\pi\sqrt{2}.$$

96. How to find the VOLUME of a RECTANGU- LAR SOLID

$$\text{Volume} = \text{length} \times \text{width} \times \text{height}$$

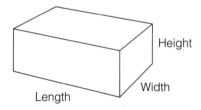

97. How to find the SURFACE AREA of a RECTANGULAR SOLID

To find the surface area of a rectangular solid, you have to find the area of each face and add them together. Here's the formula:

Let l = length, w = width, h = height:

$$\text{Surface area} = 2(lw) + 2(wh) + 2(lh)$$

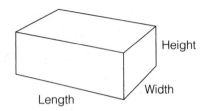

98. How to find the DIAGONAL of a RECTANGULAR SOLID

Use the Pythagorean theorem twice, unless you spot "special" triangles.

Example:

What is the length of AG?

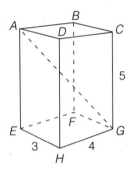

Setup:

Draw diagonal AC.

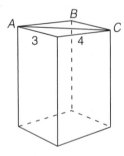

ABC is a 3-4-5 triangle, so $AC = 5$. Now look at triangle ACG:

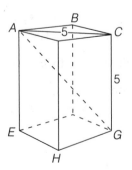

ACG is another special triangle, so you don't need to use the Pythagorean theorem. ACG is a 45-45-90 triangle, so $AG = 5\sqrt{2}$.

99. How to find the VOLUME of a CYLINDER

Volume = area of the base × height = $\pi r^2 h$

Example:

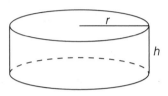

Let $r = 6$ and $h = 3$.

Setup:

$$\text{Volume} = \pi r^2 h = \pi(6^2)(3) = 108\pi$$

100. How to find the SURFACE AREA of a CYLINDER

$$\text{Surface area} = 2\pi r^2 + 2\pi rh$$

Example:

Let $r = 3$ and $h = 4$.

Setup:

$$\text{Surface area} = 2\pi r^2 + 2\pi rh =$$
$$2\pi(3)^2 + 2\pi(3)(4) =$$
$$18\pi + 24\pi = 42\pi$$